Classical and Contemporary Cryptology

Classical and Contemporary Cryptology

Richard J. Spillman
Pacific Lutheran University, Tacoma, WA

An Alan R. Apt Book

PEARSON
Prentice
Hall

Upper Saddle River, NJ 07458

Library of Congress Cataloging-in-Publication Data

Spillman, Richard J.
   Classical and contemporary cryptology / Richard Spillman.
      p. cm.
   Includes bibliographical references and index.
   ISBN 0-13-182831-2
   1. Coding theory. 2. Cryptography. I. Title.

QA268.S65 2004
652'.8--dc22

2004044651

Vice President and Editorial Director, ECS: *Marcia J. Horton*
Publisher: *Alan R. Apt*
Associate Editor: *Toni Dianne Holm*
Editorial Assistant: *Patrick Lindner*
Vice President and Director of Production and Manufacturing, ESM: *David W. Riccardi*
Executive Managing Editor: *Vince O'Brien*
Managing Editor: *Camille Trentacoste*
Production Editor: *Lakshmi Balasubramanian*
Director of Creative Services: *Paul Belfanti*
Creative Director: *Carole Anson*
Art Director and Cover Manager: *Jayne Conte*
Managing Editor, AV Management and Production: *Patricia Burns*
Art Editor: *Gregory Dulles*
Manufacturing Manager: *Trudy Pisciotti*
Manufacturing Buyer: *Lisa McDowell*
Marketing Manager: *Pamela Shaffer*
Marketing Assistant: *Barrie Reinhold*

Cover and Chapter Opening Image Courtesy of Dorling Kindersley

© 2005 Pearson Education, Inc.
Pearson Prentice Hall
Pearson Education, Inc.
Upper Saddle River, NJ 07458

The author and publisher of this book have used their best efforts in preparing this book. These efforts include the development, research, and testing of the theories and programs to determine their effectiveness. The author and publisher make no warranty of any kind, expressed or implied, with regard to these programs or the documentation contained in this book. The author and publisher shall not be liable in any event for incidental or consequential damages in connection with, or arising out of, the furnishing, performance, or use of these programs.

Printed in the United States of America

10 9 8 7 6 5 4 3 2 1

ISBN: 0-13-1828312

Pearson Education Ltd., *London*
Pearson Education Australia Pty. Ltd., *Sydney*
Pearson Education Singapore, Pte. Ltd.
Pearson Education North Asia Ltd., *Hong Kong*
Pearson Education Canada, Inc., *Toronto*
Pearson Educación de Mexico, S.A. de C.V.
Pearson Education—Japan, *Tokyo*
Pearson Education Malaysia, Pte. Ltd.
Pearson Education, Inc., *Upper Saddle River, New Jersey*

Dedication

This book is dedicated to my wife, Bonnie, and my daughters, Kimberly and Annie, who put up with a lot while I was writing it. I also want to remember my five (yes, five) dogs Jolie, Pretzel, Chica, Toby, and Bliss, who missed a lot of walks while I was writing.

I want to express my deep gratitude and thanks to the seven reviewers of the initial manuscripts; Cetin Koc, Ronald Gove, Yongge Wang, Lucia Dettori, Atul Prakash, Ashish Soni, and Martha Sloan. Each provided important insights and suggestions that significantly improve the content and coverage of this book.

Preface

The goal of this book is to introduce you to the fascinating world of cryptography. It is a multifaceted world—for some, it is a world of spies and secrets. For others, it is a world of mathematics and computers. Anyway you look at it, cryptography has an air of mystery and adventure. It also transcends traditional academic disciplines. It is not just a computer-science topic—the study of cryptography involves history, political science, engineering, languages, military science, ethics, mathematics, and technology. No single text could cover cryptography from all these perspectives, so the true student of cryptography must be prepared to develop a broad educational background. This book will only serve as the starting point for a long and satisfying search for knowledge and understanding of this very complicated, yet rewarding, topic.

Two overall principles guided the writing of this book. The first is that cryptography did not begin with the invention of the computer. While contemporary ciphers are all computer based, they owe a lot to the early work of the developers of classical ciphers. These developers had to work by hand using paper and pencil to discover weaknesses in the classical ciphers. Without the aid of a computer or even a calculator, they had to train their minds to recognize patterns and to organize data. Hence, to learn how to "think" like a cryptographer, you need to understand and appreciate the cleverness and patience that underlie the classical systems.

The second guiding principle is that a course in cryptography is not (and should not be) a programming course. While it may be helpful for students to write one or two programs that implement a cipher or an analysis tool, the time it would take learning how to write and debug code for all the important ciphers and tools would significantly reduce the time available to learn the real substance of cryptology. The task of writing cipher programs should be part of an algorithms or programming course. Hence, this book comes with a software package, Cryptographic Analysis Program (CAP), that provides access to both classical and contemporary ciphers. It also contains a set of tools for the analysis of those ciphers. The combination of the text and the software will give you real hands-on experience.

Beginning students, hobbyists, and advanced students should find something worthwhile in this text and its accompanying software program, CAP. Part One covers classical issues in cryptography and is a good place for those new to the field to begin their study. More advanced students may want to quickly scan this part for information on running CAP and perhaps spend more time on those classical ciphers or analysis techniques that are unfamiliar. Part Two covers contemporary ciphers including stream, block, and public key systems. This is the section that the more advanced students will find most useful. Part Three considers the future of cryptography and provides a short introduction to quantum systems. The world of quantum computing is so strange that it challenges our view of how the universe operates. This section is really for those who can abandon all common sense, be they beginning or advanced students.

There is a Web page for this book, which can be found at http://www.plu.edu/~spillmrj. (Follow the CAP pointers.) It contains a set of PowerPoint® files which are designed for lectures. Instructors also have access to answers to the problems in the book as well as additional problems and test questions.

The single most unique feature of this text is the accompanying software package, CAP. Together, CAP and the text are designed to create a complete learning environment. As you read about a particular cipher system, CAP allows you to explore the operation of that system. As you study an analysis technique, CAP allows you to experiment with it. CAP implements 30 different ciphers following a standardized interface so that once you become familiar with the implementation of one cipher you can easily run all the ciphers. CAP also provides a wide range of analysis tools that allow you to test the resistance of most CAP ciphers to cryptanalysis and to discover weaknesses that may be exploited in those ciphers. The usefulness of CAP is reflected in the problems at the end of each chapter. The problem sets are unique and, at times, challenging because they rely on your access to CAP. Above all, CAP is fun. It comes with a game feature so you can continue to test your cryptographic skills after you complete the text material. The CAP website (previously referenced) will contain additional challenges and post readers' high scores (if you will send in your game scores).

I hope you find the study of cryptography as interesting and rewarding as I found the writing of this book.

RICHARD J. SPILLMAN
Pacific Lutheran University,
Tacoma, WA

Contents

Chapter 1

Introduction to Cryptology

1.0 INTRODUCTION

We live in an exciting, fast-paced world and nothing is changing faster than the way we deal with information. Using the Internet, we can access and use information in ways that we never even dreamed of just a few years ago. Rather than going to the bank and standing in line waiting for a teller, we can pay bills, write checks, and shift money between accounts from home, 24 hours a day, 7 days a week. We can apply for and receive approval for loans without ever leaving home. We can buy books, food, gifts, and just about anything else over the Internet. Instead of running a garage sale in our front yard on a weekend, we can sell anything at anytime over the Net. We can buy and sell stock. We can post information for others to read and find information on just about any subject. With the advent of wireless technology, we can do all this and more from almost any location on earth using a cellular phone.

Sure, these are exciting times, but they also have a down side. The same technology that makes life so much easier has the potential to destroy our lives when used by criminals. For example, identity theft is one of the fastest growing crimes in the United States today. It thrives because the legal penalties have not caught up with the effects of the crime, besides the fact that it is easy to do. This is because most of the information "out there" about individuals is not protected. To enjoy the benefits while avoiding the pitfalls of new technology, we must have some method of protecting our identity and our personal information. How this can be done is precisely the subject matter of this book. It is about "secret writing," which has been around for centuries, but has now become a vital force for protecting and nurturing the growth of information technology. The field is called cryptography.

Cryptography is the study of codes and ciphers. David Kahn, in what has to be called the "bible of cryptography," defines it as follows: "Cryptology is protection. It is to that extension of modern man—communications—what the carapace is to the turtle, ink to the squid, camouflage to the chameleon." It is centuries old yet it remains fresh, new, and exciting. It is a field that is constantly changing and discovering new challenges. As a result, this is more than just a dry textbook only covering topics of interest to computer scientists and mathematicians. It is also a book that delves into history, political science, language, military tactics, and even games. It covers a body of knowledge that has secretly shaped the world in which we live.

1.1 CRYPTOGRAPHY

This book is a soap opera in some ways. It is the story of three people: Alice, Bob, and Eve. (These are the three names traditionally used by cryptographers to illustrate the principles of both cryptography and cryptanalysis.) It seems that Alice and Bob are constantly sending messages to each other. Eve, on the other hand, for reasons that are clouded in the past, wants to keep tabs on what Alice and Bob are saying to each other. Since both Alice and Bob are aware of Eve's intentions, they try as best they can to prevent Eve from discovering the content of their messages. This little soap opera is pictured in Figure 1.1.

The messages that Alice and Bob send to each other are called *plaintext* because they are readable by anyone. When they first started their correspondence, Alice and Bob sent each other their plaintext without any protection. However, they quickly discovered that if they did nothing to protect the messages, anyone, including Eve, could read them. So, as a result of Eve's reading their plaintext messages, Alice and Bob decided to hide the message contents in such a way that they could recover the plaintext, but Eve could not. This process of disguising a message in such a way as to hide its substance is called *encryption*. The encrypted version of the message is called the *ciphertext*. The process of recovering the plaintext from the ciphertext is called *decryption*. The encryption and decryption processes are determined by an algorithm and are controlled by a single key that only Alice and Bob share. Alice will use the key to encrypt her plaintext and then send the ciphertext on to Bob. Bob will use the same key to decrypt the ciphertext back into plaintext. If Eve intercepts the ciphertext, it appears meaningless to her because she does not have the key. This new process is illustrated in Figure 1.2.

The problem that Alice and Bob face is that Eve is both intelligent and determined. Once they try a particular encryption method, it is only a matter of time before Eve discovers a method to break the cipher. That is, Eve finds a way to either recover the plaintext

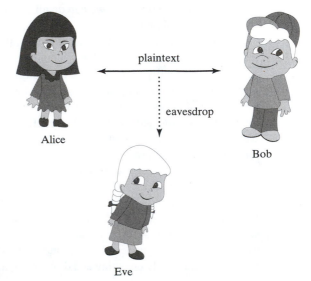

Figure 1.1: Typical communication model

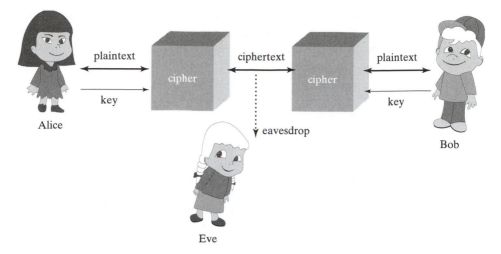

Figure 1.2: Typical communication model

without the key or a way to recover the key from the ciphertext. This forces Alice and Bob to try an even more complicated encryption method. So, the story of Alice, Bob, and Eve is a never-ending one. Alice and Bob are always trying to stay one step ahead of Eve, who is becoming increasing clever in her approach to breaking new ciphers. This book will allow you to follow this exciting story and watch as Alice and Bob develop new ciphers and Eve discovers new tools to allow her to break them. Before we can pick up the beginning of this story, however, it is necessary to define some basic terms.

1.2   IMPORTANT TERMS

Cryptology is the science (and to some extent the art) of building and analyzing different encryption–decryption methods. There are really two parts to this science. *Cryptography* is the science of building new more powerful and efficient encryption–decryption methods. This is the job of Alice and Bob. *Cryptanalysis* is the science of discovering weaknesses in existing methods so that the plaintext can be recovered without knowledge of the key. This is Eve's job. This book is about both subjects. You will learn how to protect data and how to discover weaknesses in current data-protection methods. Studying both processes will make you better at each. Understanding the different approaches to encryption will make it easier to detect weaknesses in specific ciphers. In addition, it is only through the understanding of cryptanalysis that you can ultimately judge the usefulness of any proposed encryption method. That is, every good cryptologist must spend some time in Eve's shoes in order to judge the security of their own favorite encryption algorithm.

An initial distinction must be drawn between *codes* and *ciphers* because sometimes they are mistakenly used to describe the same process. Both are methods used to hide information, but they do it in distinctly different ways. A code will substitute words, phrases, or numbers for plaintext. That is, the word "bomb" might appear in a message as the number sequence 1508. There is no algorithm or simple key that allows plaintext to be recovered from the codetext. The process of creating codetext or recovering plaintext requires a codebook that lists all the numbers (or substitution symbols) and their corresponding plaintext word, phrase, or letter. A cipher uses an algorithm and a key to hide information.

At one time codes were frequently used, but eventually the size of the codebook made it a weak link in the security of the system. Any changes in the code would require the publication and distribution of a new large codebook. A possible enemy could intercept the distribution and compromise the code. Changing the key of a cipher, however, is more secure. Distribution of a simple key is quite a bit easier and less risky than sending out large codebooks. Hence, codes are rarely used today. This does not mean that the process of managing multiple keys is easy. In fact, the process of key management is an important issue in cipher operation and will be covered in Chapter 9.

Other than codes or ciphers, another form of hiding information is called *steganography*. This method involves hiding information in ways that conceal the existence of the ciphertext. That is, the ciphertext may be embedded in a photograph or some other message. Using invisible ink is another form of steganography. Steganography fell out of use because of problems with keys, but it is making a comeback through the use of modern computer-generated image-processing techniques.

1.3   CIPHER EVALUATION

Throughout this book, the issue of what actually makes a good cipher will be continually explored. In part, you will learn what makes a good cipher by watching how Alice and Bob discover what works and what doesn't work as they continue to try to stay ahead of Eve. Each success on the part of Eve and each failure on the part of Alice and Bob will expose a weakness that will become a test for cipher quality. Each chapter will end with a summary of the current principles of good cipher design that can be derived from the plight of Alice, Bob, and Eve.

However, any discussion of what makes a good cipher must begin with the First General Principle of Cryptography—that is, it will always be assumed that ***the eavesdropper has knowledge of the underlying algorithm used to encrypt data***. This means that data are never secure just because the algorithm is new or unknown. Data are secure only if the key to the cipher algorithm remains secure. Never count on the hope that the enemy does not know how you encrypt your data. Always assume that they know every detail of the algorithm. This is sometimes called Kerckhoffs's law, and it is one of the six requirements of any cipher system that Flemish cryptographer Auguste Kerckhoffs listed in his 19th-century work *La Crypthographie Militaire*. All six are still considered to be fundamental to any cryptographic algorithm:

1. The system should be unbreakable in practice if not theoretically unbreakable.
2. Compromise of the system should not inconvenience the correspondents.
3. The key should be easy to remember without notes and should be easy to change.
4. The cryptograms should be transmissible by telegraph.
5. The apparatus or documents should be portable and operable by a single person.
6. The system should be easy, neither requiring knowledge of a long list of rules nor involving mental strain.

Claude Shannon devised another general evaluation concept in the late 1940s. He took the position that a good cipher will involve both *confusion* and *diffusion*. The confusion property means that the cipher should hide any local pattern—that is, any identifying characteristics of the language should be obscured by the cipher. The cipher should hide features of language that might give away the key to the cipher. The diffusion property requires that the cipher mix up different segments of the plaintext so that no character is left in its original position. Many of the classical ciphers that we will encounter early in this text fail on one or both of these properties. Often it is their failure to satisfy both of Shannon's conditions that allows them to be broken through the process of cryptanalysis.

As with most technologies, the evaluation of a cipher system all comes down to economics in the end. A cipher does not have to be "unbreakable" to be secure. (With one exception, it is doubtful that any cipher is truly unbreakable.) If the value of the information to be obtained is less than the cost of breaking the cipher, the data are secure. Or, if the time required to break the cipher is longer than the useful lifetime of the information, the data are secure. Hence, the ultimate security of any cipher is based on the principle that it is "more work than it is worth" to try and break it.

1.4   CRYPTANALYSIS

While Alice and Bob are faced with the challenge of creating a safe and secure cipher, Eve has to come up with ways to compromise their work. Eve will be attacking the intercepted ciphertext using all the tools and auxiliary information she can gather. This book will follow the exploits of Eve and teach you how to discover weaknesses in ciphers, which is the goal of cryptanalysis. However, it is important to understand that cryptanalysis is a classical double-edged sword. The knowledge you gain can be used for good or for evil. There are important reasons to learn about cryptanalysis—it is a necessary tool for the evaluation of new ciphers and it plays a vital role in preserving our national security. On the other hand, it can become a tool for compromising the privacy of others. Eve has no business attacking the communications between Alice and Bob. No matter how intelligent or skilled she appears to be, ultimately she is evil. You need to commit yourself to using the knowledge you gain to protect and not to harm.

There are three ways that Eve will attack the ciphers of Alice and Bob. The first is called a *ciphertext-only* attack. When all that Eve can get her hands on is the transmitted ciphertext, she will use any information she can gain from the ciphertext alone to try to produce the plaintext. The second is a *known-plaintext* attack. In this case, Eve has both the ciphertext and all or part of the plaintext available. Perhaps she has discovered that Alice and Bob always start or end their messages with the same sentence. Using this information and the ciphertext, Eve might be able to discover the key. Knowledge of the key for one set of plaintext–ciphertext may help her pry into other communications between Bob and Alice. The third is a *chosen-plaintext* attack. In this case, Eve has managed to influence the nature of the message between Alice and Bob. Perhaps she has given Alice some juicy information that she knows Alice will send to Bob. She has chosen the information so that the plaintext and the ciphertext have some important properties that make the job of discovering the key easier. Eve can use the information plus Alice's ciphertext to try and discover Alice's key.

Obviously, the ciphertext-only attack is the most difficult, while the chosen-plaintext attack is the easiest. Throughout this book, different ciphers will be compromised using one or more of these attack methods. As you learn how to break ciphers, it is important that you maintain a moral and ethical perspective. I understand that only a few paragraphs earlier this same subject was broached, but it is too important to leave to just one comment. There are only two good reasons to use cryptanalysis skills to break a particular ciphertext: for reasons of national security or to support law-enforcement efforts. Even then it should be done only with specific and lawful authority. On the other hand, there is very good reason to study the weaknesses of cipher systems in general: to ensure that only the strongest, most secure ciphers are actually used to protect sensitive information.

1.5   A BRIEF HISTORY OF CODES AND CIPHERS

The process of protecting information has a long and fascinating history. There are several excellent books on the history of encryption (see the reference section), but perhaps the bible of cipher history is the book by David Kahn, *The Codebreakers*. His book combines the intriguing history of ciphers with just enough technical detail and description to make it all come to life. I encourage anyone interested in the field of cryptology to read Kahn's book.

Some of the earliest codes and ciphers have been found on ancient Egyptian tombs. Their real use is lost in history, but it is speculated that this "secret writing" was intended to add an air of mystery to the life of the person in the tomb and thereby enhance their prestige. It did not take long for "secret writing" to move beyond enhancing prestige to become an important part of the process of governing a nation and conducting warfare. The Hebrews developed three different types of ciphers, all of which worked on the principle of substitution: the atbah, the atbash, and the albam. Each letter of the alphabet was paired with another alphabetic letter. The ciphertext was created by replacing each plaintext letter with its mate. The pairing was the key and each cipher had a different form of pairing. The atbah begins by numbering the letters of the Hebrew alphabet in order, much like in English, in which "a" is 1, "b" is 2, and so on. The first nine Hebrew characters are paired so that their values add up to 10; the remaining are paired so that their values sum to 28. Each plaintext letter in a message is substituted by its paired letter. The atbash pairs the last letter in the alphabet with the first, the next to the last with the second, and so on. The albam splits the alphabet in half and equates the two halves.

It is said that one method of secret writing used by the early Greeks was to shave the head of a slave, tattoo the message on his head, wait for the hair to grow back, and send him on his way. This is an example of steganography. The message is not encoded, just hidden from view.

The Spartans were some of the first people to use encryption for military messages. They developed a device called a skytale. (The actual spelling is scytail, but it is pronounced skytale, so that has become its name.) It was a rod of fixed dimensions. A piece of cloth or parchment would be wrapped around the skytale and a message would be written down the rod. When the cloth was unwound, the letters would be in the wrong order. (This is an example of a transposition cipher.) In order to recover the plaintext, the cloth would have to be wrapped around a similar skytale. (See the example in Figure 1.3.) This

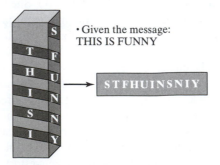

Figure 1.3: Skytale

is a fundamentally different way to encipher messages than is the method used by the Hebrews. The Spartans did not replace plaintext letters with ciphertext letters—they just rearranged the order of the plaintext letters.

David Kahn, in his classic book *The Codebreakers*, credits the Arab world with the creation of the science of cryptology—the combination of cryptography and cryptanalysis. In fact, they coined the word "cipher." An early major work on cryptology is found in a 14-volume encyclopedia completed in the early 1400s by the Arab scientist al-Qalqashandi. This work includes examples of both substitution and transposition type ciphers, as well as one of the first written accounts of approaches to cryptanalysis.

During the Dark Ages in Europe, the scientific arts, including cryptology, saw little advancement. But as Europe began to emerge from the Dark Ages, the science of codes and ciphers experienced a rapid growth. As governments formed large networks of spies and developed ciphers to communicate with them, the realization hit that it would be very useful to read the ciphers of their enemies. Hence, there emerged a new kind of government organization (one that continues today to be a significant part of most governments) called a black chamber. The function of a black chamber was to intercept and decipher important messages. These chambers became very successful and lead to the development of some of the most important initial steps in general cryptanalysis. One of the more successful black chambers was the English Deciphering Branch, which regularly read U.S. and European mail during the 1700s.

The United States did not have an official black chamber until the 1900s. This did not mean that cryptography was overlooked in the United States. Among the many accomplishments of Thomas Jefferson was the invention of a powerful (for its time) cipher machine called a wheel cipher. The wheel cipher used a set of independent "wheels," each of which had the alphabet written on it in a random order. The wheels could be rotated so that the plaintext appeared on one line and the ciphertext could be selected from any of the other lines. (See Figure 1.4.)

During WWI, the United States finally established its own black chamber called MI-8 which was headed by Herbert O. Yardley. After the war, he continued to run the agency from New York City. MI-8 was very successful in breaking Japanese codes after WWI. As a result, the U.S. government had the upper hand during early disarmament talks. All this changed in 1929, when the American Black Chamber was dissolved and its duties were assumed by the Army and the Navy.

Both the British (at Bletchley Park) and the American effort to break the Axis codes during WWII were very successful. The U.S. government was able to read most of the Japanese coded traffic and the British (with the help of codebreakers from Poland) were able to read the German Enigma traffic. Needless to say, the ability to read both Japanese and German messages played a significant part in the Allied victory.

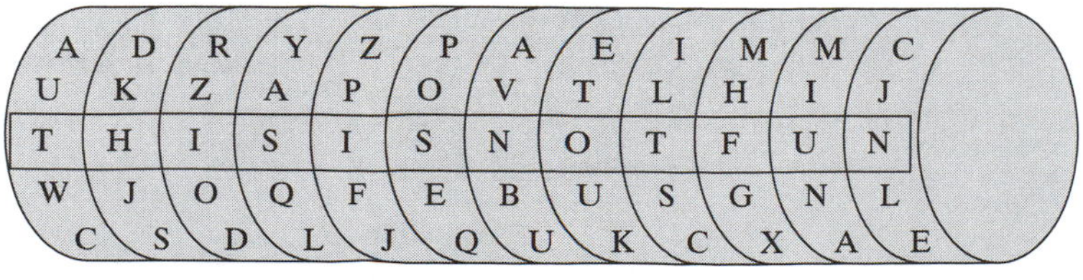

Figure 1.4: Example of a wheel cipher

Today, the United States has one of the most powerful and successful black chambers in the history of the world. It is called the National Security Agency (NSA) and it is in charge of both the development of new ciphers and the analysis of existing ciphers.

Actual stories of the use and impact of ciphers throughout history will be presented as certain classical and contemporary methods are discussed. For now, it is sufficient to remember that the science of cryptology has a long and interesting history.

1.6   CLASSICAL AND CONTEMPORARY CIPHERS

This book divides the subject of ciphers into two broad classes (as indicated by the title): classical and contemporary ciphers. Classical ciphers are ciphers that work with individual letters, while contemporary ciphers are those that work with the binary representation of plaintext. Drawing the distinction in this way makes it clear that classical ciphers are of historical (and foundational) interest, while contemporary ciphers are of more practical use today. Each class of ciphers can be further subdivided based on the nature of the algorithm used to generate the ciphertext. One such breakdown is shown in Figure 1.5.

As shown in Figure 1.5, there are two basic categories of classical ciphers that have been used throughout history. One consists of *substitution* ciphers in which each plaintext letter is replaced by another letter—that is, every plaintext "a" might be replaced by a ciphertext "c". This was the approach of the Hebrews. The other is a *transposition* cipher in which the letters in the plaintext are not changed, but their order is rearranged in the ciphertext much like the Spartan skytale—that is, the word "next" might appear as "xent" in such a ciphertext.

What Figure 1.5 does not show (simply because the chart would become too complicated) is the breakdown of these two types of classical ciphers. In the category of classical substitution ciphers, for example, there are two approaches. One is called a *monoalphabetic* cipher and the other is called a *polyalphabetic* cipher. The characteristic of a monoalphabetic cipher is that each plaintext letter is mapped to exactly one ciphertext letter—that is, if a plaintext "a" is replaced by a ciphertext "n" once, then it is always replaced by "n". On the other hand, in a polyalphabetic cipher, several different ciphertext letters may replace the same plaintext letter. For example, the ciphertext "a" may represent plaintext characters "n" or "s" or "y". It appears that a polyalphabetic cipher is more difficult to produce and to break than is a monoalphabetic cipher. However, it will become apparent later that even polyalphabetics have their weakness.

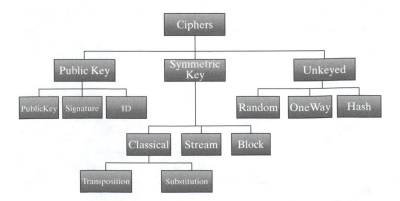

Figure 1.5: Cipher types

1.7   INTRODUCTION TO CAP

Many of the topics covered in this book will be illustrated through the use of a computer package called the Cryptographic Analysis Program or CAP. CAP is included with the book and runs on a Windows®-based PC. While you will learn how to use many of the features of CAP as they become relevant to the material covered in the various chapters, this section will only serve as a short introduction to using CAP.

CAP is a Windows program that will allow you to make and to break ciphers. It covers both the classical ciphers and cryptanalysis techniques discussed in this book, as well as some of the more contemporary systems. It even includes a challenge game that you can play on your own to test your cipher-breaking skills and an automated cryptanalysis system that will guide you step-by-step through the process of breaking a cipher.

When you double-click on the CAP icon, the main CAP window will open. (See Figure 1.6.) From this window, you can navigate though the various features of CAP.

The two major fields in the CAP main window are the Plaintext and Ciphertext boxes. Both boxes are like small word processors, so you can type text directly into one of the boxes and save it to a file. Later, the saved file can be opened into either box.

To illustrate the use of CAP, consider one of the simplest substitution ciphers. It is called the Caesar cipher because Julius Caesar used it to send messages back to Rome about the progress of the war with the Gauls. Caesar's key was to shift letters by 3 positions. Later, Augustus Caesar used a key with a shift of 1 (A to B , B to C, ... Z to A). Beginning with the 26 letters of the alphabet written out in order, ABCDEFGHIJKLMNOPQRSTUVWXYZ,

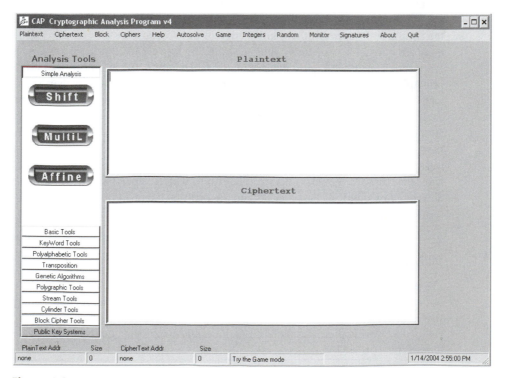

Figure 1.6: CAP main screen

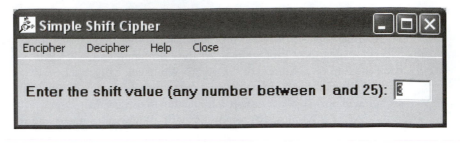

Figure 1.7: CAP Simple Shift Cipher window

Caesar would substitute each plaintext letter with the letter three spaces to our right—that is, every plaintext "a" is replaced by a "d", every plaintext "b" is replaced by an "e", and so on. The letters on the end are wrapped around so that every plaintext "x" is replaced by an "a", every plaintext "y" is replaced by a "b", and finally, every plaintext "z" is replaced by a "c" CAP implements this shift cipher automatically. Simply enter the plaintext in the plaintext box. Select the Simple Shift option from the Cipher menu. The key box for this cipher will appear, requesting a shift number. (See Figure 1.7.) Caesar used a shift of 3, but you can select any shift from 1 to 25.

Click on the Encipher button to create the ciphertext. If you entered ciphertext, then click on the Decipher button to recover the plaintext. While the other ciphers available as part of CAP are more sophisticated than this simple shift cipher, they work the same way within CAP. Enter the text (either plaintext or ciphertext), select the cipher, enter the key in the key box, and select Encipher or Decipher.

The analysis tools provided by CAP are equally easy to use. For example, to break the simple shift cipher without knowledge of the key, just try all possible shifts. After all there are only 25 ways letters could be shifted by this cipher. Since the key is so small, the effort required to break this cipher is minimal. The simple shift cipher does not satisfy the principle of "it's more work than its worth"; hence, it is a very weak cipher. You don't even have to do this analysis by hand because CAP offers a tool that will do it automatically. For example, Eve knows that Alice and Bob have elected to use a shift cipher as their first attempt to communicate with each other in private, but she does not know which key they have selected. Using a ciphertext-only attack, Eve has managed to intercept a short message from Bob to Alice. Using CAP, Eve enters the ciphertext into the ciphertext window and runs the Shift Analysis option. The result, which appears in the Shift Analysis window, quickly identifies the plaintext and the fact that Alice and Bob selected 3 as their key. (See Figure 1.8.)

1.8   SUMMARY

The art and science of cryptology have a long and fascinating history. From the early days of writing, we have tried to find ways to communicate thoughts, feelings, and plans in a way that preserves privacy and secrecy. We have also tried to gain an advantage over others by discovering their secrets. The pursuit of these opposing goals has influenced the history of the world.

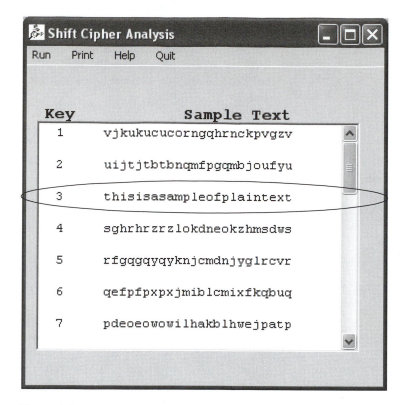

Figure 1.8: CAP Shift Analysis window

History aside, cryptology is also fascinating because it is a blend of so many different fields of science. From languages to mathematics to physics to computer science, cryptology borrows ideas and processes from them all. This book is your introduction to a world that has long been shrouded in secrecy. It will unlock the past and open your eyes to the future.

This chapter is the first of many that will add on to the cipher structure shown in Figure 1.5. Already, some new and important approaches to ciphers have been identified and are summarized in Figure 1.9.

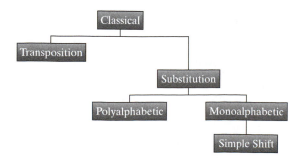

Figure 1.9: New cipher structures

1.9 IMPORTANT TERMS

Caesar cipher	A simple shift cipher in which each character is replaced by a character n positions ahead in the alphabet
Cipher	A method to disguise a message based on some algorithm that uses a key
Ciphertext	A disguised message
Code	A method to disguise a message by substituting words, phrases, or numbers for plaintext
Cryptanalysis	The art and science of breaking codes and ciphers
Decryption	The process of recovering a disguised message
Encryption	The process of disguising a message
Monoalphabetic cipher	A cipher with a fixed substitution pattern in which each plaintext letter is replaced by exactly one ciphertext letter
Plaintext	A readable message
Polyalphabetic cipher	A cipher in which the substitution pattern allows multiple letters to replace a single plaintext letter
Steganography	Methods of hiding a message that conceal the existence of the message
Substitution cipher	A cipher that substitutes one character for another
Transposition cipher	A cipher that rearranges the order of the letters in the plaintext

RESOURCES

There are a large number of excellent introductory books on the subject of cryptology, including the following:

The Code-Breakers by David Kahn (Scribner, 1996)

The Code Book by Simon Singh (Doubleday, 1999)

Codebreakers, The Inside Story of Bletchley Park, ed. by F. Hinsley and Alan Stripp (Oxford Press, 1993)

Codebreaking by R. Kippenhahn (Overlook, 1999)

Secrets and Lies by Bruce Schneier (John Wiley, 2000)

Codes Ciphers and Other Cryptic and Clandestine Communication by F. Wrixon (Black Dog & Leventhal, 1998)

Aegean Park Press also publishes a long list of books related to cryptology.

PROBLEMS

1. What is the First General Principle of Cryptology?
2. Given the following plaintext, use CAP to create the ciphertext resulting from a shift cipher with a key of 7:

   The solution to a shift cipher is easy.

3. Using CAP, find the key and the plaintext for the following shift ciphertext:

   aopzpzaoljvyyljazvsbapvu.

4. Search the Web and find at least two sites devoted to cryptology and write a short summary of their contents.

5. Define *black chamber*.

6. What is the difference between a code and a cipher, and why are codes rarely used today?

7. Write a short evaluation of the shift cipher in terms of its relationship to Shannon's two requirements for a good cipher.

8. What would be the substitution pattern for the standard English alphabet if it was used to create an atbash-type cipher?

9. Bob and Alice decide that because Eve can break a simple shift cipher they will use it twice—that is, they will create ciphertext by shifting every letter by 3. Then they will encipher the first ciphertext using a shift cipher with a key of 5. Is this a good idea? Why or why not?

Part 1

Classical Cryptology

Part One introduces the basic vocabulary of cryptology. Important terms such as *plaintext, ciphertext, codes, ciphers, substitution, transposition, polygraphic*, and others are defined. The classification of classical ciphers is presented and each chapter deals with the construction and analysis of progressively more complicated ciphers.

Perhaps more important than the classification and vocabulary, Part One also establishes the discipline of cryptology. As the historical development of ciphers and their weaknesses are presented, you should also gain an understanding of the patience and dedication that is required to master this exciting field of study.

Chapter 2

Classical Monoalphabetic Ciphers

2.0 INTRODUCTION

A classical cipher is loosely defined as any cipher that does not require a computer for its implementation. This does not mean that it cannot be implemented on a computer (after all, many of the classical ciphers in this book are implemented in CAP), just that it is possible to encipher and decipher text using the cipher by hand. Most classical ciphers were developed before computers became common place, and some are still in use today, often by hobbyists. Even though these classical ciphers are not recommended for any serious applications, the study of the nature of these algorithms and their weaknesses sets the stage of a better understanding of more contemporary ciphers. Besides, they are fun to play with and they illustrate in a simple way many of the concepts that drive current cryptology.

As defined in Chapter 1, a monoalphabetic cipher is a substitution cipher in which each plaintext letter is replaced by one and only one ciphertext character. For example, a plaintext "a" might always appear as a ciphertext "n" in a given cipher. The Caesar cipher of Chapter 1 is a good example of a weak monoalphabetic cipher. Using a shift of 3, the Caesar cipher always replaces "a" with "d", "b" with "e", "c" with "f", and so on.

This chapter will consider some of the classical monoalphabetic ciphers that have been used throughout history. You will learn how to construct these ciphers and how to break them using the tools found in CAP.

2.1 KEYWORD CIPHER

As you might remember from Chapter 1, Alice and Bob first tried to use a simple shift cipher to protect their communications from Eve. However, Eve was able to use an exhaustive search attack (with the help of CAP) to discover both the key and the plaintext. It didn't take Alice and Bob long to realize that Eve was regularly reading their messages, so they decided they needed to find a cipher that was more powerful than a simple shift.

Alice and Bob realized that, since the simple shift cipher is easy to break by trying all 25 keys, any replacement substitution cipher would have to have more keys. One type of cipher that satisfies this requirement is the keyword cipher. A keyword cipher is constructed using a two-step process:

1. Select a keyword—if the keyword has any repeated letters, drop all but the first occurrence. For example, if the selected keyword is "success", then use "suce".
2. Write the keyword below the alphabet and fill in the rest of the space with the remaining letters of the alphabet in their standard order.

For example, with the keyword "magicnet", the two alphabets would be written as follows:

```
a b c d e f g h i j k l m n o p q r s t u v w x y z
m a g i c n e t b d f h j k l o p q r s u v w x y z
```

These two alphabets define the keyword substitution pattern. With this keyword, a plaintext "a" is always replaced by a ciphertext "m", a plaintext "b" is always replaced by a ciphertext "a", and so on. In this case, a typical plaintext-message–ciphertext-message pair would appear as follows:

Plaintext	h e l p	i	a m	l o s t
Ciphertext	t c h o	b	m j	h l r s

One modification, which appears to make the cipher more difficult to break (it really doesn't), is to allow the keyword to start anywhere along the alphabet (not just under "a"). For example, if the keyword "pacific" begins under "k" then the substitution key looks like this:

```
a b c d e f g h i j k l m n o p q r s t u v w x y z
q r s t u v w x y z p a c i f b d e g h j k l m n o
```

Note that the last two letters of "pacific" are dropped because both "i" and "c" have already been used. In this case, our plaintext–ciphertext pair becomes

Plaintext	h e l p	i	a m	l o s t
Ciphertext	x u a b	y	q c	a f g h

Variations on this type of cipher were common in 14th-century Europe. By the 15th century, when cryptanalysis techniques began to emerge, European governments still relied on keyword ciphers, much to the delight of the black chambers. Even today, monoalphabetic-keyword-type ciphers can still be found, but only in the hands of amateurs (like Bob and Alice).

CAP provides an easy tool to create any keyword cipher. Run CAP, enter some plaintext, and then select Keyword under the Cipher menu. CAP will open up a Key Entry box as shown in Figure 2.1. Enter your keyword and its starting position, then hit the create key button. CAP will display your new key pattern and you are ready to encipher or decipher with it. To encipher the plaintext shown in Figure 2.1, just click on the Encipher key. The new ciphertext will appear automatically in the Ciphertext window.

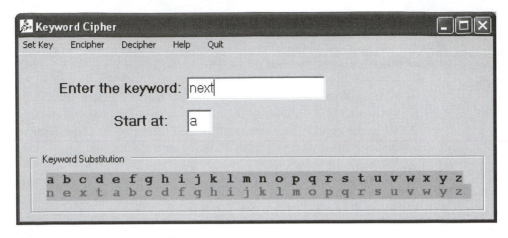

Figure 2.1: CAP Keyword Cipher

2.1.1   Cryptanalysis of Keyword Ciphers

Well, Alice and Bob started using a keyword cipher, which caused Eve some problems. Whenever she placed some intercepted ciphertext into CAP and tried a simple shift analysis, she discovered that none of the shifts produced plaintext. So, through other means (remember, Alice and Bob cannot rely on their choice of cipher remaining secret), Eve discovers that they are using a keyword cipher.

A keyword cipher is certainly stronger that the simple shift cipher, since trying all keywords and possible keyword positions is obviously more difficult than just trying all 25 shift cipher keys. It might take some time, but it would not be difficult to run a modern dictionary attack (like the type used against password systems) against any keyword cipher—that is, have a computer try every word in the dictionary until it finds one that solves the cipher. The point is that an exhaustive search attack (trying all possible keywords) against a keyword cipher may be feasible today, but it is not the method of choice. Assuming that you want to be more clever than to rely on a brute-force attack (and every cryptanalyst wants to be as clever as possible), it is easy to break a keyword cipher using some important and interesting cryptanalysis tools. In fact, the process of breaking a keyword cipher will be covered in detail precisely because it illustrates and motivates the use of some of the most basic tools of cryptanalysis. These tools will not only prove useful in breaking the keyword cipher, they will also be used to analyze other ciphers. Perhaps more important than their actual use is the approach to thinking about ciphers that these tools encourage. Cryptanalysis always has been and remains a mental discipline, in spite of the aid of computers. Learning how to break a keyword cipher is your opportunity to develop the required mental skills.

Assume that Eve has intercepted the following ciphertext and now knows that Alice and Bob used a keyword cipher to create it:

```
GJXXN   GGOTZ   NUCOT   WMOHY   JTKTA   MTXOB   YNFGO   GINUG   JFNZV
QHYNG   NEAJF   HYOTW   GOTHY   NAFZN   FTUIN   ZANFG   NLNFU   TXNXU
FNEJC   INHYA   ZGAEU   TUCQG   OGOTH   JOHOA   TCJXK   HYNUV   OCOHQ
UHCNU   GHHAF   NUZHY   NCUTW   JUWNA   EHYNA   FOWOT   UCHNP   HOGLN
FQZNG   OFUVC   NZJHT   AHNGG   NTHOU   CGJXY   OGHTN   ABNTO   TWGNT
HNTXN   AEBUF   KNFYO   HHGIU   TJUCE   AFHYN   GACJH   OATAE   IOCOH
UFOXO   BYNFG
```

Eve's goal is to discover the keyword and the plaintext knowing only that the cipher is a keyword cipher. This is an example of a ciphertext-only attack as defined in Chapter 1. Other attacks can be made using additional information. For example, a known plaintext attack is much simpler as will be shown later.

2.1.2 Frequency Information

To begin the process of breaking a keyword cipher (or any cipher for that matter) it is use-ful to stop and consider what we already know. In attacking this keyword ciphertext, Eve knows three obvious, but very important, things:

1. The underlying plaintext is standard English.
2. The cipher is a keyword cipher.
3. Therefore, each plaintext letter has been replaced by a unique ciphertext letter.

Now, this may not seem like very much to go on, but actually Item 3 is the weapon that Eve will use to pry open this cipher.

The most basic observation of cryptanalysis is that every letter of a language has a personality of its own. That is, if every plaintext "t" is changed to a ciphertext "m", then in the ciphertext, "m" assumes the personality of "t". To the trained observer, the personality of a letter gives away its real identity. These personality characteristics in-clude: the frequency of occurrence, contact with other letters, position within words, and so on. So the first step in attacking this ciphertext is to try and determine the personali-ties of the ciphertext letters and match them with the known personalities of correspond-ing plaintext letters.

The easiest personality characteristic to observe is the frequency of occurrence. In standard English, the most frequent character is "e", while characters like "x" and "z" are quite rare. Of course, the actual frequency of characters depends on the type of text. For example, scientific text has a different frequency distribution than literary text has. How-ever, most analysis of frequency is based on a typical frequency table of 400 letters of stan-dard English text:

Letter	A	B	C	D	E	F	G	H	I	J	K	L	M	N	O	P	Q
Count	32	6	12	16	42	8	6	24	26	2	2	14	12	28	32	8	1

Letter	R	S	T	U	V	W	X	Y	Z
Count	26	24	36	12	4	6	2	8	1

In Order	ETAONIRSHDLUCMPFYWGBVJKQXZ

Using frequency information to break a cipher is not a recent discovery. As early as the ninth century, the Arab scientist and philosopher al-Kindi wrote about this process. By the 1500s, European cryptanalysis appeared to be using frequency information to break monoalphabetic ciphers. Aware of this technique, Eve decides that it would be worthwhile to count the number of occurrences of each letter in her intercepted ciphertext. The result of this count is as follows:

A	B	C	D	E	F	G	H	I	J	K	L	M	N	O	P	Q	R	S	T	U	V	W	X	Y	Z
17	4	13	0	7	17	23	26	5	12	3	2	2	36	25	1	5	0	0	23	20	3	6	9	13	8

Initially, Eve was tempted to match the letters in the order listed with the standard English frequency order. Since one important principle of cryptanalysis is to always do what you are tempted to do, she gave this a try. The result is as follows:

Standard   ETAONIRSHDLUCMPFYWGBVJKQXZ
Cipher   NHOGTUAFCYJXZEWIQBKVLMPDRS

Based on this matchup, every ciphertext "n" might be a plaintext "e", every ciphertext "h" might be a plaintext "t", and so on. The only way to discover whether this is correct is to make these substitutions in the challenge text and see if words appear. Unfortunately, when Eve tried this, the results were disappointing as the ciphertext became:

OLUUE OOANC EIHAN PJATD....

It doesn't look any better than the original ciphertext. This should not surprise us, since the original frequency sample and the underlying challenge plaintext are based on a small collection of different words. As a result, the actual frequencies may vary slightly (an "i" might be more frequent than an "a" in one sample, even though it is typically less frequent), but they rarely stray far from their area in the frequency table. All this means is that the task of matching frequencies is a little more difficult than first imagined (as are all things in cryptanalysis).

So, rather than matching frequencies exactly, consider the concept of frequency groups. Standard English characters break up into four frequency groups:

High-Frequency Group	E T A O N I R S H
Medium-Frequency Group	D L U C M
Low-Frequency Group	P F Y W G B V
Rare Group	J K Q X Z

Letters tend to move around within their group, but rarely do they swap groups. So what do you look for in a single frequency report? First, look for hills and valleys—that is, some letters with high frequency and some letters with low frequency—since that is an indication that the underlying cipher is a monoalphabetic substitution. Second, look for a break between the high-frequency group and the medium-frequency group. This should appear as a drop of about two percent between two adjacent letters. Third, the most frequent letter is usually "e", but it could be either "t" or "a" as well. Of course this is only the case when there are enough letters in the ciphertext to produce an "average" frequency analysis. If there are only a few letters available, then any pattern may appear.

With this information, Eve went back to the original frequency distribution in the ciphertext. She began by listing the frequency counts for the ciphertext characters in order from high frequency to low frequency:

N	H	O	G	T	U	A	F	C	Y	J	X	Z	E	W	I	Q	B	K	V	L	M	P	D	R	S
36	26	25	23	23	20	17	17	13	13	12	9	8	7	6	5	5	4	3	3	2	2	1	0	0	0

Eve noticed that there is a large drop between ciphertext "f" and "c" (from 17 to 13), so it is highly likely that the high-frequency letters are represented by "n", "h", "o", "g", "t", "u", "a", and "f" in the ciphertext. Given the large number of "n"s in the ciphertext compared with all the other letters, it is a good guess that "n" represents a plaintext "e".

The single frequency information is helpful, but further data are required to break this cipher. Another useful personality characteristic is the set of preferred associations called *digrams*. Each letter has a set of letters that it either appears before or after in standard English text. For example, the pairs "th", "he", and "er" are quite common. Examining each pair of letters in the challenge ciphertext, Eve discovered that the most common digrams are "hy", "ot", "yn" and "nf". From this data, Eve concluded that it is quite likely that ciphertext "hy" is really "th", which means that "yn" (also a high-frequency digram) is probably "he". This is nice because single frequency information also suggested that "n" is really "e". Other data that can be used to help identify the ciphertext include standard observations about plaintext letters. Some of the more useful observations include the following:

- "r" forms digrams with more different letters more often than any other letter.
- The three vowels "a", "i", and "o" avoid each other, except for "io".
- "ea" is the most frequent digram involving vowels.
- Eighty percent of the letters that precede "n" are vowels.
- "h" frequently appears before "e" and almost never after it.

Applying these rules to the challenge ciphertext results in the following possible substitutions:

Plain	a	b	c	d	e	f	g	h	i	j	k	l	m	n	o	p	q	r	s	t	u	v	w	x	y	z
Cipher	U			N			Y	O						T	A					H						

Remember, this is only a guess based on Eve's current analysis of the ciphertext. Some of the substitutions may be correct, but others may be wrong. *Always be willing to give up on an assumption and try something else if it appears that you are on the wrong track.*

Once some possible substitutions have been identified, there are several ways to proceed. One is to look at the frequency of *trigrams*—collections of three letters. Another is to try to identify possible words in the ciphertext. For example, Figure 2.2 uses the current partial solution to search for possible words. In fact, an examination of Figure 2.2 suggests several possible words. For example, in the first plaintext row, the trigram "_ith" appears. This might be the word "with", which would mean that a ciphertext "m" corresponds to a plaintext "w". Another possible word appears at the end of the third plaintext row with the string "int_ition". This could be the word "intuition", which means that a ciphertext "j" pairs with a plaintext "u".

Eve is now fairly close to breaking this cipher. She continues to look for words, and with the help of other information about the characteristics of letters, she finally discovers the key and the plaintext. For this cipher, the keyword turns out to be "New York City" beginning at the letter "e":

Plaintext	a	b	c	d	e	f	g	h	i	j	k	l	m	n	o	p	q	r	s	t	u	v	w	x	y	z
Ciphertext	u	v	x	z	n	e	w	y	o	r	k	c	i	t	a	b	d	f	g	h	j	l	m	p	q	s

```
G J X X N G G O T Z N U C O T W M O H Y J T K T A M T X O B Y N F G O G I N U G
      E     I N   E A   I N     I T H   N   N O   N   I   H E     I     E A
J F N Z V Q H Y N G N E A J F H Y O T W G O T H Y N A F Z N F T U I N Z A N F G
      E       T H E   E   O     T H I N     I N T H E O     E   N A   E   O E
N L N F U T X N X U F N E J C I N H Y A Z G A E U T U C Q G O G O T H J O H O A
E   E   A     E   A   E       E T H O   O   A A A     I   I N T   I T I O
T C J X K H Y N U V O C O H Q U H C N U G H H A F N U Z H Y
N     T H E A   I   I T   A T   E A   T T O   E
```

Figure 2.2: Possible words in the challenge ciphertext

Eve is lucky that she was able to break Alice and Bob's cipher in the 21st century. It seems that some early cryptanalysts were suspected of possessing supernatural powers. The highly skilled 16th-century French cryptanalyst Francois Viete was charged by the King of Spain with being "in league with the devil."

2.1.3   Using CAP to Break a Keyword Cipher

While the process involved in breaking a keyword cipher can be fun for those who enjoy such things, it is still tedious to accomplish by hand. Therefore, CAP provides several tools that will automate this approach, leaving the cryptanalyst with just the fun part. These tools include a frequency analysis system, a special letter analysis tool, a word search, and a keyword worksheet. Figure 2.3 shows the main CAP window with the Analysis Tools section circled. To get to any of CAP's tools, select one of the Analysis Tools buttons on the left side, and then select the specific tool.

2.1.3.1   Frequency Analysis in CAP

The CAP Frequency Analysis window is shown in Figure 2.4. The menu options in this window allow the user to perform single frequency, digram, and trigram counts of either the ciphertext or the plaintext. These reports can be both sorted in order of frequency and displayed in the form of a graph.

2.1.3.2   Letter Identification in CAP

CAP also provides two special tools for letter identification that automate the application of various rules or regularities in standard English. The vowel ID tool is shown in

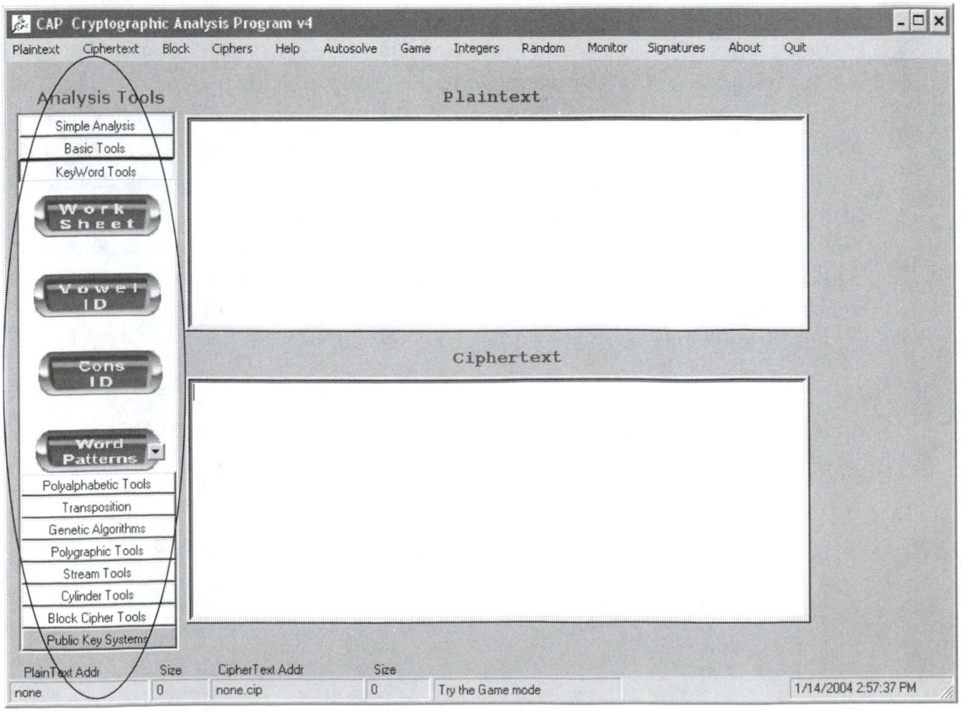

Figure 2.3: CAP Analysis Tools section

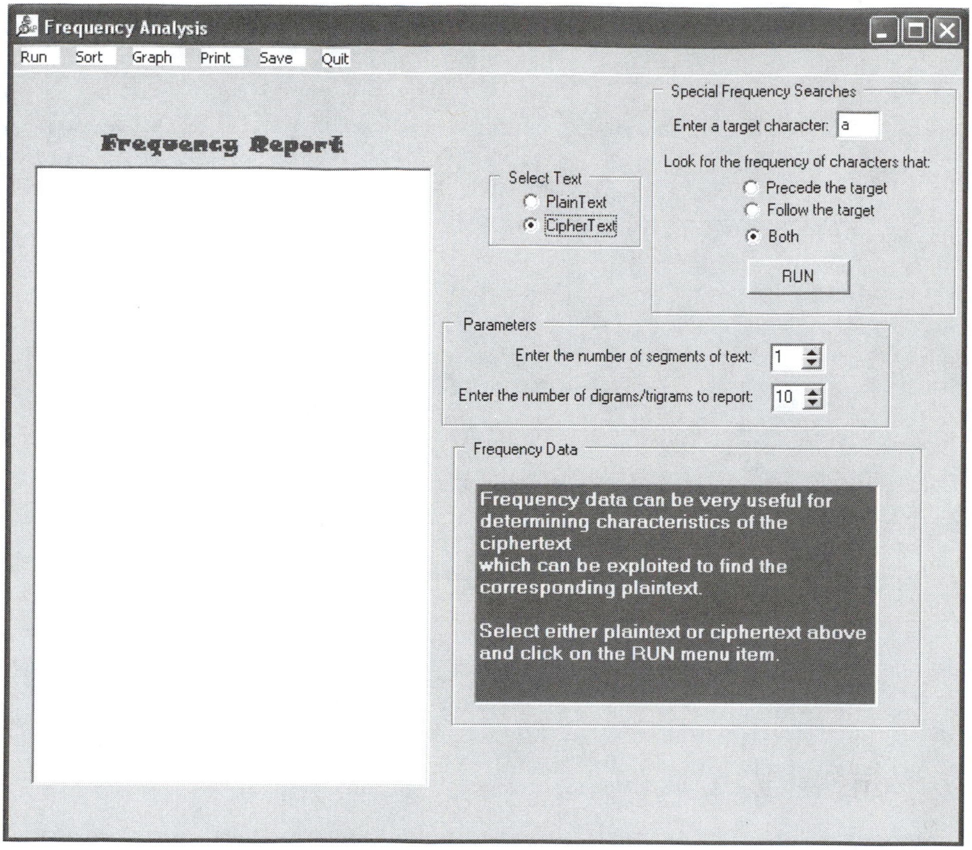

Figure 2.4: CAP Frequency Analysis window

Figure 2.5. To use this tool, simply click in the box next to each action step. As CAP searches the ciphertext for patterns that match the rule, it will assign weights to each letter. Letters with higher weights are more likely to be vowels.

The Consonant Identification window shown in Figure 2.6 performs much like the Vowel ID window. It provides a checklist of rules to apply that may identify possible consonants. It should be noted that the recommendations of both windows are just possible substitutions. Different rules may generate different possibilities for vowels or consonants. Therefore, it may be necessary to try several different substitutions for each vowel and consonant. CAP will just narrow down the number of possibilities that must be explored.

2.1.3.3 Word Identification in CAP

CAP also provides a tool that will aid in the search for words. This is an automatic tool that uses your current best guess for some of the substitutions and looks for patterns that might suggest a specific word. The Word Patterns screen is shown in Figure 2.7.

This tool is useful in a ciphertext-only attack on a keyword cipher because it does not assume the presence of any word—it just looks for letter patterns that follow the patterns of any word in its dictionary. As an alternative, CAP does provide a tool for a known-plaintext attack. Shown in Figure 2.8, this window looks for possible substitutions that match the known plaintext word(s).

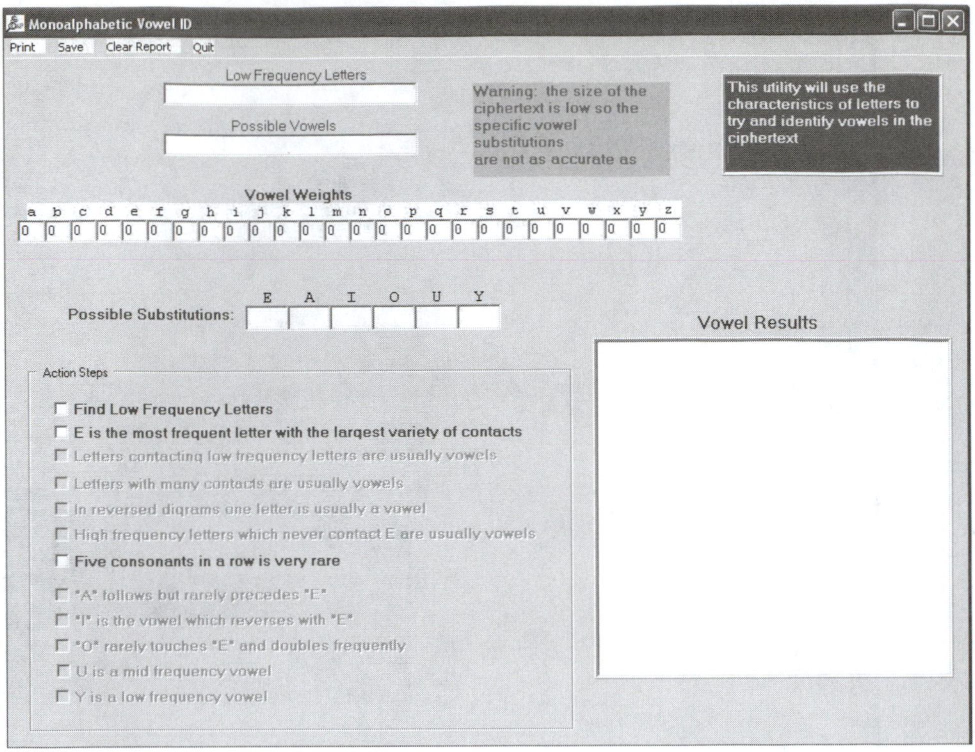

Figure 2.5: CAP Monoalphabetic Vowel ID window

2.1.3.4 Keyword Worksheet

CAP provides one final tool, a worksheet that can be used to try different substitutions and observe the effect. An example of this worksheet is shown in Figure 2.9 and is perhaps the most useful tool for breaking a keyword cipher. It allows you to try different possible substitutions and then look for whole or partial words. This will give you clues about other substitutions. For example, in the figure, the word "test" appears, suggesting that you might be on the right track. Partial words, such as the "t—s" at the beginning, might suggest the word "this", so "h" goes to "d" and "i" goes to "f".

2.2   AFFINE CIPHER

Another form of monoalphabetic cipher is called the affine cipher. In the affine cipher, the letters of the alphabet are assigned numbers—for example, $a = 0, b = 1, c = 2, \ldots, z = 25$. The key to an affine cipher is a pair of numbers (a, b) each between 0 and 25. The greatest common divisor (GCD) of a and 26 must be 1. That is GCD $(a, 26) = 1$. This means that the only number that divides both a and 26 must be 1. For example, $a = 2$ will not work because 2 divides both a and 26. However, 5 will work because 1 is the only number that divides both 5 and 26. Now, let p be the number of the plaintext letter and c the number of the ciphertext letter. Then, the affine cipher relates these two numbers using the following formula:

$$c = ap + b \pmod{26}$$

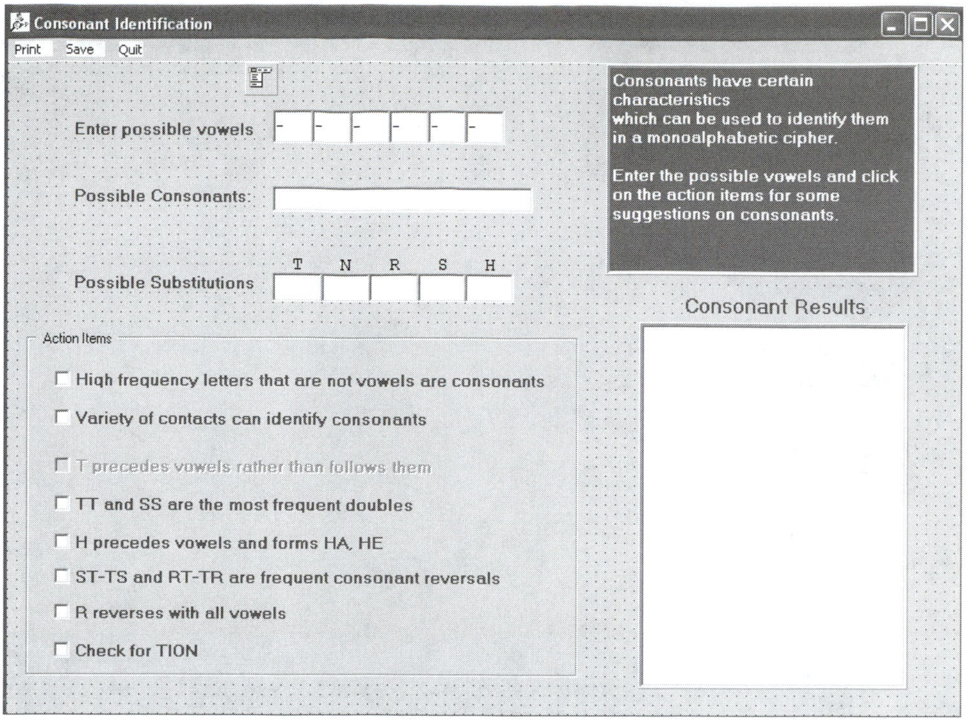

Figure 2.6: CAP Consonant Identification window

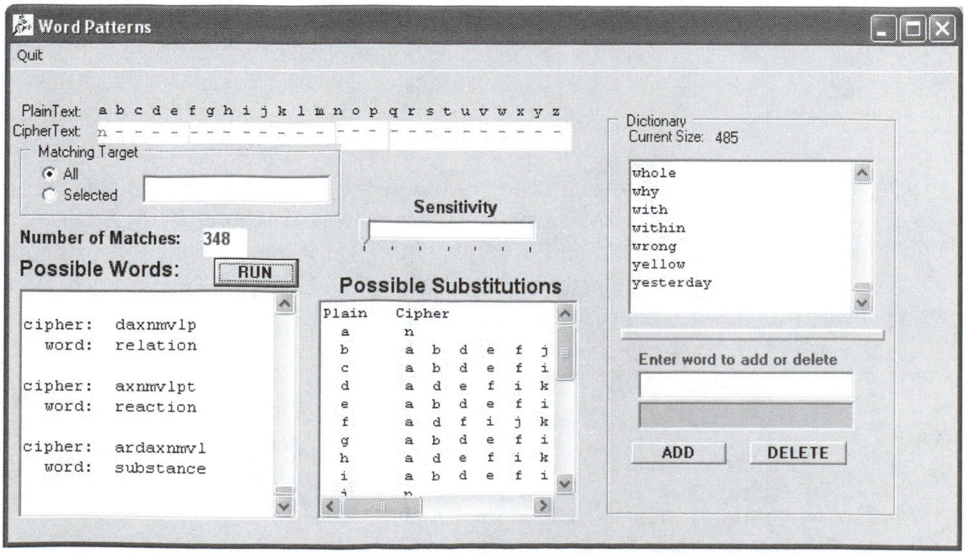

Figure 2.7: CAP Word Patterns window

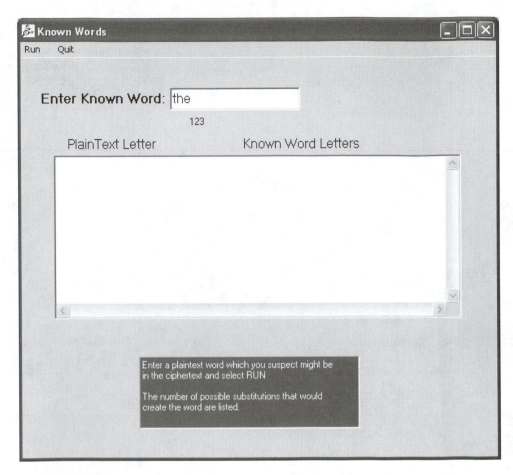

Figure 2.8: CAP Known Words window

and

$$p = a^{-1}(c-b) \ (\text{mod } 26).$$

The mod 26 operation means divide the number by 26 and keep the remainder.

For example, select the key (7, 3). Seven works because GCD (7, 26) is 1. Now, the inverse of 7 mod 26 is 15, since $7 \times 15 = 105$ and 105 mod 26 = 1. So, with this key, the word "hot" can be encrypted using an affine cipher. Converting the letters of "hot" to numbers gives 7 14 19. Using the affine equations yields:

$$c(H) = 7 \times 7 + 3 \text{ mod } 26 = 52 \text{ mod } 26 = 0, \text{ which is "a",}$$
$$c(O) = 7 \times 14 + 3 \text{ mod } 26 = 98 \text{ mod } 26 = 23, \text{ which is "x",}$$
$$c(T) = 7 \times 19 + 3 \text{ mod } 26 = 133 \text{ mod } 26 = 6, \text{ which is "g".}$$

So, with this key, "hot" becomes "axg".

CAP has an affine cipher option which will transform plaintext directly into affine ciphertext. As with all CAP ciphers, select the Affine Cipher under the Cipher menu and the window shown in Figure 2.10 will pop up.

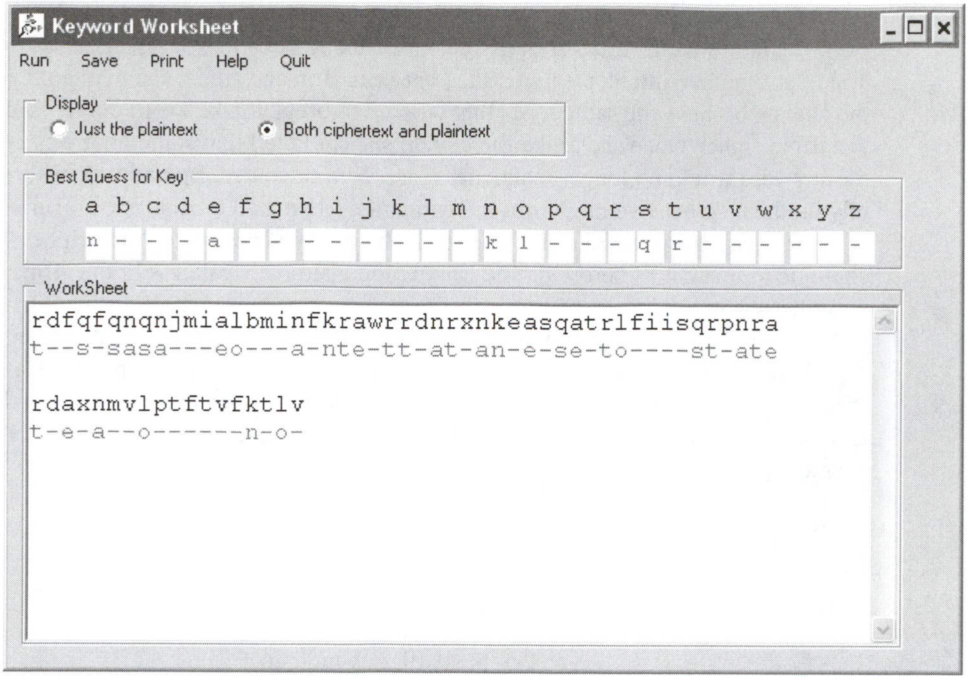

Figure 2.9: CAP Keyword Worksheet

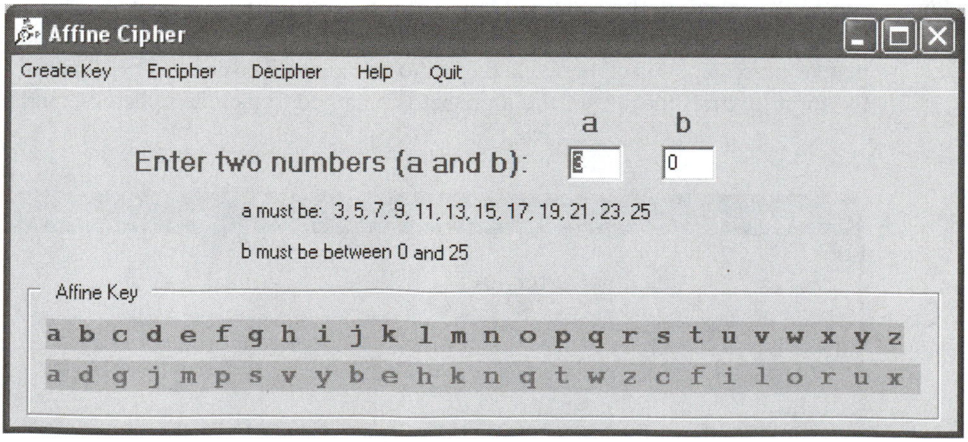

Figure 2.10: CAP Affine Cipher window

2.2.1   Cryptanalysis of the Affine Cipher

The affine cipher is nothing more than a monoalphabetic substitution since each plaintext character is mapped to only one ciphertext character. As a result, the same tools that solved the keyword cipher could be applied to the affine cipher. The only difference is that the key substitution pattern is not based on a keyword. However, it is actually easier to break an affine cipher by solving the affine equations given a known plaintext attack.

Bob and Alice, after discovering that Eve has now compromised their keyword cipher, decide to try to mix up their monoalphabetic substitution using an affine cipher. The next time Eve intercepts a message between Bob and Alice, she may not even notice the change because the same tools that worked to break the keyword cipher still work on the affine cipher. Once she broke the cipher, she could tell that something was up because the keyword would no longer make any sense. But, of course, Bob and Alice should never rely on the fact that Eve might not know that they switched to an affine cipher.

Once Eve discovered that Alice and Bob have switched to an affine cipher, she could continue to break it as before or she can exploit a simple weakness in the affine cipher to make her job easier.

She begins by running a frequency analysis followed by any of the other keyword tools in order to identify with a high degree of certainty the substitution for at least two letters. Say, for example, that she has determined that for a given affine ciphertext that plaintext "e" is represented by "c" and plaintext "t" is represented by "f". Translating these characters to numbers and setting up the affine equations Eve knows:

$$2 = a*4 + b \bmod 26 \text{ [since } (e - \text{character 4) is replaced by } (c - \text{character 2)]}$$

and

$$5 = a*19 + b \bmod 26$$
$$[(\text{since } (t - \text{character 19) is replaced by } (f - \text{character 5)]}.$$

Solving these two equations for a and b produces $a = 21$ and $b = 22$. If you don't want to solve these equations by hand, CAP provides a specific tool that will determine the affine key from knowledge of two substitutions shown in Figure 2.11. Keep in mind, however, that, as presented, this cipher is also open to an exhaustive search. Try all possible keys of the form (a, b). If the size of the alphabet is enlarged to include uppercase and lowercase

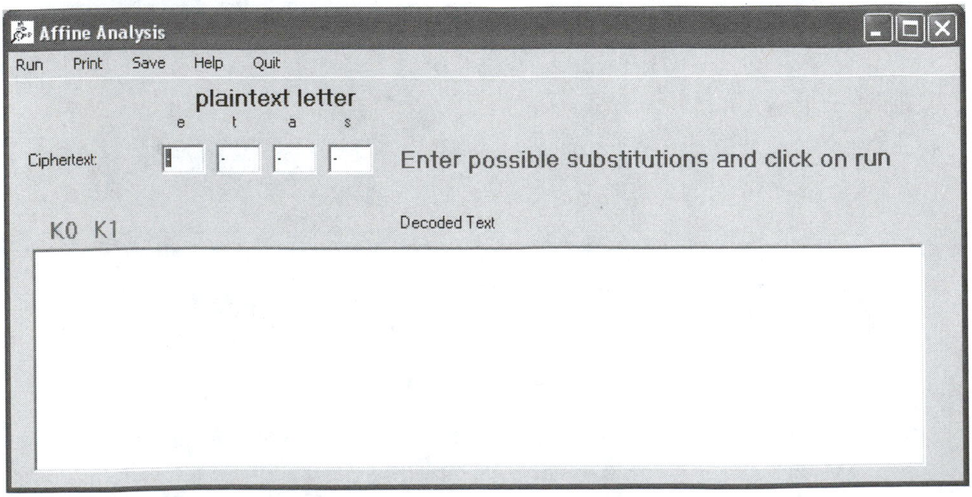

Figure 2.11: CAP Affine Analysis window

letters, the key space for the affine cipher will also increase. But by and large, it is always open to an exhaustive key search.

Poor Bob and Alice have actually selected a weaker cipher as they moved from the keyword to the affine. This is not an unusual occurrence. Often times, what appears to be a more powerful cipher ends up having more weaknesses than the prior cipher.

2.3   MULTILITERAL CIPHER

A multiliteral cipher is another weak monoalphabetic cipher that is worth examining because it tries to do something unique. It replaces each plaintext letter with a pair of letters. The resulting ciphertext is twice as large as the plaintext and looks very strange. While it certainly should not be a cipher that anyone would use, it does illustrate some interesting features that will appear again in some stronger ciphers. The multiliteral cipher key is a 5×5 matrix. The five columns and the five rows are each labeled by the same five-letter keyword. This keyword cannot have any repeating letters. The alphabet is written in the matrix. Of course, the matrix has only 25 slots, but the alphabet has 26 letters, so the letters "i" and "j" occupy the same cell. This means that on decode all the "j"s become "i"s, but that does not make the decoded plaintext difficult to read. For example, if the keyword is "codes", then the key matrix becomes

```
      c   o   d   e   s
  c   a   b   c   d   e
  o   f   g   h   i   k
  d   l   m   n   o   p
  e   q   r   s   t   u
  s   v   w   x   y   z
```

Each plaintext letter is replaced by the pair of letters that identify the row and column of the letter. In this case, the ciphertext pair "od" replaces the plaintext letter "h". So the plaintext word "hat" becomes the ciphertext "od cc ee". The decoding process is a simple reverse lookup in the matrix. CAP provides a tool (are you surprised?) for enciphering and deciphering using a multiliteral cipher. The Multiliteral Cipher window is shown in Figure 2.12.

2.3.1   Cryptanalysis of a Multiliteral Cipher

This is an easy cipher to break because the code word is made up of only five distinct letters. Therefore, the ciphertext also consists of only five distinct letters. Unfortunately, Alice and Bob in their frustration over the move to an affine cipher, decide to try this strange multiliteral cipher. It does not take Eve long to discover the change. The fact that Alice and Bob's messages now contain just five letters is a dead giveaway. Now, all Eve has to do is arrange the letters into a reasonable word and it most likely will be the code word. Of course, CAP provides a multiliteral analysis tool that does just that for Eve. Its window is shown in Figure 2.13. Selecting the KeyWords menu option will try all possible arrangements of the five letters. In the figure, the keyword turns out to be "power". So again Alice and Bob fail to securely send messages to each other.

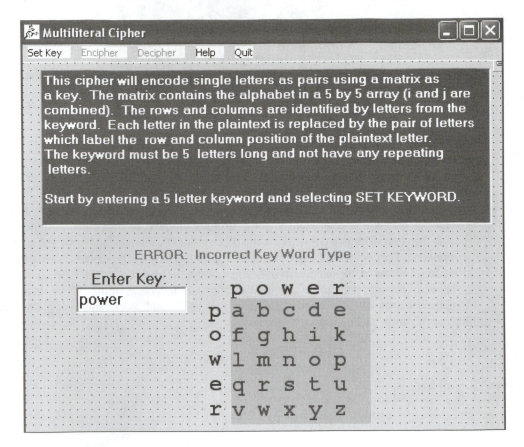

Figure 2.12: CAP Multiliteral Cipher

2.4 MONOALPHABETIC CIPHERS—A SHORT HISTORICAL VIEW

One of the earliest monoalphabetic ciphers was developed by the Greek writer Polybius around 200 B.C. (It predates the Caesar cipher.) The cipher is called a Polybius square because it arranges the letters of the alphabet in a square with the rows and columns numbered. Each letter is replaced by the corresponding row and column numbers. Using English, a Polybius square would look like this:

	1	2	3	4	5
1	a	b	c	d	e
2	e	g	h	i	k
3	l	m	n	o	p
4	q	r	s	t	u
5	v	w	x	y	z

Notice that, since there are only 25 slots, the "j" is dropped just as it was in the multiliteral cipher. Since "j" is a low-frequency letter, in those few cases in which it appears in the plaintext, it can be replaced by the letter "i" without affecting the readability of the text. Unlike the simple shift cipher, the concept of the Polybius square survived for many centuries. In the next chapter, it will be the source of the Nihilist cipher.

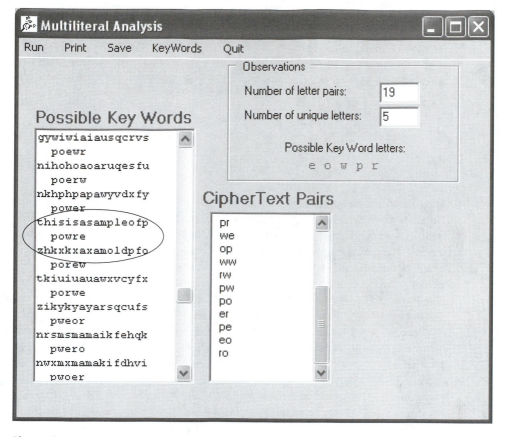

Figure 2.13: CAP Multiliteral Analysis window

A family of skilled cryptographers, the Argentis (led by Giovanni and his nephew Matteo), worked for the Pope during the late 1,500s and early 1600s. Apparently, they were the first to use a keyword substitution. However, like the Polybius Square, letters were substituted by numbers. One of their keys was

p   i   e   t   r   o   a   b   c   d   f   g   h   l   m   n   q   s   u   z
10 11 12 13 14 15 16 17 18 19 20 21 22 23 24 25 26 27 28 29

Both of these ciphers are subject to the standard keyword attacks. Using numbers in the ciphertext rather than letters does not hide the underlying frequencies, it just transfers them to the numbers. In spite of the known weakness to frequency analysis, monoalphabetics survived much longer than they should have—even being used at times by the South during the Civil War.

One variation on a monoalphabetic cipher that was used throughout Europe during the Middle Ages is called a *nomenclator*. A nomenclator involves a letter substitution that can be monoalphabetic (but can be more complicated, as will be discovered in Chapter 3) combined with some substitutions representing words or phrases. The most famous nomenclator is the cipher used by Mary, Queen of Scots in 1586.

Mary, Queen of Scots, was the cousin of England's Queen Elizabeth I. Unfortunately for Mary, she was considered to be the legitimate Queen of England by English

Catholics which made her a threat to Elizabeth's throne. As a result, she was imprisoned by Queen Elizabeth in 1568. For the next 18 years, Mary was moved from castle to castle always under house arrest. Eventually, Anthony Babington, an English Catholic, began to plot Mary's rescue. Requiring her cooperation with the plot, Babington corresponded with Mary using text enciphered in a nomenclator, part of which is shown here:

$$
\begin{array}{cccccccccccccccccccccccccc}
a & b & c & d & e & f & g & h & i & k & l & m & n & o & p & q & r & s & t & u & x & y & z \\
O & \divideontimes & \wedge & \# & \alpha & \square & \theta & \infty & | & \overset{\lambda}{\delta} & \eta & /\!/ & \varnothing & \nabla & \varsigma & m & f & \Delta & \varepsilon & C & 7 & 8 & 9
\end{array}
$$

$$
\begin{array}{ccc}
\text{from} & \text{of} & \text{when} \\
\divideontimes\!\divideontimes & \underline{m} & +\!\!+
\end{array}
$$

The nomenclator also included nulls and symbols for other words such as not, so, and, but. Gilbert Gifford, who had been smuggling letters to Mary for quite some time, offered to take Babington's coded letters to Mary and return with her replies. Unfortunately for both Babington and Mary, Gifford was a double agent who was really working for Sir Francis Walsingham, Principal Secretary to Queen Elizabeth. Among other duties, Walsingham ran a cipher school in London. His chief cryptanalyst was Thomas Phelippes. It didn't take long for Phelippes to decipher Mary's nomenclator, and soon Walsingham was reading all the details of the plot to rescue Mary, assassinate Elizabeth, and place Mary on the throne. While he had enough evidence to force Elizabeth to execute her cousin, Walsingham wanted more—he wanted the names of potential assassins. What he did is a classic example of a problem that is not directly addressed by cryptography—one that is still a significant problem today (and is addressed in detail in Chapter 9). He intercepted one of Mary's messages and added a postscript using the nomenclator. The added postscript asked for the names of the other conspirators. When Babington received the altered message, he was not at all suspicious—after all, it was coded so it must be from Mary. A short while after the transmission of the altered message, Babington and Mary were arrested and charged with treason. Mary's defense was that she knew nothing about Babington's plot. How could she direct an assassination from her confinement? The deciphered letters exposed her lie and she was executed on February 8, 1587.

2.5   SUMMARY

Of course there are a wide variety of other monoalphabetic ciphers that have been developed and used. However, they all suffer from the same weaknesses displayed by the ciphers covered in this chapter. With the failure of all four monoalphabetic ciphers, Bob and Alice decide that it is time to step up their efforts and find a more powerful cipher. Their story continues in the next chapter. For now, it is useful to consider what all three of our players have learned so far in their battle to protect and expose data.

Eve has discovered the power of a frequency analysis of the ciphertext. With a bit of creative thought and frequency data for single, double, and triple letter combinations, she was able to identify the substitutions that Alice and Bob used in their monoalphabetic ciphers. She also learned that it sometimes takes a great deal of patience even with the help of powerful analysis tools to break some ciphers, while others just seem to fall into her hands. This patience and the willingness to try different ideas until she finds one that works will equip her for the more challenging ciphers yet to come.

Alice and Bob have learned that monoalphabetic ciphers are far too weak. They need to find something that is more complicated. Since they now understand the power of frequency analysis, they will seek ciphers that defeat a frequency attack.

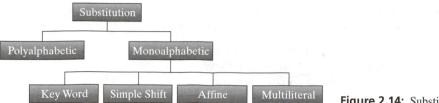

Figure 2.14: Substitution Ciphers

It should also be noted that a monoalphabetic cipher that substitutes numbers for letters or some other symbol for letters is not any stronger than a plain keyword cipher. The numbers or the symbols will still take on the personality of the plaintext letters, and any skilled cryptanalyst will be able to break the cipher.

The updated cipher structure chart is shown in Figure 2.14.

2.6   IMPORTANT TERMS

Digram	A pair of adjacent letters in the text
Frequency Analysis	The process of comparing the frequency of occurrence of plaintext characters to the observed frequency of ciphertext characters
GCD	Greatest common divisor—given two numbers, the GCD is the largest number that divides them both
Monoalphabetic cipher	A cipher in which each plaintext character is replaced by exactly one ciphertext character

RESOURCES

Encryption Techniques with BASIC and C++, by Held, Gilbert (Worldware Publishing, 1999)

Code Breaking: A History and Exploration, (Chapters 4 and 5) by Kippenhahn, Rudolf (Overlook Press, 1999)

Classical Cryptography Course, v1 and v2 by Randall Nichols (Aegean Park Press, 1996)

Cryptologia, a quarterly journal devoted to cryptology, www.dean.usma.edu/math/pubs/cryptologia/

Downloadable cryptology course, http://www.und.nodak.edu/org/crypto/crypto/lanaki.crypt.class/

A whirlwind tour of cryptology, http://www.digicrime.com/~mccurley/talks/msri2/msri2.html

Cryptographic history, http://www.nsa.gov/docs/history/

American Cryptogram Association, http://www.cryptogram.org/

PROBLEMS

1. Alice sent the following message to Bob last night:

    I think Eve has discovered how to break this latest cipher. She mentioned something to me yesterday that indicated that she might have read our last message. I recommend that we try something different.

    (a) Alice used a keyword cipher with the keyword "please" beginning at the letter "n". Recreate her original ciphertext.

    (b) Run a single character frequency analysis on your ciphertext and identify the best choices for "e" based on that analysis—compare the result to the known substitution.

2. Repeat Problem 1 with Alice relying on an affine cipher with key (5,11).

3. Eve intercepted the following message between Alice and Bob:

   qihihpkgqigqukybmpqiyqukfigqubgqukktmex
   fimgbgobtftymtbnqutqkskmkftbgpigkimfimkpqkjp
   tuktniyrppukpkkfpqihkthekqiorkppvutqvktmk
   nibgohkyimkvkkskgdgivbquivatgvkkskmvbgbgqubp
   htqqekiyvbqphrqbvbeegiqobskrjuijkvkvbeecrpq
   utskqiqmxutmnkmqutgkskmqidkkjirmfkpptokpptyk
   tgnpirgn

   She knows that the message was enciphered using a keyword cipher, but it is clear that they are
   no longer using the keyword "please". Find the keyword and the plaintext.

4. Eve intercepted another message, this time from Bob to Alice. She knows they are still using a
   keyword cipher, but have once again changed their keyword. Use what you know about their messages from the previous problems and any CAP tools you need to find the keyword and the plaintext in this message:

   tmhjf pasal tmltd abfrs tmbtd akmlt dfltd ahbta rlmml
   emlmt oahbr hfehb tarhj javaf smljy dukhl sdaph llmtp
   mltfl uatmo asmju piyfh ksura wawfj jbfle hiayt dhtsd
   aphll mtora himrh ttdav aryja hstwa wfjjp mkaun wftdt
   danar baptp fndar systa khlel avard hvatm wmrry homut
   darhc hflom o

5. Bob and Alice discover that Eve is breaking their keyword cipher so they decide to try two keyword ciphers together—that is, they encipher the plaintext with one keyword and then encipher
   the ciphertext again using a different keyword. Does this really help? Why or why not?

6. Fill in the following information:

Cipher	Summarize its operation	Summarize its weakness
Keyword		
Affine		
Multiliteral		

7. Encipher the following text using a multiliteral cipher with the keyword "guide", and then run a
   frequency analysis:

   A multiliteral cipher is easy to break and it gives itself away by its very structure.

   What can you conclude from the analysis?

8. Identify the ciphertype and find the plaintext for the following ciphertext:

   ccicooiofcoioefocficifoficoffcociciiccccfifciifeccfifcciifceio
   ccfciofcccoecfooiooifciefioecffcciifceoififioeioieifooecofoeef
   oecifiicceiooccccfecciicifoeccfifciiffoeiocioe

9. Find the plaintext for the following affine ciphertext:

   xdftv pxkdh hxkxq qrkhp rcihu rdhxd rhumt dtseh mixkx
   dmxky xuyjh fntuy prcih utkph ftvix ehdtb hrkrm rxsrk
   qtubx mrtkt kmihc tddrg shdvg dmrmv mrtkd

10. Eve intercepts the following message between Alice and Bob:

rdeqe qftqr cntem gjkru rkoui ejpyk trdcr oubeq rocre kjsko rduju xrqui uqruo
crqmd kkheq mkiej btlqk kjdcv uyktp umepu pwdem dmhcq quqyk twehh aurcg
ejbyu resqk huriu gjkwq kemcj qurtl iymhc qqqmd upthu cjpwu mcjrc gucrh ucqrk
jumhc qqrkb urduo ptoej brduq loejb huriu gjkww dcreq bkejb kjcqq kkjcq lkqqe
ahu

She suspects that the message is a keyword cipher and she believes the word "registration" is
somewhere in the message. Using this information, find the plaintext.

11. Eve has recovered the following partial key of a keyword cipher:

a b c d e f g h i j k l m n o p q r s t u v w x y z
s e   i   b d f g   k l m n   z

Can you complete the key?

Chapter 3

Classical Polyalphabetic Ciphers

3.0 INTRODUCTION

As defined in Chapter 1, a polyalphabetic cipher is a substitution cipher in which each plaintext character is represented by more than one ciphertext character and each ciphertext character represents more than one plaintext character. For example, a plaintext "e" might appear as a ciphertext "f" one time and as ciphertext "m" another time; a ciphertext character "s" might represent a plaintext "g" one time and a plaintext "c" another time. A polyalphabetic is easily confused with a homophonic cipher. In a homophonic cipher, the cipher text consists of a set of symbols (perhaps numbers) and each plaintext letter is mapped to more than one ciphertext symbol. The difference between a homophonic and a polyalphabetic is that each homophonic symbol represents one and only one plaintext letter. For example, in a homophonic cipher, the letter "a" may be replaced by the numbers 1, 27, and 56, while the letter "b" may be replaced by the numbers 2, 28, and 57. In the ciphertext, 27 always represents an "a"; but this would not be the case in a polyalphabetic cipher. A homophonic cipher is no stronger than a traditional monoalphabetic cipher. The collection of symbols that represent a given plaintext character retain the personality of that character.

The 15th-century architect, Leon Battista Alberti, is thought to be the first to suggest the use of a polyalphabetic technique. He designed a cipher disk on which the outer portion of the disk rotates around the inner portion. The inner ring contained the plaintext alphabet and the outer ring contained the ciphertext alphabet. The cipher process consisted of setting an initial position for the outer ring to use to determine the substitution pattern. After a few characters were enciphered, the outer ring would be rotated creating a different substitution pattern. This process was repeated resulting in a polyalphabetic transformation.

The polyalphabetic ciphers that were introduced in the 15th century had to compete with what had become the standard for encryption in the Middle Ages: the nomenclators. Nomenclators were a cross between code and cipher. Certain words and phrases were replaced by codes and individual letters could be replaced by a choice of one or more symbols.

King Philip of Spain adopted a particularly complex nomenclator in 1556. It had a multiple-letter substitution pattern—two substitution choices for each consonant and three for each vowel. The code portion provided two and three letter groups for common words and titles. Common digraphs and trigraphs could be replaced by either a symbol or a number.

Polyalphabetic ciphers were developed to counter the frequency analysis tools that proved so successful in breaking monoalphabetic ciphers. The goal of the polyalphabetic cipher is to spread the personality characteristics of each plaintext letter over several ciphertext letters. The result is that personality data such as single, double, and triple frequencies no longer reveal the actual plaintext characters. In a similar way to the approach taken in Chapter 2 for monoalphabetic ciphers, this chapter will explore some of the more famous classical polyalphabetic ciphers and develop a new set of analysis tools.

It is worth repeating that even though these classical ciphers are no longer secure, examining their structure and their weakness reveals some of the fundamental processes of cryptology. (Besides, it's fun.) As a result, it is important that you study this chapter and the other classical chapters as well because they will prepare you for the development and analysis of contemporary ciphers in later chapters.

3.1   VIGENERE CIPHER

The Vigenere cipher is a well-known example of a polyalphabetic cipher with an interesting history. The Vigenere cipher is actually a simplification of an autokey cipher (the autokey concept will be introduced later in this chapter) developed in the mid-1500s by Blaise de Vigenere. Its history was lost until it was rediscovered in the late 19th century. For some reason, cryptologists at the time attached Vigenere's name to a weaker version of his autokey cipher. To make matters worse, this lesser cipher was clouded in the legend that it was unbreakable long after its fundamental weakness had been exposed. Nevertheless, the Vigenere cipher became one of the most famous polyalphabetic ciphers in history and today stands as the primary example of a polyalphabetic approach.

The Vigenere cipher is another keyword-based system, but instead of using the keyword to define the substitution (as in the monoalphabetic keyword cipher), the keyword is written above the plaintext repeating it as often as necessary so that each plaintext character is associated with a keyword character. For example, if the keyword is "hold" and the plaintext is "this is the plaintext", then the keyword–plaintext character association is given by

```
h o l d h o l d h o l d h o l d h o
t h i s i s t h e p l a i n t e x t.
```

Every plaintext character is paired with one of the keyword characters. For example, the first plaintext character "t" is paired with the key character "h". Near the end of the plaintext, the character "t" is paired with the key character "l". These letter pairings are used to determine the resulting ciphertext character by means of the Vigenere table shown in Figure 3.1. The operation of this cipher is not very different from that of Alberti's cipher disk. The key character identifies the row to use in the table and the plaintext character identifies the column. The character in the table at the identified row–column intersection is the ciphertext character used to replace the plaintext character. For example, the first pair in the aforementioned sample plaintext (with the keyword hold) is "ht". Look in the Vigenere table down column "t" and over row "h" to find the resulting ciphertext character "a".

	a	b	c	d	e	f	g	h	i	j	k	l	m	n	o	p	q	r	s	t	u	v	w	x	y	z
a	a	b	c	d	e	f	g	h	i	j	k	l	m	n	o	p	q	r	s	t	u	v	w	x	y	z
b	b	c	d	e	f	g	h	i	j	k	l	m	n	o	p	q	r	s	t	u	v	w	x	y	z	a
c	c	d	e	f	g	h	i	j	k	l	m	n	o	p	q	r	s	t	u	v	w	x	y	z	a	b
d	d	e	f	g	h	i	j	k	l	m	n	o	p	q	r	s	t	u	v	w	x	y	z	a	b	c
e	e	f	g	h	i	j	k	l	m	n	o	p	q	r	s	t	u	v	w	x	y	z	a	b	c	d
f	f	g	h	i	j	k	l	m	n	o	p	q	r	s	t	u	v	w	x	y	z	a	b	c	d	e
g	g	h	i	j	k	l	m	n	o	p	q	r	s	t	u	v	w	x	y	z	a	b	c	d	e	f
h	h	i	j	k	l	m	n	o	p	q	r	s	t	u	v	w	x	y	z	a	b	c	d	e	f	g
i	i	j	k	l	m	n	o	p	q	r	s	t	u	v	w	x	y	z	a	b	c	d	e	f	g	h
j	j	k	l	m	n	o	p	q	r	s	t	u	v	w	x	y	z	a	b	c	d	e	f	g	h	i
k	k	l	m	n	o	p	q	r	s	t	u	v	w	x	y	z	a	b	c	d	e	f	g	h	i	j
l	l	m	n	o	p	q	r	s	t	u	v	w	x	y	z	a	b	c	d	e	f	g	h	i	j	k
m	m	n	o	p	q	r	s	t	u	v	w	x	y	z	a	b	c	d	e	f	g	h	i	j	k	l
n	n	o	p	q	r	s	t	u	v	w	x	y	z	a	b	c	d	e	f	g	h	i	j	k	l	m
o	o	p	q	r	s	t	u	v	w	x	y	z	a	b	c	d	e	f	g	h	i	j	k	l	m	n
p	p	q	r	s	t	u	v	w	x	y	z	a	b	c	d	e	f	g	h	i	j	k	l	m	n	o
q	q	r	s	t	u	v	w	x	y	z	a	b	c	d	e	f	g	h	i	j	k	l	m	n	o	p
r	r	s	t	u	v	w	x	y	z	a	b	c	d	e	f	g	h	i	j	k	l	m	n	o	p	q
s	s	t	u	v	w	x	y	z	a	b	c	d	e	f	g	h	i	j	k	l	m	n	o	p	q	r
t	t	u	v	w	x	y	z	a	b	c	d	e	f	g	h	i	j	k	l	m	n	o	p	q	r	s
u	u	v	w	x	y	z	a	b	c	d	e	f	g	h	i	j	k	l	m	n	o	p	q	r	s	t
v	v	w	x	y	z	a	b	c	d	e	f	g	h	i	j	k	l	m	n	o	p	q	r	s	t	u
w	w	x	y	z	a	b	c	d	e	f	g	h	i	j	k	l	m	n	o	p	q	r	s	t	u	v
x	x	y	z	a	b	c	d	e	f	g	h	i	j	k	l	m	n	o	p	q	r	s	t	u	v	w
y	y	z	a	b	c	d	e	f	g	h	i	j	k	l	m	n	o	p	q	r	s	t	u	v	w	x
z	z	a	b	c	d	e	f	g	h	i	j	k	l	m	n	o	p	q	r	s	t	u	v	w	x	y

Figure 3.1: Vigenere table

Repeating this process produces the following ciphertext:

Key:	h	o	l	d	h	o	l	d	h	o	l	d	h	o	l	d	h	o
Plaintext:	t	h	i	s	i	s	t	h	e	p	l	a	i	n	t	e	x	t
Ciphertext:	a	v	t	v	p	g	e	k	l	d	w	d	p	b	e	h	d	h.

Notice that the ciphertext letter "v" appears twice, once as a replacement for plaintext "h" and another time as a replacement for plaintext "s". This is an example of the fundamental nature of polyalphabetic ciphers—the same ciphertext character represents more than one plaintext character.

To decipher a Vigenere cipher, this lookup process is reversed. The key is written over the ciphertext and the key–ciphertext character pairs are used along with the Vigenere table to identify the corresponding plaintext character. To accomplish this, find the row identified by the key. Scan across the row until the ciphertext character is located. The plaintext character is the one that labels the column with the ciphertext character. For example, the key–ciphertext character "hp" becomes the plaintext character "i".

Of course, CAP provides a Vigenere cipher method. As always, enter the plaintext code, select Vigenere and enter a key. CAP will do the rest.

3.1.1 Cryptanalysis of the Vigenere Cipher

The Vigenere cipher proved to be a powerful system for several hundred years. It resisted all attempts to break it, which accounts for the legend of its unbreakable nature that survived long after its ultimate demise. It survived for so long, in part, because the standard cryptanalysis tools for monoalphabetic ciphers do not work against this class of polyalphabetic ciphers. Since the frequencies in the ciphertext are all smoothed out, high-frequency characters do not give themselves away. You can imagine the joy of Bob and Alice when they stumbled on to the Vigenere cipher. Buying into the legend, they immediately began to use it to send messages to each other. One of their first messages was intercepted by Eve. The ciphertext Eve recovered looked like this:

hptns bzjke mgmtc hlxrc wtbjx htapi wnqrl ecnqv oykga esixi mlvck eobqw
tzxgz eqzqq rpifm nrinp ofzkq pzzve neugw slogw ivvqa wpuch edwoi rpinq
idbco edqpx hpxcw tmcvr ohqvl iysyi acmqr tzxqj tsmrv omtgq fpmnj rpmvs
spvfq elvax htviw iykgm tywym sdmey rpiie iyavl eckqr seipx aebcg kdqns
ovnqa aclvs hpitm nrnts mjwww ozvdc tsmye yswys femph ojwwx htvma edpqy
lokje nrmqy raiuw wzzfw iykgx htaem psmte pamcv sewdi spkwv exiaf ehmee
nowkx oykge mzvvl lpboi kywya hlbas ucbjs urpvw oybjm stauy elzg

Unaware of the change in cipher, Eve tried her normal tools beginning with a frequency count. Much to her surprise, the results were like nothing she had ever seen. The expected hills and valleys were missing. (See Figure 3.2.)

Suspecting that the cipher was no longer monoalphabetic, which is a good guess whenever the frequency distribution appears to be smoother than expected, Eve decides that Alice and Bob have probably switched ciphers to one that is polyalphabetic. She confirms her guess using a test developed in the 1920s called the *Index of Coincidence* (IC).

While a smooth frequency distribution is one hint that the underlying cipher is polyalphabetic, the IC is another tool that can be used to distinguish between monoalphabetic and polyalphabetic ciphers. Developed in 1922 by William Friedman, perhaps America's greatest cryptologist, the Index of Coincidence represented one of the first cryptanalysis tools that drew upon the power of mathematical statistics.

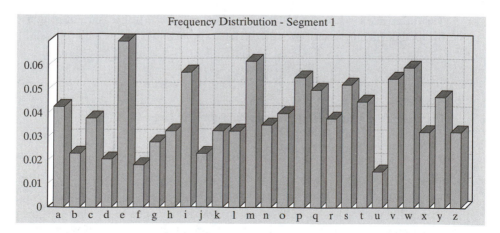

Figure 3.2: Eve's frequency report

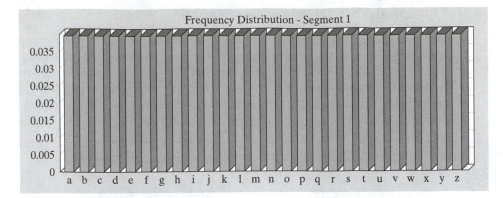

Figure 3.3: Flat frequency report

The IC is based on the idea of a measure of roughness, MR, which is an indication of just how rough is the frequency distribution of letters. For example, a totally smooth distribution of letters would produce a very uninteresting frequency distribution. (See Figure 3.3.) A rough distribution would look more like standard English with the hills and valleys in the frequency distribution. The key to assigning a number to the idea of roughness is to consider the probability of randomly selecting a letter from a segment of ciphertext. If the ciphertext is totally smooth, then every letter is equally likely to be selected. Therefore, the probability of, say, selecting "a" is 1/26. The probability of selecting a "y" is also 1/26. However, since standard English text is not totally smooth, the probability that a randomly selected letter would be "a" is greater than the probability that a randomly selected letter would be "y." So a measure of roughness could be the difference between the actual probability of selecting letters from the text and the probability of selecting letters from a totally smooth distribution. If p_α is the probability of selecting the letter α from a sample of ciphertext, then the measure of deviation from the probability of selecting α from a totally smooth text is

$$(p_\alpha - 1/26)^2.$$

The difference is squared so that it is always positive. The measure of roughness, MR, is the total deviation, so sum over all the letters from a to z:

$$\text{MR} = \sum_{\alpha=a}^{z} \left(p_\alpha - \frac{1}{26}\right)^2.$$

Expanding the square and doing a little arithmetic gives

$$\text{MP} = \sum_{\alpha=a}^{z} p_\alpha^2 - 0.038.$$

For a sample of ciphertext, MR can be determined if p_α^2 can be estimated. Since p_α is the probability that the letter α will be selected out of the ciphertext, then p_α^2 is the probability of selecting α out of the entire ciphertext times the probability of selecting α out of the remaining ciphertext (the ciphertext after the first α has been removed). If the ciphertext has n letters and f_α is the number of α's in the ciphertext, then

$$p_\alpha = f_\alpha/n,$$

so

$$p_\alpha^2 = (f_\alpha/n)[(f_\alpha - 1)/(n - 1)].$$

The only term that depends on the ciphertext in the MR is the sum over p_α^2, so the Index of Coincidence is defined to be

$$IC = \frac{\sum_{\alpha=a}^{z} f_\alpha(f_\alpha - 1)}{N(N - 1)}.$$

The IC for a monoalphabetic cipher is about 0.066. For totally smooth text, it is 0.038. If the IC value is between 0.038 and 0.066, then the underlying cipher is most likely polyalphabetic. In fact, the IC value can suggest the length of the polyalphabetic key word, using the following table:

Key Length	IC
1	0.0660
2	0.0520
3	0.0473
4	0.0450
5	0.0436
6	0.0427
7	0.0420
8	0.0415
9	0.0411
10	0.0408
11	0.0405
12	0.0403

Eve ran the IC test from CAP on the intercepted ciphertext. The IC value was 0.041, which clearly indicates that Bob and Alice have switched to a polyalphabetic cipher and their keyword is between 5 and 10 letters in length. With this evidence, Eve decides to try to find some tools that will break the most famous polyalphabetic—the Vigenere cipher.

Well, it doesn't take Eve long to discover a wide range of tools that pry open any Vigenere cipher. The most famous of the tools is one called the Kasiski method. For more than 300 years, the Vigenere cipher was thought to be unbreakable until a Polish army officer published a short book on cryptanalysis in 1863. In his book, he outlined a procedure that will determine the length of a Vigenere keyword. It turns out that the length of the keyword is the Achilles' heel of the Vigenere cipher. With the length identified, it becomes a simple matter to determine both the keyword and the underlying plaintext. Unfortunately, Frederick Kasiski died in 1881 without realizing the monumental contribution he made to the art of cryptanalysis. His breakthrough was based on a simple observation: "The conjunction of a repeated portion of the key with a repetition in the plaintext produces a repetition in the ciphertext."

What this observation says is that if a string of letters is repeated in the plaintext such that it is always enciphered with the same part of the keyword, then the ciphertext will also contain a repeated string. Perhaps an illustration will make this remarkable yet simple idea clear:

```
R U N R U N R U N R U N R U N R U N R U N R U N R U N
t o b e o r n o t t o b e t h a t i s t h e q u e s t
K I O V I E E I G K I O V N U R N V J N U V K H V M G .
↑ ⟵ 9 characters ⟶ ↑        ↑⟵6 characters⟶↑
```

In this case, the keyword is "RUN." Notice that the repeated plaintext characters "tobe" are enciphered by the keyword string "RUNR." This produces the repeated ciphertext string "KIOV." In this example, the plaintext characters "th" are also repeated and enciphered by the same segment of the keyword "UN" producing the identical ciphertext string "NU." What is interesting about this observation is not the ciphertext characters themselves, but the distance between the repeated strings of ciphertext. Since the repeated ciphertext is produced by repeated segments of both the plaintext and the key, the distance between the ciphertext repetitions will reflect the number of times the key is repeated. That in turn will provide vital information on the length of the key. As will be seen later, this is a fatal weakness in these types of ciphers, because, with knowledge of the key length, the actual key can be determined.

For the example, the length of the keyword "RUN" is 3. Notice that the distance between the repeated ciphertext strings "KIOV" is 9. The distance between the repeated ciphertext "NU" is 6. Those distances are both multiples of the keyword length ($6 = 2 \times 3$ and $9 = 3 \times 3$). This is not surprising because, for the keyword to align itself with the repeated plaintext, it has to repeat itself an integral number of times. So here is the process suggested by Kasiski:

1. Find repetitions in the ciphertext.
2. Count the number of characters between the repetitions.
3. Find the factors of the numbers discovered in Step 2.
4. The most common factor is likely to be the keyword length.

Now "accidental" repetitions may appear in the ciphertext. They are a coincidence and they will give false clues to the length of the keyword. However, the effect of accidental repetitions is diffused, whereas that of true repetitions is concentrated on one number. Hence, the most common factor (or factors) is your best guess for the keyword length.

Once the keyword length has been determined, the only remaining problem is how to use that information to find the actual keyword. Solving this problem requires you to think about what you really know when you know the length of the keyword. In cryptanalysis in general, every piece of information about the ciphertext has implications. Some of those implications may prove to be very useful. Some may not, but they all deserve to be considered. In this case, the length of the keyword reveals how the ciphertext can be broken down into a collection of monoalphabetic ciphers. For example, if Eve were to discover that Alice and Bob's keyword is six characters long, then she knows that every sixth letter is enciphered by the same keyword letter as shown in Figure 3.4:

If the keyword is "abcdef" then:

Repeated keyword:	abcdef	abcdef	abcdef	abcdef	abcdef	abcdef
Ciphertext:	lpksof	jbnnmp	flsrne	oivqrl	xbkqtz	ucxots

So, ljkfoxusjk... are all enciphered by the same letter "a"

Figure 3.4: Exploiting keyword length

Hence, the problem of breaking a Vigenere cipher in which the keyword length is known to be n becomes the problem of breaking n different monoalphabetic ciphers. Since monoalphabetic ciphers can be easily solved providing the ciphertext is large enough to produce a reasonable statistical sample, the Vigenere cipher is also easy to solve.

3.1.2   Cryptanalysis of the Vigenere Cipher with CAP

Eve still has yet to break the Vigenere ciphertext she recently intercepted from Alice and Bob. However, using CAP, she begins entering the ciphertext and running a Kasiski analysis. The result of her run is shown in Figure 3.5. CAP suggests that the best length for the keyword is 5, which is consistent with the IC test. If the keyword is actually of length 5, then every fifth character has been enciphered with the same keyword letter. Eve uses this information to divide the ciphertext into five sets of letters. The first set consists of ciphertext characters $1, 6, 11, \ldots$, the second set contains ciphertext characters $2, 7, 12, \ldots$, and so on. Each set represents a monoalphabetic cipher, so Eve applies the standard cryptanalysis

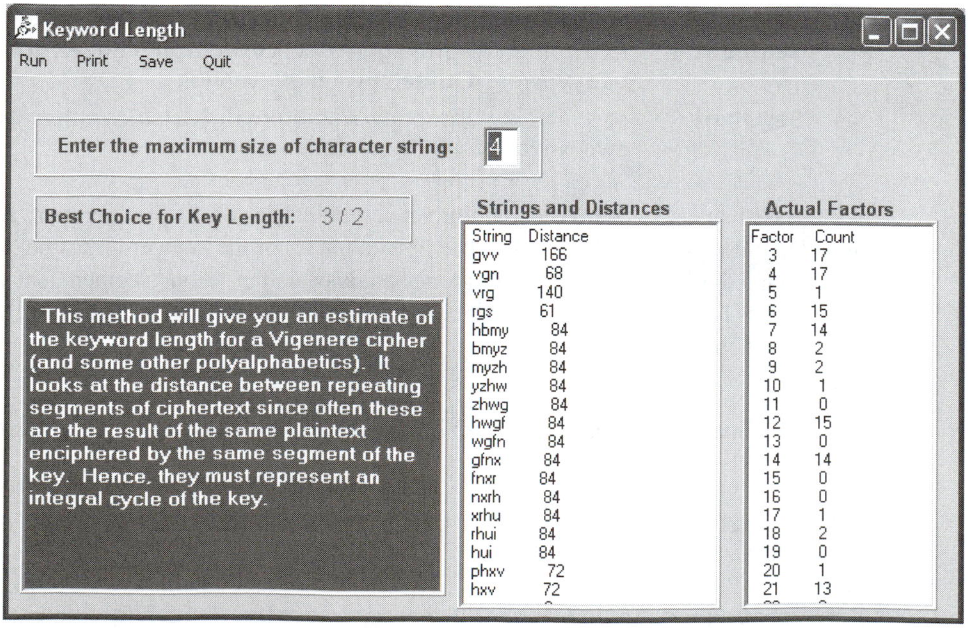

Keyword Length

Run   Print   Save   Quit

Enter the maximum size of character string: 4

Best Choice for Key Length: 3 / 2

This method will give you an estimate of the keyword length for a Vigenere cipher (and some other polyalphabetics). It looks at the distance between repeating segments of ciphertext since often these are the result of the same plaintext enciphered by the same segment of the key. Hence, they must represent an integral cycle of the key.

Strings and Distances

String	Distance
gvv	166
vgn	68
vrg	140
rgs	61
hbmy	84
bmyz	84
myzh	84
yzhw	84
zhwg	84
hwgf	84
wgfn	84
gfnx	84
fnxr	84
nxrh	84
xrhu	84
rhui	84
hui	84
phxv	72
hxv	72

Actual Factors

Factor	Count
3	17
4	17
5	1
6	15
7	14
8	2
9	2
10	1
11	0
12	15
13	0
14	14
15	0
16	0
17	1
18	2
19	0
20	1
21	13

Figure 3.5: Results of a Kasiski run

approach to such ciphers. Although she manages to break the first of the five, she discovers that it requires a lot of work. This is because she can no longer look for words, since the text consists of every fifth character of the plaintext.

After some study of the problem, Eve discovers that there is another easier way to deal with the monoalphabetic subciphers formed from a Vigenere cipher. This method is called a *low-frequency analysis*. The process begins by writing the targeted subcipher in a column. Create a second column by shifting each letter in the first by one position in the alphabet. Create a third column by shifting each letter in the second by one position. Continue this process until there are 25 columns. These columns represent all possible shifts of the original ciphertext. One of these shifts is the actual plaintext. Since the columns are formed by a selection of the letters in the original plaintext, it is not feasible to scan the column looking for words or even possible words. However, there is another characteristic of English that can be exploited to identify which one of the 25 columns contains the actual plaintext. It is based on the observation that the low-frequency letters in standard English text ("j", "k", "q", "x", "z") should have a combined frequency of about two percent. Any column in which these five letters appear more than two percent of the time is probably not the correct plaintext column. By eliminating those columns, the problem is reduced to either a single column or a just a few columns. Either way, it now becomes an easy task to solve for the plaintext.

Of course, Eve is excited to try this new technique. First, she breaks up the ciphertext into five segments as before in which each segment consists of every fifth character from the starting character. The result for her ciphertext is as follows:

Segment 1	hbmhwhweoemeternopnsiweriehtoiattofrsehitsriesakoahn-motyfohenrwihppsseenomlkhuuose
Segment 2	pzglttncyslozqprfzelvpdpddpmhyczsmpppltyydpyceedvcpr-jzssejtdorazytsaepxhoyzpylcrytl
Segment 3	tjmxbaqnkivbxziizzuovuwibqxcqsmxmtmmvvvkwmiakibqn-linwvmwmwvpkMizkammwkimwkvbwbbpbaz
Segment 4	nktrjprqgxcqgqfnkvggqconcpcvvyqqrgnvfaigyeivqpcnqvt-twdyypwmqjQufgetcdwaekgvoyajvjug
Segment 5	seccxilvaikwzqmpqewwahiqoxwrlirjvqjsqxwmmyelrxgsasm-swceshxayeywwxmevivfexeliasswmy

Based on her standard monoalphabetic cryptanalysis of the first segment, Eve determined that it represents plaintext, so the first character of the keyword must be "a". When she attempted to use the new low-frequency analysis on the second segment, she produced these results for the first three rows (the number of low frequency characters is given at the end of each string)

Shift 0:
pzglttncyslozqprfzelvpdpddpmhyczsmpppltyydpyceedvcprjzssejtdorazytsaepx-hoyzpylcrytl 10

Shift 1:
qahmuuodztmparqsgafmwqeqeeqnizdatnqqqmuzzeqzdffewdqskattdkueps-bazutbfqyipzaqzmdszum 23

Shift 2:
rbinvvpeaunqbsrthbgnxrfrffrojaebuorrrnvaafraeggfxertlbuuelvfqtcbavucgrzjqa-branetavn 6

Since the segment consists of 83 characters, the expected number of low-frequency characters, "j", "k", "q", "x", "z" is 1.66. The first three shifts resulted in substantially more than one or two of these characters. In fact, it turns out the best fit to the expected number is a shift of 15. This shift would indicate that the second letter of the keyword is "l", since another shift of 11 would return the ciphertext to plaintext. So far, then, Eve's best guess is a keyword of "al...". Do you have any idea what the actual keyword might be? Well, Eve decides to pass on the analysis of the remaining segments and just try the keyword "alice". It turns out that it works! (This is one reason why keywords should not consist of names or anything else that might be associated with ourselves.)

Of course, CAP provides all the tools necessary to perform both the Kasiski and the low-frequency analysis. If Eve had entered her ciphertext into CAP and run a low-frequency analysis for a keyword length of 5, CAP would have automatically selected the correct keyword as shown in Figure 3.6.

The standard Vigenere table is not the only way in which this cipher may be implemented. In fact, there are several alternatives that vary in the nature of the table construction. One of the most common is the Beaufort cipher, which uses a 27×27 alphabet square in which the standard alphabet is repeated on all four sides. There is a Variant Beaufort cipher that uses the standard Vigenere table, but reverses the process of reading the table. In the Variant Beaufort, the key letters label the row and the ciphertext letters label the columns. So to encipher, you find the key letter row, read across to the plaintext letter in the table, and read up to the ciphertext letter. Other variations include using a keyword to set up the table rather than just using the standard alphabet. For example, if the table

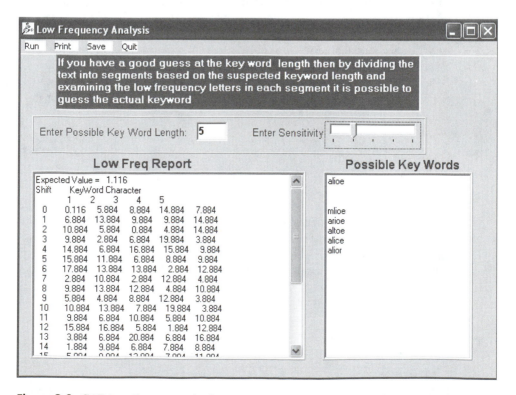

Figure 3.6: CAP Low Frequency Analysis run

keyword is "cipher", then the first row of this alternative Vigenere table would be

c i p h e r a b d f g j k l m n o q s t u v w x y z.

The remaining rows are created by rotating the first row. As a result, the second row would be

i p h e r a b d f g j k l m n o q s t u v w x y z c.

It turns out that none of these variations offers any more security than the original—the same tools and process that break the standard Vigenere work equally well on these variations.

In a surprising turn of events, the cipher that was supposed to eliminate the weaknesses of the monoalphabetic is actually easier to break. Unfortunately that did not mean that the cipher fell out of use. Even after procedures for breaking it became known it remained in use for quite a while. During the Civil War, the South used it. To make matters even worse, during the entire war they used only three keys: Manchester bluff, complete victory, and come retribution. The United States used a version prior to WWI as well.

3.2   AUTOKEY CIPHER

It doesn't take Alice and Bob long to realize that they have failed again. They like the idea of a polyalphabetic cipher, but now know that they at least have to modify it somehow in order to prevent Eve from reading their messages. The problem with the Vigenere cipher (just one of many) is that the keyword repeats itself. This allowed Eve to determine the length of the keyword and then break down the ciphertext into easily deciphered segments. If the keyword could be longer, then perhaps the cipher would be more secure. So Alice reads about another type of polyalphabetic cipher called an *autokey cipher*. In this case, the keyword is used just once and the plaintext provides the remaining letters for the cipher. This is actually more in line with the original cipher suggested by Vigenere. For example, using the keyword "alice" and a standard Vigenere table produces the following plaintext–ciphertext:

a l i c e i h o p e t h i s w o r k s b e t t e
i h o p e t h i s w o r k s b e t t e r t h a n...
i s w r i b o w h a h y s k x s k d w s x a t r

This is not a new idea. In 1550, Girolamo Cardano, a physician and mathematician, published a description of a flawed autokey method that appeared to be more secure than a simple Vigenere cipher. At the very least, it does not display the same weakness involving repeating segments of the key. Of course, CAP will implement this version of a polyalphabetic cipher as well—just select the Autokey option under the Ciphertext menu. Surprisingly, this is not as secure as it might appear to be, but it is an example of an approach to encryption involving "running" keys. We will encounter this concept again in the chapter on stream ciphers.

A variation on this process uses the ciphertext rather than the plaintext to provide the repeated key. In this case, the aforementioned message would appear as follows:

a l i c e i s w r i b z f j e p q p b f t j i f
i h o p e t h i s w o r k s b e t t e r t h a n...
i s w r i b z f j e p q p b f t j i f w m q i s

While this autokey method might seem like a good fix for the Vigenere cipher, it does have one major downside. An error anywhere in the encryption or decryption propagates throughout the remaining text. For example, if Alice were sending a message to Bob and accidentally recorded the wrong ciphertext letter, then when Bob tried to decipher the message everything would be unreadable from the point of the error to the end of the message. The other ciphers we have looked at so far do not have this problem. In those ciphers, if a wrong ciphertext character were recorded, only the corresponding plaintext character would be wrong. With just a single incorrect character, the plaintext remains quite readable.

3.2.1 Cryptanalysis of the Autokey Cipher

Alice and Bob agree to use the autokey cipher based on the ciphertext—that is, the ciphertext becomes the key (a poor choice, as they will discover later). Eve, who still is able to intercept all the traffic between Alice and Bob, quickly saves the first of their autokey ciphertexts:

tzjqf bzvwq bctkk gqnxn ukgxo iezqv madqf zevin mspzc
dwkhq xompf esdim mkrvq erfpb hgqjh bvjqh ucxbl unfdp

Since Eve is initially unaware of the change in ciphers, she tries the standard Vigenere analysis tools. Of course, since this is not exactly a Vigenere cipher, she is unable to recover the plaintext. Assuming that they have changed their cipher, Eve tries to identify the new algorithm Alice and Bob have selected. The frequency distribution of the ciphertext still suggests a polyalphabetic cipher (since the frequencies do not display the standard hills and valleys of a monoalphabetic cipher). But, the keyword length appears to be quite long and undetectable by the Kasiski method. This suggests to Eve that it is possible that they have chosen to use an autokey cipher.

Deciding to act on this assumption, Eve tries the easiest approach first. She guesses that the ciphertext is used as the running key. So she decides to exploit the obvious weakness of such a cipher—that is, since the ciphertext is also the key for later segments of the plaintext, the only problem is determining where the original keyword ends and the ciphertext-as-key begins. This is a prime candidate for a brute force attack. First, decipher the ciphertext using the ciphertext shifted over by one position as the key. If that does not produce readable plaintext, then repeat the process with the ciphertext shifted over by two characters, then three characters, and so on, until the plaintext appears. Of course this means that the beginning part of the ciphertext is not correctly decoded. This could be easily accomplished by matching pattern words—if it is even necessary at all.

As always, CAP provides an automatic tool for this kind of analysis. The results of Eve's CAP run are shown in Figure 3.7.

The analysis suggests a keyword of length 5 and provides all the plaintext after the first five characters. Eve guesses that Alice and Bob have selected the same keyword again and tries "alice", which works.

Alice and Bob quickly discover their error and decide that they really should have used the plaintext as the running key. Now, this removes the weakness of the ciphertext-key approach to an autokey cipher, but it does introduce some new weaknesses.

Once again, Eve intercepts traffic in the new autokey cipher:

ucbew cpgqy pbynp mljmg kmuqw wjckg cldjy ktavj hxspp
vvzwj wpsml vxmnv msumn jmikv txygg nabma jkbcm lvvwo gvy.

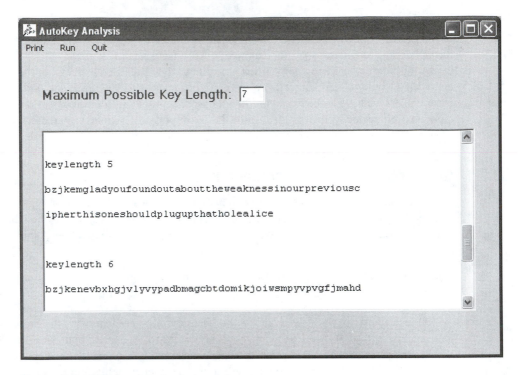

Figure 3.7: CAP Autokey Analysis window

After trying the autokey–ciphertext approach, Eve determines that Alice and Bob have again made a change. Suspecting that they are now using the plaintext for the running key rather than the ciphertext, Eve does the obvious (which is?). She tries the keyword "alice". Since it doesn't work, Eve knows that Alice and Bob are getting a little better at this protection thing.

But from Eve's standpoint, all is not lost. There are several tools available to pry open an autokey–plaintext cipher, especially if the underlying one is a Vigenere cipher. The first tool will estimate the length of the keyword. Of course, the Kasiski method for Vigenere keyword length does not work on an autokey–plaintext cipher; however, another observation about the nature of this class of ciphers reveals an alternative approach to keyword length determination.

Even though the length of the keyword does not define a repetitive period in the encryption of a sample of plaintext, it does define the "group length," which is the distance between the encryption of a plaintext character and its use as a key character to encrypt another plaintext character. For example, if the keyword is "alice", then the group length is 5. As shown next, the first plaintext character is encrypted by "a" and then five characters later it is used to encrypt the plaintext character "e".

In this same example, "h" is encrypted and then used five characters later to encrypt "x". In general, every character will be enciphered by the letter five characters to its left and every character will encipher the letter five characters to its right. Knowledge of the keyword length is equivalent to knowing the group length.

Just as was the case with a standard Vigenere cipher, knowledge of the keyword length may be exploited to break up the cipher into segments that can be analyzed individually. If it is known that the keyword length is 5, then every fifth letter is part of a single segment. The first segment begins with the first plaintext letter. This letter is enciphered using the first keyword character. Then, the first plaintext letter is used to encipher the sixth plaintext letter, which in turn is used to encipher the 11th plaintext letter, and so on. The second segment is constructed the same way, but this time beginning with the second plaintext letter. Once the segments are known, this cipher is open to a brute force attack. The process requires trying each of the possible 26 characters for the first keyword letter to reconstruct the plaintext. Since only one of the 26 reconstructed plaintext segments will be correct, a low-frequency character analysis could be applied to identify the best out of the 26 candidates. In this way, either the keyword can be immediately identified or a set of possible characters for the keyword can be suggested. Either way, the cipher is compromised.

Using the Block Analysis tool in CAP, Eve discovered several possible keyword lengths. (See Figure 3.8 for her output.) She then used the Autokey Solution tool with the

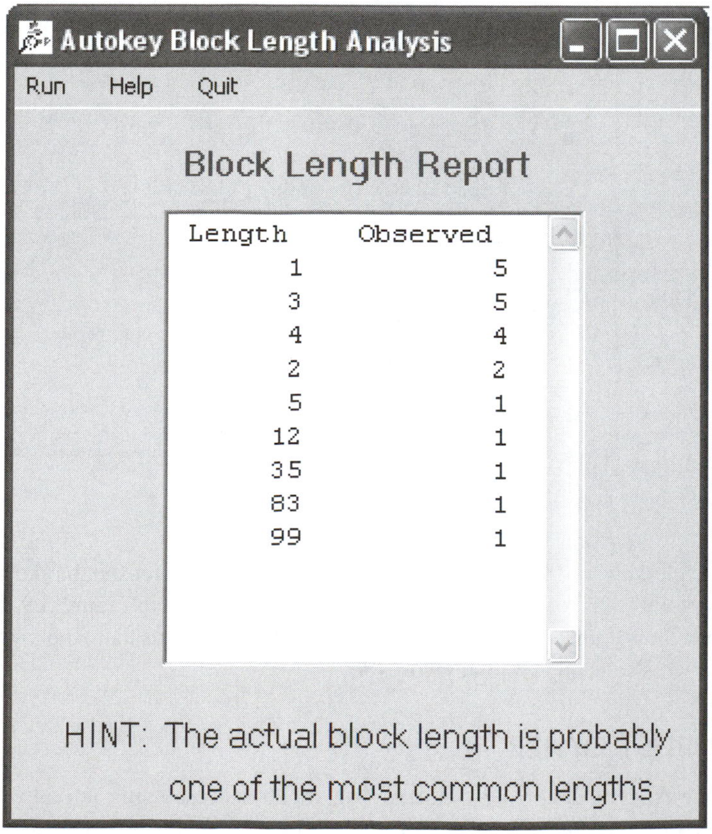

Autokey Block Length Analysis

Run   Help   Quit

Block Length Report

Length	Observed
1	5
3	5
4	4
2	2
5	1
12	1
35	1
83	1
99	1

HINT: The actual block length is probably one of the most common lengths

Figure 3.8: Autokey Block Length Analysis

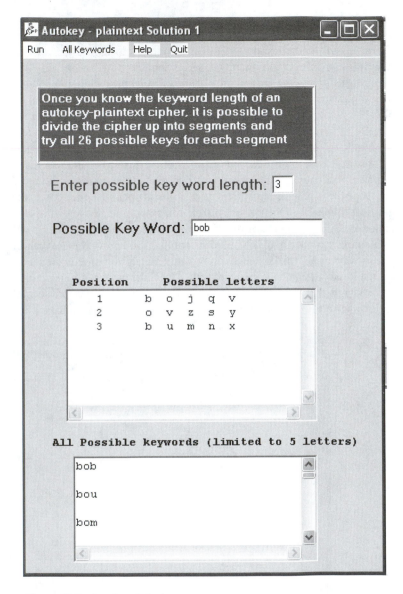

Figure 3.9: Autokey Solution

possible keyword length of 5, but it did not produce a reasonable keyword. Her second attempt with this tool worked beautifully as can be seen in Figure 3.9. The keyword appears to be "bob", which does decipher the ciphertext. It seems that Bob and Alice are still having problems selecting good keywords.

3.4   NIHILIST CIPHER

Since Alice and Bob were not having much success using polyalphabetics that relied on only one type of transformation, they did some research and came up with another approach called a *Nihilist cipher*. This cipher seems to be more secure than others they have tried because it involves more than one enciphering operation.

The Nihilist cipher is adopted from a method used by the Russian underground during the time of the czars. It was developed for use among prisoners. Most Russian prisoners at the time were kept in solitary confinement and forbidden from communicating with other prisoners. In its original use, prisoners would tap on the walls and the number of taps would designate a letter position on a checkerboard. They became very skilled at this cipher, communicating at the rate of 10 to 15 words a minute.

This checkerboard process ultimately formed the core of the Nihilist cipher. The first step in the Nihilist cipher is to select a keyword to construct a Polybius square—that is, write out the keyword (dropping any repeated letters) in a 5 × 5 array. Once the keyword is written, continue to fill in the array using the remaining letters of the alphabet in order (dropping "j" so that there are only 25 characters in the square). The rows and columns are numbered from 1 to 5. Supposing that the keyword is "example", then the Polybius square looks like this:

	1	2	3	4	5
1	e	x	a	m	p
2	l	b	c	d	f
3	g	h	i	k	n
4	o	q	r	s	t
5	u	v	w	y	z

The second step is to select another keyword and use the Polybius square to convert it into numbers. For example, if the second keyword is "next", using the previous square, it becomes the number sequence 35 11 12 45. Now, convert the plaintext into numbers using the same square. If the plaintext is "stop that", it becomes the number sequence 44 45 41 15 45 32 13 45. From this point on, the Nihilist cipher can be used just like a Vigenere cipher—that is, write the keyword-sequence numbers repeatedly above the plaintext-number sequence. To construct the ciphertext, simply add the corresponding keyword–plaintext pairs. If the sum is greater than 100, subtract 100 from the result. To decipher, subtract the keyword numbers from the corresponding ciphertext numbers and look up the result in the square. If the ciphertext number is less than 12, add 100 to it before performing the subtraction.

This seems like a difficult process to implement manually. If you don't have a lot of time on your hands (as did the prisoners of the czar in Russia), you might want to use the tools provided by CAP to explore this cipher. As with all the CAP cipher tools, enter the plaintext, select the Nihilist cipher, enter the keys (one for the square and one for the summation process), and select Encipher.

The Nihilist cipher suffers from some of the same weaknesses as the Vigenere cipher. Breaking it is complicated somewhat by the fact that numbers are used instead of letters. But with some careful thought, the use of numbers can also be exploited. Eve discovers some ways in which this cipher can be broken, but she refuses to share them with anyone else. It is left to you as an exercise.

3.5 CYLINDER CIPHER

Giving up on the Nihilist cipher, Alice and Bob turn to another class of polyalphabetics—this one based on a cylinder. Chapter 1 introduced the concept of a wheel (or cylinder cipher) based on Thomas Jefferson's enciphering device. Perhaps one of the most famous cylinder-type ciphers was developed by Etienne Bazeries in 1891. Bazeries was a brilliant and successful cryptanalyst. Yet, as good as he was at breaking ciphers, he was less skilled at creating them. He did develop a cylinder cipher that now bears his name—the Bazeries cylinder. In 1891, he tried to get the French army to adopt it, but failed. Thirty years later, however, in 1922, the U.S. Army used his method.

The Bazeries cylinder consists of 20 wheels, each with the alphabet in a different order. (See Figure 3.10.) The wheels are arranged in a preselected order. (This order is the key to the cipher.) The wheels are turned so that the plaintext appears on one line and one of the other lines is selected for the ciphertext. For example, if only three wheels are used in the order 1 5 3 and the plaintext word is "hat", then a possible ciphertext is "sxh" as shown in Figure 3.11.

Rather than construct a set of 20 metal wheels, in this age of computers, Bob and Alice use CAP to encipher–decipher text with the Bazeries cylinder. As always, they enter the plaintext into CAP and select the Bazeries Cylinder option under the Cipher menu. A special window opens. (See Figure 3.12.) The key is the order of the 20 wheels. CAP opens with a default order of 1, 2, ..., 20. Of course, Bob and Alice do not want to rely on the default, so they enter a different order. In fact, their key is 2, 5, 10, 20, 1, 3, 19, 17, 18, 15, 4, 9, 11, 16, 6, 7, 14, 13, 8, 12. With this key in place, they proceed to communicate with each other, confident that at long last they have defeated Eve.

It is important to note that CAP adds one other feature to the Bazeries cipher. In the CAP version, the user does not select the line of the cylinder to use as ciphertext; instead, CAP will vary the line selected. The first block of 20 ciphertext characters will be formed from the line adjacent to the plaintext. The second block will be formed by skipping ahead one line from the plaintext on the cylinder. The third block will be formed by skipping ahead two lines, and so on. After skipping ahead 24 lines, the process will repeat. This is important to remember when applying the CAP tools to break this cipher.

1	a b c d e f g h i j k l m n o p q r s t u v x y z
2	b c d f g h j k l m n p q r s t v x z a e i o u y
3	a e b c d f g h i o j k l m n p u y q r s t v x z
4	z y x v u t s r q p o n m l k j i h g f e d c b a
5	y u z x v t s r o i q p n m l k e a j h g f d c b
6	z x v t s r q p n m l k j h g f d c b y u o i e a
7	a l o n s e f t d p r i j u g v b c h k m q x y z
8	b i e n h u r x l s p a v d t o y m c f g j k q z
9	c h a r y b d e t s l f g i j k m n o p q u v x z
10	d i e u p r o t g l a f n c b h j k m q s v x y z
11	e v i t z l s c o u r a n d b f g h j k m p q x y
12	f o r m e z l s a i c u x b d g h j k n p q t v y
13	g l o i r e m t d n s a u x b c f h j k p q v y z
14	h o n e u r t p a i b c d f g j k l m q s v x y z
15	i n s t r u e z l a j b c d f g h k m o p q v x y
16	j a i m e l o g n f r t h u b c d k p q s v x y z
17	k y r i e l s o n a b c d f g h j m p q t u v x z
18	l h o m e p r s t d i u a b c f g j k n q v x y z
19	m o n t e z a c h v l b d f g i j k p q r s u x y
20	n o u s t e l a c f b d g h i j k m p q r v x y z

Figure 3.10: Bazeries cylinder wheels

1	5	3
h	a	t
i	j	v
j	h	x
k	g	z
l	f	a
m	d	e
n	c	b
o	b	c
p	y	d
q	u	f
r	z	g
s	x	h
t	v	l
u	t	o
v	s	j
x	r	k
y	o	l
z	i	m
a	q	n
b	p	p
c	n	u
d	m	y
e	l	q
f	k	r
g	e	s

Figure 3.11: Bazeries encoding of "hat"

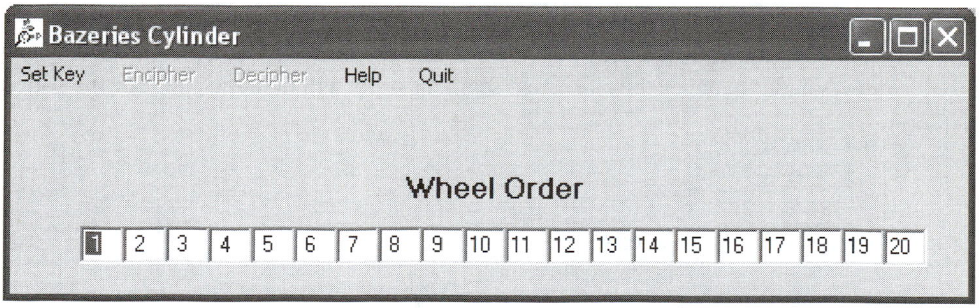

Figure 3.12: Bazeries Cylinder in CAP

3.5.1 Cryptanalysis of the Bazeries Cylinder

For a while, Bob and Alice are safe because Eve is stumped by the new cipher. She knows that it is still a polyalphabetic (how?), but she has trouble deciphering it. However, once she discovers that it is a Bazeries cylinder, she knows how to break it. In fact, the trick to breaking this cipher was discovered in 1893 by Marquis de Viaris. Therefore, it is known as the de Viaris method.

This method assumes two facts: first, that the cipher is a Bazeries cylinder with known cylinder content; and second, that at least one word of the plaintext is known. As a result, this is a known-plaintext-type attack. The goal is to determine the actual order of the cylinders.

Eve has discovered this attack method and decides to try it on the following intercepted ciphertext:

ekjdahdujcmvjbtfllhjrfgtfwfespbftpnxxgvaxpirabhusltcuuecdzab
        hgyfrsaahdihhhsjylnn

Since this is a message from Bob to Alice, Eve assumes that the word "alice" appears somewhere in the text. Now Eve has all the information she needs to apply the de Viaris attack. The process involves scanning the ciphertext with the known word and looking for an arrangement of the cylinders that will produce both the known word and the ciphertext segment pairs. In this case, Eve begins by matching the first five letters of the ciphertext with the known word:

a l i c e
e k j d a h d u j c m v j b t f l l ...

The question is: Can the cylinders be arranged so that the known word appears on one line and the ciphertext match appears on another line? If an arrangement cannot be found, then the known word is moved over one character and the search for an arrangement begins again:

** a l i c e**
e k j d a h d u j c m v j b t f l l ...

For the first possible alignment of the known word and the ciphertext, Eve creates a table of all possible cylinders. The table lists the known word at the top, and the first row consists of the letters following the known letter in Cylinder 1. The second row consists of the letters following the known letter in Cylinder 2, and so on. If there is a match—that is, if a letter on the cylinder matches the ciphertext segment—she will note the row. For the pattern

a l i c e
e k j d a,

Eve's table looks like this:

	a	l	i	c	e
1	b	m	j	d	f
2	e	m	o	d	g
3	e	m	o	d	b
4	z	k	h	b	d
5	j	k	q	b	a
6	z	k	e	b	a
7	l	o	j	h	f
8	v	s	e	f	n
9	r	f	j	h	t
10	f	a	e	b	u
11	n	s	t	o	v
12	i	s	c	u	z
13	u	o	r	f	m

14	i	m	b	d	u
15	j	a	n	d	z
16	i	o	m	d	l
17	b	s	e	d	l
18	b	h	u	f	p
19	c	b	j	h	z
20	c	a	j	f	l

If each column has at least one match, then this is a possible known-word–ciphertext match. If at least one column does not have a match, then the known word could not have been enciphered by the current alignment of ciphertext characters. Therefore, the known word must be shifted over to the adjacent ciphertext characters. In this case, Eve found that there is a possible match for each known-word character, so she tries to discover an arrangement of the cylinders that will work for all five characters. (If that fails, she shifts the known word over by one character.) An analysis of Eve's table indicates that Cylinder 2 or 3 could be in the first position, since either one will correctly match "a" with "e". Cylinders 4, 5, or 6 could be in position two because they will correctly match "l" with "k". Other possibilities include Cylinders 1, 7, 9, 19, or 20 in position three; Cylinders 1, 2, 3, 15, 16, or 17 in position four; and Cylinder 5 in position five. While this does not fully specify the cylinder order, it does significantly reduce the number of possible orders. In this case, the first five cylinders can be in only one of the following orders:

Cylinder Position	1	2	3	4	5
Cylinder Number	2	4	1	1	5
	3	6	7	2	
			9	3	
			19	15	
			20	16	
				17	

For example, a possible order is 2, 4, 1, 3, 5, and another is 2, 4, 1, 15, 5. This defines just over 60 possible cylinder orders and Eve must try each one. Of course they all work on the first five letters of the ciphertext and produce "alice". So to test them, Eve has to move ahead 20 characters in the ciphertext because that is where the wheel order repeats.

Next, those segments of the ciphertext enciphered by the first five wheels consist of the first five characters

ekjda hdujc mvjbt fllhj rfgtf wfesp bftpn xxgva xpira bhusl tcuue cdzab hgyfr saahd ihhhs jylnn.

When Eve tries the order 2, 4, 1, 3, 5, the result is

alice hdujc mvjbt fllhj pherh wfesp bftpn xxgva ssful bhusl tcuue cdzab cktex saahd ihhhs jylnn,

which does not look very promising. But when she tries the order 2, 6, 1, 3, 5, the ciphertext becomes

alice ciphe succe mvjbt fllhj pherh wfesp bftpn xxgva ssful bhusl tcuue cdzab cltex saahd ihhhs ytext.

This looks like a possibility in which the second word may be cipher, the third word may be successful, and the final word may be text. This opens up additional letters to match with the cylinder patterns. Eve does this and eventually discovers that the cylinder pattern used by Alice and Bob is 2, 6, 1, 3, 5, 4, 7, 8, 9, 10, 11, 12, 13, 14, 15, 16, 17, 18, 19, 20.

This is a lot of work to do by hand, so CAP provides some tools to help. The first tool will search for a possible word match. It will indicate the possible cylinders for each letter of the known word as shown in Figure 3.13. The second tool will use a possible cylinder arrangement to help identify other words in the ciphertext as shown in Figure 3.14.

3.6   ROTOR CIPHERS

Since the cylinder cipher was eventually broken by Eve, Alice and Bob decided that they needed to rethink this entire process. After looking into the history of ciphers, Bob came across the description of a rotor cipher similar to the type used by Germany during WWII. While he found it interesting, he decided not to use it because it was broken by the Allies during WWII.

A rotor cipher is an electromechanical system that implements a complicated polyalphabetic transformation. A rotor is a disk with electrical contacts on both sides, one for each letter of the alphabet. The internal path of the wires that connect the two sides defines a monoalphabetic substitution. A simple rotor is shown in Figure 3.15. Since each rotor is wired internally to represent a possible substitution pattern for the 26 letters of the alphabet, the number of possible rotors is

$$26! = 403,291,461,126,605,635,584,000,000.$$

By using several rotors connected in series and rotating them at different rates, a powerful polyalphabetic system can be constructed.

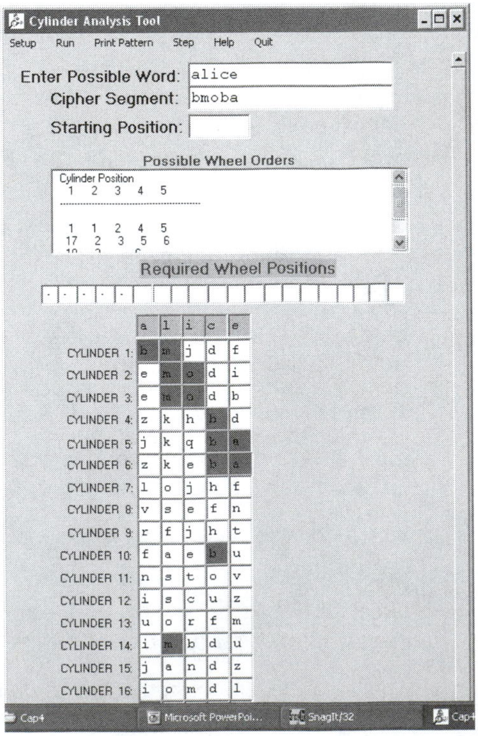

Figure 3.13: Possible word search in a Bazeries cylinder

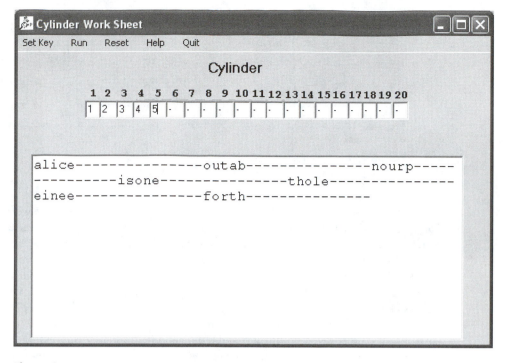

Figure 3.14: Bazeries Cylinder Work Sheet

Figure 3.15: A simple rotor

An example of a limited dual-rotor system is shown in Figure 3.16. Initially, "A" is mapped to "B", but after Rotor 2 rotates by one position, "A" is mapped to "E". After Rotor 2 has rotated 25 positions, Rotor "A" rotates by 1. As a result, there are $26 \times 26 = 676$ possible substitution patterns. By adding more rotors, the possibilities increase significantly.

During WWII, Germany used a rotor system of this type, called Enigma. Unknown and it turns out, unsuspected, by Germany, England had broken Enigma just prior to the outbreak of war. England had a head start on the cryptanalysis of the German machine because they had access to the work of three brilliant Polish mathematicians.

Poland, fearful of the growing power of Germany in the early 1920s, began to study German ciphers. The Polish Cipher Bureau experienced a great deal of success and was able to regularly read encrypted German communications until 1928, when Germany began to use the Enigma. Shortly after the move to the Enigma, Poland received a break. It seems that Germany sent an Enigma machine to their embassy in Poland. Polish postal

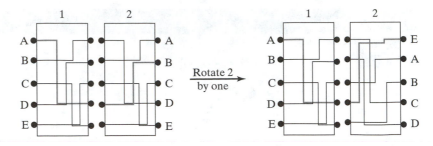

Figure 3.16: A dual-rotor system

employees, unbeknownst to the Germans, turned it over to Polish agents who were able to examine its construction and operation for several days before delivering it to the embassy. Even with this valuable information, it still required years of work to break the new cipher.

By the early 1930s, Marian Rejewski, Henryk Zygalski, and Jerzy Rozycki discovered a weakness in the Enigma machine that allowed them to re-create the machine from the ciphertext. This ranks among the most astonishing success stories in the history of cryptanalysis. Their work was passed on to England just before Germany overran Poland. England's codebreakers used the Polish data to break the German cipher. It became one of the most closely guarded secrets of the war and remained secret for long after the war was over.

Germany used several variations on the basic Enigma structure, but fundamentally it consisted of three rotors, a reflector, and a plugboard. Actually, there were five rotors, three of which were selected for use in the machine at any one time. The reflector was used to create a longer path by using each rotor twice. The plugboard was a fixed substitution, which usually involved only a few characters. The entire system is illustrated in Figure 3.17 in which "a" is mapped to "c".

CAP provides a simple three-rotor system without the plugboard. Select Rotor under the Cipher menu and the CAP Rotor Cipher window shown in Figure 3.18 will pop up.

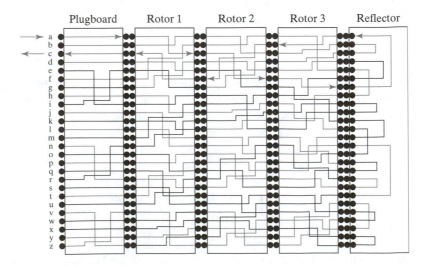

Figure 3.17: A three-rotor Enigma system

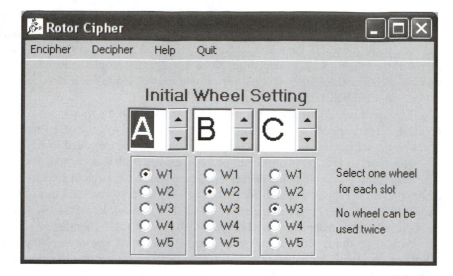

Figure 3.18: CAP Rotor Cipher Window

3.6.1 Breaking Enigma

During WWII, several methods for attacking Enigma as well as general rotor systems were discovered. However, one method that made it easier to ultimately find the Enigma key was to take advantage of the process used by Germany to set up the key. Each Enigma operator looked up the common daily key in a code book that contained one month of keys. The daily key consisted of the order of the three rotors; the initial starting positions of each rotor; and the plugboard settings. This process had a critical weakness. Following it meant that every transmission made by the German armed forces on a given day had the same key. With so much traffic available, the Germans were afraid that the Allies might be able to discover the key and read all the messages for that day. It was a realistic fear. It is the reason why even with today's powerful ciphers, keys are changed on a regular basis. So, to patch this security weakness, each message had its own key, which would be selected by the operator. Of course, the operator needed to transmit the new key, since the recipient only knew the official daily key. This became one of the first practical encounters with the problem of key management. The contemporary approach to this problem is addressed in Chapter 9. The steps to establishing a common key and sending an encrypted message were the following:

1. Set the machine to the official daily key.
2. Enter the three letters that represented the operators key for the message.
3. Repeat Step 2—that is, enter the operator's key again.
4. Reset the wheels to the starting position defined by the operator's key.
5. Send the message.

For example, the official key for the day might be a specific plugboard setting; Wheels 2, 1, and 4; and an initial wheel setting of "X T B". The operator would select a random initial setting, say, "J Y Q". With the Enigma set to the daily key, the operator would enter the random setting twice: "J Y Q J Y Q". Then the operator would set the wheels to "J Y Q" and transmit the message. On the receiving end, using the official daily key, the recipient would decode the first six characters to "J Y Q J Y Q" and then reset the initial wheels to "J Y Q" to decode the rest of the message. Sending the randomly selected operator key twice improved the reliability of the decoding, since the recipient would know something went wrong if the same three letters did not repeat themselves. However, it also opened a window of opportunity that the Allies could exploit.

For one thing, it was a safe bet that the operators would get lazy and use the same three letters for their code over and over again, or they would select an easy pattern such as repeating the same letter three times. Both mistakes could be exploited over the long run.

However, an even more important problem existed with this method. The concept at work here is that by encoding the operator-selected key twice, the first six letters of the ciphertext reveal something about the daily key to a skilled cryptanalyst. For example, if the first six letters of an Enigma message are "RTY UIO", then we know that the first letter of the operator's key is mapped by the daily key to "R" and to "U" after three rotations.

You might think: "It's only six characters—what could anyone possibly learn from so little information?" As with so much in cryptology, the answer may surprise you. Given the first six characters of enough messages, the initial position of the rotors for the daily key can be exposed.

For example, say that the Allies intercepted a series of messages from different sources on a given day. The first six characters of each of the messages are

"RTY UIO DEF PCQ NZK WAE PTI SVX SHQ LKG LCM DVY".

There are several interesting patterns in these characters. For example, in the first and last messages, "R" maps to "U" and "U" maps to "R": **RTY UIO UCM RVY**". This forms a cycle, "RU". In the remaining messages, "D" maps to "P", "P" maps to "S", "S" maps to "L", and "L" maps back to "D". This forms the cycle "DPSL". It turns out that the nature of the cycles produced by the daily keys can be used to identify the actual key. The attack used was to catalog all the cycles produced by each possible key. Once the cycle structure for a given day was discovered by examining the first six letters of that day's messages, the daily key was found by looking it up in the catalog. The net effect was that a method or protocol for using Enigma that was intended to make it more secure actually weakened it. What the Allies were able to exploit was the way the cipher was used more than the cipher itself.

3.6.2 Using CAP to Break a Rotor Cipher

Today's computers are powerful and fast enough to run a brute force attack against a rotor cipher, especially if there is some known plaintext. CAP implements just such an attack. Select Rotor Attack under the Polyalphabetic tools menu, and the window shown in Figure 3.19 will open. Enter the known plaintext and click on Run. Then, be patient because the attack may take some time.

3.7   THE RISE OF THE MACHINES—A BRIEF HISTORY

In the late 1890s and early 1900s, machines began to take over the process of enciphering plaintext. Not the computer-based machines that rule today, this was a revolution of primarily mechanical devices consisting of gears and wheels with the electronics limited to wires, lights, switches, and plugs. Some ideas just seem to have a life of their own waiting in the wings for their time. Apparently, the late 1910s was the time for the rotor machine. Almost simultaneously and independently, several cryptographers came up with the same

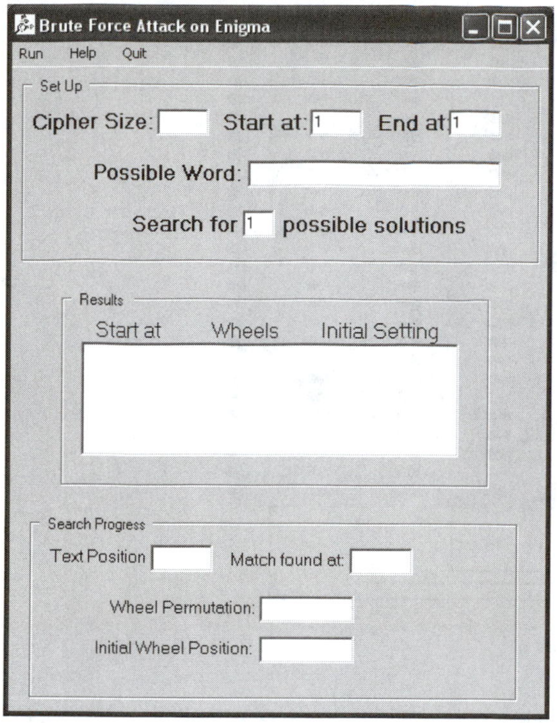

Figure 3.19: CAP's Brute Force Attack on a rotor cipher

idea. The concept of the rotor (which ultimately found its way into the Enigma machine) was born and became the foundation of a new class of polyalphabetic ciphers.

Arvid Damm patented a rotor idea in Sweden in 1919 that became the basis of the B-211 machine designed by Boris Hagelin. Hagelin's machines were among some of the most widely used cryptographic systems in Europe for decades. While Damm and Hagelin were working on rotor machines in Europe, Edward Hebern patented a rotor system in the United States in 1917. His rotor mechanism was used in his "electronic code machine" which had an impact on the design of U.S. cipher machines through WWII.

Of course the most famous (or infamous) rotor machine was the Enigma. The Allies were able to break that machine and use the information they gained to their advantage throughout the war. The obvious questions are: What did the United States use to protect military communications? Did Germany break it? For top-level communications, the U.S. military used the ECM Mark II (also called the ECM or the SIGABA). Like most cryptographic systems of the time, the ECM was a rotor-based machine. However, it was much more complicated than Enigma. It had 15 rotors (compared with the 3 to 5 rotors of Enigma) arranged in three banks of five. Five of the rotors had 26 contacts on a side to represent letters of the alphabet. These rotors formed the cipher bank (shown in Figure 3.20), and much like the Enigma, the signal for the plaintext letter entered on one side, followed a path through the five rotors, and emerged from the other side as the ciphertext signal. One major difference between the Enigma and the ECM is the rotational behavior of the rotors. In the Enigma, the first rotor advanced one position with each letter. When it had advanced 26 positions, the second rotor advanced one position, and so on. The rotors in the ECM rotated in a random fashion under the control of the other two banks of five rotors.

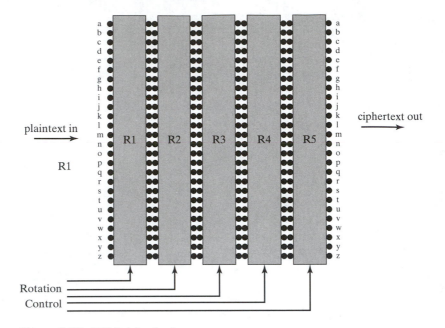

Figure 3.20: ECM cipher bank

The control bank consists of five rotors with 26 contacts as well, as shown in Figure 3.21. The first four inputs to the control were fixed to "ON". These signals would follow a given path through the five rotors to produce "ON" signals on some set of the outputs 1 to 9. As noted in Figure 3.21, some of the outputs are connected together such as outputs "k", "j", and "i", which form the overall output 5. This means that if any one or a combination of "k", "j", and "i" are "ON", then output 5 is "ON". In other words, the outputs are "OR"ed together. In the control bank, only Rotors 2, 3, and 4 are free to rotate. Rotor

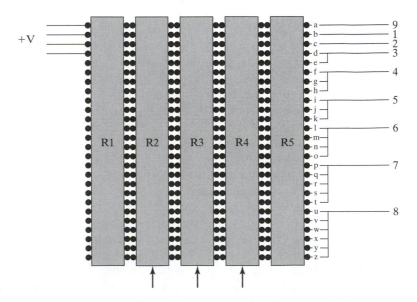

Figure 3.21: ECM control bank

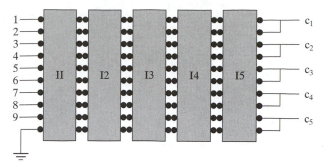

Figure 3.22: ECM index bank

3 rotates one step with every letter. Once Rotor 3 completes a full cycle of 26 steps, Rotor 4 rotates by one step. Once Rotor 4 completes 26 steps, Rotor 2 rotates by one step.

The control bank sends its 10 outputs to the index bank. It is the job of the index bank (shown in Figure 3.22) to translate those 10 signals into a set of five commands—one to each of the five cipher rotors. The commands determine which of the cipher rotors will rotate after a plaintext letter is enciphered. The result is a random-appearing rotation schedule for the cipher block.

Evidence gathered after WWII revealed that, though the Axis had tried, they were never successful in breaking the ECM. This was due in part to the increased complexity of the machine and in part to the care taken in using the machines in the field. The difference between the success of the Allies and the failure of the Axis involved not only the choice of cipher, but also the method by which keys were managed. Remember this difference because you will encounter it again in great detail in Chapter 9.

The U.S. Navy continued to use the ECM until 1959. It was retired at that time because the machine proved to be too slow for the communication requirements of the new Navy. It was time for the nature of cipher machines to change and lose their mechanical features in favor of fully electronic devices. The resulting ciphers are explored in Chapters 6, 7, and 8.

3.8   SUMMARY

As was the case with the monoalphabetic ciphers in Chapter 2, there are a wide variety of polyalphabetic ciphers that have been developed and used. They all have the characteristic that a plaintext letter is mapped to more than one ciphertext letter. This process interferes with frequency analysis. As a general rule, polyalphabetics are certainly more secure than are monoalphabetics, but they are still too weak to rely on for any reasonable level of security (as Alice and Bob discovered).

This round of the battle between Alice, Bob, and Eve goes to Eve again, but she did have to work harder to succeed. There were brief periods of time during which Alice and Bob seemed to have the upper hand, but Eve eventually broke all the new ciphers. In the process, all three learned more about ciphers and their weaknesses.

Alice and Bob learned how to disrupt a simple frequency analysis by using ciphers that replaced a plaintext letter by more than one ciphertext letter, thereby smoothing out the frequency of ciphertext characters. They also learned how to extend the length of a key by creating a running key, using either previously enciphered plaintext or prior ciphertext (the autokey cipher). They began to explore the use of more mechanized cipher systems such as cylinder- and rotor-based structures. While all of these eventually fell to the efforts of Eve, they did introduce important ideas about the structure of cipher systems that will

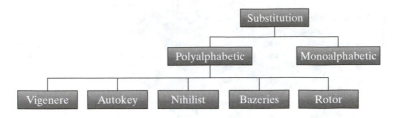

Figure 3.23: Polyalphabetic ciphers

prove very valuable later. Perhaps the most important lesson they learned was that, just because a cipher appears to be complicated, it does not mean that it is secure.

Eve discovered that frequency analysis, while still a valuable tool, does not always work. She also learned the importance of looking for patterns in the ciphertext. Repeated segments of ciphertext turned out to be the key to breaking the Vigenere cipher. She discovered that it sometimes takes a great deal of patience even with the help of powerful analysis tools to break some ciphers, while others just seemed to fall into her lap. This patience and the willingness to try different ideas until she finds one that works will equip her for the more challenging ciphers yet to come.

At this point you may be wondering about Eve. How does she seem to always know when Bob and Alice have changed their cipher? How does she discover the new cipher type so quickly? The answer is that Eve may not be as quick as you might think. Sometimes she discovers the change in a cipher only when she is no longer able to break the messages between Bob and Alice. The process of identifying the new cipher can sometimes be long and difficult for her. Like any good cryptanalysts, she needs to understand the nature of any potential new cipher and know what clues to look for in the ciphertext that might give the cipher type away. Also, she is good at social engineering, which is the technical term for a con job. She may call Bob or Alice with some long story about how she wants to send them an important message, but she doesn't know what cipher she should use and asks for their recommendation. She may look through their garbage to find any notes they may have made about cipher algorithms. She may trick the local librarian into releasing a list of books that they have read, hoping that one is about a particular cipher algorithm. Any way she goes about this task, she is ultimately successful.

Overall, this chapter introduced five new ciphers that fit into our cipher structure chart as shown in Figure 3.23.

3.9   IMPORTANT TERMS

Autokey	A method to extend the length of a key by using either the plaintext or the ciphertext as part of the key
de Viaris method	A known-plaintext method to attack cylinder ciphers that scans for the correct arrangement of cylinders
Enigma	One of the ciphers used by Germany during WWII
Index of Coincidence (IC)	Developed by William Friedman, the IC is a measure of the roughness of a text. It is a test for a polyalphabetic cipher, since the smoother the text (a small IC), the more probable it is that it is based on a polyalphabetic cipher

Homophonic cipher	A cipher in which each plaintext letter is replaced by more than one ciphertext symbol
Kasiski method	Discovered by a Polish army officer in the 1800s, this method can be used to find the length of a polyapha-betic key by looking for segments of repeated ciphertext
Polyalphabetic cipher	A cipher in which each plaintext letter is replaced by more than one ciphertext letter
Rotor cipher	A polyalphabetic cipher that uses a set of rotors each of which implements a monoalphabetic cipher. The rotors combine and rotate to create a new substitution pattern after each letter encryption.

RESOURCES

Polyalphabetic ciphers are covered in some of the references found at the end of Chapters 1 and 2. In addition, the reader might want to look at the following texts:

Codes, Ciphers & Other Cryptic & Clandestine Communication by Fred Wrixon (Black Dog and Leventhal, 1998)

Making, Breaking Codes by Paul Garrett (Prentice Hall, 2001), especially Chapter 3

Codes and Ciphers by Robert Churchhouse (Cambridge, 2002), especially Chapter 3

PROBLEMS

1. Create the table for a keyword version of the Vigenere table using the keyword "neverhome" and use it to encipher the word "alphabet".

2. Describe how you might break the Nihilist cipher.

3. Using a Vigenere cipher with the keyword "section", create the ciphertext for the paragraph that follows and run a frequency analysis. Comment on what you observe.

   Bob, I think Eve may be on to something that will break this cipher. We need to look at the weaknesses that might exist in a Vigenere cipher. If she has broken it, what shall we do? Do you have any idea of where we should turn? Yours, Alice

4. What is the Index of Coincidence for the ciphertext you created in Problem 3 and what does it suggest about the keyword?

5. Fill in the following information:

Cipher	Summarize its operation	Summarize its weakness
Vigenere		
Autokey		
Cylinder		
Rotor		

6. You have intercepted the following ciphertext between Bob and Alice:

   blakgzomitfraojuilwviifsvialmxfhsadsocmpuhwdkhefmtfbmbkianmpp
   ivmcioowtxhsbyfcsvvsyfmzupwzjbpkbjfpjwdmeequbrwawmtgnqvrkpqst
   cmatbmbjpwuipxeuwofuhekuhtmvuejipelgvifrcmatdggqvhsdgbnqawhgw
   avjofaapujadpb

   You know that Bob and Alice are using a Vigenere cipher. Find the plaintext.

7. You have intercepted the following ciphertext between Alice and Bob:

cotqv iwosr vcjop sleky xkpkr xrzao vclkw yskhf vkkav
gwnaw cestd zvmar wrzlq dsfdh kmmwe chyic yrewn rmazi
lipzy srrkq qlvax acuwg rbkwa dmoig oolwb pglwd peoem
ilvyi gwgnf dvwty uymsy glsws cyzxl tadhk aufyb kiicy
zctw

All you know is that Alice and Bob have changed to some form of autokey cipher. Find the plaintext.

8. Encipher the plaintext that follows, using a cylinder cipher with cylinders in the following order:

20 1 19 2 18 3 17 4 16 5 15 6 14 7 13 8 12 9 11 10.

Alice, how was your vacation? I hear that LA is really hot this time of year. Did you get all the rest you need? We have all missed you at work and are looking forward to your return on Monday. Yours, Bob

What is the IC for the ciphertext? Run a frequency analysis of the ciphertext and comment on the results.

9. You have intercepted the following ciphertext between Alice and Bob:

yncnz xrfls nnsln tgaac wruyv bsdjj nqrqj aeexf dfjoy
rbyeu eutcb vspst iifsx aujfj kdlun pvcaf ajazj ncadn
yutly aabnr pohaj jlxzx nixth bsbht fkppo bdlgu cnual
chunu ojbdt ltpsm euqpl twele

You know that Alice and Bob are using a cylinder cipher, but you do not know the order. You suspect that the word *Tuesday* is in the text. You can probably guess some other words as well. Find the plaintext.

10. Encipher this plaintext, using a rotor cipher with the first three rotors (Rotors 1, 2, 3, in that order) and the starting positions given by "A B C":

Alice, waiting until Tuesday is fine I hope the doctor's appointment does not mean that something is wrong. I think we need to explore other options for our ciphers. It is possible that Eve has made a major breakthrough. I no longer trust our current system. You know this is really becoming a pain. Yours, Bob

What is the IC for this ciphertext? Run a frequency analysis of the ciphertext and comment on the results.

11. Using the Enigma wiring from Figure 3.17, rotate R1 one step "up", redraw following the figure and determine where "a" will be mapped.

12. Eve intercepted the following message between Bob and Alice:

gcckk dejjk ubecv tsews byqrj xgydi vsjat pjpyc
oqveq keaoq tajqn ngzrs xybnq gxpgi ws

Eve suspects that Bob and Alice used a rotor cipher and that the word "alice" is somewhere in the beginning of the text. Find the plaintext and the key arrangement.

13. What is the difference between a homophonic cipher and a polyalphabetic cipher?

14. Construct your own homophonic cipher by replacing letters with numbers in the range 0 to 100.

Chapter 4

Classical Polygraphic Ciphers

4.0   INTRODUCTION

One look at the title of this chapter and you may feel like you are getting lost in a world of "poly" this and "poly" that. Well, you are, but it is not that bad. To make it easier, there will be an occasional pause in the narrative to remind you of where we currently are in the world of ciphers. This is one of those times. Remember that a *monoalphabetic* cipher is one in which each character is replaced by one other character. A *polyalphabetic* cipher, on the other hand, replaces each plaintext character by more than one ciphertext character. Yet, both monoalphabetic and polyalphabetic ciphers work with single characters. Any cipher that enciphers one letter at a time is called a *monographic cipher*. A *polygraphic cipher*, on the other hand, works on groups of characters. Each combination of n characters in the plaintext is replaced by another group of n characters in the ciphertext. The simplest example is a digraphic substitution that enciphers pairs of letters at a time. For example, the pair "at" may be replaced by "ui" in the ciphertext, while the pair "an" is replaced by "wq", and so on. A digraphic cipher is stronger than a monographic one because there are more digraphs (pairs of letters) than individual letters. For the standard English alphabet, there are only 26 letters, but there are 625 possible digraphs (26×26). As a result, it is harder to identify digraphs by their personality characteristics. This makes simple frequency analysis almost useless. The strength of the cipher increases if three letters are enciphered at a time (trigraphic cipher), since there are 17,576 trigrams in English ($26 \times 26 \times 26$).

The problem with polygraphic ciphers is determining how to map groups of plaintext letters into groups of ciphertext letters. For a digraph cipher, it could be done by creating a table that lists all 625 plaintext pairs and their corresponding ciphertext pairs. In fact, there have been ciphers constructed in just that way, but they are difficult to manage. A table of this form for a trigraph cipher would be prohibitive. (It would become a code and not a cipher.) What is needed is some algorithm that is key based and generates the polygraphic pair substitutions much like the ciphers in the previous two chapters. It should come as no surprise that several such ciphers have been developed. These ciphers illustrate some of the underlying characteristics of contemporary block ciphers that will be covered later.

4.1 PLAYFAIR CIPHER

Bob and Alice decide that in their never-ending battle to protect their communications from Eve that neither monoalphabetic nor polyalphabetic ciphers are secure. They go back to their resources and discover a powerful digraphic cipher called *Playfair*. It turns out that Playfair is considered to be the premier example of a digraph substitution much like Vigenere is the primary example of a polyalphabetic.

The Playfair cipher was actually developed by Charles Wheatstone, a prolific inventor and scientist during the 1800s. The cipher is named after Wheatstone's friend Lyon Playfair. This is in part because it was Baron Playfair who introduced the cipher to the British government at a dinner party on January 1854 and who worked hard to get it accepted by the government. While Playfair never claimed the cipher for himself, it took on his name. Its use is unclear, but there is some evidence that Britain employed the cipher during the Boer War. The Australian Coast Watchers used Playfair during WWII to transmit their observations of Japanese ship traffic.

Not only is the Playfair cipher more challenging than are the standard monoalphabetic and polyalphabetic ciphers we have studied so far, it is surprisingly simple to implement. It is based on a keyword that is written in a 5 × 5 square (dropping any repeated letter and the letter j). The remaining slots in the square are filled in with the unused letters of the alphabet in their natural order. For example, the keyword "telegram" could be used to construct the following square:

The square is used to transform plaintext letter pairs into ciphertext letter pairs by looking up the plaintext pairs in the square and selecting ciphertext pairs based on the application of one of three rules:

- If the two plaintext characters appear in the same row in the square, select the characters to the right.
- If the two plaintext characters appear in the same column in the square, select the characters below.
- If the two plaintext characters appear in different rows and columns, then they form two points of a square—select the characters on the other two points.

Before these rules will work, the plaintext has to be preprocessed to remove the letter "j" and any double letters. This is done by replacing all "j"s with "i"s and placing a dummy letter (usually "x" or "q") between all double letters. In addition, if there is an odd number of letters in the plaintext, the dummy letter is added to the end so that the number of characters is even. For example, using the Playfair square formed from the keyword telegram previously shown, the plaintext "next time, jay, try something different" is processed in this way:

1. The "j" is changed to "i": next time, iay, try something different.
2. A "q" is inserted between the double "f" in "different": next time, iay, try something difgferent.
3. Since there are 34 letters, there is no need to add a "q" to the end to make the length even. Of course, the plaintext now appears strange, but it is still very readable.
4. Take the first pair of plaintext letters, in this case "ne", and look them up in the table—as shown next, they form two corners of a square. The ciphertext pair consists of the other two corners, which are "hr".

5. Repeating this process results in the substitution of "xt" by "vl", "ti" by "fl". The fourth plaintext pair is "me". These two letters appear in the same column in the table so they are replaced by the letters below them. In this case, "me" is replaced by "hm".

The final result is the following ciphertext: hrvlf lhmfb vgzgu phmef kfrck hoirm tlfr. At one point in the process, the plaintext pair "in" is replaced by the ciphertext pair "kf". This is because the table raps around itself so the letter after "n" is "f".

While this is actually an easy cipher to work with by hand, it can become tedious. Therefore, Alice and Bob rely on CAP to automatically encipher and decipher when using the Playfair cipher. They select Playfair under the Cipher menu, and a Playfair Cipher window opens such as the one shown in Figure 4.1. They enter the keyword, select Set

Figure 4.1: CAP Playfair Cipher window

Key and the Playfair square appears. Then, all they have to do is select Encipher or Decipher—the rest is automatic.

4.1.1 Cryptanalysis of Playfair

Playfair is a powerful cipher compared with those we have examined so far. However, it is not without its weaknesses. It turns out that there are two approaches to breaking this cipher—one is a probable-word attack and the other is a keyword-discovery attack. Either one (or both in concert) can be used to compromise Playfair.

The first step for any attack is to verify that the underlying cipher is indeed a Playfair cipher. This can be done by examining the features of Playfair ciphertext. There are four specific characteristics to look for:

1. There must be an even number of characters in the ciphertext.
2. The rare consonants "j", "k", "q", "x", and "z" will appear more frequently than in plaintext.
3. When divided into digraphs, repeated letters such as "SS" or "EE" will not appear.
4. The frequency distribution of digraphs will approximate that of plaintext.

Since Bob and Alice have selected Playfair as their new cipher, Eve is initially confused by the ciphertext she manages to intercept. Eventually, she decides that Bob and Alice are using a new cipher based on a completely different approach to encryption. Aware of the kinds of books that Bob and Alice are reading, she suspects that the new cipher might be a Playfair system, so she looks for the aforementioned characteristics in the latest ciphertext sample (shown here—already divided into pairs):

pk km km ew dw qn bs hl uf gq zk zp tl fc ls fq tn ca zw ae ns fq tn zw ps el kz kc xc rb ke tm wg co ab fk vn cl uf ui df ch hq kc mp.

Just as CAP helped Alice and Bob create the cipher, CAP will perform the tests to check for a Playfair cipher. Eve selects the PolyID button under the Polygraphic Tools menu and runs each of the three tests by clicking the three check boxes. The results are shown in Figure 4.2. Since this ciphertext is consistent with the characteristics of Playfair, she decides to try to break it based on a known-plaintext attack because she has reason to believe that the phrase "*a sample of*" is somewhere in the ciphertext.

The general process for a known-plaintext attack on Playfair is shown in Figure 4.3. The attack process begins by finding a ciphertext pattern that matches the known plaintext. This is done by passing the plaintext over the ciphertext and checking for consistency in the application of the Playfair rules—specifically verifying that none of the peculiarities of Playfair are violated. Among those peculiarities are the following:

1. No single letter in the plaintext can ever be represented by itself—that is, "a" can never be represented by "a".
2. Two reversed digraphs in the plaintext (such as "RE" and "ER") will always be represented by reverse digraphs in the ciphertext.
3. Every single letter from the plaintext can be enciphered by one of only five other letters—the one directly below it in the Playfair square or the other four in its row.

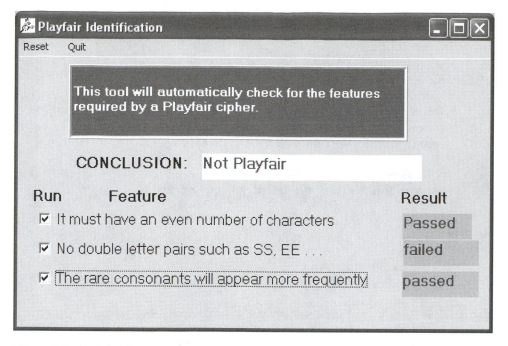

Figure 4.2: CAP Playfair Identification

If the pairs produced by the current lineup of the known plaintext with the ciphertext violate any of these conditions, then the known plaintext is shifted over one character and the conditions are checked again. If the pairs do not violate these conditions, then it is possible (only possible) that the corresponding segment of ciphertext might represent the known plaintext.

Eve begins by lining up the known plaintext with the first characters in the ciphertext as shown here:

as am pl   eo f–
pk km km ew dw qn bs hl uf gq zk zp.

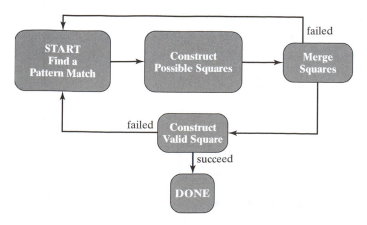

Figure 4.3: Playfair attack

This violates Condition 1 because both "m" and "e" are represented by themselves. So, Eve slides the known plaintext over by one character:

```
-a    sa mp    le   of
pk km km ew dw qn bs hl uf gq zk zp.
```

This requires that two different plaintext pairs map to the same ciphertext pair ("sa" maps to "km" and "mp" maps to "km"), which cannot happen in Playfair, so Eve rejects this lineup and moves the known plaintext to the right again.

```
   as am    pl eo f-
pk km km ew dw qn bs hl uf gq zk zp.
```

This still maps to different plaintext pairs to the same ciphertext pair, so it is rejected. Eve again makes a one-character shift to the right, producing the following pairings:

```
    a   sa mp    le  of
pk km km ew dw qn bs hl uf gq zk zp.
```

This might work. Not only does it not violate the rules, but it also suggests that the plaintext letter before the known phrase must be "s". (Why?) This generates four possible plaintext–ciphertext pairings: "sa" = "KM"; "mp" = "EW"; "le" = "DW"; and "of" = "QN". These possible pairings are used in the next step to try to create possible Playfair squares. However, after some effort on Eve's part, they do not lead to a solution. She therefore returns to this stage and slides the known plaintext over by one character. While some other possible pairings are suggested, Eve has no success until the known plaintext is aligned with the ciphertext as shown here:

```
         as am    pl eo f-
pk km km ew dw qn bs hl uf gq zk zp.
```

This alignment does not violate the rules, so Eve uses the new set of four plaintext–ciphertext pairings to try to reproduce the Playfair square. These new pairings are "as" = "EW"; "am" = "DW"; "pl" = "QN"; and "eo" = "BS". Each pairing reflects a possible arrangement of the Playfair square. For example, if "as" = "EW", then "aesw" must be in the same row, in the same column, or at the corners of a rectangle. The second step of this process is to construct the possible squares as shown in Figure 4.4.

If these pairings are correct, then it must be possible to merge these four arrangements into one complete square. In her previous attempts, Eve was unable to come up with a consistent merger, but now it looks more promising. The merging process is based on the knowledge discovered from these incomplete squares. For example, from Square 1, it is clear that

1
as = EW

A	E	S	W
E			
S		A	E
W		W	S

2
am = DW

A	D	M	W
D			
M		A	D
W		W	M

3
pl = QN

P	Q	L	N
Q			
L		P	Q
N		N	L

4
eo = BS

E	B	O	S
B			
O		E	B
S		S	O

Figure 4.4: Implication of possible Playfair pairs

in the final Playfair square "a" and "e" must be in the same row or column. Square 2 also requires that "a" and "d" be in the same row or column. Square 4 requires that "e" and "b" be in the same row or column. Taken together, these three facts imply that "a", "b", "d", and "e" must all be in the same row or column. With this information, it is possible to make an initial guess for part of the structure of the Playfair square. Since the alphabet is written in order after the keyword is entered, it is possible that the letters "a", "b", "c", "d", and "e" are not in the keyword and that they all appear together in the second row. Eve finds this to be an interesting possibility and one that she wants to explore further. As a short aside, Eve is displaying one of the most important characteristics of a cryptanalyst—the willingness to follow a hunch. This hunch results in the following partial Playfair square:

```
- - - - -
A B C D E
- - - - -
- - - - -
- - - - -
```

Now, the other possibilities suggested by the four partial squares shown in Figure 4.4 could be used to help complete the construction of the key. Squares 1 and 2 both require that "w" be in the same row or column as "a". Square 4 requires that "s" and "e" be in the same row or column. Square 3 requires that "d" and "m" are in the same row or column. These three facts suggest that the underlying Playfair square may look like this:

```
W - - M S
A B C D E
- - - - -
- - - - -
- - - - -
```

One look at this possible structure and Eve guesses that the keyword is "Worms", which produces the following Playfair square:

```
W O R M S
A B C D E
F G H I K
L N P Q T
U V X Y Z
```

Eve verifies that she has found the correct key by using it to decipher the ciphertext. It works, and yet another of Bob and Alice's ciphers bites the dust.

Even if Eve did not have a segment of known plaintext available, she still could have broken this cipher by discovering the keyword using a method developed during WWI. Major Frank Moorman, chief of the U.S. Army's Radio Intelligence Service (G.2.A.6), suggested this method to break Playfair by guessing the letters of the keyword. Of course, just blind guessing would not be a very effective method, but Major Moorman had something else in mind. He used the characteristics of the keyword to aid in the guessing process. Specifically, he knew that the keyword would likely have two vowels for every three consonants and that the keyword would contain some of the more common letters. This fact used in conjunction with the observation that the letters in the ciphertext that combine with the largest number of other letters are most likely letters of the keyword (because the keyword letters are some of the more commonly used letters in the plaintext) allowed him to develop a method to break Playfair using a ciphertext-only attack.

His approach was to analyze the ciphertext to find the set of letters that formed combinations with the greatest number of other letters. These are likely to include most of the letters in the keyword. The remaining letters are placed in a Playfair square. Using digram information and trial-and-error arrangements, it is possible to discover the keyword.

4.1.2   Cryptanalysis of Playfair with CAP

As is usually the case, CAP provides you with some fundamental tools for breaking a Playfair cipher. Once it is clear that a Playfair cipher is a good possibility (which can be determined by using CAP's Playfair ID tool), if a probable word is known, the CAP Playfair Known Word tool will search the ciphertext for possible matches. For example, in Figure 4.5, CAP found a possible match for the word "plaintext" starting at location 5 in the ciphertext. The four possible pairs could be used to set up a likely arrangement of the Playfair square that can then be used to verify the matches and search for other possible

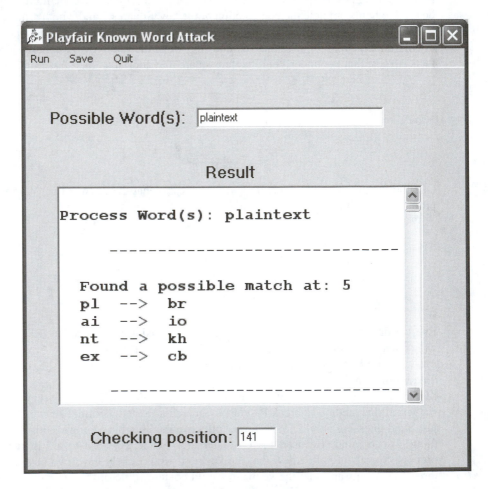

Figure 4.5: CAP Playfair Known Word Attack screen

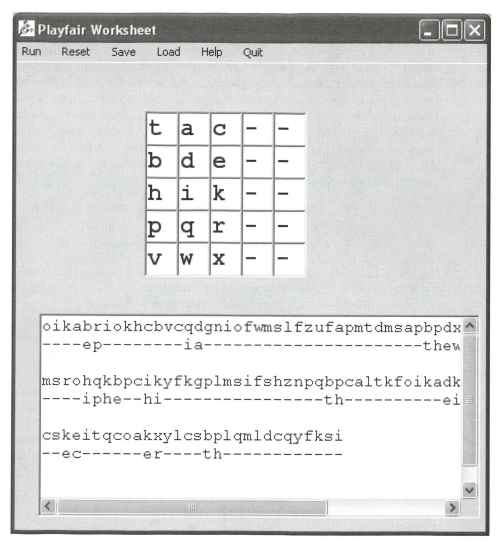

Figure 4.6: CAP Playfair Worksheet

words using the CAP Playfair Worksheet as shown in Figure 4.6. If the first match found does not work, CAP lists all possible matches, so move on to the second. Admittedly, this may take some time and certainly a lot of patience, but the effort will be rewarded with the identification of the Playfair key.

4.2   THE HILL CIPHER

The Playfair cipher highlights the usefulness of enciphering multiple letters at a time. Once the Playfair cipher became well known, other cryptologists attempted to devise ciphers for trigrams and larger (three or more characters at a time). In part because of the difficulty of maintaining a three-dimensional table, their efforts failed. A successful polygraphic method had to wait until mathematical principles could be applied to the science of cryptology.

The use of mathematics to create a general polyalphabetic cipher first appeared in 1929 in the form of the Hill cipher. This cipher was named after its inventor, Lester S. Hill, a mathematics professor at Hunter College in New York. In 1929, he published a short paper entitled "Cryptography in an Algebraic Alphabet" in which he outlined a cipher algorithm based on systems of simultaneous equations. It works on a block of m plaintext letters to produce a block of m ciphertext letters. Each plaintext letter is assigned a numerical value usually $a = 0, b = 1, \ldots, z = 25$, though Hill used a random-number assignment. The numerical values of each letter in the block are combined to create a new set of numerical values that represent the ciphertext letters. For example, if $m = 3$, then the numerical value of three plaintext letters, say, p_1, p_2, and p_3, are transformed to the ciphertext values c_1, c_2, and c_3 by the following equations:

$$c_1 = (k_{11}p_1 + k_{12}p_2 + k_{13}p_3) \bmod 26$$
$$c_2 = (k_{21}p_1 + k_{22}p_2 + k_{23}p_3) \bmod 26$$
$$c_3 = (k_{31}p_1 + k_{32}p_2 + k_{33}p_3) \bmod 26$$

The key to the cipher is the set of values selected for the k_{ij}'s. The mod operation means divide the result of the sum by 26 and keep the remainder.

One possible system is given by the following three equations:

$$c_1 = (17p_1 + 17p_2 + 5p_3) \bmod 26$$
$$c_2 = (21p_1 + 18p_2 + 21p_3) \bmod 26$$
$$c_3 = (2p_1 + 2p_2 + 19p_3) \bmod 26$$

Using these three equations, the plaintext word *now* is first converted to numerical form: 13 14 22. These values are substituted into the equations to produce the numerical form of the ciphertext: 23 20 4. Converted back to letters, the ciphertext is *xue*.

The easiest way to visualize this cipher is in the form of matrices. The enciphering key is a matrix, M, and the deciphering key is its inverse M^{-1}. For the previous example, the key is given by

$$M = \begin{pmatrix} 17 & 17 & 5 \\ 21 & 18 & 21 \\ 2 & 2 & 19 \end{pmatrix} \qquad M^{-1} = \begin{pmatrix} 4 & 9 & 15 \\ 15 & 17 & 6 \\ 24 & 0 & 17 \end{pmatrix}$$

Encrypt "n o w"
13 14 22
$$\begin{pmatrix} 17 & 17 & 5 \\ 21 & 18 & 21 \\ 2 & 2 & 19 \end{pmatrix} \begin{pmatrix} 13 \\ 14 \\ 22 \end{pmatrix} = \begin{pmatrix} 23 \\ 20 \\ 4 \end{pmatrix} \bmod 26$$
$$\uparrow$$
x u e

For this process to work, the key matrix must have an inverse, so the key values cannot be selected at random. It is easy to generalize beyond the specific example of an $m = 3$ Hill cipher and express the system in more mathematical terms. The key is written in the form of an $m \times m$ invertible matrix:

$$K = \begin{pmatrix} k_{11} & k_{12} & \cdots & k_{1m} \\ k_{21} & k_{22} & \cdots & k_{2m} \\ & & \cdots & \\ k_{m1} & k_{m2} & \cdots & k_{mm} \end{pmatrix}$$

The text is divided into blocks of size m given by an $m \times 1$ vector. For example, block i consists of the characters $p_1, p_2, \ldots, p_m$ and is written as follows:

$$b_i = \begin{pmatrix} p_1 \\ p_2 \\ \cdots \\ p_m \end{pmatrix}.$$

The ciphertext is given by

$$Kb_i = \begin{pmatrix} k_{11} & k_{12} & \cdots & k_{1m} \\ k_{21} & k_{22} & \cdots & k_{2m} \\ & & \cdots & \\ k_{m1} & k_{m2} & \cdots & k_{mm} \end{pmatrix} \begin{pmatrix} p_1 \\ p_2 \\ \cdots \\ p_m \end{pmatrix} = \begin{pmatrix} c_1 \\ c_2 \\ \cdots \\ c_m \end{pmatrix}.$$

4.2.1 Hill Cipher in CAP

Neither Alice nor Bob wanted to spend the time to develop their own keys for the Hill cipher (they didn't want to have to test each possible key to determine whether it had an inverse), so they turned to CAP to generate a random key with an inverse. CAP will do so whenever they need one. To take advantage of this feature of CAP, select Hill Cipher under the CAP Cipher menu. A window will pop up with all the options required to create a Hill cipher for groups of two to six characters as shown in Figure 4.7. First, set the matrix size, then select Autokey under the Key menu item to generate a new matrix key with an inverse. This key can then be saved for future use. Once the key is available, the ciphertext or plaintext can be generated in the same manner as any other cipher in CAP—click on Encipher

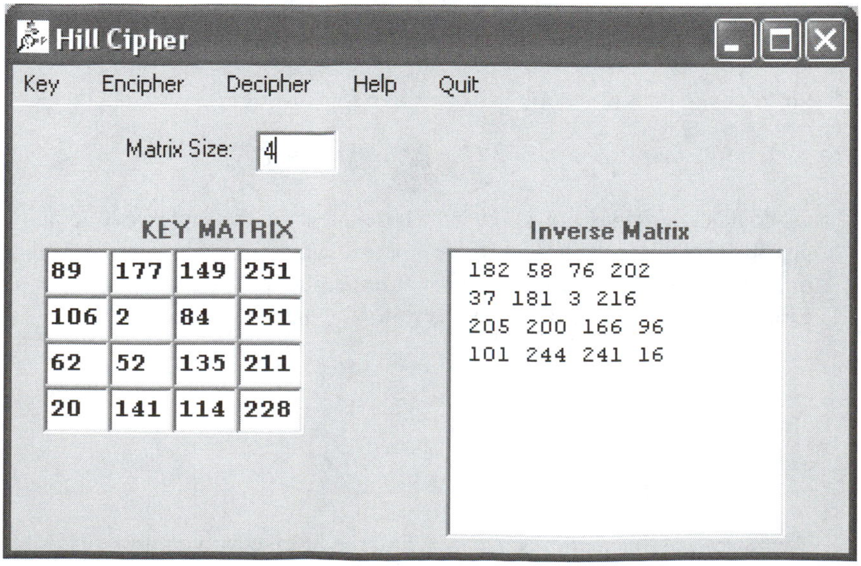

Figure 4.7: CAP Hill Cipher screen

or Decipher. When you run CAP's version of a Hill cipher, you will notice numbers larger than 25. This is because CAP uses the decimal value of the ASCII code to represent each character. Since ASCII is 8 bits wide, the numbers in the CAP Hill matrices will range from 0 to 255.

4.2.2 Cryptanalysis of the Hill Cipher

The Hill cipher is highly resistant to a ciphertext-only attack. In fact, the larger the matrix, the more resistant the cipher becomes. However, it is easy to break using a known-plaintext attack. The process is much like the method used to break an affine cipher in that the known plaintext–ciphertext group is used to set up a system of equations that, when solved, will reveal the key.

For example, assume that Alice and Bob used a Hill cipher with a key matrix of size 4 to encipher some plaintext. Eve intercepts the following ciphertext (which is just a stream of numbers) and guesses that it represents a Hill cipher:

```
209   37   59  255  110  196  247   90   52   34    1   68   11  130   43
 23   20   26  219  119   93  164   12   63  110  202  124  137  112  158
232   23  127  118  128  123  115   89   62  224  199   10  199  142  104
242  120    4  142   26  230  159  129  164  133  153   31  256  210   62
```

Knowing that Alice and Bob used CAP, Eve only needs two pieces of information to break this cipher: the matrix size and some known plaintext. She strongly suspects that the ciphertext contains the words "she can not attack us". While she doesn't know the key matrix size, she does know that it must be between 2 and 6 because of the limitation of CAP, so she tries each size. When it comes time to test for a key matrix of size 4, Eve converts the known plaintext phrase into a 4×4 matrix, M. She knows that if this phrase was enciphered by Alice and Bob's key matrix, K, then the resulting ciphertext matrix, C, is really the product of M and K. In other words,

$$C = M \times K.$$

So, knowing both C and M, Eve can solve for K using

$$K = M^{-1} \times C.$$

Of course, Eve does not know which segment of the ciphertext actually enciphers the phrase. Therefore, she has to create a possible key for each portion of ciphertext until she finds a key that, when applied to the entire ciphertext, actually produces plaintext. In this case, the known phrase becomes the following matrix:

$$\mathbf{M} = \begin{pmatrix} 115 & 104 & 101 & 99 \\ 97 & 110 & 110 & 111 \\ 116 & 97 & 116 & 116 \\ 97 & 99 & 107 & 117 \end{pmatrix}.$$

The inverse of this matrix (CAP will find the inverse for you using the Matrix Ops option under the Polygraphic Analysis tool) is given by

$$\mathbf{M}^{-1} = \begin{pmatrix} 254 & 104 & 101 & 99 \\ 236 & 236 & 195 & 75 \\ 224 & 10 & 109 & 18 \\ 202 & 52 & 155 & 61 \end{pmatrix}.$$

Eve proceeds to multiply this inverse matrix by matrices formed from the ciphertext. Each result is a possible key, which she uses to decipher the ciphertext. Most of the time, the possible key does not work, but the one time that the possible message matched the ciphertext, Eve discovered a working key:

$$\mathbf{K} = \begin{pmatrix} 4 & 6 & 154 & 69 \\ 129 & 34 & 179 & 103 \\ 26 & 32 & 78 & 121 \\ 41 & 22 & 30 & 54 \end{pmatrix}.$$

By hand, this would be a difficult process, but, as usual, CAP provides the necessary tools to make it easier. Select the Hill Attack button under the Polygraphic Tools menu and the window shown in Figure 4.8 will pop up. Enter your best guess for the size of the key matrix and the word or words you believe are in the plaintext. When you click on Run, CAP will give you a list (usually quite long) of possible key matrices along with some deciphered ciphertext created using that key. Search for a segment of deciphered text that is readable—if you find one, then you have discovered the key.

There are two limitations to this procedure. The first is that enough known plaintext must be available to create a full matrix. The second is that the segment of plaintext that is being tested must match the matrix boundaries.

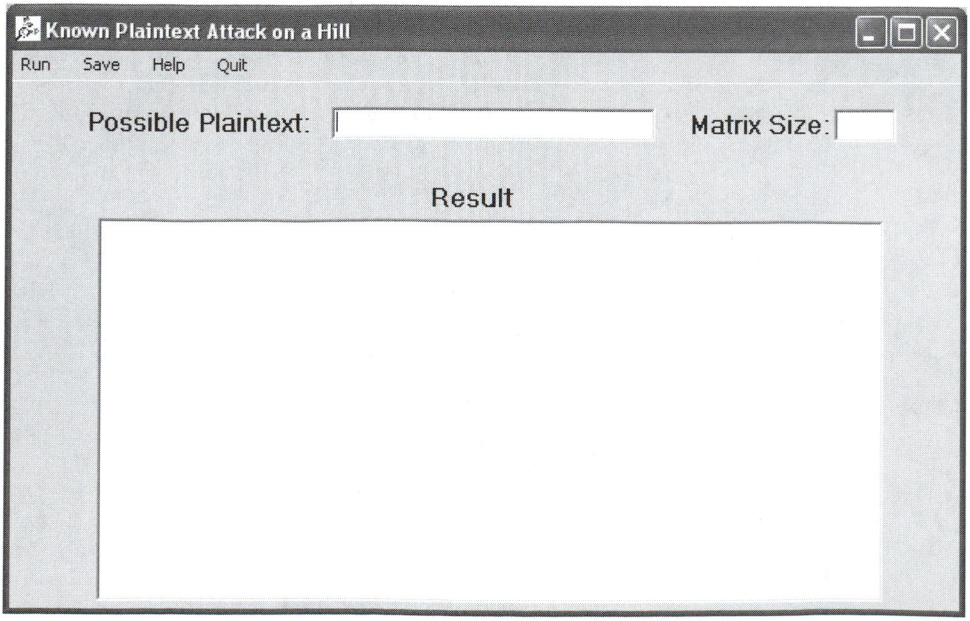

Figure 4.8: Hill Known-Plaintext Attack in CAP

4.3   BEALE CIPHERS—A BRIEF HISTORICAL INTERLUDE

The story of the Beale ciphers is not really a story about polygraphic ciphers, though it is possible that the yet undeciphered portion of the Beale ciphers may involve something that is polygraphic. Rather, the story is offered at this point more because it illustrates the impact of cryptography and cryptanalysis on the lives of individuals. The story should have more impact now that you have gained a fundamental understanding of the inner workings of cryptography than it would have had it been presented in the first chapter.

Robert Morris, a Virginia tavern keeper, broke open a locked box after keeping it for almost 20 years. The box had been given to Morris in 1821 by a friend, Thomas Jefferson Beale, with instructions to open it if he didn't return within 10 years. Morris never heard from T.J. Beale again. When he finally opened the box, he was shocked by what he discovered. The box contained two letters addressed to him and several sheets of paper filled with numbers. The letters explained that Beale and 30 friends had discovered a vast gold and silver mine 250 miles north of Santa Fe in 1817. Over the space of a couple of years, Beale and some of his friends had returned to Virginia and buried over a ton of gold and silver. The paper filled with numbers hid the location of the gold and the names of the next of kin of each of the 30 men that worked with Beale. Morris was to dig up the gold and distribute it to the people on the list. The letters also promised that the cipher key would arrive in the mail, but it never did.

Morris was left with a map to a fortune in gold and silver that he could not read. He tried for years to break the cipher, but never made any headway. Eventually, he told James Ward about the ciphers and let him try to analyze them. Amazingly, Ward found the key to the second of the three ciphers. The second cipher consisted of numbers from 1 to 1322:

115, 73, 24, 807, 37, 52, 49, 17, 31, 62, 647, 22, 7, 15, 140, 47, 29,
107, 79, 84, 56, 239, 10, 26, 811, 5, 196, 308, 85, 52, 160, 136, 59,
211, 36, 9, 46, 316, 554, 122, 106, 95, 53, 58, 2, 42, 7, 35, 122, 53,
31, 82, 77, 250, 196, 56, 96, 118, 71, 140, 287, 28, 353, 37, 1005, 65,
147, 807, 24, 3, 8, 12, 47, 43, 59, 807, 45, 316, 101, 41, 78, 154,
1005, 122, 138, 191, 16, 77, 49, 102, 57, 72, 34, 73, 85, 35, 371, 59,
196, 81, 92, 191, 106, 273, 60, 394, 620, 270, 220, 106, 388, 287, 63,
3, 6, 191, 122, 43, 234, 400, 106, 290, 314, 47, 48, 81, 96, 26, 115,
92, 158, 191, 110, 77, 85, 197, 46, 10, 113, 140, 353, 48, 120, 106, 2,
607, 61, 420, 811, 29, 125, 14, 20, 37, 105, 28, 248, 16, 159, 7, 35,
19, 301, 125, 110, 486, 287, 98, 117, 511, 62, 51, 220, 37, 113, 140,
807, 138, 540, 8, 44, 287, 388, 117, 18, 79, 344, 34, 20, 59, 511, 548,
107, 603, 220, 7, 66, 154, 41, 20, 50, 6, 575, 122, 154, 248, 110, 61,
52, 33, 30, 5, 38, 8, 14, 84, 57, 540, 217, 115, 71, 29, 84, 63, 43,
131, 29, 138, 47, 73, 239, 540, 52, 53, 79, 118, 51, 44, 63, 196, 12,
239, 112, 3, 49, 79, 353, 105, 56, 371, 557, 211, 505, 125, 360, 133,
143, 101, 15, 284, 540, 252, 14, 205, 140, 344, 26, 811, 138, 115, 48,
73, 34, 205, 316, 607, 63, 220, 7, 52, 150, 44, 52, 16, 40, 37, 158,
807, 37, 121, 12, 95, 10, 15, 35, 12, 131, 62, 115, 102, 807, 49, 53,
135, 138, 30, 31, 62, 67, 41, 85, 63, 10, 106, 807, 138, 8, 113, 20, 32,
33, 37, 353, 287, 140, 47, 85, 50, 37, 49, 47, 64, 6, 7, 71, 33, 4, 43,
47, 63, 1, 27, 600, 208, 230, 15, 191, 246, 85, 94, 511, 2, 270, 20, 39,
7, 33, 44, 22, 40, 7, 10, 3, 811, 106, 44, 486, 230, 353, 211, 200, 31,
10, 38, 140, 297, 61, 603, 320, 302, 666, 287, 2, 44, 33, 32, 511, 548,
10, 6, 250, 557, 246, 53, 37, 52, 83, 47, 320, 38, 33, 807, 7, 44, 30,

31, 250, 10, 15, 35, 106, 160, 113, 31, 102, 406, 230, 540, 320, 29, 66,
33, 101, 807, 138, 301, 316, 353, 320, 220, 37, 52, 28, 540, 320, 33, 8,
48, 107, 50, 811, 7, 2, 113, 73, 16, 125, 11, 110, 67, 102, 807, 33, 59,
81, 158, 38, 43, 581, 138, 19, 85, 400, 38, 43, 77, 14, 27, 8, 47, 138,
63, 140, 44, 35, 22, 177, 106, 250, 314, 217, 2, 10, 7, 1005, 4, 20, 25,
44, 48, 7, 26, 46, 110, 230, 807, 191, 34, 112, 147, 44, 110, 121, 125,
96, 41, 51, 50, 140, 56, 47, 152, 540, 63, 807, 28, 42, 250, 138, 582,
98, 643, 32, 107, 140, 112, 26, 85, 138, 540, 53, 20, 125, 371, 38, 36,
10, 52, 118, 136, 102, 420, 150, 112, 71, 14, 20, 7, 24, 18, 12, 807,
37, 67, 110, 62, 33, 21, 95, 220, 511, 102, 811, 30, 83, 84, 305, 620,
15, 2, 10, 8, 220, 106, 353, 105, 106, 60, 275, 72, 8, 50, 205, 185,
112, 125, 540, 65, 106, 807, 138, 96, 110, 16, 73, 33, 807, 150, 409,
400, 50, 154, 285, 96, 106, 316, 270, 205, 101, 811, 400, 8, 44, 37, 52,
40, 241, 34, 205, 38, 16, 46, 47, 85, 24, 44, 15, 64, 73, 138, 807, 85,
78, 110, 33, 420, 505, 53, 37, 38, 22, 31, 10, 110, 106, 101, 140, 15,
38, 3, 5, 44, 7, 98, 287, 135, 150, 96, 33, 84, 125, 807, 191, 96, 511,
118, 40, 370, 643, 466, 106, 41, 107, 603, 220, 275, 30, 150, 105, 49,
53, 287, 250, 208, 134, 7, 53, 12, 47, 85, 63, 138, 110, 21, 112, 140,
485, 486, 505, 14, 73, 84, 575, 1005, 150, 200, 16, 42, 5, 4, 25, 42, 8,
16, 811, 125, 160, 32, 205, 603, 807, 81, 96, 405, 41, 600, 136, 14, 20,
28, 26, 353, 302, 246, 8, 131, 160, 140, 84, 440, 42, 16, 811, 40, 67,
101, 102, 194, 138, 205, 51, 63, 241, 540, 122, 8, 10, 63, 140, 47, 48,
140, 288

What Ward discovered is that the numbers refer to the words in the Declaration of Independence. Each plaintext letter corresponded to the first letter of the numbered word. The resulting plaintext confirmed Robert Morris's story:

I have deposited in the county of Bedford about four miles from Bufords in an excavation or vault six feet below the surface of the ground the following articles belonging jointly to the parties whose names are given in number three herewith, the first deposit consisted of ten hundred and fourteen pounds of gold and thirty eight hundred and twelve pounds of silver deposited nov eighteen nineteen. The second was made dec eighteen twenty one and consisted of nineteen hundred and seven pounds of gold and twelve hundred and eighty eight of silver also jewels obtained in St Louis in exchange to save transposition and valued at thirteen thousand dollars. The vault is roughly lined with stone and the vessels rest on solid stone and are covered with others. Paper number one describes the exact locality of the value so that no difficulty will be had in finding it.

The crucial cipher—the one containing the location of the treasure—is found in paper one and is given next:

71, 194, 38, 1701, 89, 76, 11, 83, 1629, 48, 94, 63, 132, 16, 111, 95,
84, 341, 975, 14, 40, 64, 27, 81, 139, 213, 63, 90, 1120, 8, 15, 3, 126,
2018, 40, 74, 758, 485, 604, 230, 436, 664, 582, 150, 251, 284, 308,
231, 124, 211, 486, 225, 401, 370, 11, 101, 305, 139, 189, 17, 33, 88,
208, 193, 145, 1, 94, 73, 416, 918, 263, 28, 500, 538, 356, 117, 136,
219, 27, 176, 130, 10, 460, 25, 485, 18, 436, 65, 84, 200, 283, 118,
320, 138, 36, 416, 280, 15, 71, 224, 961, 44, 16, 401, 39, 88, 61, 304,
12, 21, 24, 283, 134, 92, 63, 246, 486, 682, 7, 219, 184, 360, 780, 18,
64, 463, 474, 131, 160, 79, 73, 440, 95, 18, 64, 581, 34, 69, 128, 367,
460, 17, 81, 12, 103, 820, 62, 116, 97, 103, 862, 70, 60, 1317, 471,

540, 208, 121, 890, 346, 36, 150, 59, 568, 614, 13, 120, 63, 219, 812,
2160, 1780, 99, 35, 18, 21, 136, 872, 15, 28, 170, 88, 4, 30, 44, 112,
18, 147, 436, 195, 320, 37, 122, 113, 6, 140, 8, 120, 305, 42, 58, 461,
44, 106, 301, 13, 408, 680, 93, 86, 116, 530, 82, 568, 9, 102, 38, 416,
89, 71, 216, 728, 965, 818, 2, 38, 121, 195, 14, 326, 148, 234, 18, 55,
131, 234, 361, 824, 5, 81, 623, 48, 961, 19, 26, 33, 10, 1101, 365, 92,
88, 181, 275, 346, 201, 206, 86, 36, 219, 324, 829, 840, 64, 326, 19,
48, 122, 85, 216, 284, 919, 861, 326, 985, 233, 64, 68, 232, 431, 960,
50, 29, 81, 216, 321, 603, 14, 612, 81, 360, 36, 51, 62, 194, 78, 60,
200, 314, 676, 112, 4, 28, 18, 61, 136, 247, 819, 921, 1060, 464, 895,
10, 6, 66, 119, 38, 41, 49, 602, 423, 962, 302, 294, 875, 78, 14, 23,
111, 109, 62, 31, 501, 823, 216, 280, 34, 24, 150, 1000, 162, 286, 19,
21, 17, 340, 19, 242, 31, 86, 234, 140, 607, 115, 33, 191, 67, 104, 86,
52, 88, 16, 80, 121, 67, 95, 122, 216, 548, 96, 11, 201, 77, 364, 218,
65, 667, 890, 236, 154, 211, 10, 98, 34, 119, 56, 216, 119, 71, 218,
1164, 1496, 1817, 51, 39, 210, 36, 3, 19, 540, 232, 22, 141, 617, 84,
290, 80, 46, 207, 411, 150, 29, 38, 46, 172, 85, 194, 39, 261, 543, 897,
624, 18, 212, 416, 127, 931, 19, 4, 63, 96, 12, 101, 418, 16, 140, 230,
460, 538, 19, 27, 88, 612, 1431, 90, 716, 275, 74, 83, 11, 426, 89, 72,
84, 1300, 1706, 814, 221, 132, 40, 102, 34, 868, 975, 1101, 84, 16, 79,
23, 16, 81, 122, 324, 403, 912, 227, 936, 447, 55, 86, 34, 43, 212, 107,
96, 314, 264, 1065, 323, 428, 601, 203, 124, 95, 216, 814, 2906, 654,
820, 2, 301, 112, 176, 213, 71, 87, 96, 202, 35, 10, 2, 41, 17, 84, 221,
736, 820, 214, 11, 60, 760

Ward discovered that the Declaration of Independence did not work on this cipher. Others have tried the Constitution, books of the Bible, Shakespeare, and other texts, but nothing has worked. Some have given up and claimed that it is all a hoax. They may be right. Others have claimed to have solved it, but no one has produced the treasure.

Whether it is true or not, the Beale ciphers have consumed the lives of many individuals. Ward blamed his financial problems on the ciphers. As late as 1966, a banker invested in a backhoe to dig a large number of holes without any luck. A hill was bulldozed to the ground without finding anything. It appears that the mystery of hidden gold and a secret cipher still has the power to capture our imagination and even take over our lives.

4.4   SUMMARY

This chapter introduced the concept of a polygraphic cipher—that is, a cipher in which two or more characters are enciphered at a time. The result is a cipher that is resistant to single-frequency analysis as well as introducing other problems for the cryptanalyst. However, these ciphers are not completely secure. They are open to a known-plaintext attack.

Another round of the battle between Alice, Bob, and Eve concludes with no one having a decisive advantage. Alice and Bob were able to use both the Playfair cipher and the Hill cipher for a short time, blocking Eve's attempts to read their messages. However, Eve eventually discovered the weakness of these polygraphic systems and was back to her old tricks of exposing the communication between Alice and Bob.

Every one involved learned something new about the process of protecting information. Alice and Bob discovered a new class of ciphers that offered some real promise. Once again, they also learned that complications do not mean security. Now they are aware of the difficulties of using a substitution method to keep their communications secure, and they are ready to try something completely different. (That adventure will begin in the next chapter.)

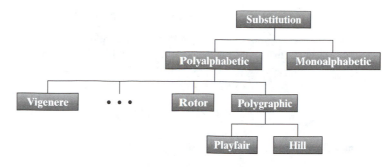

Figure 4.9: Polygraphic ciphers

Eve discovered the power of a known-plaintext attack. While the standard tools of cryptanalysis seemed to lead to a dead end, guessing a portion of the plaintext proved very valuable. She also discovered the usefulness of the tiny weakness of a cipher that will not map a plaintext character to itself. What seemed like a little thing to Bob and Alice when they were using the Playfair cipher turned out to be the crack that helped Eve break into their system. As always, Eve's understanding of the importance of patience and perseverance was reinforced by her experience with polygraphic ciphers. She came away with a renewed commitment to follow her hunches.

Overall, this chapter introduced two new ciphers that fit into our cipher structure chart as shown in Figure 4.9.

4.5   IMPORTANT TERMS

Hill cipher	A polygraphic cipher based on matrix multiplication
Playfair cipher	A cipher that encrypts pairs of characters using a keyword square
Polygraphic cipher	A cipher in which two or more characters at a time are enciphered

RESOURCES

Nova Presentation at http://www.pbs.org/wgbh/nova/decoding/playfair.html

Cryptological Mathematics by Robert Lewand (Mathematical Association of America, 2000), Chapter 3

Making, Breaking Codes by Paul Garrett (Prentice Hall, 2001), Chapter 8

Cryptography and Data Security by Dorothy Dennings (Addison-Wesley, 1982)

PROBLEMS

1. Using the example Hill cipher matrix in the text, find the ciphertext for "new" and compare it with the ciphertext produced for "now". Comment on the result.
2. Fill in the following information:

Cipher	Summarize its operation	Summarize its weakness
Hill		
Playfair		

3. Create a Playfair cipher using the keyword "classroom" and use it to encrypt the following text:

> Bob, I find this Playfair cipher easy to use but when it is deciphered I don't like all the j's and the q's. Sure I can read the plaintext just fine but it looks so strange that I wonder if some mistake has been made. How do you feel about the deciphered text? Does it bother you as much as it bothers me? Yours, Alice

Find the IC for the ciphertext and run a single frequency analysis on it as well. Comment on what you observe.

4. Create a Hill cipher using the following 3×3 key:

$$
\begin{array}{ccc}
113 & 13 & 197 \\
97 & 131 & 126 \\
146 & 219 & 50
\end{array}
$$

Use it to encipher the same plaintext used in Problem 3. What is the inverse key? Find the IC for the ciphertext and run a single frequency analysis on it as well. Comment on what you observe.

5. Find the plaintext for the following Playfair ciphertext (you know that the word "frequency" is somewhere in the text):

gkfam omyug cqrup hdsau zhoic tgnqs pltrq ihcuf iqmwp
kuklh haelq tauaz hpiqr tgpxm azlux tcfop gdaco fbkia
ytdqa lnaos typhm ecvbi lsecu plugm ctqpo pzdmy uflhp
cxfyg poeas mlhli ceau

6. Find the plaintext for the following Hill ciphertext (you know that the phrase "no more secrets" occurs somewhere in the plaintext):

129	228	145	221	241	236	190	156	27
107	71	193	29	30	226	250	191	54
141	210	111	31	106	1	105	30	50
234	0	180	159	121	149	46	218	11
21	142	133	118	124	220	191	3	18
65	203	133	219	17	14	188	100	181
94	197	149	225	40	213	179	92	190
190	99	147	229	9	176	160	207	87

7. What is the size of the key space for the Playfair cipher? If you could program a computer to examine one key every 10^{-6} sec, how long would it take on average to break a Playfair cipher by brute force?

8. Problem 7 overstates the size of the key space because most Playfair users would select a word for their key. Assuming that it is highly likely that a Playfair key will be selected from a dictionary of 10,000 words, what is the size of the key space and how long will the program reference in Problem 7 take to break Playfair?

9. Playfair could be strengthened if the keyword could start at any position in the matrix. Repeat Problem 8 using this assumption. Suggest at least one other way in which the size of the key space for Playfair could be increased.

Chapter 5

Classical Transposition Ciphers

5.0 INTRODUCTION

Having tried and failed to protect their communications using a wide range of substitution ciphers, Bob and Alice decide that they need to try something completely different. After hitting the books once again, they come across a new class of ciphers (new to them at least) that do not involve substitution at all—transposition ciphers. Rather than hiding text contents by replacing letters with other letters, transposition ciphers rearrange the existing letters in the text. They are like giant jigsaw puzzles in that all the pieces are there, but are not arranged in the correct order. The goal of the developer of such a cipher is to come up with a way in which the pieces can be put in order easily *if you know the key*. Without the key, the puzzle is impossible to solve. Of course, the goal of the cryptanalysis is to assemble the puzzle without the key or to discover the key from the characteristics of the puzzle. Both goals can be difficult to achieve.

The skytale cipher used by the ancient Spartans (described in Chapter 1) was an example of the early use of transposition ciphers. While the history of transpositions is somewhat clouded, these types of ciphers have been employed from time to time. During the Civil War, the North used a form of a transposition to hide the content of telegraph messages from Confederate wiretappers.

The methods used by the North involved the transposition of words rather than of individual letters. The plaintext was written out in lines and then transcribed in columns—going up some columns and down others. For example, the plaintext message might have been something like "We will attack at dawn with the first division on the right and the second division on the left. Surprise is important, so make all preparations under the cover of darkness". This message might be written out in seven columns:

| We | will | attack | at | dawn | with | the |
| first | division | on | the | right | and | the |

second	division	on	the	left	surprise	is
important	so	make	all	preparations	under	the
cover	of	darkness	nulls	fill	up	the

Nulls are added to fill up the columns. So if the columns are read in the following order—up one, down three, up four, down two, up six, down seven, up five—the ciphertext is:

> "cover important second first we attack on on make darkness nulls all the the at will division so of up under surprise and with the the is the the fill preparations left right dawn".

To improve the cipher, certain words that might give away the meaning were replaced with codewords. Thus, "attack" might be replaced with "blue" in the preceding example. In addition, more complicated patterns were developed. In contrast, the South used some very weak ciphers including a Caesar cipher and the Vigenere cipher (with only three different keys).

There are two general types of transposition ciphers that differ in terms of the unit of analysis. *Monographic* transpositions work with individual letters (like the Spartan skytale) while *polygraphic* transpositions work with combinations of letters such as words or phrases (like the North's cipher). Of the two, monographic transpositions are typically stronger and will be the focus of this chapter.

The key for a transposition cipher is usually some geometric figure that is used as a form to rearrange the letters. For example, you have already been introduced to a transposition cipher in Chapter 1—the skytale used by the ancient Greeks. The key was the skytale pole that was used as the form for scrambling the letter order. Other geometric forms that are used include squares and rectangles. The plaintext is written into the form in one direction (down the skytale for example) and then read off in another direction (left to right after the paper was unwrapped from the skytale).

Rather than writing the plaintext and reading the ciphertext in an up-and-down process, the rail-fence cipher uses diagonals. For this cipher, the plaintext is written into a rectangle in a zigzag pattern and the ciphertext is read off in rows. For example, if the rectangle has a depth of 3 and a length of 11, the plaintext "this is a test" is written in the pattern shown in Figure 5.1. The ciphertext is produced by reading the rows in that figure—"tiehsstsiat".

This same process could be applied to other geometric figures as well. The plaintext could be written as a triangle within a fixed-size rectangle and then read off in columns. Such a cipher is illustrated in Figure 5.2 using the plaintext "You must do that now" written in the form of a triangle inside a 7 × 4 rectangle. The ciphertext—read off in columns—is "tuhosayuttmdnoow".

Figure 5.1: Example rail-fence cipher

Figure 5.2: A triangle form transposition

5.2   PERMUTATION CIPHER

A simple implementation of a transposition cipher is called a permutation cipher. This is much like shuffling a deck of cards in order to randomize the deal. In this case, the plaintext is divided into blocks of some fixed length, say, d, and a permutation function, f, of the integers 1 to d is selected. Then the letters in each block are rearranged according to f. The key for this cipher is the pair (d, f). For example, say d is 4 and f is given by (2, 4, 1, 3). This means that character 1 goes to position 2, character 2 goes to position 4, character 3 goes to position 1, and character 4 goes to position 3. To apply this permutation cipher to the plaintext "codes and ciphers are fun", first break up the plaintext into blocks of four letters: "code sand ciph ersa refu nxxx". Note the use of nulls to fill out the last block. Now, rearrange each block according to the specification of the function f. For the first block, "c" goes to position 2, "o" goes to position 4, "d" goes to position 1, and "e" goes to position 3. This produces "dceo". The process is repeated on each block to produce the following ciphertext: "dceonsdapchipchisearfruexnxx".

Bob and Alice are impressed with both the simplicity and the apparent strength of the permutation cipher, so they decide to give it a try. Finally they have a cipher that cannot be cracked by single-character frequency analysis, or so they think. They check out CAP and discover that it provides a tool for implementing the selected cipher.

Using CAP is easy, but somewhat limited. In CAP, the maximum block size is 10. When Bob and Alice want to use a permutation cipher, they enter their plaintext and select Permutation under the Cipher menu. A window will pop up allowing them to enter their key. (See Figure 5.3.) They begin by entering the block size and then the permutation. An example is shown in Figure 5.4. In this case, the block size is 7. The permutation will map character 7 to position 1, character 3 to position 2, character 6 to position 3, and so on.

5.2.1   Cryptanalysis of a Permutation Cipher

A permutation cipher is open to both a ciphertext-only and a known-plaintext attack. A ciphertext-only attack examines blocks of the ciphertext looking for possible rearrangements that might produce a recognizable word. Once the pattern is discovered for one block, it is applied to all the blocks in the ciphertext. If a cryptanalyst is especially skilled in anagramming, this could be a simple task.

Figure 5.3: Initial Permutation Cipher window

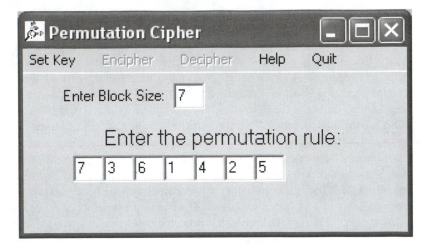

Figure 5.4: Example of a permutation cipher key

A known-plaintext attack is even easier. Using a word that might be in the plaintext, the attack involves three steps:

1. Find a block of ciphertext that contains the same letters as the known word.
2. Determine a permutation between the known word and the ciphertext block.
3. Test the result on other blocks of the ciphertext.

Eve uses a known-plaintext attack to break the following ciphertext:

eialciithsansaehitcpoierhwipetzkors.

Eve suspects that the word "Alice" is in the plaintext, so she matches up blocks of size 5 with this word. If any ciphertext block has the same set of letters, it might be possible to reconstruct the permutation. In this case, Eve hits pay dirt right at the start because the initial block has all the letters of the word "alice":

a l i c e
e i a l c

From this match, Eve guesses that letter 1 goes to position 3, letter 2 goes to position 4, letter 3 goes to position 2, letter 4 goes to position 5, and letter 5, goes to position 1. Trying this on the remainder of the ciphertext reproduces the plaintext.

In this case, Bob and Alice selected a poor key for their permutation. If the block size were larger perhaps the cipher would have been stronger. Certainly, a larger block size would make searching for a match more difficult to do by hand. However, even for larger block sizes, CAP will do the difficult work for Eve.

To access the CAP tool for breaking a simple permutation, go to the Transposition segment of the Analysis Tools and click on the Permutation button. This will open a window like the one shown in Figure 5.5. Enter the known word and CAP will return with possible substitutions. Select the result that is the most promising and test it.

CAP does provide a ciphertext-only-attack worksheet that will allow the user to input the suspected size of the block and use anagramming techniques to try to discover the actual permutation.

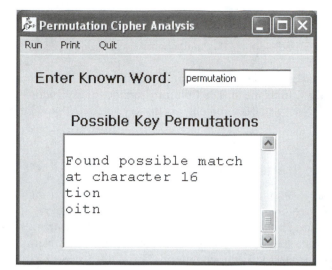

Figure 5.5: Known-word attack on a permutation cipher

5.3   COLUMN PERMUTATION CIPHER

Even though Eve managed to break the permutation cipher, Bob and Alice see some real promise in a transposition approach. So they decide to use a more complicated scheme involving more of the plaintext at a time. They select a column permutation cipher. With this cipher, the plaintext is written into a fixed-size rectangle by rows and the ciphertext is read off in columns in a predetermined order. For example, if the rectangle consists of four columns and five rows, then the phrase "encryption algorithms" could be written as follows:

```
1 2 3 4
e n c r
y p t i
o n a l
g o r i
t h m s
```

Reading off the columns in some specified order forms the ciphertext. For this example, if the order is 4, 1, 2, 3, then the ciphertext is "rilis eyogt npnoh ctarm". This cipher requires that the rectangle be filled, so if there are not enough letters in the plaintext, nulls such as "x" or "q", are added.

The key to this kind of cipher is the number of columns and the order in which they are selected. If there are a large number of columns, it might be difficult to remember the order so that it can be expressed as a keyword whose length identifies the number of columns and whose alphabetic order of its letters determines the column order.

For example, the keyword "general" has seven letters, which means that there are seven columns in the rectangle. Since "a" is the lowest order letter of the alphabet in "general", a number 1 is placed in column 6; the first "e" is the next letter in alphabetic order in "general", so a 2 is placed in column 2. The second "e" produces a 3 in column 4. The final result is as follows:

```
g e n e r a l
4 2 6 3 7 1 5
```

So the column order given by the keyword "general" is 4 2 6 3 7 1 5.

CAP offers a completely filled column transposition algorithm. "Completely filled" means that the matrix must have characters in each position—that is, the last row must be completely filled in. If the text does not support this, null characters are added to complete the last row.

The process is the same as any other CAP cipher. Enter the plaintext and select Column Transposition from the Cipher menu. The Column Transposition window will pop up as shown in Figure 5.6. Notice that all you enter is the keyword, CAP will determine the column order.

5.3.1 Cryptanalysis of Column Transpositions

As usual, Eve had some difficulty with the new cipher that Alice and Bob were using. She had to find some way to break a column transposition, but she found that attacking it directly was not feasible. A brute-force attack that tried all possible column and row sizes involved a lot effort with very little payoff. She needed to break down the problem into smaller steps. In fact, she decided to tackle a column transposition in three-steps. First, she

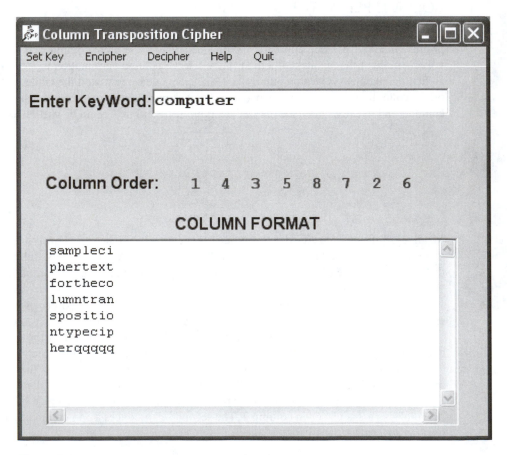

Figure 5.6: CAP Column Transposition Cipher form

would try to discover some possible sizes for the underlying rectangle (how many rows and columns?). Second, she would try to discover which of the possible rectangles was the correct one. Third, knowing the correct rectangle, she would try to rearrange the columns to recover the message. By attacking the problem in this three-step manner, she was soon back to reading the messages between Bob and Alice.

5.3.1.1 Possible Column Sizes

This is the first and the easiest task. Because the transposition is a completely filled column transposition, the number of characters in the ciphertext must be the product of the number of rows times the number of columns (or some factor of that number if the plaintext is spread across multiple rectangles). For example, say Eve intercepted the following message:

```
NETEF   LTDSR   TSSTF   MDCET   DRHXS   WHOHO   EEADU   OUUFI   RRRRS
NEROT   CFIEM   EDSHA   RTCPJ   AOEGE   WNLHO   EPMWA   WERUV   AAINA
TSDDS   OEOAC   EHNTL   HFLAU   RAEEN   OTOTS   SOSYS   TNNCG   EMETT
YDYRR   NEOOE   RESTH   INR
```

This message has 153 characters. 153 can be factored as $3 \times 51, 51 \times 3, 17 \times 9$, or 9×17. Assuming that this message was transposed into a single rectangle, one of the four products must define its size—that is, the rectangle has 3 rows and 51 columns, 51 rows and 3 columns, 17 rows and 9 columns, or 9 rows and 17 columns. There are no other possible rectangles that are completely filled by 153 characters. Since 3×51 or 51×3 offers a poor distribution of columns to rows, it is unlikely that either of these sizes defines the actual rectangle. The most likely rectangle size is either 17×9 or 9×17. So, the next step is to discover which of these two is the correct size. If neither is correct, then Eve can go back and try the other two possible sizes.

5.3.1.2 Determining the Correct Rectangle

Eve has narrowed it down to two possible rectangles. (If neither one works, then she can go back and try the 3×51 and 51×3 options, even though they represent poor choices by the cipher designer.) The problem Eve now faces is which of the two rectangles is the correct one. She could try to rearrange the columns of both to find the one that produces recognizable words, but half her work would be wasted on the wrong rectangle. Instead, it would be useful to find the most likely rectangle and then spend all her effort on that one first. It turns out that it is possible to evaluate each rectangle and discover the most likely candidate with very little effort.

The process is based on the observation that each line in the rectangle represents a line of standard English. All the letters in the plaintext are still in the ciphertext line—they are just in the wrong order. So Eve can rely on a general property of English to detect the most likely arrangement of the ciphertext. Any line of plaintext English should consist of about 40 percent vowels. The best candidate will be the rectangle whose distribution of vowels best matches the 40 percent per-line criteria.

For the 9×17 rectangle, there are nine columns, so each row should have about 3.6 (9×0.4) vowels. Eve loads the ciphertext into this rectangle and counts the number of vowels per line. She finds the absolute value of the difference between the actual number of vowels and the expected number of vowels (3.6) and adds up those differences to create a score for the rectangle. Her calculations for this case are shown next:

1	2	3	4	5	6	7	8	9	Vowels	Difference
N	C	U	F	G	A	N	S	E	2	1.6
E	E	O	I	E	A	T	S	Y	7	3.4
T	T	U	E	W	I	L	O	R	4	.4
E	D	U	M	N	N	H	S	R	2	1.6
F	R	F	E	L	A	F	Y	N	3	.6
L	H	I	D	H	T	L	S	E	2	1.6
T	X	R	S	O	S	A	T	O	3	.6
D	S	R	H	E	D	U	N	O	3	.6
S	W	R	A	P	D	R	N	E	2	1.6
R	H	R	R	M	S	A	C	R	1	2.6
T	O	S	T	W	O	E	G	E	4	.4
S	H	N	C	A	E	E	E	S	4	.4
S	O	E	P	W	O	N	M	T	3	.6
T	E	R	J	E	A	O	E	H	5	1.4
F	E	O	A	R	C	T	T	I	4	.4
M	A	T	O	U	E	O	T	N	5	1.4
D	D	C	E	V	H	T	Y	R	2	1.6
									TOTAL	20.6

For the 17×9 rectangle, Eve repeats the process:

1	2	3	4	5	6	7	8	9	10	11	12	13	14	15	16	17	Vowels	Difference
N	R	E	O	U	N	M	P	L	E	T	C	A	O	N	Y	E	8	1.2
E	T	T	H	U	E	E	J	H	R	S	E	U	T	N	D	R	6	.8
T	S	D	O	F	R	D	A	O	U	D	H	R	S	C	Y	E	6	.8
E	S	R	E	I	O	S	O	E	V	D	N	A	S	G	R	S	7	.2
F	T	H	E	R	T	H	E	P	A	S	T	E	O	E	R	T	6	.8
L	F	X	A	R	C	A	G	M	A	O	L	E	S	M	N	H	5	1.8
T	M	S	D	R	F	R	E	W	I	E	H	N	Y	E	E	I	7	.2
D	D	W	U	R	I	T	W	A	N	O	F	O	S	T	O	N	6	.8
S	C	H	O	S	E	C	N	W	A	A	L	T	T	T	O	R	5	1.8
																TOTAL	8.4

The best score is the smallest difference, so the 17×9 rectangle appears to be the most likely choice.

5.3.1.3 Restoring the Column Order

The final step in breaking a column transposition is to discover the correct order of the columns. This is an anagramming process that takes advantage of several characteristics of letters. One big help is what are called *pilot letters*. These are letters that can be followed by a limited set of other letters. For example, in English, "q" is always followed by "u". Other rules include the following:

- "j" can only be followed by a vowel.
- "x" can be preceded only by a vowel and except at the end of a word, it can only be succeeded by a vowel or by "c", "h", "p", or "t".

There are other rules that may also be helpful. For example, certain letters (usually of medium or low frequency) combine with other letters to form digrams of high frequency:

- "h" (medium frequency) combines with "t" to form "th" (highest frequency).
- "h" combines with "c" (medium frequency) to form "ch".

To begin the anagramming process, write out the ciphertext in the column format selected. Then look for pilot letters or other possible letter pairings. In Eve's case, the ciphertext looked like this:

1	2	3	4	5	6	7	8	9	10	11	12	13	14	15	16	17
N	R	E	O	U	N	M	P	L	E	T	C	A	O	N	Y	E
E	T	T	H	U	E	E	J	H	R	S	E	U	T	N	D	R
T	S	T	O	F	R	D	A	O	U	D	H	R	S	C	Y	E
E	S	R	E	I	O	S	O	E	V	D	N	A	S	G	R	S
F	T	H	E	R	T	H	E	P	A	S	T	E	O	E	R	T
L	F	X	A	R	C	A	G	M	A	O	L	E	S	M	N	H
T	M	S	D	R	F	R	E	W	I	E	H	N	Y	E	E	I
D	D	W	U	R	I	T	W	A	N	O	F	O	S	T	O	N
S	C	H	O	S	E	C	N	W	A	A	L	T	T	T	O	R

There are no "q"s in the ciphertext, but there is a "j" in row 2, column 8. This "j" must be matched with a vowel, and the two best candidates are the two "u"s in columns 5 and 13. Since this is a trial-and-error process, Eve tries matching column 8 with column 5 and then with column 13. The other rows should produce feasible letter pairings, and the match that produces the best possible set of pairs is the one that Eve will continue to work with. The question is: "How can she objectively determine which set of pairings is the best?" The answer is supplied by a table of centiban weights.

The U.S. government studied a collection of 5000 digrams and compiled a table of the log of twice the frequency of each digram. The larger the centiban weight, the more common is the digraph. Eve selects the two columns that produce the largest centiban total when the centiban score for each pair is summed. For the two possible matches, she produced the following results:

8	5	rank		8	13	rank
P	U	33		P	A	61
J	U	25		J	U	25
A	F	38		A	R	82
O	I	42		O	A	48
E	R	94		E	E	81
G	R	42		G	E	61
E	R	94		E	N	99
W	N	25		W	O	67
N	S	71		N	T	93
		464				617

From this table, Eve concludes that the best match is columns 8 and 13. Now the task remains to find the columns that should be placed before and after this pair. This can be accomplished by continuing the pairing process. For example, the "U" pair formed from columns 8 and 13 should be followed by a consonant—preferably an "n" or an "s"—so columns 15 and 11 are candidates:

8	13	15	rank		8	13	11	rank
P	A	N	89		P	A	T	83
J	U	N	68		J	U	S	58
A	R	C	53		A	R	D	64
O	A	G	45		O	A	D	73
E	E	E	81		E	E	S	86
G	E	M	61		G	E	O	58
E	N	E	87		E	N	E	87
W	O	T	67		W	O	O	45
N	T	T	67		N	T	A	74
			618					628

Using the centiban test on the two possibilities gives the 13–11 pairing a slight advantage. The three "e"s in row 5 of the 8–13–15 group is an unlikely occurrence, giving further weight to the 13–11 pairing. However, should 13–11 ultimately fail, it is worth a try to come back and explore the 8–13–15 group. With three columns selected, it becomes easier to begin to look for possible words, as well as to continue with the centiban tests. In Eve's case, the choice of the next column to place is made by looking at the current status of her work:

8	13	11		1	2	3	4	5	6	7	9	10	12	14	15	16	17
P	A	T		N	R	E	O	U	N	M	L	E	C	O	N	Y	E
J	U	S		E	T	T	H	U	E	E	H	R	E	T	N	D	R
A	R	D		T	S	D	O	F	R	D	O	U	H	S	C	Y	E
O	A	D		E	S	R	E	I	O	S	E	V	N	S	G	R	S
E	E	S		F	T	H	E	R	T	H	P	A	T	O	E	R	T
G	E	O		L	F	X	A	R	C	A	M	A	L	S	M	N	H
E	N	E		T	M	S	D	R	F	R	W	I	H	Y	E	E	I
W	O	O		D	D	W	U	R	I	T	A	N	F	S	T	O	N
N	T	A		S	C	H	O	S	E	C	W	A	L	T	T	O	R

Column 2 looks like a good choice to follow column 11 because it would create the word "just" in row 2 and possibly the word "enemy" in row 7. With a little more work, Eve ultimately deciphers the message. (It is left up to you to discover the final message.)

5.3.2 Using CAP to Break a Column Transposition

Breaking a column transposition by hand could be difficult, but with the services of CAP, many of the required tools are just a mouse click away. From the Analysis bar in the main CAP window, select the Transposition button. There are several tools available within that bar. Begin with the Vowel Analysis option, which produces the window shown in Figure 5.7. It will automatically count the number of characters in the ciphertext and report possible transposition sizes. To perform a vowel analysis, simply enter one of the possible column sizes and click on Run. From the Vowel Results Summary box, find the best choice for the column size.

The anagramming process and the use of the centiban test are also part of the CAP tool set. Select Anagram from the Analysis bar and CAP will open the window shown in Figure 5.8.

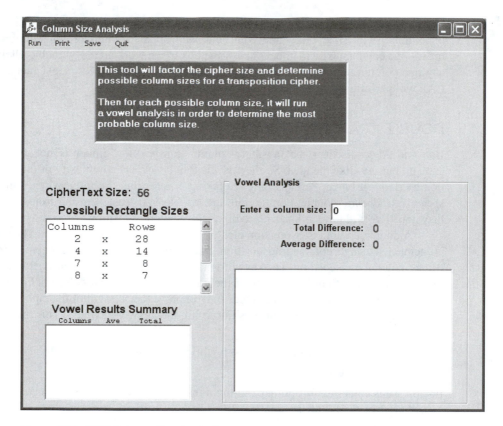

Figure 5.7: CAP Column Size Analysis

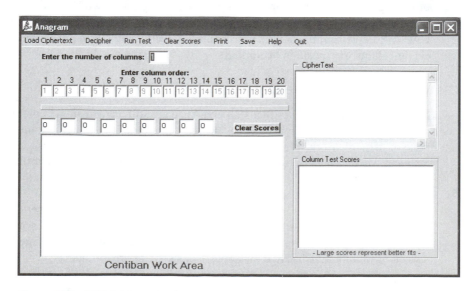

Figure 5.8: CAP Anagram tool

This is one of the more complicated tools provided by CAP. Begin by entering the number of columns. In the small boxes above the centiban work area, enter column numbers in any order—the column text will appear below the box in the work area. By double-clicking on any two column numbers in those boxes and then selecting the Run Test menu option, CAP will perform a centiban test and report the results.

5.4   DOUBLE-TRANSPOSITION CIPHER

Bob and Alice discover that a single-column transposition cipher is not complicated enough, but they like the idea. So they decide to increase the complexity of the transposition by doing it twice. Perhaps they are taking a note from the three witches in Shakespeare's *Macbeth*: "double, double, toil and trouble." At least, toil and trouble are what they hope Eve will have as she tries to break this new transposition.

A double-column transposition cipher works just as the name implies. The plaintext is enciphered using a column transposition, and the resulting ciphertext is enciphered again using a column transposition. The keyword may be the same for both transpositions. Hopefully, the result is a thorough mixing of the positions of the plaintext letters. For example, given the plaintext "Using a cipher twice may improve the strength of the cipher or it may not", encipher it in a column transposition using the keyword "what". This produces the first ciphertext:

nircy   rttgf   ceiyq   sahwm   mveeh   hpomo   ugpte   iohrt   tirtn
iceia   pesno   ehrat

Encipher this ciphertext in another column transposition using the keyword "next". Doing so will produce the following final result:

irfyh   vhoth   iianr   qnygi   amhmp   otnis   hqcte   smeog   ittee
etqrt   cqwep   uerrc   poaq

As expected, the effect of the double use of the column transposition is an additional level of mixing. Bob and Alice hope that this added complication will invalidate the tools that Eve constructed to break a single-column transposition cipher. They also like the fact that CAP will implement the double transposition directly, without requiring them to use two single-column transposition operations.

5.4.1   Cryptanalysis of the Double-Transposition Cipher

Eve first mistakenly believes that Bob and Alice are still using a single-column transposition cipher because the ciphertext has all the characteristics of such a transposition. But none of her tools work, so Eve is once again forced to find a new weakness in the system Bob and Alice have selected. After some trial and error, she decides that there is a good chance that they have selected a double transposition. She also discovers that there are some weaknesses associated with a double transposition.

One such weakness involves the creation of several same-size ciphertexts using the same pair of keys. Aware of this weakness, Eve decides to gather the encrypted messages between Bob and Alice over a few days time and collect a group of the same length. After a week of waiting, Eve has five messages that satisfy her requirements:

1. egota   iptai   qunlt   vsoit   nqxns   seoqb   iyhoh   sicsq   lscar
    xtnti   kewte   arbtr   mwldi   anfxo   oldao   repoi   eirdu   baalr
    cx

2. ttcay yaeah qinsn aoiok aqxun utvqg nhele treeq hoeml
   xcrur wbryh ifaif aywec osixr awonl cinbo althe iegbe
   nx

3. tdhit htbaa qewwi rioon rqxnm udeqe aeset tahyq dnsve
   xiekd rawrh eobot ocher otuxn owhfo maute kotly bello
   nx

4. oohoe ihtmt qtdnd daaoe wqxmt mxeqo odaoe wtaaq mywbn
   xcwni herie iaaru euhem ttvxe eaeel rwrte ftech ioaew
   rx

5. ocahl weihb qtsnn eaoli eqxbf lsaqn ioofo hwtoq onwtu
   xhtet tauio ecbne bantc tdaxa ekoro aeovo ofnws btvue
   wx

All are 92 characters in length, and if Bob and Alice used the same two keywords for all five, Eve can break the cipher. Eve begins by placing all five messages "in depth"—that is, one on top of the other. The result is a 92 × 5 matrix that represents a giant single-column transposition:

egota iptai qunlt vsoit nqxns seoqb iyhoh sicsq lscar xtnti
kewte arbtr mwldi anfxo oldao repoi eirdu baalr cx
ttcay yaeah qinsn aoiok aqxun utvqg nhele treeq hoeml xcrur
wbryh ifaif aywec osixr awonl cento althe iegbe nx
tdhit htbaa qewwi rioon rqxnm udeqe aeset tahyq dnsve xiekd
rawrh eobot ocher otuxn owhfo maute kotly bello nx
oohoe ihtmt qtdnd daaoe wqxmt mxeqo odaoe wtaaq mywbn xcwni
herie iaaru euhem ttvxe eaeel rwrte ftech ioaew rx
ocahl weihb qtsnn eaoli eqxbf lsaqn ioofo hwtoq onwtu xhtet
tauio ecbne bantc tdaxa ekoro aeovo ofnws btvue wx

All Eve now has to do is rearrange the columns so that each row is in plaintext form. It all boils down to a large anagramming problem.

With the five ciphertexts arranged as a large single-column transposition, it becomes clear that "q" and "x" were used as nulls (note several columns of just "q" or just "x"). These columns should be moved to the end of the text. The arrangement of the remaining columns can be accomplished by looking for pilot letters and possible words.

5.4.2 Using CAP to Break a Double Transposition

Luckily for Eve, she does not have to solve the double transposition by hand, because CAP provides some useful tools for attacking this cipher. Under the Transposition tool, there is a MultiColumn button that will open the window shown in Figure 5.9. To use this tool, enter each ciphertext sample in the main Ciphertext window. Then select Load Next Ciphertext under the Ciphertext menu in the Double Column Analysis window. This will line up each sample and define the columns. Finally, use the Centiban Tests and the Worksheet to arrange the columns in the best order.

This chapter only covers a few of the many types of transposition ciphers. CAP actually implements some additional transpositions.

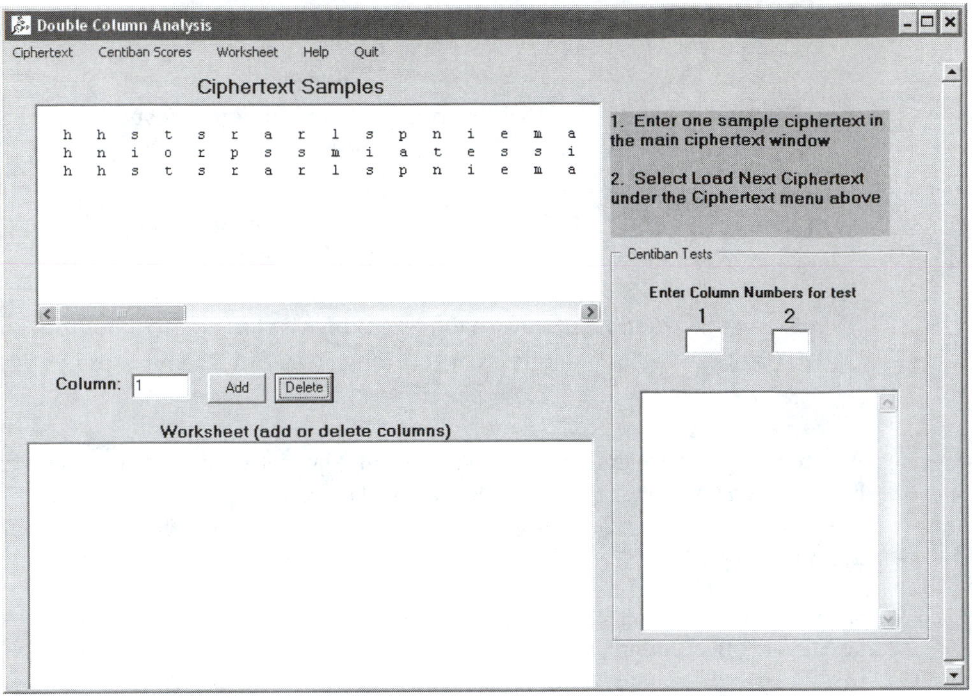

Figure 5.9: Double Column Analysis

5.5   A BRIEF HISTORY OF TRANSPOSITIONS

Transpositions have a varied and interesting history, from the skytale of the Greeks to the Union ciphers used during the Civil War. But their use did not end with the restoration of the Union. Transposition continued to find a niche in cryptography for many years. In fact, they are still used today as part of substitution–permutation networks, which are covered in Chapter 7.

For example, during WWI, the Germans used a famous and complicated double-transposition cipher. It began with a keyphrase that was translated into a number sequence using the alphabetic method described earlier. If the keyphrase is "next time", then the number sequence is as follows:

```
n e x t t i m e
5 1 8 6 7 3 4 2
```

The plaintext, "Bob I need to see you at the office now Alice", is written under the following number sequence:

```
5 1 8 6 7 3 4 2
b o b i n e e d
t o s e e y o u
a t t h e o f f
i c e n o w a l
i c e
```

The columns are written under the same number sequence and as many null letters as there are words in the keyphrase are added:

```
5 1 8 6 7 3 4 2
o o t c c d u f
l e y o w e o f
a b t a i i i e
h n n e e o b s
t e e x j
```

Finally, the letters are taken off in column order: "oebne ffesd eiouo ibola htcoa excwi ejtyt ytne".

This usually produced an incompletely filled column transposition, which made things more difficult for cryptanalysts. However, before the outbreak of WWI, the French prepared their cryptographic service, providing it with increased manpower and resources. From their initial efforts arose a powerful radio traffic analysis system—just in time for a war that required the use of radio. The French effort paid off and they were able to break and read many of the German messages sent using this double-transposition cipher. It seems that the Germans could never get a break during wartime.

During the war, the German army moved from transpositions to substitutions. By 1916, they were back to transpositions. This time they adopted a turning grille. Turning grilles first appeared in a book by C.F. Hindenburg in 1796. They quickly became very popular. Because of this, they were used frequently near the end of the 18th century and later by Germany during WWI. A typical turning grille and some sample plaintext ("this is an example of a turning grille for us") are shown in Figure 5.10. If the turning grille is placed above the plaintext, the first set of ciphertext letters is exposed, as shown in Figure 5.11. These letters are written down in row order: "hinxetios".

Figure 5.10: An example of a turning grille and some plaintext

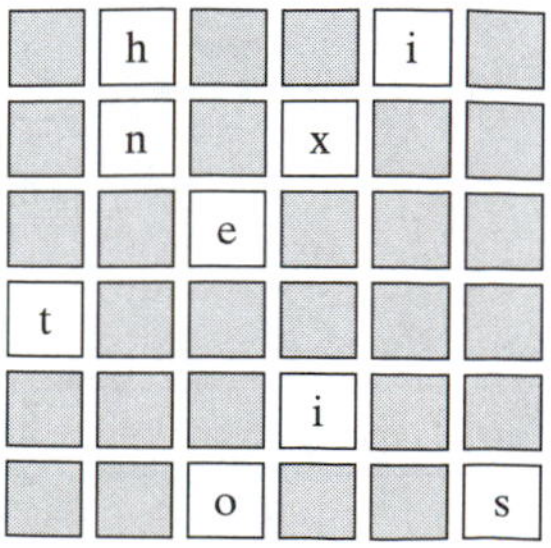

Figure 5.11: The first application of the turning grille

The grille is rotated clockwise by 90 degrees to expose the second set of ciphertext letters as shown in Figure 5.12. Now the ciphertext is "hinxetios **iampouile**". The grille is rotated another 90 degrees (Figure 5.13) and the third part of the ciphertext is exposed: "hinxetios iampouile **tseanrlfu**". The final rotation is shown in Figure 5.14, and the final ciphertext is "hinxetios iampouile tseanrlfu salfrnggr".

The multiple anagramming attacks that work so well against the double transposition also work against a turning grille. The French did not find this new wrinkle in German cryptography to be much of a challenge. Within four months, the Germans decided they had to abandon the turning grilles.

Lest you conclude that the French were masters of the cryptography game during WWI, it is worthwhile to note that they actually used a weaker transposition algorithm than the Germans—called an *interrupted columnar transposition*. In this type of cipher, certain predetermined diagonals were read off first, then the columns were read, skipping any character that had already been used. For example, in the following pattern, the diagonals are transcribed first, followed by the columns:

```
4   2   7   1   3   5   6
t   h   i   s   i   s   a
w   e   a   k   c   i   p
h   e   r   i   t   w   a
s   b   r   o   k   e   n
```

This results in the ciphertext "haik aito sk eeb ic twhs swe pan irr" (each segment is shown—that would not be done in the actual ciphertext).

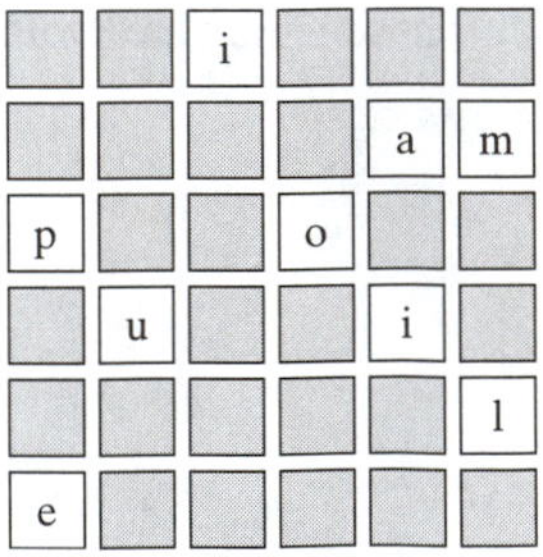

Figure 5.12: The first rotation of the turning grille

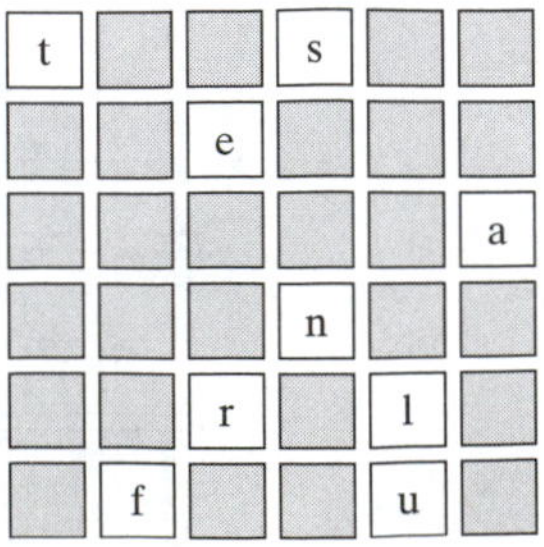

Figure 5.13: The second rotation of the turning grille

Figure 5.14: The final rotation of the turning grille

5.6 SUMMARY

This chapter introduced a different approach to encryption—the transposition cipher. Instead of substituting one letter or group of letters for another, this approach rearranges the letters in the plaintext. This makes decryption like a giant jigsaw puzzle in which all the letters have to be put back into the correct order. The key to this type of cipher is usually a geometric figure. The plaintext is written into the figure in one order and read out in a different order. The new ciphers fit into our growing cipher structure chart as shown in Figure 5.15.

This new round of the battle between Alice, Bob, and Eve is again a toss-up. Alice and Bob discovered a new method of protecting their messages, but Eve discovered a new set of tools for attacking their ciphers at every turn. Specifically, Eve discovered the utility of using several ciphertext messages together to help break the double-column transposition cipher. This will prove to be very useful later when she will encounter more difficult systems. Alice and Bob learned that, just because they implement two ciphers back-to-back, they do not necessarily gain any advantage. However, they do sense some promise in such an approach and will investigate other ways in which they may combine ciphers to perhaps achieve a higher degree of protection.

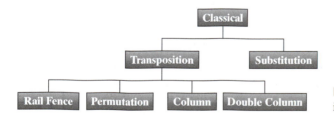

Figure 5.15: Transposition ciphers found in Chapter 5

5.7 IMPORTANT TERMS

Anagramming	The process of rearranging the order of letters to produce words
Centiban scores	Scores that rank the value of letter digrams
Column cipher	A transposition cipher in which the plaintext is written into a rectangle in rows and the ciphertext is formed by reading off the columns in some specified order

Double-column cipher	A transposition cipher that applies a column transposition to create an intermediate ciphertext to which another column transposition is applied to create the final ciphertext
Monographic transposition	A transposition cipher that rearranges letters
Polygraphic transposition	A transposition cipher that rearranges words or groups of letters
Transposition cipher	A cipher that rearranges the order of the plaintext

RESOURCES

Making, Breaking Codes by Paul Garrett (Prentice Hall, 2001), Chapter 3

Decrypted Secrets by F. L. Bauer (Springer, 1997), Chapter 6

PROBLEMS

1. The ciphertext that follows was produced by a rail-fence transposition of depth 4 with 14 columns:

   aellneepiedhcs

   Recover the plaintext.

2. Fill in the following information:

Cipher	Summarize its operation	Summarize its weakness
Permutation		
Column transposition		
Double column		

3. Bob and Alice get the idea that, since one permutation will help, why not do two back-to-back? Is this a good idea—that is, is it more secure than a single permutation? Why or why not?

4. Complete Eve's work to break the transposition cipher in Section 5.3.

5. Complete Eve's work to break the double-transposition cipher in Section 5.4.1.

6. The following ciphertext was created with the use of a permutation cipher:

   eacil dieen whple hitht rieps tmatu iicno ipreh ecsna geotm tetit bonur zozzb

   Suppose we know that the code contains the word "alice". Find the plaintext.

7. The following ciphertext was created with a column transposition cipher:

   anrjc   esdhs   qenns   bcdet   eeiok   utlri   nqlee   uabto   ihucf
   yoqie   hssrh   nnoio   otoqe   mliea   stwlt   ummbq   iopnv   kited
   hmaeo   q

   Find the plaintext.

8. Eve discovers that Bob and Alice have switched to a double-transposition cipher. She collects the following set of ciphertext:

   ymqscaqhbgoxewlocrenqrbxlpqvoorktilqufaeqtooriox
   qkidiuqseunxllsotidlqyixocqkaioatboqdibiqaccwisx
   jryccoqnbutxirdadseuqnbxlwqfesoitiyqoaaoqeotvunx
   usanwaqrembxsloioihiqtixoaqnaeaysbgqttbtqacaddhx
   saidcdqgbtlxdwucsneiqibxloqdokljeiuqwfayqnoinaix

   Find the plaintext for each.

Part 2

Contemporary Ciphers

Historically, the ciphers covered in Part One were developed and, for the most part, implemented by hand. Most of the cryptanalysis techniques covered in Part One were also applied by hand. Of course, with CAP, the computer now does all the work—something you should appreciate.

With Part Two, we formally enter the world of computers. Ciphers and the analysis tools can no longer be implemented by hand. The whole approach to the world of ciphers will take advantage of the characteristics of computers—characteristics that significantly complicate the whole field of cryptology. Yet, as you will discover, everything that is done has its roots in classical cryptology. What you learned in Part One will remain valuable because you can use that knowledge as a foundation for the study of contemporary ciphers.

Chapter 6

Stream Ciphers

6.0 INTRODUCTION

Early in the history of human beings, messages were delivered by hand. Transportation was limited to either walking or riding on horseback. As a result, messages were slow to arrive at their destination. When a message was important enough to require some sort of protection, it might be enciphered (also by hand). Because of the method of transmission, every important message also came with a guard, whether it was enciphered or not. If a message was intercepted, either the guard returned to report the loss or didn't return at all. Either way, it was a good bet that the enemy had the message in their possession.

With the development of the telegraph, messages could be delivered quickly over long distances. A human was no longer needed to act as a courier. However, the enemy could tap the lines and receive the message at the same time as the intended recipient. Without a guard carrying the message, no one would know that it had been intercepted. The telegraph lines could be guarded to try and minimize the loss, but confidence in the security of messages dropped, making cryptology even more important as a means of protecting vital information.

Then along came the radio. Now messages could be quickly sent over vast distances without the need for wires. The source and destination of messages could be more mobile—moving from place to place while remaining in contact. The cost of this revolution was the total lack of security. The enemy could receive a message just as easily as the intended recipient. The assumption had to be made that the enemy was always "listening." Cryptology became vital to the protection of information—it was the only way to insure that someone listening could not understand the message.

Today, the computer has revolutionized everything. There is no limit to the form, amount, or distance over which information can be shared (or intercepted). Cryptology is now essential to protect our personal privacy as well as our national security. Computers not only changed the way information is managed, they also changed the way in which it is hidden. New ciphers are based on computer characteristics rather than on language structure. The focus of new ciphers is on binary digits (bits) and not on alphabetic characters.

This chapter looks at those characteristics of a computer that change the way information is both stored and encrypted. Those familiar with computer structures can skip that material and move to Section 6.1. Using the new computer representation of information, a simple cipher system based on streams of bits will be introduced. While the approach to a stream cipher outlined in this chapter does involve exploiting the characteristics of a computer, the idea of a stream cipher is not new. In fact, the autokey ciphers covered in Chapter 3 operate much like the binary stream cipher found in this chapter.

6.0.1 Computer Characteristics

The fundamental change brought about by computer technology is the means of representing information. Computers represent information internally as a set of binary bits—0's and 1's. As a result, the alphabet is no longer the method of information storage—binary bits are the currency of information today. Everything we write must be translated into computer bits for storage and manipulation and then converted back into letters and numbers for human interpretation.

Numbers are easy to represent in this binary world. Counting in binary is just like counting in decimal except the only digits available are 0 and 1. The comparison between binary numbers and decimal numbers is shown here:

Binary	Decimal	Binary	Decimal
0	0	110	6
1	1	111	7
10	2	1000	8
11	3	1001	9
100	4	1010	10
101	5		

Using the binary number system generates longer strings of digits to represent decimal numbers; however, all the arithmetic processes that work on decimal numbers (addition, subtraction, etc.) also work on binary numbers. So the switch from decimal to binary is not much of a change at all.

Computers need to be able to represent both characters and numbers. This is not as easy as it may sound, because there is no formal mathematical relation between alphabetic letters and strings of 0's and 1's. We have to define such a relationship in order to avoid chaos. Hence, everyone who makes or uses a computer has to use the same relationship. Such a relationship was defined early on in the development of computer systems. Called the ASCII (American Standard Code for Information Interchange) code, it assigned an 8-bit pattern to each letter of the alphabet. It also assigned patterns to special characters such as a line feed and a carriage return.

For example, a computer represents the character "a" as an internal pattern of 8 binary bits—specifically, 01100001. CAP has a feature that will be useful later for transforming plaintext into its equivalent ASCII code by selecting the to Binary option under the Plaintext menu.

Since the transformation from letter to ASCII code is transparent to the user (you see letters on the screen or the printer, not binary bits), it is still possible to write computer code that will perform substitution and transposition ciphers at the character level. After all, that is what CAP does all the time. However, since the computer represents plaintext as a string of 0's and 1's, it makes sense to design ciphers that work on binary strings instead of on individual letters. For example, the ASCII code for "a" is 01000001. If a cipher changes some of the 1's to 0's and 0's to 1's, it might replace the binary string for "a" with 00101101, which is the ASCII code for "+". The problem with developing such a cipher is: "How do I appear to randomly change 0's to 1's and 1's to 0's in such a way that I can recover the original binary string?" The answer lies in the use of a special function of binary bits called an exclusive-OR (XOR).

6.0.2 XOR Function

The XOR is a special binary function with two inputs and one output. The output is 1 if the two inputs are different and 0 if the two inputs are the same. This can best be summarized in the form of a truth table that lists all possible input combinations and the resulting output as shown in Figure 6.1.

This function can be used to "randomly" change bits in a binary string. Let one input to the XOR be the plaintext bit stream and the other be a random-key bit string. The resulting output is the ciphertext bit stream. For example, the word "The" in ASCII could be encrypted as follows:

```
Plaintext         T         h         e
Plaintext bits    01010100  01101000  01100101
Key bits          00001101  00110100  01101101
Ciphertext bits   01011001  01011100  00001000
Ciphertext        Y         \         "SI" shift in
```

The first thing to notice about this example is that the ciphertext is not limited to letters—it can be special or even unprintable characters. This is an example of a cipher that has two different alphabets: one for the plaintext and one for the ciphertext. This issue of multiple alphabets will be examined more closely later. Given this cipher, the problem is how do you recover "The" from the ciphertext? The answer is, "XOR the key bits with the ciphertext bits." It's as simple as that, as the following example shows:

```
Ciphertext        Y         \         "SI"
Ciphertext bits   01011001  01011100  00001000
Key bits          00001101  00110100  01101101
Plaintext bits    01010100  01101000  01100101
Plaintext         T         h         e
```

So, a bit-level cipher can be constructed by using the XOR function and a random key-stream. This is the scheme that is covered in the next section.

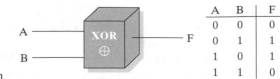

Figure 6.1: The XOR function

6.1 STREAM CIPHER

A simple stream cipher requires a "random" bit stream to serve as a key. The ciphertext is created by XORing the plaintext with this random keystream. The plaintext is recovered by XORing the ciphertext with the same random keystream. This process is illustrated in Figure 6.2.

The XOR function is simple to implement, making this a fast and efficient cipher when one is working at the bit level. The only issue that must be addressed is how to generate a random keystream. This is a problem because the keystream must appear random yet be easy to reproduce for legitimate users. A short sequence of bits that is repeated over and over would be easy to remember, but would not be very secure. On the other hand, a random bit sequence that is as long as the plaintext would not be feasible to remember. So the dilemma is how can a "random" bit sequence be generated that both parties can easily use, but is not so short as to be insecure? This is very similar to the Vigenere autokey ciphers covered in Chapter 3. In the autokey ciphers, the keystream was formed from either the plaintext or the ciphertext. In both cases, the keystream started with a keyword. The solution for a bit-level stream cipher is much the same: develop a random-bit generator that is dependent on a short key. The generator produces the keystream, but the user only has to remember how to get the generator started.

There are two general types of keystream generators: synchronous and self-synchronous. The keystream from a synchronous generator is independent of the plaintext stream. As a result, if a ciphertext character is lost during transmission, the ciphertext and the keystream will be misaligned. The keystream must be resynchronized in order to recreate the correct plaintext. A self-synchronous stream cipher produces the keystream from knowledge of the previous n ciphertext characters. If there is an error in one of the ciphertext characters, the keystream will resynchronize itself after n correct ciphertext characters.

There are several ways to produce a synchronous keystream generator. The most common is to use a hardware device called a linear feedback shift register (LFSR).

6.1.1 Linear Feedback Shift Registers

Before we can get back to the issue of stream-cipher key design, we need to take a little detour into the fascinating world of hardware circuits. This should come as no surprise, since we are looking at ciphers that are based on computers rather than on manual manipulations of letters.

One very useful hardware device is a shift register. This device saves a set of bits (register part), which are loaded into the device in one of two ways. They can be loaded in parallel—that is, if the device saves 8 bits, all 8 bits can be loaded at one time—or they can be loaded in using a shift register. A typical 8-bit shift register loads bits in one at a time. (See Figure 6.3.)

In the shift mode, each bit is moved to the right—the rightmost bit is lost; the leftmost bit is replaced with the input bit. For the shift register shown in Figure 6.3, if the shift-in bit is a 0, then, after a shift operation, the contents will appear as shown in Figure 6.4.

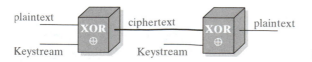

Figure 6.2: A stream cipher

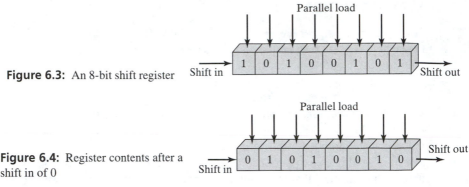

Figure 6.3: An 8-bit shift register

Figure 6.4: Register contents after a shift in of 0

As long as a bit is supplied on the shift in, this device will supply a stream of bits on the shift-out side. By itself, this device cannot solve our problem of generating a long "random-appearing" bit stream for a key. After all, it will only output on the shift-out side the same bits that were shifted into it. So, how do we provide a shift-in bit sequence that appears to be random? This is where the feedback part of the name of our key generator comes from. Select some of the cells in the shift register, XOR them, and use the result for the shift in—that is, feedback a function of the current contents of the register to the input.

Now we have an LFSR, as shown in Figure 6.5. The operation of a simple 8-bit LFSR in which the shift in is the XOR of Cells 2 and 5 is illustrated in Table 6.1.

The shift-out stream is the key (in this case, 0 1 0 0 1 1). An LFSR can run as long as necessary to produce key bits to match plaintext bits. All that is needed to decipher the ciphertext is to run the same LFSR with the same initial contents. Eventually, the cell contents will cycle back to the beginning, and then the key stream will repeat. One issue in the design of an LFSR for random-bit generation is what is the longest nonrepeating sequence of bits that can be produced from a given LFSR? This is an especially important issue in the design of the one cipher that is provably unbreakable, but you will have to wait until a

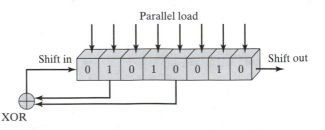

Figure 6.5: A shift register with feedback

TABLE 6.1 Sample run of an LFSR

Shift in	Cell 1	Cell 2*	Cell 3	Cell 4	Cell 5*	Cell 6	Cell 7	Cell 8	Shift out
1	1	1	0	1	0	0	1	1	1
0	1	1	1	0	1	0	0	1	1
1	0	1	1	1	0	1	0	0	0
1	1	0	1	1	1	0	1	0	0
1	1	1	0	1	1	1	0	1	1
0	1	1	1	0	1	1	1	0	0

later section to learn about it. Clearly, if the LFSR uses an n-bit register and the contents of the register never repeated until all the possible n-bit combinations have appeared, then the period (the length of the cycle before it begins to repeat) of the random numbers is $2^n - 1$. (The -1 occurs because we never want the register to contain all 0's, as you will discover if you are assigned one of the problems in this chapter.) The actual length of the period depends on the initial contents of the register and on the feedback pattern used by the LFSR. Some settings guarantee a maximum period, and others produce shorter periods. The structure of maximum-period LFSRs has been cataloged for different length registers. For example, the maximum period for a 6-bit LFSR occurs when bits 5 and 6 are XNORed (XOR with an inverter on the output) to create the feedback bit.

6.1.2 LFSR Period Analysis

A general LFSR can be represented by a function of its stored bits and the connections to the shift-in bit. For the LFSR shown in Figure 6.6, the function is

$$b_n = c_1 b_1 \text{ XOR } c_2 b_2 \text{ XOR } \dots \text{ XOR } c_n b_n,$$

where $c_i = 1$ if the ith bit is selected for the XOR operation; otherwise, it is 0.

Each LFSR has an associated characteristic polynomial, which is not the same as the function that determines the next shift-in bit. This polynomial is related to the underlying mathematical structure of the LFSR. For the example register in Figure 6.6, the characteristic polynomial is

$$p(x) = c_n x^n + c_{n-1} x^{n-1} + \dots + c_i x + 1,$$

where (as before) $c_i = 1$ if the ith bit is selected for the XOR operation; otherwise, it is 0. It turns out that an LFSR has a maximal sequence if its characteristic polynomial is "primitive" (sometimes it is referred to as "irreducible"). A polynomial of degree n, $p(x)$, is primitive if it cannot be factored and the smallest integer k for which $p(x)$ divides $x^k - 1$ is $2^n - 1$.

An example of a three-element LFSR is shown in Figure 6.7. Its characteristic polynomial is

$$p(x) = x^3 + x + 1,$$

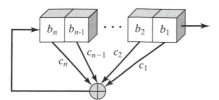

Figure 6.6: A general LFSR

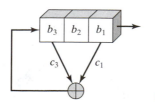

Figure 6.7: A three-element LFSR

which satisfies the requirements for a primitive polynomial. So the LFSR of Figure 6.7 has a maximal period like that shown in Figure 6.8.

By contrast, an LFSR that does not have a maximal cycle is shown in Figure 6.9. This is a four-element LFSR represented by the polynomial

$$p(x) = x^4 + x^3 + x^2 + x + 1.$$

The cycles for this example are shown in Figure 6.10. If the LFSR is initialized to one of the bit patterns in those cycles, it will always remain within that cycle producing a sub-standard random string of bits.

There are mathematical procedures for determining primitive polynomials that have been used to catalog the conditions for maximal-cycle LFSR. Using a negative XOR (XNOR) for the feedback function, the maximal-cycle LFSR of size 4 uses bits 3 and 4 for the feedback links. A size 8 maximal-cycle LFSR (again with the XNOR feedback function) uses bits 8, 6, 5, 4.

6.1.3 Random-Bit Tests

Another issue in the design of any random-number generator is just how random are the bits? If the bits are not completely random, then an attacker may be able to discover patterns in the bits that may be exploited to reveal all or most of the key. In order to avoid this problem, several different tests of randomness have been developed. These tests are used to determine whether a specific random-bit generator is safe to use.

It is impossible to mathematically prove that any given random-bit generator actually produces a truly random-bit stream. The best that can be done is to show that the bit stream has the characteristics expected of a random set of bits. As a result, there are several groups of standardized randomness tests available. The FIPS 140–1 test suite includes some obvious

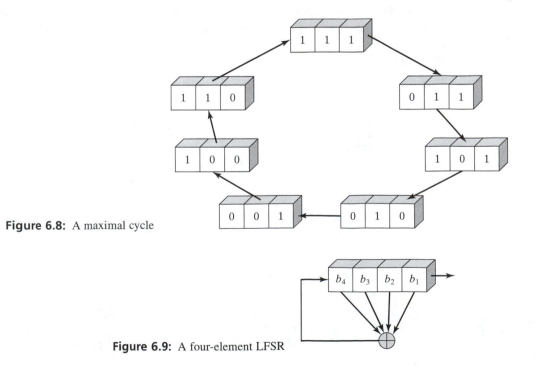

Figure 6.8: A maximal cycle

Figure 6.9: A four-element LFSR

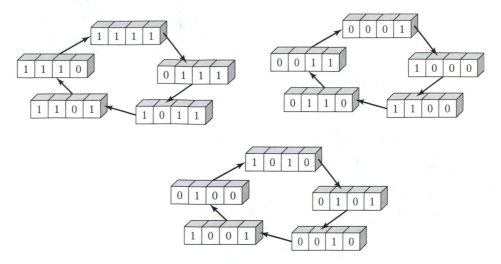

Figure 6.10: Nonmaximal cycles

and some not so obvious tests. This test suite accepts 20,000 bits from a random source. The first test is the *monobit test*, which verifies that the number of 1's and 0's are almost equal. This is what we would expect from a random-bit stream. The process counts the number of 1's: If it is within the range 9654–10,346, then the bit stream passes the monobit test.

However, passing the monobit test does not guarantee that a bit stream is truly random. Another test specified by FIPS 140–1 is the *poker test*. For the poker test, the 20,000 bits are divided into 4-bit segments. Each 4-bit segment represents a decimal number between 0 and 15. A truly random sequence of bits should result in a random distribution of the numbers 0–15. Let n_i be the number of occurrences of a number i—that is, n_1 is the number of 4-bit segments of the form 0001, and n_8 is the number of 4-bit segments of the form 1000. These values are substituted into

$$X = \frac{16}{5000} \sum_{i=0}^{15} n_i^2 - 5000.$$

The test is passed if $1.03 < X < 57.4$.

A third randomness test is called the *runs test*. A run is a consecutive sequence of either 1's or 0's. In a truly random-bit stream, there should be a random distribution of maximal-length runs. (A run is maximal length if it is not contained in a larger run.) For example, the sequence 0110111101 contains a maximal run of length 2 (the 1's that are in positions 2 and 3) and a maximal run of length 4 (1111). It also contains four maximal runs of length 1. Using the 20,000 bit test sequence, the number of maximal-length runs for each possible length is counted. If the number of each run falls within the following guidelines, then the sequence passes this test:

		1	2267–2733	
		2	1079–1421	
Length		3	502–748	Required
of run		4	223–402	interval
		5	90–223	
		6+	90–223	

The National Institute of Standards and Technology (NIST) also suggests a set of randomness tests. Some of the FIPS 140–1 tests are in this collection. CAP offers a subset of these tests that may be used to evaluate the implementation of a stream cipher or any other bit cipher. To run these tests, select Random from the main CAP menu and Test from the submenu. The Randomness Tests window shown in Figure 6.11 will open.

At a minimum, an acceptable random sequence should pass all the CAP tests.

6.1.4 Implementing a Stream Cipher in CAP

A stream cipher is not the kind of cipher system that can be implemented by hand. It requires the bit representation of the plaintext characters and a long random-bit stream. It also produces a bit representation of the ciphertext characters. Luckily for Bob and Alice, CAP provides a Stream Cipher option. Select the Stream Cipher option under the main Cipher menu, and the window shown in Figure 6.12 will pop up.

CAP's version of a stream cipher is based on an LFSR. You need to enter the size of the shift register, which must be a multiple of 4. Then, enter the initial value for the shift register in the form of a hex number (using the digits 0..9 and the letters A..F). The feedback

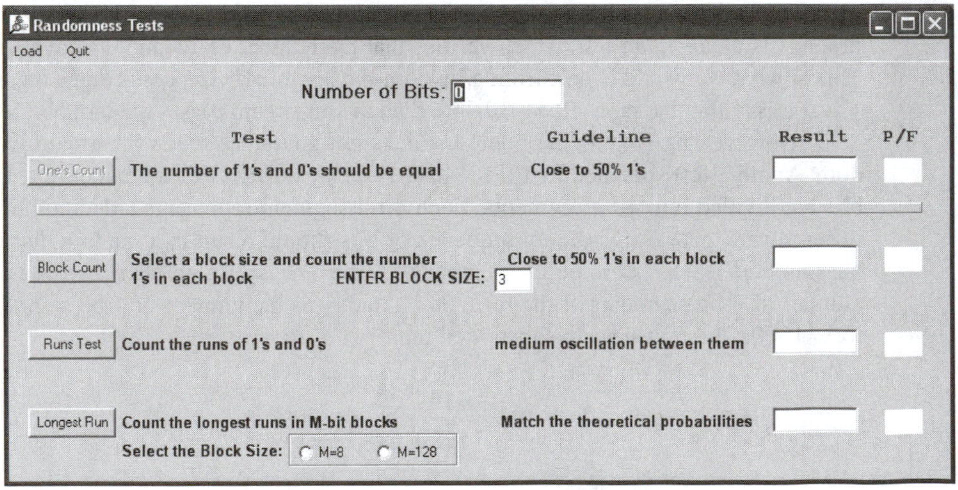

Figure 6.11: CAP randomness tests options

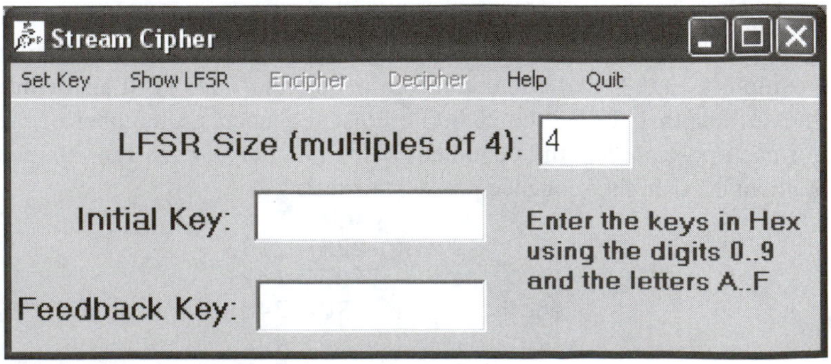

Figure 6.12: CAP Stream Cipher window

key determines which cells in the register are XORed to produce the input bit. This must also be in the form of a hex number. CAP has an added feature that is useful if you are unsure about the structure of your random-key generator. Once you have specified both the size and the two keys, select Show LFSR from the main menu. A window will open that shows your LFSR initial contents and the feedback links. (See Figure 6.13.)

From this window, you can actually run some simple randomness tests by selecting the Test menu option. You can also watch your LFSR cycle by selecting the Run option.

6.2   BREAKING A STREAM CIPHER

Bob and Alice feel like they have now entered the 21st century by finally discovering a means of protecting their communications from the prying eyes of Eve. Unfortunately, as always seems to happen, Eve is quick to catch up with their latest approach. She discovers that Bob and Alice are using a stream cipher, so she looks into ways that the cipher might be compromised. She discovers three types of attacks: an insertion attack, a bit-string-matching attack, and a known-plaintext attack.

6.2.1   Insertion Attack on a Stream Cipher

This attack is quite simple, but it requires the ability to insert a single bit into the plaintext stream and intercept the ciphertext stream. Assume that the original plaintext, key stream, and ciphertext are given by

p_1 p_2 p_3 p_4 p_5 . . .
k_1 k_2 k_3 k_4 k_5 . . .
c_1 c_2 c_3 c_4 c_5 . . .

If Eve can insert a known bit, p, into the plaintext stream, say, after the first bit, and have it transmitted with the same key, the result would be

p_1 p p_2 p_3 p_4 p_5 . . .
k_1 k_2 k_3 k_4 k_5 k_6 . . .
c_1 c_2 c_3 c_4 c_5 c_6 . . .

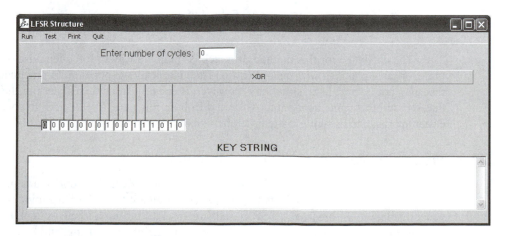

Figure 6.13: CAP LFSR structure

Using her knowledge of the known bit and the two ciphertext streams, Eve can construct a chain of equations that will reveal the key and the actual plaintext. The first compromised key bit is $k2$ because $k2 = c$ XOR p. With the knowledge of $k2$, Eve can discover the original second plaintext bit $p2$ using $p2 = k2$ XOR $c2$. With the knowledge of $p2$, Eve can discover $k3$ using $k3 = c3$ XOR $p2$. This process continues with the following chain of equations:

$$p3 = k3 \text{ XOR } c3$$
$$k4 = c4 \text{ XOR } p3$$
$$p4 = k4 \text{ XOR } c4$$
$$k5 = c5 \text{ XOR } p4$$

For example, say Eve intercepts the following bits of ciphertext 101101, which were part of this message from Alice to Bob:

Plaintext	0 1 1 1 0 1
Key	1 1 0 0 0 0
Ciphertext	1 0 1 1 0 1

Of course, Eve only knows the ciphertext, but the original plaintext and key are shown in order to verify that ultimately Eve discovers those values as well. If Eve is able to force Alice to retransmit the message with an extra 1 inserted into position 2, she would then intercept the following ciphertext bits:

Plaintext:	0 1 1 1 1 0 1
Key:	1 1 0 0 0 0 1
Ciphertext:	1 0 1 1 1 0 0

Using the only the two ciphertext streams and the knowledge that bit 2 is a "1", Eve reconstructs the original key and plaintext as follows:

$$k2 = 0 \text{ XOR } 1 = 1$$
$$k3 = 1 \text{ XOR } 1 = 0$$

$$p2 = 0 \text{ XOR } 1 = 1$$
$$p3 = 1 \text{ XOR } 0 = 1$$

The challenge for this method of attack is finding a way to force the retransmission of the original plaintext with a single bit inserted into a known position. In practical terms, that may not be a realistic situation—however, it does illustrate a weakness in the cipher that should be of some concern to Alice and Bob. In this case, Eve decides to try another easier approach to breaking a stream cipher—a probable-word attack.

6.2.2 Probable-Word Attack One: Matching Bit Strings

There are two approaches to a probable-word attack, one of which is more mathematical in nature than the other. Eve selects the mathematical attack first, since it provides a more general solution. To break an LFSR-based stream cipher using a known-plaintext attack, Eve must have a plaintext bit string, its corresponding ciphertext string, and knowledge of the size of the LFSR. (If she doesn't know the LFSR size, she can try several reasonable values and this process will still work.) To reconstruct the key generator, she only needs to discover the feedback bits.

Eve begins with the known m-bit plaintext string p_i $(i = 0 \ldots n - 1)$ and its corresponding m-bit ciphertext string c_i $(i = 0 \ldots n - 1)$. From these two strings, she can find the keystring k_i by using

$$k_i = p_i \text{ XOR } c_i.$$

In general, the keystring bits for an LFSR are given by

$$k_{m+j} = \sum_{i=0}^{m-1} a_i k_{i+j} \bmod 2,$$

where the sum mod 2 is the same thing as an XOR; m is the size of the LFSR; and the a's indicate which bits participate in the feedback—that is, if $a_4 = 1$, then the fourth bit is fed back into the LFSR.

If the number of bits in the known-plaintext stream, n, is equal to or larger than $2m$ (m is the size of the LFSR), then the a_i's can be found by solving a system of m linear equations given in matrix form by

$$(a_0, a_1, \ldots, a_{m-1}) = (k_{m+1}, k_{m+2}, \ldots, k_{2m}) \begin{pmatrix} k_1 & k_2 & \cdots & k_m \\ k_2 & k_3 & \cdots & k_{m+1} \\ \vdots & \vdots & & \vdots \\ k_m & k_{m+1} & \cdots & k_{2m-1} \end{pmatrix}^{-1}.$$

Once the a's are known, then the LFSR structure is known and the key can be regenerated.

For example, if the plaintext–ciphertext bit stream is known, the keystream can be found by XORing the two:

Plaintext   0110 0001 0110 1100
Ciphertext   1011 0100 0001 0011
Keysteam   1101 0101 0111 1111

Assuming an 8-bit shift register (so $m = 8$), the feedback links can be determined from the matrix of keystream elements:

$$\begin{pmatrix} 1 & 1 & 0 & 1 & 0 & 1 & 0 & 1 \\ 1 & 0 & 1 & 0 & 1 & 0 & 1 & 0 \\ 0 & 1 & 0 & 1 & 0 & 1 & 0 & 1 \\ 1 & 0 & 1 & 0 & 1 & 0 & 1 & 1 \\ 0 & 1 & 0 & 1 & 0 & 1 & 1 & 1 \\ 1 & 0 & 1 & 0 & 1 & 1 & 1 & 1 \\ 0 & 1 & 0 & 1 & 1 & 1 & 1 & 1 \\ 1 & 0 & 1 & 1 & 1 & 1 & 1 & 1 \end{pmatrix}$$

Find the inverse of this matrix:

$$
\begin{pmatrix}
1 & 1 & 0 & 1 & 0 & 1 & 0 & 1 \\
1 & 0 & 1 & 0 & 1 & 0 & 1 & 0 \\
0 & 1 & 0 & 1 & 0 & 1 & 0 & 1 \\
1 & 0 & 1 & 0 & 1 & 0 & 1 & 1 \\
0 & 1 & 0 & 1 & 0 & 1 & 1 & 1 \\
1 & 0 & 1 & 0 & 1 & 1 & 1 & 1 \\
0 & 1 & 0 & 1 & 1 & 1 & 1 & 1 \\
1 & 0 & 1 & 1 & 1 & 1 & 1 & 1
\end{pmatrix}^{-1}
=
\begin{pmatrix}
1 & 0 & 1 & 0 & 0 & 0 & 0 & 0 \\
0 & 1 & 1 & 0 & 0 & 0 & 0 & 1 \\
1 & 1 & 0 & 0 & 0 & 0 & 1 & 0 \\
0 & 0 & 0 & 0 & 0 & 1 & 0 & 1 \\
0 & 0 & 0 & 0 & 1 & 0 & 1 & 0 \\
0 & 0 & 0 & 1 & 0 & 1 & 0 & 0 \\
0 & 0 & 1 & 0 & 1 & 0 & 0 & 0 \\
0 & 1 & 0 & 1 & 0 & 0 & 0 & 0
\end{pmatrix}
$$

Multiply the inverse by the key bits ($k_9, \ldots, k_{16}$):

$$
(1\,1\,0\,0\,0\,0\,0\,0) = (0\,1\,1\,1\,1\,1\,1\,1)
\begin{pmatrix}
1 & 0 & 1 & 0 & 0 & 0 & 0 & 0 \\
0 & 1 & 1 & 0 & 0 & 0 & 0 & 1 \\
1 & 1 & 0 & 0 & 0 & 0 & 1 & 0 \\
0 & 0 & 0 & 0 & 0 & 1 & 0 & 1 \\
0 & 0 & 0 & 0 & 1 & 0 & 1 & 0 \\
0 & 0 & 0 & 1 & 0 & 1 & 0 & 0 \\
0 & 0 & 1 & 0 & 1 & 0 & 0 & 0 \\
0 & 1 & 0 & 1 & 0 & 0 & 0 & 0
\end{pmatrix}
$$

Since the feedback vector is (1 1 0 0 0 0 0 0), the LFSR has eight stages, with stages 0 and 1 XORed and fed back into the register.

6.2.3 Probable-Word Attack Two: Word Match

It turns out that with knowledge of a possible word in the cipher and a little bit of clever manipulation, Eve can break the stream cipher. What makes this approach different from the prior attack is that the corresponding ciphertext is not known. Eve must find the location in the ciphertext stream that matches the probable word. In order to illustrate this process without getting lost in the details, we will assume that Alice and Bob use a simple form of the LFSR—one in which the first bit and a second unknown bit are the only ones that are used in the feedback loop. While this is unlikely to be the case, keep in mind that this process will work for more complicated LFSR structures as well.

Say Alice and Bob use a 6-bit LFSR, with bits 1 and 4 XORed to produce the input bit shown in Figure 6.14.

Eve intercepts the following cipher bit stream:

1110000111111001100011100100011010111000001000 11

She suspects that the first word is "The". If she is correct, then the first few bits of the key can be determined by XORing the ASCII code for "The" with the initial bits of the cipher stream:

```
    T        h         e
010101000110100001100101
111000011111100110001110010001101011100000100011
101101011001000111101011
```

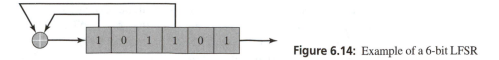

Figure 6.14: Example of a 6-bit LFSR

This only identifies the key bits up to the letter "e". In order to find the rest of the key, it is necessary to find the two bits that are XORed to produce the LFSR input bit. This is done by XORing pairs of bits in the keystream to produce a new stream of bits:

Initial Key	**10**1101011001000111101011
	1 (XOR the first pair 1 and 0)
Initial Key	1**01**1010110010001111101011
	11 (XOR the second pair 0 and 1)
Initial Key	101101011001000111101011
	110111101011001000011110

Scan both the initial key and the pairwise XOR of the initial key to find a long identical bit pattern. In this case, the identical bit patterns are as follows:

Initial Key	101101011001000111101011
	110111101011001000011110

The distance between these bit patterns identifies the second bit in the LFSR XOR. In the example, they differ by 4 bits, which means that the LFSR used by Bob and Alice uses bits 1 and 4 as feedback to produce the keystream. Using this information, Eve can reconstruct the entire keystream by XORing the current key bit with the key bit 4 bits behind it. The result is

Cipher stream	111000011111100110001110010001101011100000100011
Keystream	101101011001000111101011001000111101011001000111
Plaintext stream	010101000110100001100101011001010110111001100100
	T h e e n d

If this does not produce readable results, then the word "The" was not located correctly, and Eve must shift it over and repeat this process.

6.2.4 Using CAP to Break a Stream Cipher

CAP provides the necessary tools to run both attacks against an LFSR-type stream cipher. For example, if Eve intercepts a message between Alice and Bob, which she suspects was enciphered using an LFSR stream cipher: (but she does not know the size of the shift register, the initial values in the shift register, or the feedback links used by Alice and Bob), she can still break the cipher. While Alice and Bob think they have finally stumped Eve, Eve is sure that the message begins with the word "Alice", since it is from Bob to Alice. She will use this information to discover everything she needs to know about both the cipher and the LFSR.

6.3 OTHER STREAM-CIPHER IMPLEMENTATIONS

A stream cipher is any cipher that involves the interaction between a keystream and a plaintext stream. The keystream does not have to be generated by a single LFSR, nor does it have to consist just of binary bits. There are other ways in which this cipher process can be implemented and most involve different ways to produce a random-bit stream for the key.

Alternative methods of generating a random-bit stream that are designed to improve the random nature of the key may involve using more than one LFSR. In fact, several different LFSRs can be used where the output of one is selected at random based on yet another LFSR. These are called *nonlinear generators*. One type of hardware device that can perform the selection function is called a multiplexer (MUX). A MUX is a digital device with several inputs and one output. Its purpose is to select one of the many inputs to pass to the output. As shown in Figure 6.15, it operates like a switch. The address bits determine the placement of the switch, which in turn determines the input that is connected to the output. Varying the address bits varies the output connection.

Multiplexers come in several different sizes. The one shown in Figure 6.9 is a 4–1 MUX because it has four data inputs routed to one data output—it requires two address bits to select among the four data inputs. For example, if the address bits are 00, then data input 0 is routed to the output and the other three data inputs are blocked. A larger device is an 8–1 MUX that has eight data inputs and three address bits.

Used in combination with several LFSRs, a MUX can provide a powerful random-bit keystream. For example, a system using a 4–1 MUX with five different LFSRs is shown in Figure 6.16.

The first LFSR generates a 2-bit address that randomly selects the output of one of the other 4 LFSR bits. The result is that a bit is "randomly" selected from one of four "random" processes.

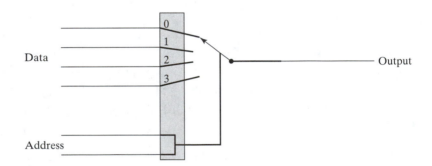

Figure 6.15: A 4–1 multiplexer (MUX) device

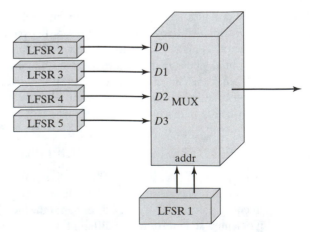

Figure 6.16: A multiple LFSR random-bit generator

To encrypt their signals, many satellite-television broadcasters use a version of this type of random-bit-stream generator. Each line of the TV signal is cut and rotated at a point determined by the output of the random generator.

6.3.1 RC4

RC4, developed by Ron Rivest of the Massachusetts Institute of Technology (MIT) (one of the developers of RSA, a cipher that will be covered later), is perhaps the most widely used stream cipher in the world. It is part of Microsoft Windows, Lotus Notes, and other software applications. It is used in the secure sockets layer (SSL) protocol to protect Internet traffic. It is also part of the wireless equivalent privacy (WEP) system used to protect wireless links. One advantage of RC4 is that it can be easily implemented in software.

The size of RC4 varies based on the value of a parameter, n. RC4 works off a secret internal state that is the permutation of all $N = 2^n$ possible n-bit numbers. Typically, $n = 8$ and that will be the value selected for our example. Overall, RC4 randomizes an array of $256 \, (=2^8)$ elements called S. Its output at each stage is a random element selected from S. To accomplish this, it uses two processes: a key-scheduling algorithm (KSA), to set up the initial permutation of S, and a pseudo random-generation algorithm (PSGA), to select the random elements and modify the original permutation of S.

The KSA begins by initializing S so that $S(i) = i$ (for $i = 0$ to 255). A key is constructed by selecting a set of numbers that are loaded into a key array $K(0)$ to $K(255)$. You do not have to select 256 numbers; you just repeat a short sequence of numbers over and over until K is filled. The array S is randomized using the following program:

```
j := 0;
for i := 0 to 255 do begin
        j := i + S(i) + K(i) (mod 256)
        swap(S(i),S(j))
end
```

Once the KSA has completed the initial randomization of S, the PRGA takes over and selects bytes for the keystream by selecting random elements of S and modifying S for the next selection. The selection process relies on two indices, i and j, which both start at 0. The following program is run to select each byte of the keystream:

```
i := i +1 (mod 256)
j := j + S(i) (mod 256)
swap(S(i),S(j))
t:= S(i) + S(j) (mod 256)
```

k := S(t)

Alice and Bob are interested in RC4, so they put together a simple example using 3-bit representations (the numbers range from 0 to 7) in which the operations are all mod 8 (instead of mod 256). The S array begins with only eight slots and is initialized to

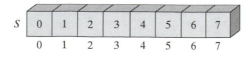

Bob and Alice select a key that consists of a set of numbers from 0 to 7 in any order. For this case, they select 5, 6, and 7 as their key. This key is written into the key array and repeated as many times as necessary to fill the array:

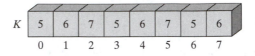

Now they are ready to construct the actual S array using the following loop:

```
j = 0;
for i = 0 to 7 do
        j = (j + S(i) + K(i)) mod 8;
        Swap (S(i),S(j));
```

The loop begins with $j = 0$ and $i = 0$. Using the update formula for j results in

$$j = [0 + S(0) + K(0)] \bmod 8$$
$$= (0 + 0 + 5) \bmod 8$$
$$= 5.$$

So the first operation on the S array is to swap $S(0)$ and $S(5)$:

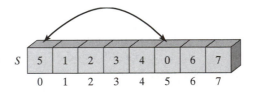

The index i is incremented to 1 and the next value for j is given by

$$j = [5 + S(1) + K(1)] \bmod 8$$
$$= (5 + 1 + 6) \bmod 8$$
$$= 4.$$

Now the S array is modified by swapping $S(1)$ and $S(4)$:

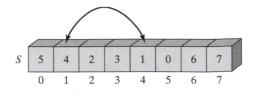

Once the loop over i is completed, the S array has been "randomized" :

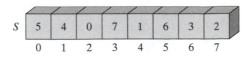

Now the S array is ready to be used to produce a sequence of random numbers. With i and j starting at 0, RC4 calculates the first random number as follows:

i = (i + 1) mod 8 = (0 + 1) mod 8 = 1
j = [(j + S(i))] mod 8 = [(0 + S(1))] mod 8 = (0 + 4) mod 8 = 4
Swap S(1) and S(4)

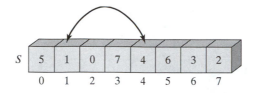

then calculate t and k as follows:

$$t = [S(j) + S(i)] \bmod 8 = [S(4) + S(1)] \bmod 8 = (1 + 4) \bmod 8 = 5$$
$$k = S(t) = S(5) = 6$$

The first random number in the stream is 6, which in binary is 110. This process continues until enough binary bits have been generated to match the plaintext bits.

CAP provides a full 256-element implementation of RC4. To access it, select RC4 under the Ciphers menu.

6.3.2   Evaluation of RC4

A typical implementation of RC4 is based on $n = 8$ (the numbers from 0 to 255). The initial key for such a system is a permutation of the integers 0 to 255. There are 256! possible permutations, which is about 2^{1600}. This is the equivalent of a 1600-bit key, making a brute-force attack all but impossible.

As Bob, Alice, and Eve have discovered over and over again, an exhaustive key search is usually not the only way to break a cipher. In the case of RC4, there are suggestions of other weaknesses that may be exploited to compromise the cipher. For example, there is a class of keys that the KSA will never produce. This class consists of all the permutations that KSA could produce if $j = i + 1$ and $S(j) = 1$. It turns out that the number of keys in the class is given by 2^{-2n} of the possible permutations. For $n = 8$, this is $<256!/2^{16}>$.

Since these are not possible, eliminating them will reduce the amount of search required for a brute-force attack (but not by enough to make it feasible). Another approach to a brute-force attack is to build hardware that is specifically designed to efficiently implement the algorithm. Such hardware may be able to speed up the process of testing possible keys. Such a device was designed and tested for RC4 by Kundarewich, Wilton, and Hu in 1999. They designed a programmable logic device that could be used to find a 40-bit RC4 key in less than 159 days. That may seem like a long time, but it is short enough to make it a feasible threat.

6.3.3   A5

The A5 stream cipher is an example of an irregularly clocked multiple LFSR system. As shown in Figure 6.17, it consists of three different-sized LFSRs, a, b, and c. a is 19 bits long, b is 22 bits long, and c is 23 bits long. The stream output is the XOR of these registers. They are irregularly clocked, which means that each register shifts on a different

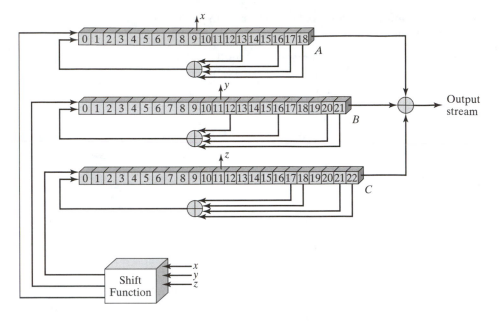

Figure 6.17: The A5 stream cipher

schedule. The clock signal for each register is determined by the values of x, y and z, where x is bit 9 of the first register, y is bit 11 of the second register, and z is bit 11 of the third register. The shift function implements a majority function on the three inputs x, y, and z. The majority function $[(maj(x,y,z))]$ is 1 if and only if two or more of the inputs are 1. As a result, a is clocked (it shifts) only if x XOR $maj(x,y,z)$ is 0. b is clocked only if y XOR $maj(x,y,z)$ is 0. Finally, c is clocked only if z XOR $maj(x,y,z)$ is 0.

The key is the initial values for the three shift registers, which means that A5 has a 64-bit key. The key size is somewhat misleading, since a known-plaintext attack would require knowledge of only two of the registers' initial values to compromise the initial value of the third. The result is that only 2^{40} steps are required to solve for registers A and B. A simpler version of A5, called A5/2, has been developed for export purposes—it is believed that A5/2 can be broken in only 2^{16} steps. Besides the small effective key size, A5 also suffers from a collision problem in which different initial-register values produce the same keystream. In fact, studies indicate that only 70 percent of the possible initial values actually produce unique keystreams.

The A5 stream cipher has been used for the protection of voice communications as part of the GSM (General System for Mobile) communications system. GSM is the largest mobile telephone system in the world with over 200 million subscribers. In the United States, it is part of the digital (Personal Communications Service) network. A GSM voice message is converted into a set of 228-bit frames. Each frame is encrypted with an A5 228-bit stream as shown in Figure 6.18.

6.3.4 Cellular Automata

A cellular automation, CA, is just an array (either one dimensional or two dimensional) of simple cells. The cells in a binary CA may be in one of two states—they contain either a 0

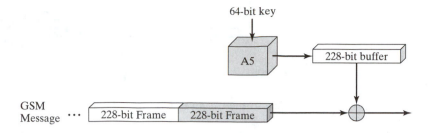

Figure 6.18: GSM use of the A5 stream cipher

or a 1. On each tick of a clock, a cell will change its state based on the states of the cells in some local neighborhood. These structures were first introduced by John von Neumann in the 1940s. Interest in CAs grew in the early 1970s when John Conway invented the Game of Life based on a CA. Since then, they have been used in a large number of applications, one of which is the generation of random bits.

A simple example of a CA is the 7-cell one-dimensional array shown below:

This CA is initialized to 0010100. Each cell changes its state based on some rule. One possible rule for the example CA could be defined by the immediate neighborhood of each cell—that is, the updated value in a cell depends on the current value in the cell and the values in the cells to its left and its right. The CA is assumed to be connected in a circle, so the cell to the left of cell 0 is cell 6, and the cell to the right of cell 6 is cell 0. A specific rule for this neighborhood could be

Neighborhood	000	001	010	011	100	101	110	111
New state:	0	0	0	1	0	1	1	1

Applying this rule to the initial CA produces the following CA:

Rules for this type of CA are identified by converting the new state bits into a decimal number. For example, the new state for the preceding rule is 00010111, which in decimal is 23. Rule 90 is 01011010.

A CA can be used to generate random bits by selecting a rule, a CA size, an initial seed, and one cell to provide the random bit. For example, an 11-cell CA with an initial seed of 01100011000, Rule 30, and using bit 7 for the random bit is shown in Figure 6.19.

Rule 30 is given by

Neighborhood	000	001	010	011	100	101	110	111
New state	0	0	0	1	1	1	1	0

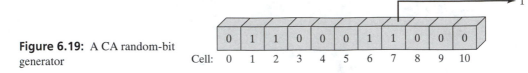

Figure 6.19: A CA random-bit generator

When this rule is applied to the example CA, the first few random bits are shown in Figure 6.20.

As with any random-number generator, the questions that need to be answered about a CA are: "When will the patterns begin to repeat" and "What is the best seed rule." Steven Wolfram, a pioneer in the field of cellular automata, studied the properties of 1-D CAs and determined that Rule 30 in combination with an initial seed with a single nonzero element produced the longest cycles.

CAP provides a small 1-D CA system for testing the possibilities of this random-number generator. The CAP window is shown in Figure 6.21. To set up the 1-D CA in CAP, first select the CA length (enter an integer from 1 to 10) and then enter a rule for each cell. One cell is selected to be the source of the random bits. The random-bit stream may be used to encipher–decipher sample text, or it may be used to generate a random-bit stream for testing purposes by selecting options under the Random menu item.

A two-dimensional CA offers a more powerful random-number generator at the expense of additional complexity. A 2-D CA is just an array of 1-D CAs as shown in Figure 6.22. As with a 1-D CA, a cell's value is updated by some function of its current value and the values of its neighbors. In this case, there are two different definitions of a neighborhood. As indicated in Figure 6.22, the von Neumann neighborhood consists of the cells above, below, to the right, and to the left of the target cell. The Moore neighborhood, on the other hand, consists of all eight cells that surround the target cell.

The rules for a 2-D CA are much like those for 1-D CA. They define how a cell is updated based on the values in its neighborhood. On the basis of a von Neumann neighborhood,

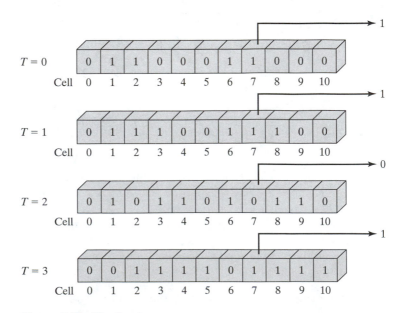

Figure 6.20: The first four stages

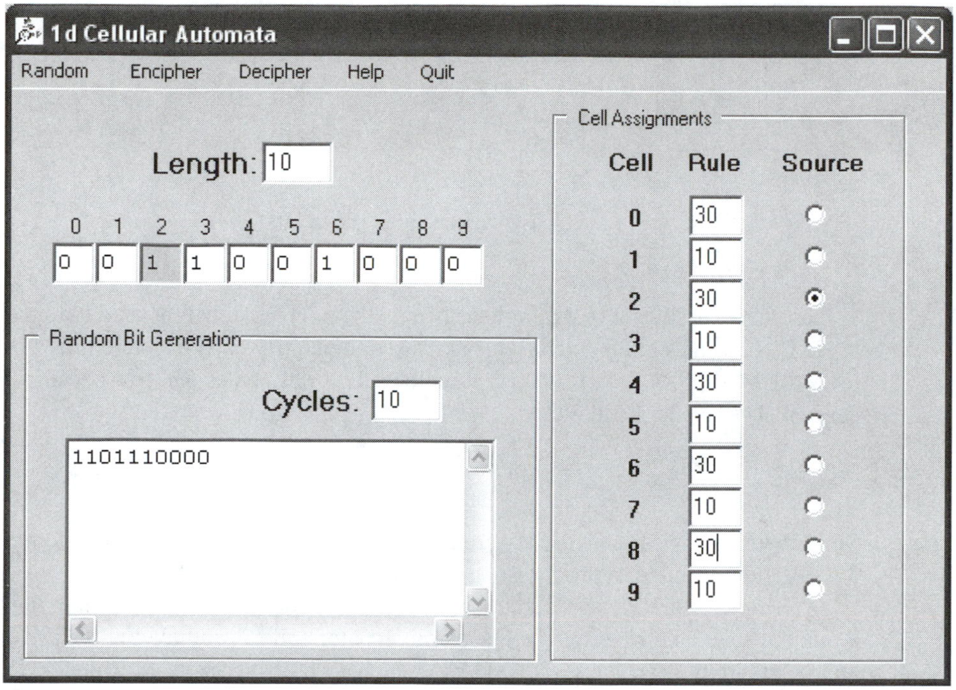

Figure 6.21: CAP implementation of a 1-D CA

a general rule structure can be defined as

$$s_{i,j}(t+1) = X \text{ XOR } [(C \times s_{i,j}(t))] \text{ XOR } [(N \times s_{i-1,j}(t))] \text{ XOR } (W \cdot s_{i,j-1}(t))$$
$$\text{XOR } [(S \times s_{i+1,j}(t))] \text{ XOR } [(E \times s_{i,j+1}(t))],$$

where X, C, N, W, S, E are binary $(0,1)$ variables. If X is 1, this is a nonlinear rule; otherwise, it is a linear rule. $C, N, W, S,$ and E are the center, north, west, south, and east cells, respectively. The cells that participate in updating the center cell are determined by values

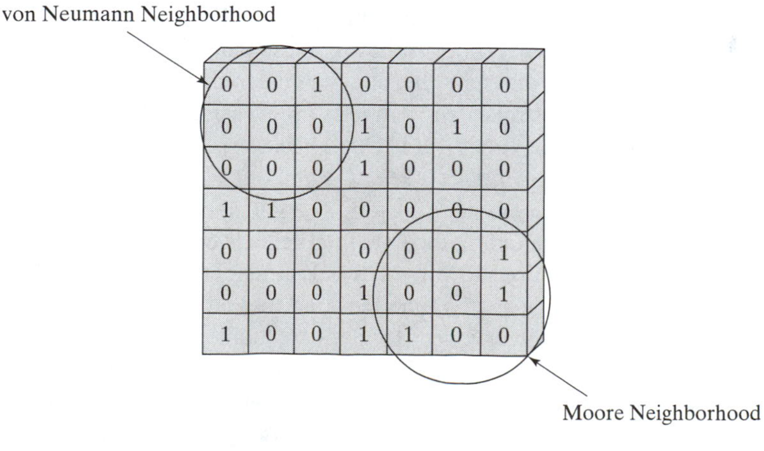

Figure 6.22: A 2-D cellular automata

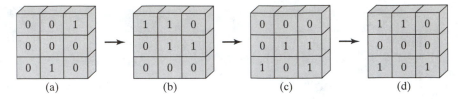

Figure 6.23: A 3 × 3 CA used to generate random bits

of these five variables. For example, if N is 1, then the north cell is used to update the center cell. The values of all six variables are used to identify each possible rule. For example, if $(X, C, N, W, S, E) = (001110)$, then the rule is defined as Rule 14 because 1110 is binary 14. The rule looks like this:

$$s_{i,j}(t + 1) = s_{i-1,j}(t) \text{ XOR } s_{i,j-1}(t) \text{ XOR } s_{i+1,j}(t)$$

Since there are six variables, there are 64 possible rules. Tommassini, et al. found that rules 31, 47, and 63 tended to produce better random numbers in an 8 × 8 CA.

A random stream is generated by assigning a rule to each cell, initializing the CA to a random state, and running the CA using a center cell to produce the bit stream. For example, Figure 6.23 shows a 3 × 3 CA in which each cell is assigned Rule 14. The value in the center cell is used to construct the random stream. The cells are randomly initialized as shown in Figure 6.23(a). After three steps, the random-bit stream is 0 1 1 0.

CAP also provides a simple 2-D CA for testing purposes. Selecting 2d Cellular Automata under the Cipher menu will open the CAP window shown in Figure 6.24. CAP will create up to a 7 × 7 CA. Rules can be assigned to individual cells, or all the cells may be assigned the same rule using the shortcut provided in the Cell Rule Assignments panel. As with the 1-D CA, this CA may be used to generate a test set of random bits or to encipher–decipher text.

6.3.5 Other Ways to Generate Random Numbers

Any random-number generator that depends on a small seed or key value to generate a random-bit stream based on some algorithm is not really random. However, there are ways in which we might tap into random events and use them to produce a random keystream.

For example, typing patterns on a computer keyboard is random. So, by monitoring the time between keystrokes and extracting the least significant bit, it is possible to generate a small random-bit stream. It is small because we cannot demand that the user type a large document just to produce a key.

There are other computer operations that can be monitored to produce random bits. Mouse movements, including the time interval between movements or the distance of each movement, could be used to provide random numbers much like the time between keystrokes. The difference in the time required to read disk blocks is also a random value. Since the location of the disk heads and the rotational speed (which is influenced by air turbulence) vary, this can be a very effective generator of random numbers.

Usually, random physical events can provide a ready source of random bits. The radioactive decay of a long half-life element as recorded by a Geiger counter works as a potential source. White noise on an empty radio channel is an easily available source as well.

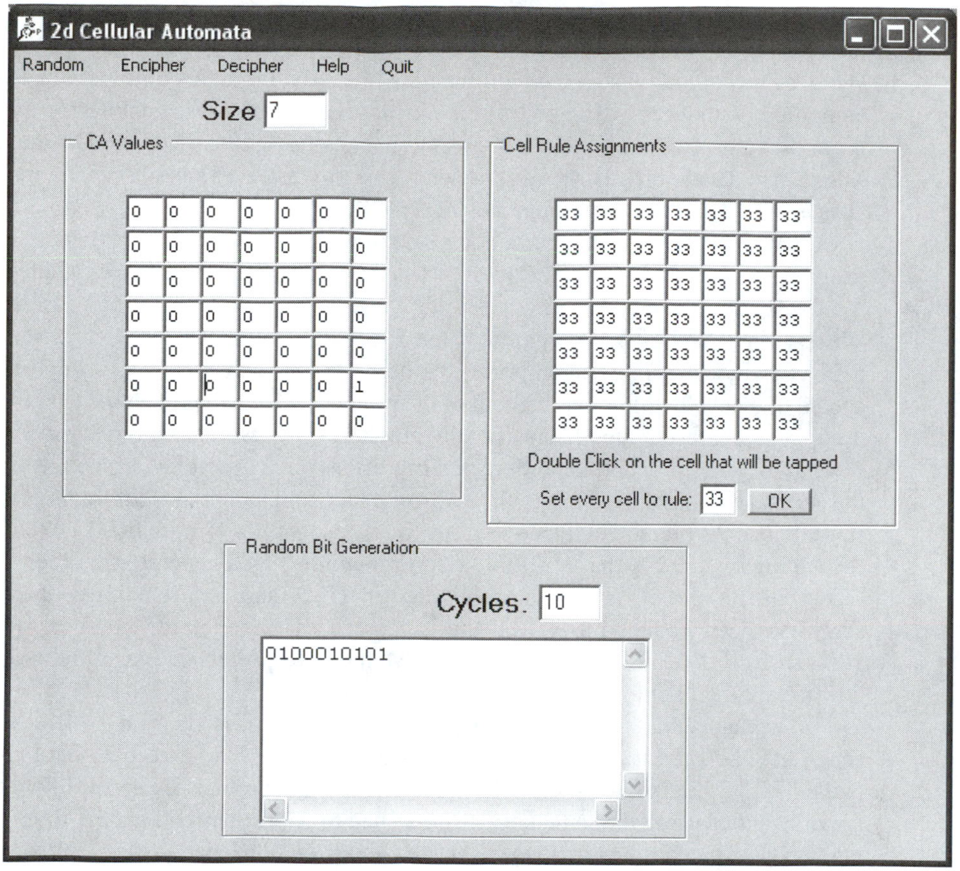

Figure 6.24: CAP implementation of a 2-D CA

6.4   AN UNBREAKABLE CIPHER

It turns out that the only provably unbreakable cipher is a stream cipher that meets certain conditions. If the keystream is both completely random and as long as the plaintext, then it is a one-time pad. Shannon proved that, under these conditions, the cipher is unconditionally secure against a ciphertext-only attack.

Of course, generation of a truly random-bit stream is very difficult. In addition, the requirement that the keystream be as long as the plaintext implies that it never repeats and is never used again. This is also hard to maintain. As a result, most stream ciphers only approximate these conditions. Therefore, they are not unbreakable.

6.5   A PRACTICAL APPLICATION

As already mentioned, the RC4 stream cipher is used to protect wireless communication links. It is worthwhile to briefly explore how it is used and some of the weaknesses that have been discovered in its application.

It used to be the case that families had one phone, one car, one TV, and one computer. Now many families have several phones, two cars, multiple TVs, and more than one computer.

Since most homes are not wired for computer use, wireless technology becomes a useful tool that allows multiple home computers to share files, printers, and even the Internet. Wireless technology also allows companies to easily add new computers or use mobile computers without rewiring or forcing employees to find a wall connector to plug into the company network. While it is a great convenience, wireless connections have a down side. Since data is broadcast, anyone with a nearby receiver can access the information. Hence, wireless connections must be encrypted.

Since multiple manufacturers design, construct, and sell wireless devices, they need to agree on a standard format for wireless transmissions. That standard is called 802.11 and it includes the wireless equivalent privacy (WEP) protocol for encrypting transmissions. WEP is more than just a requirement to use RC4—it is a complete protocol describing how RC4 is to be used. For contemporary ciphers, the protocol is often as important as the choice of cipher. In this case, the goal of the protocol is to both protect the data from eavesdropping and prevent modification of the message (preserve message integrity).

In order to prevent the undetected modification of a wireless transmission, the initial message bits are used to create a 32-bit checksum called a *cyclic redundancy check* (CRC). The 32 bits are selected so that the message bits M plus the 32 checksum bits form a binary number that is divisible (no remainder) by a generator number, G. On the receiving end, the $M + 32$ bits are divided by G. If there is a remainder, then the message has been changed and it is not accepted. The generator number for WEP is 100001001100000100011101101101111. Methods to protect message integrity will be covered in great detail in Chapter 9.

The augmented message ($M +$ the CRC checksum) is encrypted using RC4 with a secret key, K. The international standard is a 40-bit key, but some U.S. implementations (called WEP2) use a 104-bit key. Here is where another problem emerges. If two messages are transmitted using the same key, it is possible to XOR them, producing the XOR of the plaintexts. (The two identical key values drop out.) Knowledge of the XOR of the plaintexts enables a statistical attack on the system. As a result, the WEP protocol specifies a method to vary the key for each message. A 24-bit initial vector (IV) is selected and added to the key, so the actual RC4 key is IV $+ K$. Since this is a unique vector, it is also added to the ciphertext and the transmitted data is IV $+$ ciphertext.

From a cryptanalysis standpoint, it is possible to attack the WEP protocol as well as the RC4 itself. For example, on a busy network, it is highly likely that the IV will repeat (24 bits is really not enough for a secure wireless protocol), resulting in a successful statistical attack on the system. In addition, it turns out the CRC checksum methodology has a weakness in it making it possible to selectively change bits in the message but allowing the transmitted result to pass the CRC test. The moral is that it is now important not only to select a powerful cipher, but also to design a secure protocol for its use.

6.6   AN HISTORICAL PERSPECTIVE ON STREAM CIPHERS

While the autokey ciphers covered in Chapter 3 display some of the characteristics of a stream cipher, their actual emergence came with the work of Gilbert Vernam at AT&T in 1917. He was the first to suggest the use of a XOR operation on a plaintext stream. His discovery became known as a Vernam cipher. In Vernam's case, the plaintext consisted of punched tape with holes representing marks (what we now call a binary 1) and a blank spot representing a space (what we now call a binary 0). Characters were represented on the punched tape as a sequence of five marks and spaces, much like the ASCII code used today. Vernam's key was a tape with random marks and spaces. The plaintext tape would run side-by-side with the key tape. The two positions on the two tapes would be read. If they were both marks or both spaces, then the ciphertext tape (or pulse) would contain a space. If they were different, then the ciphertext tape would contain a mark. In other words, today's stream cipher is just a Vernam cipher without the paper tape.

Initially, Vernam used an 8-foot tape loop for the key with the marks and spaces determined by drawing characters from a hat. One of Vernam's coworkers, an equipment engineer at AT&T, Lyman Morehouse, realized that the key was not long enough to provide adequate security. He suggested an alternative using two key tapes of different lengths. One random tape would be used to encipher the other random tape, and the result would be used to create a secondary key for use on the actual plaintext. If one random tape contained 50 characters and the other 49, then there would be 2450 (49 $\times$ 50) combinations of random characters for the actual key. Even this improvement, however, could not meet the voracious appetite of the Vernam cipher for random-key material.

It took 30 years before the amazing significance of Vernam's discovery would be fully understood. A brilliant mathematician and engineer working at Bell Laboratories (the same place where, 30 years earlier, Vernam came up with the idea for a stream cipher), Claude Shannon began his studies of communication. The results of his work were astounding. He laid the foundation for communication theory, developed the criteria for a cipher (diffusion–confusion), formalized the concept that "the adversary learns nothing about the plaintext by seeing the ciphertext", and proved that the Vernam cipher was unbreakable. (It is said that he could even juggle four balls while riding a unicycle.) The catch was that the key had to be totally random and could never be used again (hence the name *one-time pad*). Shannon showed that with a random nonrepeating key not only was the cipher unbreakable, but even with perfect knowledge an attacker could not compromise the plaintext.

There is a rumor that the teletype hot line between Washington, DC, and Moscow used a one-time pad in its early days. It is known that Russian spies used a paper-and-pencil one-time pad to exchange information. However, because of the large key requirements, one-time pads the are not used today. Rather, they are approximated using pseudo random-key generators.

6.7   SUMMARY

Bob and Alice have finally entered the modern world. They realized that, to keep ahead of Eve, they need to take advantage of the real power of their computers to produce ciphers at the bit level rather than at the character level. They decided to use a stream cipher that mixed a binary keystream with the binary plaintext stream to create a binary ciphertext stream. While that offered a simple procedure, they quickly discovered that they needed to be assured that their keystream was completely random. One way to at least approximate a random-bit stream was to use a linear feedback shift register (LFSR). Putting the pieces together and using the resources provided by CAP, Bob and Alice were confident that they now had a secure and modern method for communicating.

As always, their confidence was put to the test by Eve's activities. Eve discovered that an LFSR is open to a known-plaintext attack, and it wasn't long before she was again reading the mail between Bob and Alice. Bob and Alice discovered the break-ins. They explored other ways to create a random-bit stream, but decided that they were all too risky. For Bob and Alice, it was time to try another type of cipher.

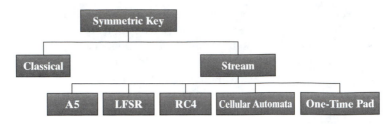

Figure 6.25: Stream ciphers found in Chapter 6

The class of stream ciphers covered in this chapter fit into the general scheme of ciphers as shown in Figure 6.25.

6.8   IMPORTANT TERMS

A5	An LFSR-based stream cipher that is used for mobile-phone security
Cellular Automata	Automation an array of simple cells whose value depends on the value of its neighbors and a specified rule
CRC	Cyclic redundancy check—a method used to insure message integrity
LFSR	Linear feedback shift register—a digital circuit that saves n bits. It shifts those bits on position to the right and fills in the leftmost bit with the XOR of a selected set of bits
MUX	Multiplexer—a digital circuit with 2^n inputs and 1 output; it selects one of the inputs to pass to the output
One-time pad	A stream cipher in which the key bit patterns never repeat—the only provably unbreakable cipher
RC4	A widely used stream cipher that is easily implemented in software
Synchronous cipher	The keystream is independent of the message stream
Self-synchronous steam cipher	The keystream depends on the previous n ciphertext characters
WEP	Wireless equivalent privacy—the protocol that uses RC4 to protect wireless transmissions

RESOURCES

Tomassini, M. and M. Perrenoud, "Cryptography with Cellular Automata," *Applied Soft Computing*, 1 (2001), pp. 151–160

Mantin, I., "The security of the stream cipher RC4." Master's thesis, The Weizmann Institute of Science, October 2001 www.wisdom.weizmann.ac.il/~itsik/RC4/thesis.html

P. D. Kundarewich, S. J. E. Wilton, A. J. Hu, "A CPLD-based RC4 Cracking System," in *IEEE* 1999, Canadian Conference on Electrical and Computer Engineering, May 1999

PROBLEMS

1. Assign all 0's to an LFSR and find the output stream.
2. How many possible keys are there for a 48-bit LFSR?
3. What is Rule 23 in a 2-D CA?
4. A maximum-length 4-bit LFSR is created when bits 4 and 3 are the feedback links. Find the actual length for each possible input from 0000 to 1111.
5. Find the cycle structure of the 5-bit LFSR represented by $p(x) = x^5 + x^3 + x + 1$.
6. Prove that in A5 at least two registers are clocked (that is, shifted) every cycle.
7. How many possible keys are there for an $n = 5$ implementation of RC4?
8. Given the following ciphertext bit stream, you know that the word "security" is somewhere in the plaintext, and you strongly suspect that the LFSR used to generate the keystream is either 8 or 12 bits long:

   000010100000011010101100110110010000000001
   110101000101111010110111111001111101110
   10000110001001100110001101010011110011110
   001000000000011010111011100110010100101
   100001110101100110110001101001101111001
   10011010001000000011101000011101110011000
   001001010000101110101011100001110000001
   110010000010101011011000110100110111111111
   100000000011110001111001000101101100111
   001001100100010111101110101101000100101101
   110011100101100010110001

   Find the plaintext and the structure of the LFSR.

9. Fix WEP and, in the process, revolutionize wireless security. Sell your results to the highest bidder, and give your instructor and the author of this book a hefty percentage in appreciation of their fine work.

Chapter 7

Block Ciphers

7.0 INTRODUCTION

Block ciphers are the most common class of ciphers in use today. They are a natural generalization of the classical substitution–transposition ciphers to the world of computer bits. As the name suggests, a block cipher works on fixed-size blocks of bits at a time (in contrast to the stream cipher that enciphers a bit at a time) as shown in Figure 7.0.

A block cipher divides the plaintext into m blocks of fixed size: $M_1, M_2, \ldots, M_m$. It performs the same transformation on each block to produce m blocks of ciphertext, $C_1, C_2, \ldots, C_m$. The block size can be any number of bits, but it is usually large (on the order of 64 or more bits). For example, in Figure 7.0, a block cipher accepts the plaintext word "this" as a block of 32 bits. It operates on that block using a 32-bit key to produce a 32-bit block of ciphertext. The ciphertext represents the character string "}kc{". The next 32 bits in the plaintext would be mapped into another 32-bit ciphertext block. These ciphers operate on the entire plaintext including spaces, punctuation, and special characters, not just on letters.

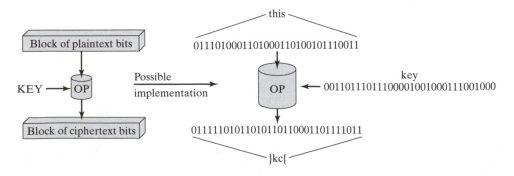

Figure 7.0: General structure of a block cipher

With a large block size, this cipher operates much like the classical polygraphic ciphers, such as Playfair, in that it maps two or more plaintext characters to a cipher block. Hence, they possess the strength of polygraphics in terms of their resistance to frequency-analysis attacks. On the other hand, if the block size is as small as 8 bits (which is a single character), then these ciphers would be no better than classical single character substitution ciphers.

It may appear that a classical cipher such as the Vigenere cipher could be called a block cipher—after all, the keyword of the Vigenere cipher could define the block size. For example, with the keyword "next", it appears that the following Vigenere cipher transformation is a block transformation operating on blocks of size 4:

```
next next  next  next  next
this isno  tago  odci  pher
glfl vwkh  gedh  bhzb  clbk
```

The reason that this is not a block cipher reveals one of the most important characteristics of a true contemporary block cipher—*all the bits in the cipher block should depend on all the bits in the plaintext block*. If a single plaintext bit changes, on average half the bits in the cipher block should change. This does not happen in the Vigenere cipher (ignoring for the moment the obvious difference between single bits and individual characters) in which a single character change in a plaintext block produces only a single character change in the cipher block. For the example, if the first plaintext block is changed from "this" to "thes", the cipher block would change from "glfl" to "glbl".

7.1   BLOCK-CIPHER MODES

Before presenting a specific block cipher, it is helpful to consider the general way in which block ciphers can be put to use. This way, the application method is not tied to a specific implementation—any block cipher (and there are lots of them) can be used in any of three standard modes: electronic-codebook mode, cipher-block-chaining mode, or output-feedback mode. There are more than just these three modes, but these are the three most commonly discussed modes. Actually, the National Institute of Standards and Technology (NIST) recommends five modes. In the next section, some of the newer modes that are receiving a lot of attention are presented.

The electronic-codebook mode (ECB) is the simplest mode of operation. In fact, it is the mode assumed at the beginning of this chapter—each block of plaintext is enciphered into a block of ciphertext. Figure 7.1 illustrates this mode of operation.

The cipher-block-chaining (CBC) mode adds an additional layer of complication to the implementation (with the goal of adding extra security). Because of its added security,

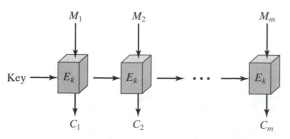

Figure 7.1: Electronic-codebook mode

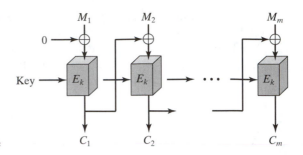

Figure 7.2: Cipher-block-chaining mode

it is the most commonly used block cipher mode. In this mode, the ciphertext from the previous block is XORed with the plaintext block and the resulting bit block is enciphered. This is something like the autokey-cipher mode covered in Chapter 3. Figure 7.2 illustrates this mode of operation. In the figure, the first plaintext block is XORed with a zero vector. That is the easiest way to start the CBC process, but not the most secure. A more secure implementation of CBC uses an initial vector (IV).

If a different IV is selected for every message transmission, then two identical messages would have different ciphertext, even when using the same key. That provides a significant increase in overall security. The problem then is: How does the receiver know the IV? One approach (not necessarily the best) is to send the IV over an insecure channel. In this case, the IV should be used only once and never repeated. Another more secure method is based on the concept of a nonce (*number used once*). The nonce is a unique number that is never reused with the same key. It does not have to be secret—it could be something like the message number. The IV is formed by encrypting the nonce with the block cipher. The receiver can recover the IV if the nonce is attached to the front of the ciphertext.

The output-feedback mode (OFM) uses a block cipher to create a random-bit stream for a stream cipher. A key and an initial input to the block cipher start the process, and additional key bits for the stream cipher are provided by enciphering the output of the block cipher as shown in Figure 7.3.

7.1.1 Contemporary Block-Cipher Modes

Several other block-cipher modes have been developed as alternatives to the three classical modes of operation. In fact, this is an interesting and fruitful field of research. The development of new block-cipher modes can increase the security of current block-cipher algorithms.

One of the newer modes is called the counter mode (CTR), having been only recently adopted as one of the NIST standards. Because of this, it is receiving a fresh look. This is another stream-cipher-implementation mode much like the OFM. The counter mode is

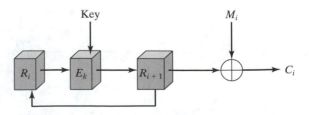

Figure 7.3: Output-feedback mode

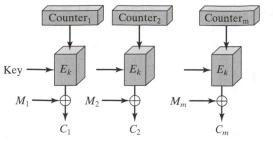

Figure 7.4: Counter mode

shown in Figure 7.4. Note that, in this mode, the block cipher is not used to encipher the plaintext. Rather, it is used to encipher the counter value, which is then XORed with the message block so this has all the characteristics of a stream cipher. The counter is updated, encrypted, and XORed with the second message block, and so on. One nice feature of this method is that all the message blocks can be encrypted (and decrypted) in parallel if all m counter values are known at the same time. This makes for a high-speed cipher.

Like the CBC mode, the CTR mode requires an initial vector (IV) for the first counter value. (The remaining counter values could be derived by counting up from the IV.) This IV should be a nonce. There are many variations on the IV-selection method. Some encipher the counter value concatenated with a nonce. Others use an IV formed from the clock, the block number, and a cycle counter.

Another new mode is called the offset-codebook mode (OCB). This mode not only describes how to encipher each block, but also provides a method of authentication (something that is covered in detail in Chapter 9). In some ways, OCB is the most complicated of the five modes covered so far. Its operation is illustrated in Figures 7.5(a) and 7.5(b).

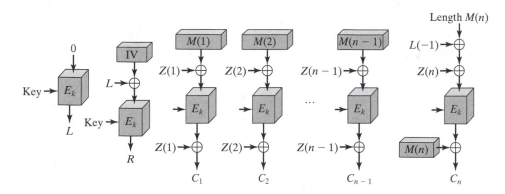

Figure 7.5A: OCB mode (part 1)

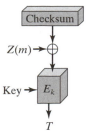

Figure 7.5B: OCB mode (part 2)

Given a message that consists of n blocks, $M(1)$ to $M(n)$, the mode begins by enciphering the zero vector using the secret key to create L. L is XORed with the IV (nonce), and that result is encrypted to create R. R and L are used to create a set of binary vectors Z, where

$$Z(1) = L \text{ XOR } R$$
$$Z(i) = Z(i - 1) \text{ XOR } L[\text{ntz}(i)].$$

The function $\text{ntz}(i)$ is the number of trailing 0's in the binary representation of i. The values $L(1) \dots L(n)$ are formed by conditionally shifting L and XORing with one of two values that depend on the size of the blocks.

For authentication purposes (that is, to ensure that the ciphertext has not been modified), the OCB mode transmits the ciphertext plus a tag value. The tag value is the first t bits of the T vector formed in Figure 7.5(b). The checksum used to find T is the XOR of the message blocks, the mth ciphertext block (C_m), and $Y(m)$. In this case, $Y(m)$ is the XOR of the enciphered length of the mth block and $L(-1)$. Authentication is achieved by comparing the received check bits with a recalculation of those bits. If they match, then the plaintext is authenticated; if not, the plaintext is assumed to be unreliable.

Even a casual examination of the overall simplified explanation of OCB exposes the complicated processes that have been developed to implement ciphers (and we haven't even considered the complicated nature of the ciphers themselves). This should indicate that while contemporary systems have their roots in classical ciphers, they have had to go to great lengths to ensure security.

7.1.2 Padding

An issue that all block ciphers must deal with regardless of the nature of the cipher itself is padding. The problem occurs because block ciphers operate on blocks of a fixed size. But what happens if the plaintext size is not an integral number of block sizes? For example, the block size might be 64 bits (8 characters), but the plaintext size is only 96 bits (12 characters). In this case, the second block contains only 32 bits of plaintext. This was not a problem for most classical ciphers. If the plaintext did not match the length of a repeated keyword in the Vigenere cipher, only a portion of the final keyword repetition was used. The Playfair cipher required padding if the number of plaintext characters was odd, but that was solved using a dummy character, such as "x" or "q". Padding was more of an issue for the transposition ciphers. During the Civil War, the North would pad their word transpositions using meaningless words. The column-transposition cipher required the use of a dummy character to fill out the column array. Padding for classical ciphers was not a great concern—however, it does become an issue for automated block ciphers. In this case, it is useful if the padding is reversible—that is, it is possible for the automated system to add padding while enciphering and detect padding while deciphering. The typical solution is to add (pad) the plaintext with enough 0's to create a full block. The problem with this is that it is not reversible. That is, plaintext "p" and plaintext "p" with 0's on the end both decipher to "p". There is no way to tell whether the plaintext came with or without the 0's.

Ferguson and Schneier suggest two padding methods that will allow for reversible decryption. One pads with an initial byte of 128 followed by enough 0 bytes to fill out the block. The other takes the number of padding bytes required, n, and pads with n bytes each with the value n.

7.2   PRODUCT CIPHERS

A block cipher is neither weak nor strong simply by virtue of being a block cipher or being implemented in one of the five modes. The classical ciphers that fall into the category of block ciphers have many weaknesses. Contemporary block ciphers also come in both strong and weak versions. Ultimately, it is the implementation of the block cipher that determines its performance. Many of today's strongest block ciphers are implemented as product ciphers. These are ciphers that involve more than one approach to encryption.

In 1973, Feistel suggested a form of product cipher that has become the architecture of choice for almost all symmetric block ciphers in use today. The overall process involves several stages of a substitution followed by a transposition. The master key is subdivided into a set of subkeys—one subkey for each stage. At each stage, the data block is divided into a left and a right segment, the segments are swapped, and one segment is mixed with the subkey for that stage. The operation of a stage of a Feistel cipher is shown in Figure 7.6. The *F* block in the figure is used to create a subkey for each stage of the cipher. Another name for this type of cipher is a substitution—permutation (SP) cipher.

The features that vary in a Feistel-type cipher are as follows: block size, key size, the number of rounds, the nature of the round function, and the subkey-generation process. Varying these design features produces a trade-off between the security of the cipher and the efficiency of its implementation. For example, a larger key or block size may make the cipher more secure, but it will also make the cipher slower to implement.

7.2.1   Evaluation of a Block Cipher

Any new cipher must be secure against attacks. But as ciphers become more complicated (such as the class of Feistel block ciphers), how can we be reasonably confident that they can protect our valuable data? As Alice and Bob have learned, just because the algorithm appears complicated does not mean that Eve cannot find a way to break it. The sad truth is that the real answer to this problem is that we can never be sure that a cipher is secure. The best way to gain some confidence in a new cipher is to allow the security community to test it. That is what was done with the advanced encryption standard selection (as will be described later).

Nevertheless, there are some features that a cipher must possess if it is to be accepted by its users. First, of course, the key space must be large enough to make a brute-force attack impossible or at least too expensive to mount. That was the problem with the Caesar

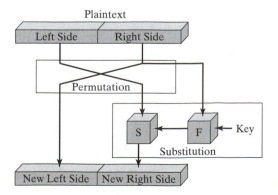

Figure 7.6: Initial stage of a Feistel cipher

cipher, which led to its rejection and the development of the keyword cipher. Second, if the cipher produces ciphertext that passes the randomness tests, it would go a long way to establishing some confidence in the cipher as well.

There are some more formal criteria for evaluating new ciphers. One of the most important strength criteria is called the *avalanche condition*: There should be no correlation between any input bits or key bits with the output bits. In other words, there should be nothing in the ciphertext content that suggests anything about the key or the plaintext. This is important because if someone started trying different keys, they should not be able to tell if they are close (within a few bits) to the actual key. Even one bit of difference between a guess and the real key should produce radically different ciphertext. There are two versions of the avalanche condition:

- Strict plaintext avalanche criterion (SPAC)—each bit of the ciphertext block should change with the probability of one-half whenever any bit of the plaintext block is complemented.
- Strict key avalanche criterion (SKAC)—for a fixed plaintext block, each bit of the ciphertext block changes with a probability of one-half when any bit of the key changes.

Back in Chapter 4, if you completed Problem 1, then you actually explored the SPAC for the Hill cipher. As specific block ciphers are introduced, the performance of the algorithm with respect to the avalanche condition will be considered.

7.3 DATA ENCRYPTION STANDARD

In the mid-1970's, the U.S. government decided that a powerful standard cipher system was necessary. The National Bureau of Standards (NBS) put out a request for the development of such a cipher. Several companies went to work and submitted proposals. The winner was IBM with their cipher system called Lucifer. With some modifications suggested by the National Security Agency, in 1977, Lucifer became known as the data encryption standard or DES. For over 20 years (much too long for any cipher to remain in use), DES was the cipher of choice in many applications. It has since been replaced by the advanced encryption standard (AES), which is covered later in this chapter. DES works on 64-bit blocks of plaintext using a 64-bit key to produce 64-bit blocks of ciphertext. It is a substitution–permutation cipher with 16 stages.

7.3.1 DES Key

While the key is 64 bits long, the user only supplies 56 bits (usually in the form of a seven-letter word that is transformed into its ASCII bits, which serve as the key). The remaining 8 bits are supplied by the algorithm and placed in bit positions 8, 16, 24, 32, 40, 48, 56, and 64, respectively. The result is that each 8-bit block of the key consists of 7 bits supplied by the user and 1 bit determined by DES. The added bits are selected so that each 8-bit block has odd parity (an odd number of 1's).

Each of the 16 stages uses a 48-bit subkey derived from the initial 64-bit key. The key passes through a PC-1 block (permuted choice 1) that extracts the original 56 bits supplied by the user. The 56 bits are divided into left and right halves. Each half is shifted left by 1 or 2 bit positions (which varies, depending on the stage). The new 56 bits are compressed using PC-2 (permuted choice 2) by throwing out 8 bits to create the 48-bit key for the given stage. This process is shown in Figure 7.7.

PC-1 selects the 56 bits from the key and rearranges them according to the following pattern:

57	49	41	33	25	17	9	1	58	50	42	34	26	18
10	2	59	51	43	35	27	19	11	3	60	52	44	36
63	55	47	39	31	23	15	7	62	54	46	38	30	22
14	6	61	53	45	37	29	21	13	5	28	20	12	4

PC-2 selects 48 bits from the 56 bits of C_i and D_i and rearranges them according to the following pattern:

14	17	11	24	1	5	3	28	15	6	21	10
23	19	12	4	26	8	16	7	27	20	13	2
41	52	31	37	47	55	30	40	51	45	33	48
44	49	39	56	34	53	46	42	50	36	29	32

The number of left shifts varies from stage to stage based on the following schedule:

Iteration	# Left Shifts
1	1
2	1
3	2
4	2
5	2
6	2
7	2
8	2
9	1
10	2
11	2
12	2
13	2
14	2
15	2
16	1

This is another characteristic of block ciphers that was not part of classical ciphers—the elaborate manipulation of the key. In classical ciphers, the key is the key, but with block ciphers, the key is put through as many transformations as is the plaintext. This allows each stage of the cipher to perform its substitution and permutation operations with a different key structure.

7.3.2 DES Stages

Each stage of DES performs the same set of operations using a different subkey and the output of the previous stage. Those operations are defined in three "boxes" called the expansion box (Ebox), the substitution box (Sbox), and the permutation box (Pbox). The order of application of these three boxes in a single stage of DES is shown in Figure 7.8.

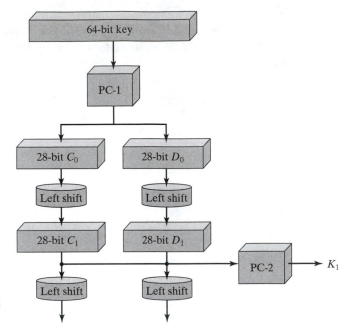

Figure 7.7: Initial stage of the DES key schedule

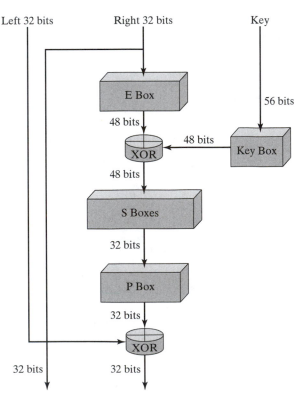

Figure 7.8: One stage of DES

Since even a single stage is quite complicated, let's follow a 64-bit plaintext block through one stage of a DES transformation. Our example block is a simple one consisting of alternating 0's and 1's. Since the input block has a known pattern, it will be instructive to consider how that pattern is distorted by a single DES stage. The input is **11001100 11001100 11001100 11001100 01010101 01010101 01010101 01010101** The left-side 32 bits are put aside to be used in the final operation of the stage. The right 32 bits serve as inputs to the Ebox.

The Ebox expands (hence the name Ebox) its 32-bit input into 48 bits by duplicating some of the input bits. The pattern for the Ebox is shown in Figure 7.9. Notice, for example, that bits 1 and 32 appear twice—once as the first two bits and again as the last two bits.

For our sample, the RHS 32-bit input is

01010101   01010101   01010101   01010101

These bits are mapped into the Ebox

```
1   0   1   0   1   0
1   0   1   0   1   0
1   0   1   0   1   0
1   0   1   0   1   0
1   0   1   0   1   0
1   0   1   0   1   0
1   0   1   0   1   0
1   0   1   0   1   0
```

to produce the following 48-bit output:

101010   101010   101010   101010   101010   101010   101010 101010.

While this might look like a major transformation of the data block, it actually provides very little protection. The actual role of the Ebox is to ensure that the final ciphertext depends on all the plaintext bits. For example, follow the bit in position 1 through the Ebox operations as shown next. The actual transformations that occur in each stage are not taken into account—what is considered is how the Ebox "moves" the impact of the initial bit

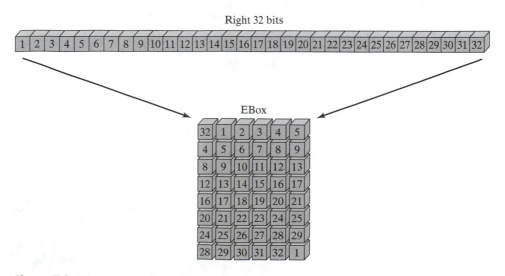

Figure 7.9: Ebox permutation and expansion

through the text. The first Ebox operation duplicates the bit and places it in positions 2 and 32. The second time the Ebox operates on this word, the influence of the initial bit is spread to locations 1, 3, and 31. By the eighth time this word has passed through the Ebox, notice that it has had some influence on every bit position (evidenced by the fact that each column has one or more "1's"). Since the left-hand side and right-hand side are swapped in each stage, this effect occurs after 16 full stages. Here are the Ebox operations:

Initial   10000000000000000000000000000000

The IMPACT ONLY of the bit value

Stage 1   01000000000000000000000000000001
Stage 2   10100000000000000000000000000010
Stage 3   01010000000000000000000000000101
Stage 4   10110000000000000000000000001010
Stage 5   01011010000000000000000001010101
Stage 6   10101111010000000000001010101010
Stage 7   01010101111000100101010101010101
Stage 8   10101010101111111010111010101010

· · ·

The next operation will XOR the Ebox output with the 48-bit subkey. If the subkey consists of the 48-bit pattern

Input   101010 101010 101010 101010 101010 101010 101010 101010
Key   001100 001110 110010 001000 001100 100011 001101 110001
Output   100110 100100 011000 100010 100110 001001 100111 011011

this operation will generate a new 48-bit block to serve as input to the Sboxes. The Sboxes are the real source of the power of DES. These boxes define the substitution pattern for DES. There are eight different Sboxes—Sbox 1 is shown in Figure 7.10. Each Sbox accepts 6 bits of input and produces 4 bits of output. An Sbox has 16 columns and 4 rows in which each element is a 4-bit block usually given in its decimal representation.

For example, Column 5, Row 1 of Sbox 1 contains a decimal 2, which is really a binary 0010. Note that the columns of an Sbox are numbered from 0 to 15 and the rows from 0 to 3. Each 6-bit input is divided into a row and a column index. The row index is given by bits 1 and 6, and bits 2 to 5 supply the column index.

The specific Sboxes used in DES are not the only substitutions that could have been used or that are used in other block ciphers. Exactly why these specific Sboxes

		Column															
		0	1	2	3	4	5	6	7	8	9	10	11	12	13	14	15
	0	14	4	13	1	2	15	11	8	3	10	6	12	5	9	0	7
Row	1	0	15	7	4	14	2	13	1	10	6	12	11	9	5	3	8
	2	4	1	14	8	13	6	2	11	15	12	9	7	3	10	5	0
	3	15	12	8	2	4	9	1	7	5	11	3	14	10	0	6	13

Figure 7.10: Sbox 1

were chosen for DES remains classified. However, examination of the DES Sbox structures reveals some important cryptographic features. For example, each row of an Sbox is a nonlinear mapping of the column number. Consider Row 0 of Sbox 1—the relationship between the column and the Sbox value is as follows:

Column	Value
0	14
1	4
2	13
3	1
4	2
5	15
6	11
7	8
8	3
9	10
10	6
11	12
12	5
13	9
14	0
15	7

The nonlinear characteristic means that there is no linear equation of the form

$$y = ax + b,$$

where a and b are constants, x is the column number, and y is the Sbox value. Graphing the column against the value (reserved for the exercises at the end of the chapter) would provide a stunning visible illustration of the nonlinear structure of Sboxes. This nonlinear feature of the DES Sboxes means that it is difficult to predict all the Sboxes' output, given a set of sample input–output values.

Another apparently important feature of the DES Sboxes is that changing a single input bit results in at least two changes in the output bits. For example, if the input to Sbox 1 is 010010, the output is found in Row 0 (binary 00) Column 9 (binary 1001), which contains the value 10 or binary 1010. If a single bit of that input is changed to, say, 110010, then the output is found in Row 2 (binary 10) Column 9 (binary 1001). The new output is 12 or binary 1100. When comparing the two outputs, notice that the middle two bits change. This is true for every case in which a single input bit changes. The impact of this is that small changes on the input produce larger changes on the output, which can only be considered a useful feature for a cipher.

The design of Sboxes for block ciphers is an open area of research; however, some basic design requirements have been discovered. For example, each row of an Sbox should contain all possible output-bit combinations. If two inputs to an Sbox differ by one bit, then the outputs should differ by at least two bits. If two inputs differ in the middle two bits, then the outputs should differ in at least two bits.

The output of the Ebox is divided into 6-bit segments, and each segment serves as an input to one of the eight Sboxes. The row and column values for each block of our sample input are given by

Sbox	1	2	3	4	5	6	7	8
Input	100110	100100	011000	100010	100110	001001	100111	011011
Row	2	2	0	2	2	1	3	1
Column	3	2	12	1	3	4	3	13

The output of each Sbox is given by the binary contents of the designated row and column. Using the eight Sboxes listed in Figure 7.11, the outputs are as follows:

Sbox	1	2	3	4	5	6	7	8
Input	100110	100100	011000	100010	100110	001001	100111	011011
Row	2	2	0	2	2	1	3	1
Column	3	2	12	1	3	4	3	13
Output	1000	0111	1011	0110	1011	0111	1000	1110

There are now just 32 bits, which are rearranged according to the permutation table shown in Figure 7.12.

Input	10000111101101101011011110001110
Output	01101101110001001110001101111101

The final operation places the original RHS 32 bits on the LHS and XORs the original LHS with the 32-bit output of the Pbox:

```
                                11001100 11001100  11001100 11001100
                     XOR        01101101 11100010  01110001 10111101
01010101 01010101  01010101 01010101  10100001 00101110  10111101 01110001
```

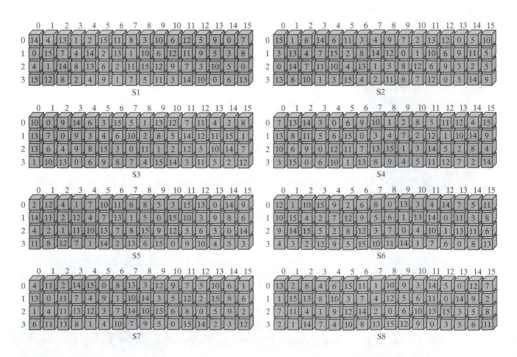

Figure 7.11: All eight Sboxes

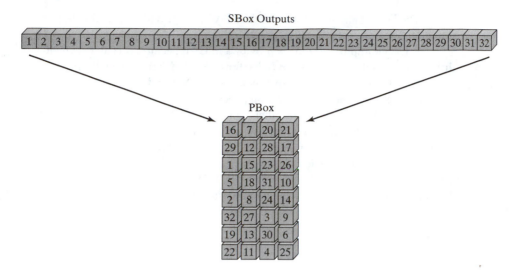

Figure 7.12: Pbox permutation

Comparing the output of a single stage of DES to the input gives

**11001100 11001100 11001100 11001100 01010101 01010101 01010101 01010101
01010101 01010101 01010101 01010101 10100001 00101110 10111101 01110001**

Notice that the two bit strings differ at 33 locations. In other words, slightly more than half the bits changed during this single stage.

7.3.3 Alternative Implementations of DES

DES could be used in any one of the five standard block-cipher implementation modes: OFM, CBC, CTR, OCB, or ECB. However, as will be seen in Section 7.3.5, DES is no longer a secure cipher. Hence, alternative implementations of DES have been suggested in an effort to improve its overall security. The most common is called triple-DES. Triple-DES comes in two versions: One uses three keys and the other only uses two. The three-key version first encrypts the message with Key1, decrypts the result with Key2, and finally encrypts that with Key3 as shown in Figure 7.13. The two-key version uses the same steps where Key3 = Key1.

7.3.4 DES in CAP

CAP provides two versions of DES—a standard DES implementation and a smaller version that is useful for experimentation. Both operate in the same way as all the algorithms found in CAP. Enter the plaintext or the ciphertext, select Ciphers and click on either DES (for the real DES implementation) or S-DES (for the simplified version).

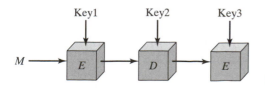

Figure 7.13: Three-key version of triple-DES

The DES implementation found in CAP also provides an evaluation option. You can run both types of avalanche tests on DES.

S-DES (simplified-DES) is provided in CAP because it is an excellent learning tool. It was developed by Dr. Edward Schaefer at Santa Clara University in 1996. It is simple enough so that you can explore the operation of DES and some of its weaknesses. The full structure including the key-generation procedure of S-DES is shown in Figure 7.14. It operates on 8-bit data blocks (in other words, single characters) using a 10-bit key (only $2^{10} = 1024$ possibilities) and two stages. In spite of the simplifications, as the figure shows, it looks much like our basic DES. The initial permutation maps the eight data bits 1 to 8 into 2 6 3 1 4 8 5 7. The final inverse permutation is 4 1 3 5 7 2 8 6. The function F has an Ebox, Pbox, and two Sboxes much like DES. The Ebox expands the 4-bit input into 8 bits in the order 4 1 2 3 2 3 4 1. The 8-bit subkey is XORed to the Ebox output. The first four bits are input to Sbox 0 and the other four bits are inputs to

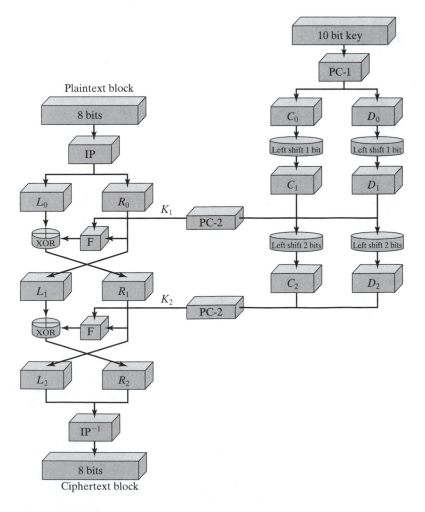

Figure 7.14: S-DES

Sbox 1. The two Sboxes are shown here:

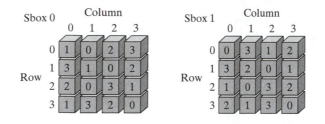

The first and last bits of each Sbox input identify the row and the middle two bits select the column. The output of each Sbox is a 2-bit binary number. The two outputs are permuted by the Pbox in the order 2 4 3 1. This output becomes the right-hand side and the original right-hand side becomes the new left-hand side for another stage of S-DES. The output of the final stage is permuted resulting in the ciphertext block.

The key-generation mechanism begins with a 10-bit key that is permuted by PC-1 into the order 3 5 2 7 4 10 1 9 8 6. It is separated into two 5-bit segments, and each segment is shifted left by one bit. PC-2 selects and rearranges eight bits from the two 5-bit segments—the bits in order are 6 3 7 4 8 5 10 9. The result is subkey 1. The two segments are now shifted left twice, and PC-2 is applied again to produce subkey 2.

CAP implements this version of S-DES. Select S-DES under the Ciphertext menu and the window shown in Figure 7.15 will pop up. The key must be an integer between 0 and 1023. When you run Set Key, the results of the key-generation process are displayed.

7.3.5 Cryptanalysis of DES

DES has a long and interesting history full of speculation and controversy. It all began when the National Security Agency (NSA) required the modification of the original specification

Figure 7.15: S-DES in CAP

for Lucifer submitted by IBM. Among the changes they requested was that the original key length of 128 bits be reduced to 56 bits. This fueled the speculation (which has never been verified) that NSA could break the 56-bit version of DES from the very beginning. If they could, no one was talking, but others outside of NSA tried for more than 20 years with varying degrees of success. Brute-force attacks seemed to be the only feasible way to undermine the algorithm. These had to wait until computer technology caught up with the key size to allow for high-speed testing of all possible keys. This happened in the late 1990s. In July of 1997, a process that borrowed time from more than 14,000 computers across the Internet was able to break a DES key in 90 days. Within 6 months, the time to break DES in this way was reduced to 39 days. In July of 1998, a special machine was built (called Deep Crack) that was able to break a DES key in 56 hours. Clearly DES was no longer a viable system, hence the NBS put out a bid for its replacement under the advanced encryption standard, AES. The outcome of that search will be covered later in this chapter.

The study of the structure of DES lead to more than just the development of a faster brute-force attack method against block ciphers. It also motivated the development of a new set of cryptanalysis tools such as linear analysis and differential analysis—both of these will be covered in a later section. In addition, several interesting properties of DES were discovered that suggested weaknesses in the algorithm. What the cryptological community learned about DES is now used to evaluate new block ciphers.

One of the early discoveries was that DES had some weak keys. These are keys that generate the same subkey for each round. There are four such DES keys:

0101	0101	0101	0101		FEFE	FEFE	FEFE	FEFE
1F1F	1F1F	0E0E	0E0E		E0E0	E0E0	F1F1	F1F1

There are also 12 semiweak DES keys. Semiweak keys generate only two subkeys that alternate rounds. Of course, weak and semiweak keys must be avoided when using DES, but, given the small number of such keys, they do not have much of an impact on the overall security of the algorithm. S-DES also has weak keys. For example, Key 0 produces the same subkeys. (Both K0 and K1 are 00000000.)

7.3.5.1 Differential Cryptanalysis

Differential cryptanalysis was introduced by Biham and Shamir in 1990, but it is thought to have been known to the National Security Agency and the original designers of DES long before 1990. It is a general method for analyzing block ciphers, so it is not just a DES attack. It falls into the category of a chosen-plaintext attack because it requires a large number of selected plaintext–ciphertext pairs. In part, the number of pairs required makes this an impractical attack, but it is useful for evaluating the overall security of a proposed block cipher. Since it can be faster than a brute-force attack, it does suggest possible weaknesses that must be considered before accepting and using a cipher.

The basic idea is to compare the differences in ciphertext pairs with those in their corresponding plaintext pairs. It is possible to make reasonable guesses about bits in the key based on these differences. Consider a simple stream cipher in which the ciphertext is the XOR of the plaintext and a key:

$$C_1 = P_1 \oplus K.$$

For example, we might use

Key	0	0	1	1	0	1	1	1	0	1
Plaintext	0	1	1	0	0	1	0	1	0	0
Ciphertext	0	1	0	1	0	0	1	0	0	1

If two ciphertext streams produced by the same key operating on different plaintext streams are XORed, the result is

$$C_1 \oplus C_2 = P_1 \oplus K \oplus P_2 \oplus K$$
$$C_1 \oplus C_2 = P_1 \oplus P_2.$$

For example, we might have

Key	0 0 1 1 0 1 1 1 0 1	Key	0 0 1 1 0 1 1 1 0 1
P1	0 1 1 0 0 1 0 1 0 0	**P2**	0 1 1 0 1 0 0 0 1 1
C1	0 1 0 1 0 0 1 0 0 1	**C2**	0 1 0 1 1 1 1 1 1 0

In this case, since the same keystream was used for both, consider the XOR of the two ciphertext steams and the XOR of the two plaintext streams:

C1 XOR C2	0 0 0 0 1 1 0 1 1 1
P1 XOR P2	0 0 0 0 1 1 0 1 1 1

As predicted, they both produce the same result. The problem with this is that, if the two ciphertext streams and one of the plaintext streams are known, then the other plaintext stream can be determined. For our example, if P1, C1 and C2 were known, then

$$P2 = C1 \text{ XOR } C2 \text{ XOR } P1$$

or

C1 XOR C2	0 0 0 0 1 1 0 1 1 1
P1	0 1 1 0 0 1 0 1 0 0
P2	0 1 1 0 1 0 0 0 1 1

Because of the linear nature of the stream cipher, the difference between the plaintext is the same as the difference between the ciphertext. Also, neither depends on the actual key. This makes it open to a known-plaintext–ciphertext attack, but it does not provide a direct mechanism for revealing the key. (Indirectly it does, but that is not the issue here.) However, block ciphers like DES are not linear. (Remember the nonlinear characteristic of the DES Sboxes?) So, for a given key, the difference between two plaintext pairs is not the same as the difference between their ciphertext pairs. In fact, the key has an impact on the relationship between these differences. While this may seem to be an advantage because it eliminates the possibility of using the little trick shown earlier, it does create another possible weakness. That is, knowledge of some actual differences may suggest possible key values. Once again, it appears that, by plugging one hole, you only open another. This is one reason that you must be careful and thoroughly study any new approach to creating a new cipher.

Since the nonlinear properties of a block cipher are the result of the structure of the Sboxes, differential cryptanalysis begins with an examination of their characteristics. For example, consider the S_0 box used in S-DES. The box can be written as an array with both binary inputs and binary outputs (remember, the first and last input bits specify the row, and the middle two bits specify the column):

Binary Input	0000	0001	0010	0011	0100	0101	0110	0111	1000
	1001	1010	1011	1100	1101	1110	1111		
Binary Output	01	11	00	01	10	00	01	11	10
	01	00	11	11	01	01	00		

Given two different inputs to S_0, X_1 and X_2, it follows that $\Delta X = X_1$ XOR X_2. If Y_1 is the output for X_1 and Y_2 is the output for X_2, then $\Delta Y = Y_1$ XOR Y_2. What we want to find is all the possible pairs (ΔX, ΔY). The number of occurrences of each pair is entered into a ***difference distribution table*** (DDT) such as the one shown in Figure 7.16 for S_0 and S_1. The rows represent ΔX values and the columns represent ΔY values (in Hex). The table indicates that, for S_0, there are no pairs with an input difference of 3 and an output difference of 0. However, there are two pairs with an input difference of 7 and an output difference of 3. The table may also be read as probability values. For example, if the input difference to S_0 is 2, then 8 out of the 16 possible output differences are also 2. In other words, on the probability of the output difference being 2 is 8/16, or $^1/_2$. An "ideal" DDT would have the same value in every cell. (In our example, the table entries would all be 4.) Since the DDT for S_0 is not ideal, it can be exploited to discover the key.

Knowledge of the DDT for the all the Sboxes used in a block cipher is only the beginning step. The overall goal of differential cryptanalysis is to find the differential characteristics of the entire cipher—that is, the difference of plaintext pairs and the difference of their resulting ciphertext. This process will be illustrated using S-DES because it is less complicated and we already have the DDTs for the two Sboxes.

Figure 7.17 shows the first stage of S-DES, in which a random pair of inputs has been selected so that the ΔX into S_0 is 1 (in binary, 0001) and the ΔX into S_1 is 0. From the DDT for S_0, there is a probability that $\Delta Y = 2$ of 8/16, or $^1/_2$. Of course, for S_1, the probability that ΔY is $= 0$ is $\frac{16}{16}$, or 1.

S_0

ΔX	ΔY 0	1	2	3
0	16	0	0	0
1	0	4	8	4
2	0	4	8	4
3	4	8	0	4
4	2	6	2	6
5	4	4	4	4
6	4	4	4	4
7	6	2	6	2
8	4	4	4	4
9	2	6	2	6
A	6	2	6	2
B	4	4	4	4
C	4	8	4	0
D	8	0	4	4
E	4	0	4	8
F	4	8	4	0

S_1

ΔX	ΔY 0	1	2	3
0	16	0	0	0
1	2	8	2	4
2	0	6	4	6
3	4	2	8	2
4	2	0	10	4
5	2	4	2	8
6	0	10	0	6
7	8	2	4	2
8	4	6	0	6
9	8	2	4	2
A	2	0	10	4
B	0	6	4	6
C	0	6	4	6
D	6	0	6	4
E	10	4	2	0
F	2	8	2	4

Figure 7.16: Difference distribution table for S-DES

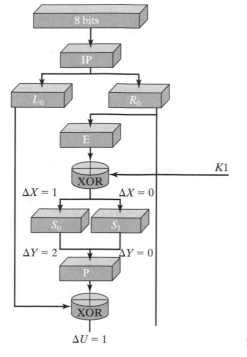

Figure 7.17: Stage one of S-DES

The differential out of stage one is permuted by P as follows:

$$(1000) \rightarrow (0001).$$

So the output differential of the first stage is 1. This is fed into the next stage of S-DES as shown in Figure 7.18. The differential input to the second stage is permuted by E and split so the differential inputs to the two Sboxes are 4 and 1. The output differential of S_0 will be 1 with a probability 6/16. (From the DDT, there are 6 cases out of 16 for which an input of 4 will produce an output of 1.) The output differential of S_1 will be 1 with a probability 8/16. Because of the final permutation P, the differential of the output stage is C.

Now, the differential pair $\Delta X_{\text{in}} = 1$ and $\Delta Y_{\text{out}} = C$ becomes our target. It will occur with a probability given by

$$\frac{8}{16} \times \frac{6}{16} \times \frac{8}{16} = \frac{384}{4096} = \frac{3}{32}.$$

To find the actual key, a large number of random plaintext pairs with a differential of 1 will be tried. Those with the correct output differential (in this case C) are called *right pairs*; those which do not produce the correct output differential are called *wrong pairs*. The right pairs are used to guess possible key bits in the last stage of the cipher. This is done by running the ciphertext backward through the stage, trying all possible subkeys for that stage. A count of the number of times a given subkey produces the correct differential is maintained. At the end of the run, the subkey with the largest count is likely to be the subkey used in the cipher. This process is then repeated in the next stage until enough subkey information is available to allow the discovery of the actual key.

Since this approach requires an exhaustive search of the subkeys, it may appear to be no better than an exhaustive search on the main key. However, the subkeys are smaller,

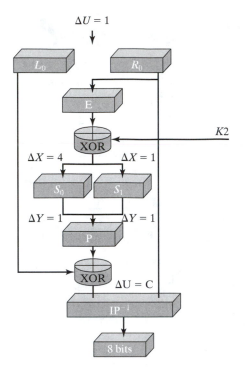

Figure 7.18: Stage two of S-DES

making this a more feasible approach. For example, the DES main key is 56 bits requiring a search of 2^{56} keys, while the subkeys are only 48 bits, reducing the search space to 2^{48} keys. Still, differential cryptanalysis does require an enormous amount of data, including a large number of known-plaintext–ciphertext pairs.

7.3.5.2 Linear Cryptanalysis

Linear cryptanalysis is a known-plaintext attack introduced by Mitsuru Matsui in 1993. Since the nonlinear structures in a block cipher are the primary source of their strength, linear cryptanalysis attempts to discover weaknesses in those structures. This is done by search for a linear approximation to the nonlinear segments. The assumption is that the values of the key which work for the approximate algorithm are likely to work for the actual algorithm. At the very least, the results will provide some strong hints as to the actual key bits.

A typical stage of a Feistel cipher was shown in Figure 7.6. The nonlinear component of that stage is the substitution operation defined by some function, f, of the key and plaintext, say $f(x, k)$. Linear cryptanalysis asks if that function could be written as a linear combination of x and k reduced to mod 2, such as

$$y = f(x, k) = \mathbf{A}x + \mathbf{B}k \ (\text{mod } 2),$$

where $\mathbf{A}$ and $\mathbf{B}$ are constant matrices. If such an $\mathbf{A}$ and $\mathbf{B}$ could be found, then, with knowledge of y and x (known-plaintext–ciphertext), the value of k can be calculated.

Consider the case of S-DES. By ignoring the initial and final permutations, its actions on the plaintext can be expressed as the application of a set of functions as shown in

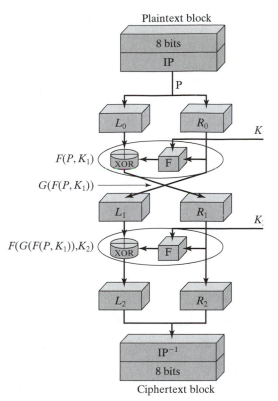

Plaintext block

Ciphertext block

Figure 7.19: Linear cryptanalysis of S-DES

Figure 7.19. The function F represents the action of the Sboxes and the function G is the swap function, so S-DES is really

$$C = F(G(F(P, K_1), K_2)).$$

The swap function G is a linear operation. Operating on the 8-bit data in S-DES, G in matrix form looks like this:

$$\begin{vmatrix} Y_0 \\ Y_1 \\ Y_2 \\ Y_3 \\ Y_4 \\ Y_5 \\ Y_6 \\ Y_7 \end{vmatrix} = \begin{vmatrix} 0 & 0 & 0 & 0 & 1 & 0 & 0 & 0 \\ 0 & 0 & 0 & 0 & 0 & 1 & 0 & 0 \\ 0 & 0 & 0 & 0 & 0 & 0 & 1 & 0 \\ 0 & 0 & 0 & 0 & 0 & 0 & 0 & 1 \\ 1 & 0 & 0 & 0 & 0 & 0 & 0 & 0 \\ 0 & 1 & 0 & 0 & 0 & 0 & 0 & 0 \\ 0 & 0 & 1 & 0 & 0 & 0 & 0 & 0 \\ 0 & 0 & 0 & 1 & 0 & 0 & 0 & 0 \end{vmatrix} \begin{vmatrix} x_0 \\ x_1 \\ x_2 \\ x_3 \\ x_4 \\ x_5 \\ x_6 \\ x_7 \end{vmatrix}$$

If F is also a linear function, then C can be rewritten as

$$C = A(G(F(P, K_1))) + BK_2 \ (\text{mod} \ 2).$$

Using the fact that G is a linear function ($y = Sx$) gives

$$C = A[S(AP + BK_1)] + BK_2 \ (\text{mod} \ 2).$$

Expanding this expression yields

$$C = ASAP + ASBK_1 + BK_2 \pmod 2.$$

This equation can be solved for the key values given knowledge of C and P—in other words, a known-plaintext–ciphertext attack.

The reality is that F is not linear, so the trick to linear cryptanalysis is to come up with a good linear approximation to F. This really means that the actual Sboxes used in the block cipher are replaced by approximate Sboxes for the purpose of cryptanalysis.

The approximate Sboxes identify the most probable linear relationships that can be exploited to discover the key bits. For example, the S_0 box of S-DES translates a 4-bit input $\{X_1, X_2, X_3, X_4\}$ into a 2-bit output $\{Y_1, Y_2\}$. Any underlying linear structure in this Sbox can be revealed by looking for examples of

$$a_1X_1 \oplus a_2X_2 \oplus a_3X_3 \oplus a_4X_4 \oplus b_1Y_1 \oplus b_2Y_2 = 0,$$

for a_i and $b_i = 0$ or 1. For example, if $a_1 = 1$, $a_2 = 1$, $a_3 = 0$, $a_4 = 0$, $b_1 = 1$, and $b_2 = 0$, then the equation becomes

$$X_1 \oplus X_2 \oplus Y_1 = 0.$$

If this equation is true for S_0, it suggests a linear relationship of the form X_1 XOR $X_2 = Y_1$. If it is true significantly more than half the time or significantly less than half the time, this suggests that an approximate linear relationship exists in S_0. So, possible linear relationships can be discovered in an Sbox by looking for values of a_1, a_2, a_3, a_4, b_1, and b_2 that are highly probable or improbable. As shown in Figure 7.20, the aforementioned relationship is true 9 times out of 16, or slightly more than half. A linear approximation table can be constructed for an Sbox by trying all possible values for a and b. Such tables are shown in S_0 and S_1 of S-DES in Figure 7.21. These example tables were constructed by subtracting 8 (half of 16) from each count in order to better see when a specific relationship is probable or improbable. For example, using S_0, it is highly probable that relationship (4, 1)

X_1	X_2	X_3	X_4	Y_1	Y_2
0	0	0	0	0	1
0	0	0	1	1	1
0	0	1	0	0	0
0	0	1	1	0	1
0	1	0	0	1	0
0	1	0	1	0	0
0	1	1	0	0	1
0	1	1	1	1	1
1	0	0	0	1	0
1	0	0	1	0	1
1	0	1	0	0	0
1	0	1	1	1	1
1	1	0	0	1	1
1	1	0	1	0	1
1	1	1	0	0	1
1	1	1	1	1	1

Figure 7.20: A linear relationship in S_0

S_0

	B: 0	1	2	3
A: 0	8	-8	-8	-8
1	-8	2	0	-2
2	-8	0	-2	-2
3	-8	0	-4	0
4	-8	0	0	0
5	-8	4	2	2
6	-8	-2	0	-2
7	-8	-2	2	-4
8	-8	0	0	0
9	-8	0	2	-2
A	-8	2	0	2
B	-8	-2	2	-4
C	-8	-2	2	0
D	-8	-2	0	2
E	-8	-4	-2	2
F	-8	0	4	0

S_1

	B: 0	1	2	3
A: 0	8	-8	-8	-8
1	-8	0	1	1
2	-8	2	-1	-3
3	-8	-2	-1	1
4	-8	2	1	-1
5	-8	-2	1	-3
6	-8	0	-5	3
7	-8	0	3	3
8	-8	0	-1	-1
9	-8	0	-1	-1
A	-8	2	1	-1
B	-8	6	1	3
C	-8	2	3	1
D	-8	-2	3	-3
E	-8	0	1	1
F	-8	0	1	1

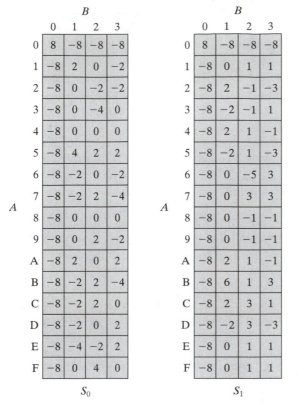

Figure 7.21: Linear approximation tables for S-DES

is true ($A = 4$, $B = 1$), since it occurs 12 out of 16 times ($12 - 8 = 4$, the entry in the table). This represents the equation $X_2 = Y_2$. For $S1$, the relationship (7, 3) is also probable. It represents the equation $X_2 \text{ XOR } X_3 \text{ XOR } X_4 = Y_2 \text{ XOR } Y_1$.

Using these results, known-plaintext–ciphertext pairs, and working backward through the block structure, bits of the keys into each stage can be found. The process involves finding the key values that most often satisfy the linear relationships. This method requires a large number of known-plaintext–ciphertext pairs; however, it is less than that required by differential cryptanalysis.

7.3.5.3 Meet-in-the-Middle Attack

Back in Section 7.3.3, an alternative implementation of DES called triple-DES was suggested. Because it uses two (or three) DES keys and three runs of DES, it is more secure than standard DES. You might have wondered what happened to double-DES. Why not use two keys and only two runs of DES to gain the same security in terms of an increase in key size yet run faster than triple-DES? Just such an implementation is shown in Figure 7.22.

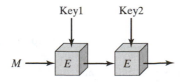

Figure 7.22: Possible double-DES implementation

If a brute-force attack on standard DES requires searching 2^{56} keys, then it appears that double-DES would require a search of $2^{56} \times 2^{56} = 2^{112}$ keys. This is large enough to provide a very high degree of protection.

The problem is that double-DES can be attacked with only a small added effort (over an attack on standard DES) if it is possible to trade memory space for time. The process involves using a known-plaintext–ciphertext pair in what is called a meet-in-the-middle attack. If there is enough memory space available, encipher the known plaintext with every possible key and save each result. Then decipher the ciphertext with every possible key and compare each result with the contents of memory. If there is a match, then both keys have been found. The method is illustrated in Figure 7.23. At most, it requires the evaluation of 2^{56} keys for the encipher process and another 2^{56} keys for the decipher process—that is, just $2 \times 2^{56} = 2^{57}$ keys, which is a far cry from 2^{112} keys.

For example, say Eve suspects that Alice and Bob are using double S-DES and that Bob begins his messages with "Alice". Eve begins by constructing a list of the enciphering of "Alice" for every possible S-DES key. Following is part of this list:

Key				Ciphertext				
0	10110	10110	10001	11001	10110	11110	10111	10100
1	01011	10000	10001	01101	10100	10101	11000	11001
2	00000	10111	01001	10110	10111	11110	00010	00000
$\vdots$								
92	11110	10011	10101	10101	10111	01110	10011	10101
$\vdots$								
1023	01000	01110	00101	01110	10001	10011	01000	00110

This table would be saved in memory. When Eve intercepts a ciphertext message sent from Bob to Alice, she would then decipher the first part of the message with every possible key. Say she intercepted the following message:

10111 10101 00001 11111 01000 01000 01000 00110.

Deciphering this message with the use of every possible key produces the following table:

Key				Result				
0	00101	11111	01011	00110	01010	01000	01110	00000
1	10001	11001	11011	10100	00011	11010	00100	00001
2	11100	01001	11101	10100	01010	01100	00001	00111
$\vdots$								
122	11110	10011	10101	10101	10111	01110	10011	10101
$\vdots$								
1023	11001	11001	10000	11010	10111	11101	11011	00101

Comparing the two lists, Eve notes that deciphering using key 122 produces the same result as enciphering using key 92, so Bob and Alice must be using the key pair (92, 122).

This concept of a meet-in-the-middle attack is not limited to compromising double-DES. It turns out that meet-in-the-middle approaches may be used against other ciphers and even against key-management systems (as you will learn in Chapter 9).

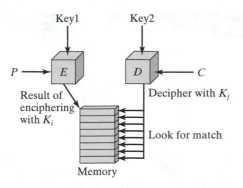

Figure 7.23: Meet-in-the-middle attack

7.3.5.4 Side-Channel Analysis

Block ciphers like DES are sometimes implemented in smart cards. These are credit-card-like devices that are used to maintain bank accounts or provide a positive identification for the user. The key used in these devices can be discovered by means other than traditional cryptanalysis. It turns out that information about the operation of the underlying cipher can be leaked by observing certain performance characteristics. These are called side-channel attacks. For example, when a key bit of 1 is being processed, the chip draws more power from the power supply. By monitoring the power drain, the key bits can actually be exposed. There is also a timing version of this attack that monitors the number of microseconds it takes to complete the algorithm. The timing values will expose parts of the key as well.

This attack mode is covered in greater detail in Chapter 8. When you encounter it again, remember that side-channel analysis is also a viable attack method to use against block ciphers.

7.3.5.5 Bob, Alice, and Eve

Bob and Alice are still searching for a perfect cipher that will forever block Eve's attempts to read their mail. They became interested in using DES, but felt like the key was too long for them to safely remember, so they settled on S-DES instead. This may seem like an unrealistic option, but all too often real users make decisions like this for reasons that are equally as stupid.

It doesn't take Eve long to discover the new cipher and to start searching for simple ways to break it. Her first try is an exhaustive key attack using the tool provided by CAP. As shown in Figure 7.24, it worked quite well.

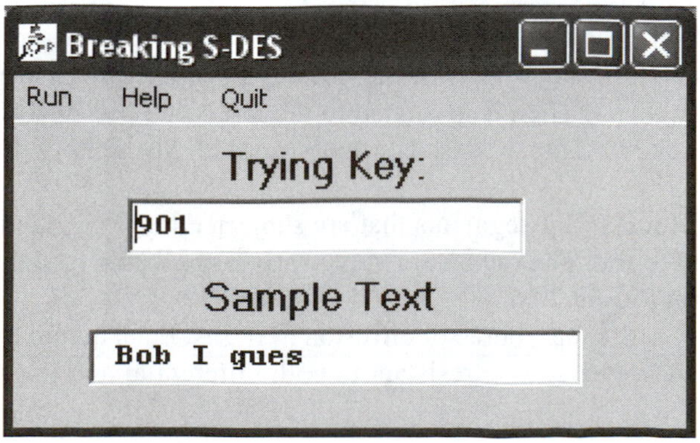

Figure 7.24: Using CAP to break S-DES

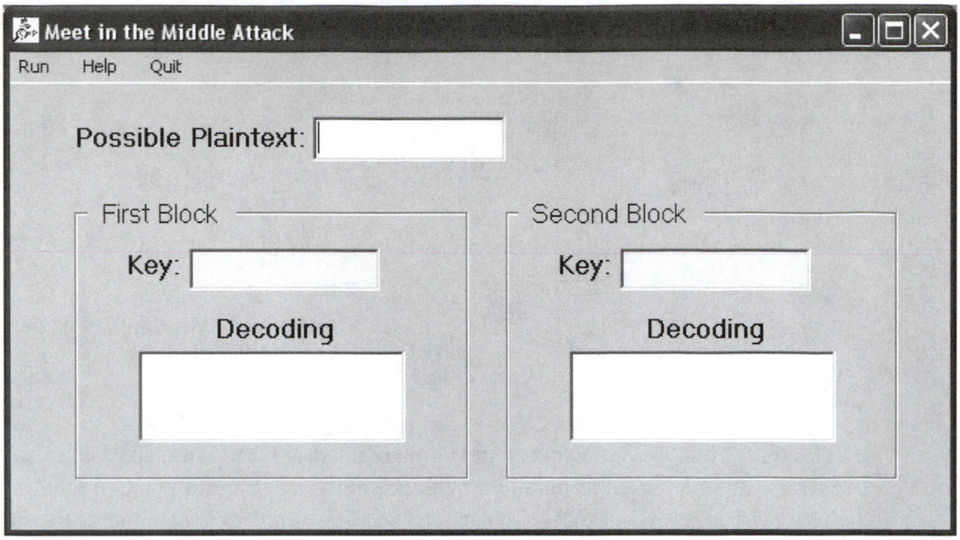

Figure 7.25: A Meet-in-the-Middle Attack using CAP

As usual, Bob and Alice began to suspect that their choice of S-DES was not very wise, so they decided to upgrade to double S-DES (CAP provides this cipher). After all, it promised a key space of 2^{20}, which they hoped would keep Eve busy for a long time. However, Eve was ready with a meet-in-the-middle attack (also using CAP—see Figure 7.25).

7.4 IDEA

The International Data Encryption Algorithm (IDEA) was first publicly released by X. Lai, J. L. Massey, and S. Murphy in a 1991 paper. It was meant to be a stronger alternative to DES. Its major use today is as the encryption algorithm built into PGP (pretty good privacy). IDEA encrypts 64-bit plaintext blocks into ciphertext using a 128-bit key. However, the difference between IDEA and DES is more than just key size. IDEA modified the Feistel structure by using three different mixing operations: XOR, 2's complement addition, and multiplication mod $2^{16} + 1$. Some of these ideas were to appear later in the Advanced Encryption Standard. (See Section 7.5.)

IDEA requires fifty-six 16-bit subkeys, which are generated from the original 128-bit key by successive rotations of 25 bits—that is, the initial 128-bit key, K, is broken up into the first eight 16-bit subkeys. Then K is rotated to the left by 25 bits and divided into the next eight 16-bit subkeys. This process continues until all 56 subkeys are generated.

The plaintext is divided into four 16-bit segments that are subjected to eight rounds of IDEA plus a final transformation round. The round structure involves applications of the three mixing operations as shown in Figure 7.26.

The M–A (multiply–add) box is the real source of diffusion in IDEA. Each output bit depends on all the input bits. IDEA appears to be resistant to both differential and linear cryptanalysis.

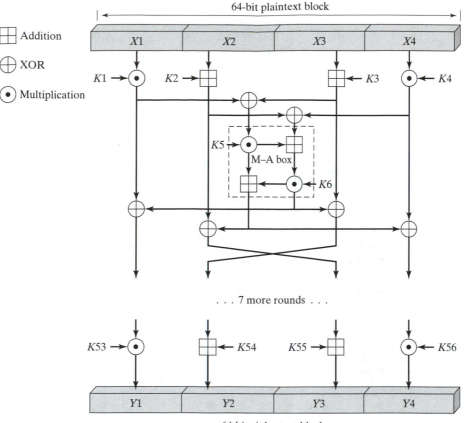

Figure 7.26: IDEA

7.5   ADVANCED ENCRYPTION STANDARD

Since DES was becoming less reliable as new cryptanalysis techniques were developed, the National Institute of Standards and Technology (NIST) put out a notice in early 1999 requesting submissions for a new encryption standard. The requirements were as follows:

- A symmetric block cipher with a variable length key (128, 192, or 256 bits) and a 128-bit block.
- It must be more secure than triple-DES.
- It must be in the public domain—royalty free worldwide.
- It should remain secure for at least 30 years.

Fifteen algorithms were submitted from 10 different countries. They were subjected to a long public analysis process before the final algorithm was selected.

NIST went about the process of selecting a new block-cipher standard in just the right way. They required public disclosure of the algorithm and solicited comments from the cryptology community. At a series of three public conferences, the algorithms were presented and discussed, and weaknesses were exposed. After the second conference, the list of 15 ciphers was reduced to five finalists: MARS, submitted by IBM; RC6, submitted by RSA Laboratories; Rijndael, submitted by Joan Daemen and Vincent Rijment; Serpent, submitted by Anderson, Biham, and Knudsen; and Two Fish, submitted by Schneier, Kelsy, Whiting, Wagner, Hall, and Ferguson. All five were excellent algorithms having survived a rigorous six months of examination. These five were reexamined, and after another six months of testing, the winner was announced. It was Rijndael (pronounced "rain-doll").

7.5.1 Rijndael Structure

Rijndael is a flexible algorithm with a variable block size (128, 192, or 256 bits), a variable key size (128, 192, or 256 bits), and a variable number of iterations (10, 12 or 14). The number of iterations is dependent on the block–key size and varies from 10 to 14. As a result of its flexible nature, there are really three versions of Rijndael: AES-128, AES-192, and AES-256. The general structure of Rijndael is shown in Figure 7.27. Rather than using just a substitution and a permutation at each stage (as DES does), Rijndael consists of multiple cycles of substitution, shifting, column mixing, and a key add operation. In this way, Rijndael is more like IDEA—it does not contain a typical Feistel round involving a permutation. (*Note*: this section will use the terms "AES" and "Rijndael" interchangeably.)

The process begins by grouping the plaintext bits into a column array by bytes. This is sometimes called the "State within AES." The first four bytes form the first column; the second four bytes form the second column, and so on. The resulting array is shown in Figure 7.28. If the block size is 128 bits, this becomes a 4 $\times$ 4 array. For larger block sizes, the array has additional columns. The key is also grouped into an array using the same process.

The substitution layer uses a single Sbox (rather than the eight Sboxes used in DES). The Rijndael Sbox is a 16 $\times$ 16 array shown in Figure 7.29. Each element in the current column array serves as an address into the Sbox: The first four bits identify the Sbox row and the last four bits identify the Sbox column. The Sbox element at that location replaces the current column-array element.

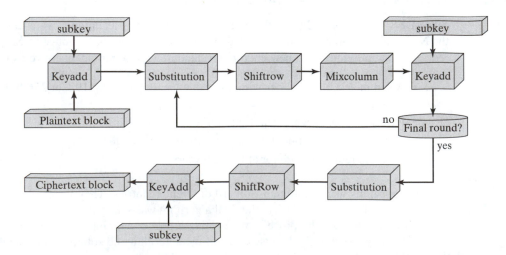

Figure 7.27: General Rijndael structure

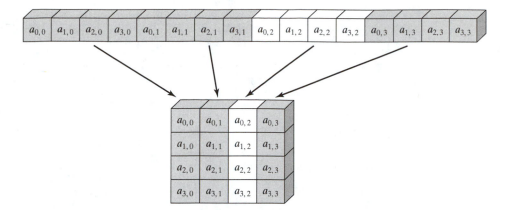

Figure 7.28: Rijndael grouping

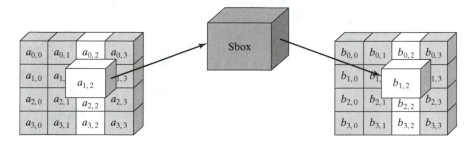

Figure 7.29: Rijndael substitution operation

The Rijndael Sbox actually performs an algebraic transformation on the input to produce the output. In matrix form, it is given by the following expression:

$$
\begin{vmatrix} b_0 \\ b_1 \\ b_2 \\ b_3 \\ b_4 \\ b_5 \\ b_6 \\ b_7 \end{vmatrix}
=
\begin{vmatrix}
1 & 0 & 0 & 0 & 1 & 1 & 1 & 1 \\
1 & 1 & 0 & 0 & 0 & 1 & 1 & 1 \\
1 & 1 & 1 & 0 & 0 & 0 & 1 & 1 \\
1 & 1 & 1 & 1 & 0 & 0 & 0 & 1 \\
1 & 1 & 1 & 1 & 1 & 0 & 0 & 0 \\
0 & 1 & 1 & 1 & 1 & 1 & 0 & 0 \\
0 & 0 & 1 & 1 & 1 & 1 & 1 & 0 \\
0 & 0 & 0 & 1 & 1 & 1 & 1 & 1
\end{vmatrix}
\begin{vmatrix} a_0 \\ a_1 \\ a_2 \\ a_3 \\ a_4 \\ a_5 \\ a_6 \\ a_7 \end{vmatrix}
+
\begin{vmatrix} 1 \\ 1 \\ 0 \\ 0 \\ 0 \\ 1 \\ 1 \\ 0 \end{vmatrix}
$$

Byte a is multiplied by the given matrix, and the result is added to the fixed vector value 63 (in binary) to produce the output value. This can be expressed in a typical Sbox format as shown in Figure 7.30. For example, if the input state consists of the array (displayed in Hex), then the output is as shown:

Input				Output			
12	2a	21	0b	c9	e5	fd	2b
45	bd	04	c1	6e	7a	f2	78
23	0a	00	1c	26	67	63	9c
89	11	2a	fc	a7	82	e5	b0

	0	1	2	3	4	5	6	7	8	9	a	b	c	d	e	f
0	63	7c	77	7b	f2	6b	6f	c5	30	01	67	2b	fe	d7	ab	76
1	ca	82	c9	7d	fa	59	47	f0	ad	d4	a2	af	9c	a4	72	c0
2	b7	fd	93	26	36	3f	f7	cc	34	a5	e5	f1	71	d8	31	15
3	04	c7	23	c3	18	96	05	9a	07	12	80	e2	eb	27	b2	75
4	09	83	2c	1a	1b	6e	5a	a0	52	3b	d6	b3	29	e3	2f	84
5	53	d1	00	ed	20	fc	b1	5b	6a	cb	be	39	4a	4c	58	cf
6	d0	ef	aa	fb	43	4d	33	85	45	f9	02	7f	50	3c	9f	a8
7	51	a3	40	8f	92	9d	38	f5	bc	b6	da	21	10	ff	f3	d2
8	cd	0c	13	ec	5f	97	44	17	c4	a7	7e	3d	64	5d	19	73
9	60	81	4f	dc	22	2a	90	88	46	ee	b8	14	de	5e	0b	db
a	e0	32	3a	0a	49	06	24	5c	c2	d3	ac	62	91	95	e4	79
b	e7	c8	37	6d	8d	d5	4e	a9	6c	56	f4	ea	65	7a	ae	08
c	ba	78	25	2e	1c	a6	b4	c6	e8	dd	74	1f	4b	bd	8b	8a
d	70	3e	b5	66	48	03	f6	0e	61	35	57	b9	86	c1	1d	9e
e	e1	f8	98	11	69	d9	8e	94	9b	1e	87	e9	ce	55	28	df
f	8c	a1	89	0d	bf	e6	42	68	41	99	2d	0f	b0	54	bb	16

Figure 7.30: Rijndael Sbox

In this example, the first input term 12 is replaced by the Sbox element in Row 1 Column 2, which is c9. The rest of the outputs are determined in the same manner. This Sbox design was selected for a variety of reasons, some of which are the following: it is invertible, it has no fixed points (that is, there are no cases in which Row i Column j contains the value ij), and it is simple to describe yet has a complicated algebraic structure. (Do you believe that?)

A row-shift operation is applied to the output of the Sbox in which the four rows of the column array are cyclically shifted to the left. The first row is shifted by 0, the second by 1, the third by 2, and the fourth by 3, as shown in Figure 7.31. As is evident from the figure, this has the effect of completely rearranging the columns so that each column contains a byte from each of the previous columns. At this point, the columns are ready for a process that will mix up the bits within the columns.

Column mixing is accomplished by a matrix-multiplication operation. The shifted column array is multiplied by a fixed matrix (given in hex) such as

$$
\begin{vmatrix} c_0 \\ c_1 \\ c_2 \\ c_3 \end{vmatrix} = \begin{vmatrix} 02 & 03 & 01 & 01 \\ 01 & 02 & 03 & 01 \\ 01 & 01 & 01 & 03 \\ 03 & 01 & 01 & 02 \end{vmatrix} \begin{vmatrix} b_0 \\ b_1 \\ b_2 \\ b_3 \end{vmatrix}
$$

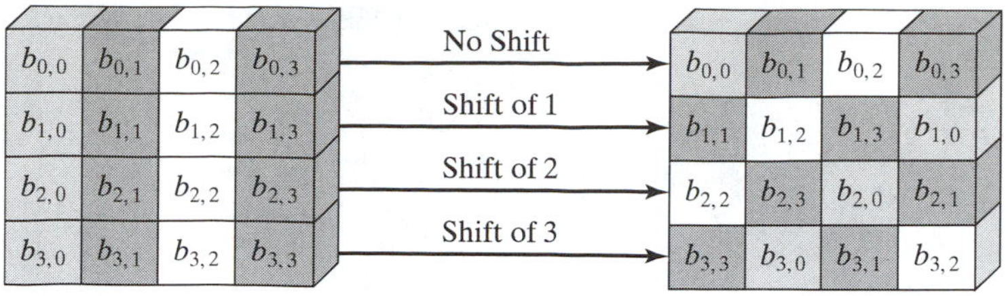

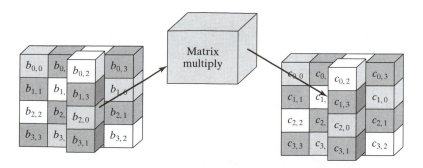

Figure 7.31: Rijndael shift operation

and is illustrated in Figure 7.32. For example, if the first column of the current state of the system contained the bytes 11, 09, 01, and 35 (in Hex), then the multiplication operation would look like this:

$$
\begin{vmatrix} 73 \\ 6b \\ ba \\ a7 \end{vmatrix} = \begin{vmatrix} 02 & 03 & 01 & 01 \\ 01 & 02 & 03 & 01 \\ 01 & 01 & 01 & 03 \\ 03 & 01 & 01 & 02 \end{vmatrix} \begin{vmatrix} 11 \\ 09 \\ 01 \\ 35 \end{vmatrix},
$$

So the new first column would contain the bytes 73, 6b, ba, and a7. This operation guarantees that the original plaintext bit pattern becomes highly diffused over several rounds. It also ensures that there is very little correlation between the inputs and the outputs. Both are important features for the ultimate security of the algorithm. A different matrix is used for the decryption operation.

The final stage of a single iteration XORs a subkey derived from the original key to the current state as shown in Figure 7.33. This completes one iteration of the algorithm. Each stage was selected for both its simplicity and its ability to create a diffused output—in combination, they do an astounding job.

It might be helpful now to trace through one iteration of AES to observe the impact of all these operations. Say Alice wants to send Bob this short message: "Bob look at this". Counting the three spaces, this message is exactly 16 characters (or 128 bits in ASCII) long. Rather than look at this at the bit level (you don't want to have to read 128 bits and I don't want to write them), follow the actions of AES at the byte level in Hex. In this case, the message is presented to AES as

42   6f   62   20   6c   6f   6f   6b   20   61   74   20   74   68   69   73.

Figure 7.32: Rijndael MixColumn operation

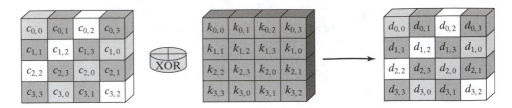

Figure 7.33: Rijndael KeyAdd operation

This is written as a 4×4 array:

$$
\begin{array}{cccc}
42 & 6c & 20 & 74 \\
6f & 6f & 61 & 68 \\
62 & 6f & 74 & 69 \\
20 & 6b & 20 & 73 \\
\end{array}
$$

The array serves as input to the Sbox. The first input is 42, which addresses Row 4 Column 2 of the Sbox. The content of that cell is 2c. Looking up each element in the Sbox produces an output array:

$$
\begin{array}{cccc}
2c & 50 & b7 & 92 \\
a8 & a8 & ef & 45 \\
aa & a8 & 92 & f9 \\
b7 & 7f & b7 & 8f \\
\end{array}
$$

This substitution provides the first layer of confusion within AES. This is followed by the next stage, which will rotate the rows:

$$
\begin{array}{cccc}
2c & 50 & b7 & 92 \\
a8 & ef & 45 & a8 \\
92 & f9 & aa & a8 \\
8f & b7 & 7f & b7 \\
\end{array}
$$

This operation provides the first layer of diffusion within AES by mixing up the order of the rows. This is followed by the multiplication stage, which mixes up and transforms the columns. In this example, the first column is transformed by the relation:

$$
\begin{vmatrix} 72 \\ d1 \\ ad \\ 66 \end{vmatrix} = \begin{vmatrix} 02 & 03 & 01 \\ 01 & 02 & 03 \\ 01 & 01 & 01 \\ 03 & 01 & 01 \end{vmatrix} \begin{vmatrix} 2c \\ a8 \\ 92 \\ 8f \end{vmatrix}.
$$

Multiplying each column produces

$$
\begin{array}{cccc}
72 & 19 & 66 & 4b \\
d1 & d1 & be & 91 \\
ad & d0 & d0 & 07 \\
66 & 46 & 23 & 74 \\
\end{array}
$$

The subkey is used at this point. For our example, let the subkey (in Hex) be

$$
\begin{array}{cccc}
01 & a3 & 90 & 12 \\
e1 & 44 & 20 & 11 \\
cc & 73 & 04 & a9 \\
59 & 06 & 30 & b4 \\
\end{array}
$$

Now XOR the subkey with the current state to produce

$$
\begin{array}{cccc}
72 & 19 & 66 & 4b \\
d1 & d1 & be & 91 \\
ad & d0 & d0 & 07 \\
66 & 46 & 23 & 74 \\
\end{array}
\quad \text{XOR} \quad
\begin{array}{cccc}
01 & a3 & 90 & 12 \\
e1 & 44 & 20 & 11 \\
cc & 73 & 04 & a9 \\
59 & 06 & 30 & b4 \\
\end{array}
\quad = \quad
\begin{array}{cccc}
73 & bA & f3 & 59 \\
30 & 95 & 9e & 80 \\
61 & a0 & d4 & a6 \\
3f & 40 & 13 & c0 \\
\end{array}
$$

A quick comparison of the initial input and the first-round output reveals

42 6f 62 20 6c 6f 6f 6b 20 61 74 20 74 68 69 73
73 30 61 3f ba 95 a0 40 f3 9e d4 13 59 80 a6 c0.

At the bit level, there are 76 bit changes out of 128, and this is just one round—there are 10 more to go.

7.5.2 Key Schedule

The key is grouped into a column array and then expanded by adding 40 new columns. If the first four columns (given by the key) are $W(0)$, $W(1)$, $W(2)$ and $W(3)$, then the new columns are generated in a recursive manner.

If i is not a multiple of 4, then column i is determined by

$$ W(i) = W(i - 4) \text{ XOR } W(i - 1). $$

If i is a multiple of 4, then column i is determined by

$$ W(i) = W(i - 4) \text{ XOR } T[W(i - 1)], $$

where $T[W(i - 1)]$ is a transformation of $W(i - 1)$ and implemented as follows:

1. Cyclically shift the elements of $W(i - 1)$ by one byte—that is, abcd goes to bcda.
2. Use each of these four bytes as input into the Sbox to create four new bytes efgh.
3. Calculate a round constant $r(i) = 2^{(i-4)/4}$.
4. Create the transformed column as follows: $[e \text{ XOR } r(i), f, g, h]$.

The round key for the ith round consists of the columns $W(4i)$, $W(4i + 1)$, $W(4i + 2)$, $W(4i + 3)$.

This process is illustrated in Figure 7.34. For example, if the initial 128-bit key is (in Hex)

3ca10b21 57f01916 902e1380 acc107bd,

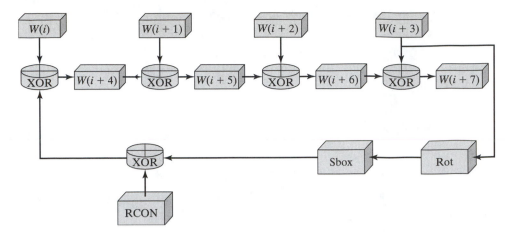

Figure 7.34: Rijndael key generation

then the four initial values are $W(0) = 3ca10b21$; $W(1) = 57f01916$; $W(2) = 902e1380$; and $W(3) = acc107bd$. The index of the next subkey segment, $W(4)$, is a multiple of 4, so

$$W(4) = W(0) \text{ XOR } T[W(3)].$$

The process of calculating $T[W(3)]$ uses the four steps previously outlined:

1. Cyclically shift $W(3)$: $acc107bd \rightarrow c107bdac$.
2. Transform $c107bdac$ using the Sbox: $c1\ 07\ bd\ ac \rightarrow 78\ 85\ 7a\ 91$.
3. Find the round constant $r(4) = 2^0 = 01$ (in Hex).
4. XOR $r(4)$ with the first byte 78: $78 \text{ XOR } 01 = 79$.

So, $T[W(3)] = 79857a91$ and

$$W(4) = 3ca10b21 \text{ XOR } 79857a91 = 452471b0.$$

The remaining three subkey segments are given by

$$W(5) = W(1) \text{ XOR } W(4) = 57f01915 \text{ XOR } 452472b0 = 12d468a5$$
$$W(6) = W(2) \text{ XOR } W(5) = 902e1380 \text{ XOR } 12d468a5 = 82fa7b25$$
$$W(7) = W(3) \text{ XOR } W(6) = acc107bd \text{ XOR } 82fa7b25 = 2e3b7c98$$

The first round key is $452471b012d468a582fa7b252e3b7c98$.

7.5.3   AES Operation

AES (Rijndael) is intended to replace DES in all applications that currently use DES. It should be secure enough to also replace triple-DES applications as well. Like DES, AES can be used in any of the five block-cipher modes: CBC, ECB, OFB, CTR, and OCB. (Don't you love all these acronyms?) In addition, AES has been suggested for use in a new block cipher as stream-cipher mode called the integer counter mode (ICM). The ICM mode is illustrated in Figure 7.35. It uses AES (or some other block cipher) to encipher a

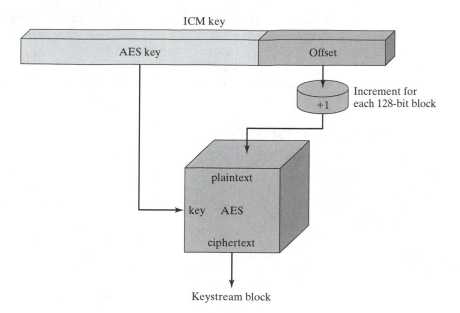

Figure 7.35: AES in the integer count mode

128-bit initial value to create a 128-bit stream. The initial value is then incremented and another 128-bit stream is produced. This process continues until enough bits have been generated.

As Rijndael is particularly small, fast, and believably secure with its 128-bit key size, it is likely to be used not only in applications for which security comparable to triple-DES is desired, but also when limited computational resources are available. That is, it appears to have a tremendous potential for use in the handheld- and wireless-computing markets.

7.5.4 AES Security

During the AES selection process, all the proposed algorithms were subjected to cryptanalysis. In the relatively short time available to the participants, no one was able to come up with a technique to break Rijndael (or the other finalists for that matter). Hence, Rijndael appeared to be secure. Since the adoption of AES, cryptanalysts continue to probe the algorithm searching for weaknesses. They have had varying degrees of success.

It appears that AES is secure against both differential and linear cryptanalysis. This should come as no surprise, since Rijndael was designed with these attacks in mind. However, other attacks have emerged that have been successful against reduced rounds of AES. These are variations on the concept of differential and linear cryptanalysis. The impossible differentials (ID) attack has been used to break a six round version of AES-128. Square attacks have been successful against seven rounds of both AES-128 and AES-192. Collision attacks have also worked on seven round versions of AES-128 and AES-192. All these attacks have failed when applied to the full 10 rounds of AES-128, but they do suggest that there may be an exploitable weakness yet to be found.

In January 2003, a paper was published on the Internet that may have disclosed one of those future exploitable weaknesses. It claimed to have discovered a bias in the AES output bits that could be exploited by what is called a plaintext-dependent repetition-code attack. As should be expected, the paper caused quite an uproar in the cryptographic community. It was not long before a response appeared which claimed that the attack on AES was not valid and that no bias could be found in the AES output bits. While it appears that there were some fundamental errors in the initial paper, the whole process does illustrate the ongoing effort to discover and validate any weaknesses in AES.

7.5.5   Hardware Implementation

Contemporary block ciphers such as DES and AES may be implemented in either hardware or software. While software implementations may be more flexible, more and more applications are emerging that require hardware implementations. In fact, the AES candidates were evaluated in terms of the efficiency of their implementation in both hardware and software.

There are two major reasons why cipher algorithms are being implemented in hardware. The first is that software implementations are too slow for many applications. This is especially true as block ciphers become more complicated. Current software encryption rates hover at less than 100 MBit/sec for block ciphers and are even slower for public key algorithms (as will be demonstrated in the next chapter). The second reason is that hardware implementations are more secure. The algorithm (and perhaps the key) is fixed in hardware, which is much more difficult to modify than software.

Another consideration is that the speed advantage offered by a hardware implementation may expose a weakness in the cipher that was not evident or exploitable given a slower software implementation. For example, DES was shown to be unreliable through the design of a computer based on DES hardware chips. It is important to construct hardware implementations to allow for the continuous monitoring of the overall security of a block cipher.

There are two ways in which AES (and other block ciphers for that matter) is typically imbedded in hardware. One is called an ASIC implementation and the other is an FPGA implementation. ASIC stands for application specific integrated circuit and is the method used to create a fixed implementation on silicon. The algorithm is transformed into a hardware design and fabricated on a chip. FPGA stands for field programmable gate array and is the more flexible of the two methods. An FPGA consists of an array of pre-designed and programmable logic elements connected by programmable wires.

For high speed, the custom-designed ASIC approach is recommended. In this case, the algorithm is translated into hardware and placed on a silicon chip. One such chip was designed and constructed by Verbauwhede, Schaumont, and Kuo in 2003. The overall chip architecture is shown in Figure 7.36.

The input and output are supplied in 16-bit chunks. This is because the ASIC chip does not have enough pins for the AES-256, which would require 256 input pins and 256 output pins. As a result, the input unit is designed to save the input until it reaches 128, 196, or 256 bits. The key-schedule unit performs all the calculations required for the determination of the subkeys in hardware. The encryption unit will implement a single round of AES in one clock cycle. In order to accomplish this, it must operate on the data in parallel. This includes the substitution step, which means that the hardware contains 32 Sboxes.

A block diagram of the encrypt segment of the hardware for AES-128 is shown in Figure 7.37. Notice that there is a separate Sbox for each 16-bit input and that the shift operation is performed by the wiring pattern. There are four matrix-multiplication units that, along with the 16 Sboxes, provide the parallel computational ability of the chip. This specific chip

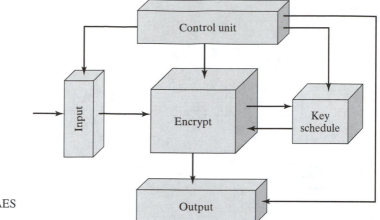

Figure 7.36: Possible AES hardware structure

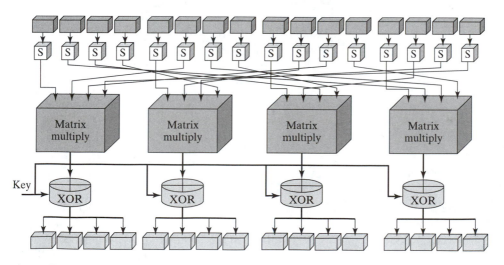

Figure 7.37: AES encrypt hardware

consists of 173,000 logic gates, runs at 125 MHz, and offers a throughput of 2.29 GBits/sec. It is not the only ASIC implementation of AES. Several have been reported in the literature, but few are now available commercially.

As already noted, an alternative to an ASIC implementation is a field programmable gate array implementation. An FPGA is predesigned with a collection of logic devices interconnected in an array like the structure shown in Figure 7.38. The logic blocks consist of a sophisticated set of circuit components with the ability to implement a wide range of Boolean functions. They also have some memory capability. These blocks are "programmable" in the sense that internal connections can be set or cleared that define the specific logic structure of the block. The wires between the blocks allow signals to be sent along programmable links. That is, the inputs or outputs of the blocks can be programmed to connect to a specific wire or to bypass a specific wire. The wire paths can be directed from the vertical to the horizontal by the switch matrix.

Programmable connections

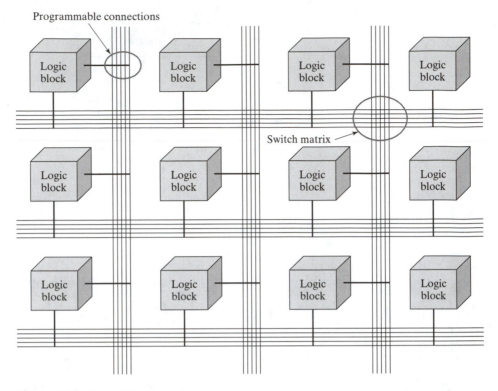

Figure 7.38: Typical FPGA structure

This is a short explanation of a very complicated device, but it could be looked at as a system in which a flexible hardware structure is "programmed" to implement a specific function rather than using a fixed hardware structure to run a set of program instructions. There are a wide range of FPGA "families" and technologies that are supplied by several different manufacturers. Commercial FPGAs with gate counts in excess of two million are available.

As part of the AES evaluation, researchers at several universities designed FPGA implementations of Rijndael. The designs ranged in speed from 294 MBits/sec to 414 MBits/sec. A typical FPGA implementation is faster than a software implementation, but is slower than a custom ASIC chip. However, FPGAs are easier to design and are less expensive than ASIC.

7.5.6 Other Finalists

Rijndael was selected as the new AES for a combination of reasons. It was not necessarily the most secure, the fastest, or the smallest, but it was the decision of NIST that Rijndael was the best choice overall. None of the finalists could be classified as "losers." They all offered interesting ideas and worthwhile alternatives to DES. Since they were examined in great detail during the competition, their strengths and weaknesses are well documented. It is clear that the other finalists will continue to be used. Hence, it is worthwhile to briefly explore a few of the features of some of the other AES candidates.

7.5.6.1 RC6

RC6 was one of the AES finalists submitted by Rivest, Robshaw, Sidney, and Yin. It was probably the simplest of the AES algorithms operating on plaintext blocks consisting of 128 bits, using a key size of 128, 192, or 256 bits and 20 rounds of encryption.

RC6 requires 44 round keys that are generated from the initial 128 bits using a complex series of operations. The initial key is divided into four words and placed in the array $L(0\ldots3)$. The 44 subkeys are initialized in the array $S(0\ldots43)$ using two natural constants—e (the base of natural logarithms) and ϕ (the golden ratio). The procedure is as follows:

$$S[0] = \text{b7e15163 (Hex value)}.$$

For $i = 1$ to 43, do
$$S[i]: = S[i - 1] \times \text{9e3779B9 (Hex)}$$
$$A = B = i = j = 0.$$
For $k = 1$ to 132, do
$$A = S(i) = [S(i) + A + B] <<< 3$$
$$B = L(j) = [L(j) + A + B] <<< (A + B)$$
$$i = (i + 1) \bmod 44$$
$$j = (j + 1) \bmod 4.$$

Once the subkey array S is available, the actual encryption begins by dividing up the 128 plaintext bits into four 32-bit blocks labeled A, B, C, and D. Blocks B and D are modified by

$$B = B + S(0)$$

and

$$D = D + S[1].$$

This is followed by 20 rounds of encryption that involve XOR, multiplication, shifts, and additions. The ith round is shown in Figure 7.39. The Fbox performs a multiplication and an addition operation defined by

$$t = [B \times (2B + 1)]$$

and

$$u = [D \times (2D + 1)].$$

After 20 rounds, Blocks A and C are modified in the final step by

$$A = A + S(42)$$

and

$$C = C + S(43).$$

The process of using some of the key material at the beginning and the end of the cipher is called *whitening*. It has been shown to increase the difficulty of key-search attacks in part because it hides the actual inputs and outputs to the multiround network.

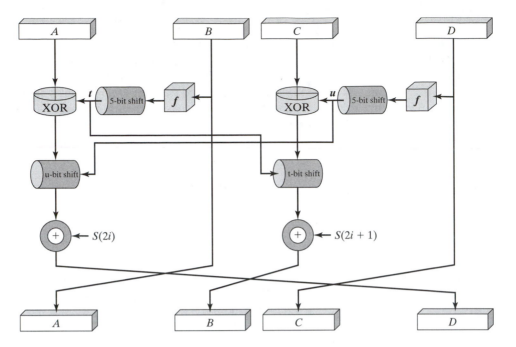

Figure 7.39: An RC6 encryption round

7.5.6.2 Twofish

Twofish, submitted by Schneier, et al., is another AES finalist that has some of the features of both RC6 and Rijndael. It operates on 128-bit blocks using a variable-length key of up to 256 bits. It runs the plaintext through 16 rounds of a Feistel network, applying some unique operations such as key-dependent Sboxes and a matrix-multiplication operation.

Twofish uses a very complex key-schedule algorithm to create 40 subkeys (K_0 to K_{39}).

The subkeys are used both in the Fboxes of the Feistel rounds and to create key dependent Sboxes. This dynamic nature of the Sboxes offers the advantage that attackers cannot analyze them in advance.

Like RC6, Twofish begins and ends with a whitening process. The plaintext is divided into four 32-bit blocks and each block is XORed with a subkey. [Block A is Xored with $K(0)$, Block B with $K(1)$, Block C with $K(2)$, and Block D with $K(3)$.] After the final round, each block is XORed with $K(4)$ to $K(7)$. Each of the 16 rounds make use of an XOR operation, a single bit shift, a special function, f, and a mixing schedule. A single round is shown in Figure 7.40.

The f function consists of a set of Sboxes, a matrix-multiplication operation, and addition with subkeys as shown in Figure 7.41. Each Sbox accepts 8 bits of input and produces 8 bits of output. The outputs are multiplied by a 4 × 4 MDS matrix.

7.5.6.3 Evaluation and Performance

By the time the five AES finalists were announced, all the algorithms had undergone extensive public testing. The finalists all appeared to provide a high level of security, but this was not the only criterion for the selection of a winner. The speed of encryption and the nature of a hardware implementation were also important issues. If an algorithm is too slow

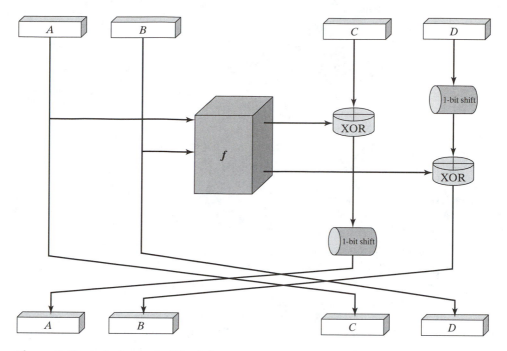

Figure 7.40: A single round of Twofish

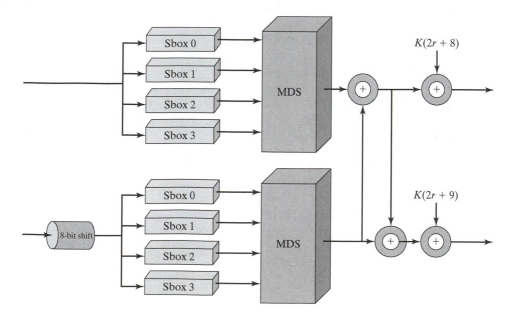

Figure 7.41: A Twofish Fbox

in its encryption process, it will not be accepted by users even if it provides the highest level of security.

In terms of speed, NIST set up a minimum test configuration for all the candidates that called for an evaluation of their performance on a 200-MHz Pentium Pro system

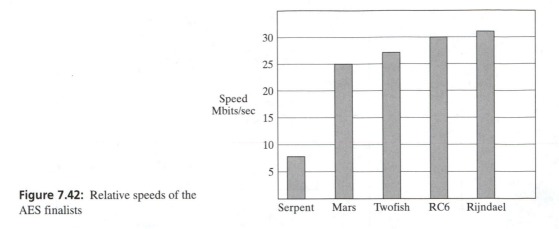

Figure 7.42: Relative speeds of the AES finalists

with 64 MB of RAM running Windows 95. The algorithm was required to be written in Borland C++ 5.0. One set of speed results for the five finalists is shown in Figure 7.42. Rijndael and RC6 are almost tied for first in this test. Overall, software implementations of the finalists were tested across six different Intel systems, three Alpha systems, an HP system, and a Sun Sparc system. Rijndael ranked first on five of the tests, Twofish ranked first on two tests, and RC6 came in first on the remaining four. Clearly, implementation and architecture play significant roles in the ultimate speed of a cipher.

Speed is not only an issue for the encipher–decipher run—it is also an issue for the key setup. It is evident that these block ciphers use sophisticated methods to generate a set of subkeys from the initial key. The result of one test for the AES finalists is shown in Figure 7.43. The results are not surprising: RC6 has the simplest key-setup algorithm and Twofish has the most complicated.

Since AES will be implemented in both software and hardware, other evaluation issues were the size and the performance of a hardware implementation. Several groups designed chips and others placed the algorithm on FPGAs (field programmable gate arrays). One feature that was considered was the area requirement on the chip or the FPGA. A graph of the size results found by the George Mason University team that implemented each algorithm on a Virtex FPGA is shown in Figure 7.44. Surprisingly, Twofish was as small as the much simpler RC6.

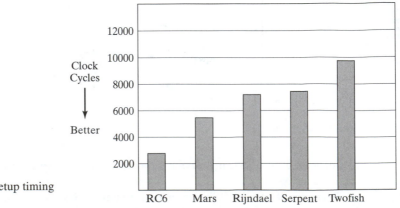

Figure 7.43: Key-setup timing for AES finalists

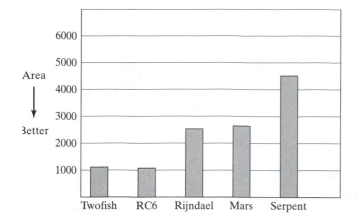

Figure 7.44: FPGA area requirements for AES finalists

7.6   USING BLOCK CIPHERS

Up to this point, the assumption has been that we are all like Bob and Alice—that is, if we want to have secure communications, we select a common cipher and key and then use those to protect our messages. There is nothing wrong with this process, and it is sometimes the way in which things are done. However, most computer users have no idea how to select a cipher or create a key, yet everyone needs to have some degree of privacy in their on-line communications. The way to protect those who might be naïve or who do not have the time or ability to select their own algorithm and key is to automate the process. This way, everyone using a specific network is protected in a transparent, but effective, manner.

One way in which a cipher is used has already been covered in Chapter 6. Remember that the WEP protocol uses the RC4 stream cipher. That may be fine for wireless connections, but what about wired networks? It turns out that there are several procedures for automatically protecting network communications, one of which is called IPSec. The goal of IPSec is to proscribe a method that provides secure communications over the Internet. IPSec is a fairly detailed process, but it will be simplified in this presentation in order to focus on the use of encryption. In Chapter 9, some of the authentication processes in IPSec will be covered. But for the complete story, consult a network-security text.

7.6.1   A Quick Overview of Network Connections

The Internet consists of millions of computers and other devices interconnected in an almost haphazard manner. For example, Figure 7.45 illustrates the use of routers, servers, company networks, and home systems. If these varied systems are to all work together, every system must follow a common protocol: Every system must understand the format of messages, the order in which messages are sent and received, and the actions taken when a message is transmitted or received (among other things).

There are several ways in which this goal is accomplished, but a complete discussion would require looking at the layered structure of a network link that would take us off our primary task—understanding how block ciphers are used. Instead, consider one transmission protocol, called TCP (transmission control protocol).

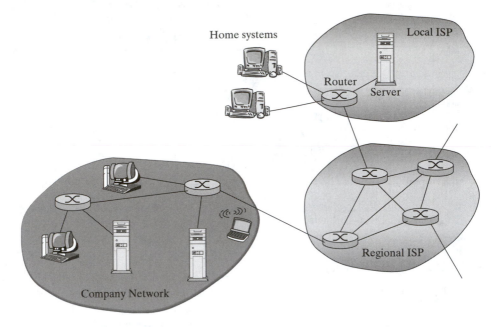

Figure 7.45: A very small version of the Internet

Messages are sent on the Internet in *packets*. A packet is collection of bytes that contains the message in addition to addressing and control information. Before a set of packets can be sent between two machines, however, a connection between them must be established. This is done by TCP. When a host wants to make a connection, TCP sends out a specific packet (called a *request message*) to the destination machine. The structure of such a packet is shown in Figure 7.46.

The TCP header contains a port number, which is a value associated with the application. For example, a file transfer application (FTP) uses Port 21. When the destination host receives the connection request, it returns a message containing its own unique socket and port numbers, thus identifying a virtual connection between the two hosts. Keep in mind that this is a simplified description of a complicated process.

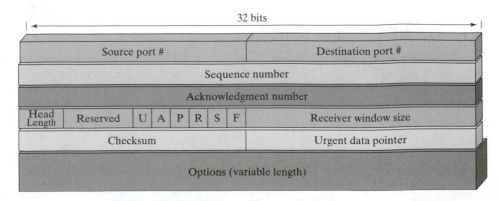

Figure 7.46: A TCP packet header

7.6.2   IPSec Connections

If the connection is to be secure, it may adopt the IPSec protocol, which will add additional header information to the data packet. The purpose of the additional information is to establish a *security association* (SA) between the two machines. An SA is a record of all the information required to support a secure connection. It includes authentication and encryption keys, specific ciphers, IP addresses, and so on. In addition to the SA, IPSec utilizes two basic security protocols. This means that it actually adds two additional headers to the data packet. The first is the authentication header (AH), which uses a hash function to validate the authenticity of the data packet (more on hash functions in Chapter 9). The second is the encapsulating security payload (ESP), which uses encryption to maintain the integrity of the data packet. The ESP uses the agreed-upon block cipher (triple-DES, AES, IDEA, ...) to encrypt the data packet before transmission and to decrypt it upon receipt. Hence (and here is where block ciphers finally come into the picture), IPSec sets up an SA that uses ESP to secure a data packet with AES. (How is that for using acronyms?) The header information added to a simple message data packet by this protocol is shown in Figure 7.47.

In the figure, there are several other headers added to the data packet as well. The app header contains information about the fundamental application associated with the data. The IP header contains information about both the source and the destination Internet address, the total message length, and so on. The AH header contains authentication information. (Remember this will be covered in Chapter 9.) The ESP header contains information about the encryption algorithm and any parameters that are necessary for its operation. The ESP tail contains padding so that the encrypted segment size matches the required block size of the selected cipher. Notice that everything except the IP and ESP headers is encrypted. It would not make sense to encrypt the IP header because none of the routers on the path between the two machines would be able to read the destination address.

The most important aspect of all this is that it is done without the intervention of the user. When Bob and Alice log on to the Internet and elect to use IPSec, the choice of algorithm and key is made by the system. The question is: How is this done? For the answer, you will have to wait until Chapter 9. For now, realize that the process of protecting information has gone beyond the simple choice of a cipher and a key. There is a lot more involved when these processes become automated.

7.7   BLOCK CIPHERS' SHORT HISTORY

Considering the historical scope of cryptography, block ciphers have been around for only a short time. Stories about their use equivalent to the incident involving Mary, Queen of

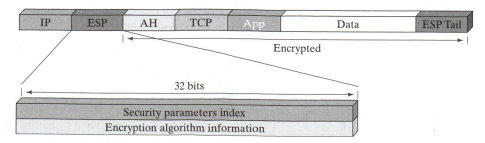

Figure 7.47: An encrypted data packet in IPSec

Scots, have yet to be written. However, in their short history, block ciphers have raised some interesting and perplexing moral and ethical dilemmas. One of the most difficult surrounds the story of the Clipper chip.

The problem began long before it was forced into the public eye by AT&T in 1992. (Notice the role AT&T has played in the history of cryptography?) That was when AT&T announced the 3600 Telephone Security Device (TSD)—a commercial DES-encrypted phone add-on. The government (especially the FBI and the National Security Agency, NSA) has expressed opposition to the TSD. Since legal phone taps are a vital source of intelligence in the fight against crime and terrorism, the government fears that the TSD will severally hamper its ability to do its job. NSA's first step was to convince AT&T to use a new hardware encryption chip called the Clipper chip in return for a guarantee of government purchases. Then NSA bought out the entire TSD production run and paid AT&T to retrofit them with Clipper. That was just a stopgap measure. The overall approach was announced by the White House on April 15, 1993.

It turns out that the U.S. government had been considering the possibility of something like AT&T's TSD for quite some time. To prepare for the eventuality, NSA developed a secret encryption algorithm called Skipjack and embedded it in the Clipper chip. Skipjack was classified until 1998. It is a DES-like block cipher operating on 64-bit blocks using an 80-bit key. It has 32 rounds of encryption. Since it was initially secret, there was a lot of concern in the cryptological community that there was a backdoor known only to NSA. Since its release, no backdoor has been found, but a number of weaknesses have been exposed. The real interest in Skipjack, however, is not the algorithm itself, but the proposed key-management process.

The U.S. government wanted two things to happen: (1) Communication vendors would voluntarily adopt the Clipper chip and (2) Clipper-chip keys would be stored in a key-escrow system. If these were accomplished, then the government could ensure that wiretapping would remain a viable intelligence-gathering tool. In order to ensure that communication vendors adopted the Clipper chip, all communications equipment purchased by the government would be required to contain it. The hope was that the market forces created by such a large customer would encourage the use of the Clipper chip. Adoption of the key-escrow system—which is at the core of the Clipper-chip process—was more problematic.

Each Clipper chip contained a unique identification number (UID), an 80-bit family key (KF) common to all Clipper chips, and an 80-bit unique chip key (KU). It also generated (and here is where the controversy arose) a law enforcement access field (LEAF) that was transmitted with each session. The LEAF contains all the information needed to recover the session key. The process of setting up the LEAF involves the following steps:

1. Encrypting the session key, KS, with the chip key, KU.
2. Creating a master key consisting of the UID $\|\{KS\}_{KU}\|$, hash encrypted with the family key KF, where the hash is a 16-bit authenticator.

Knowledge of KU and KF would allow for the recovery of the session key, KS. This is where the key-escrow system comes into play. For each Clipper chip, the manufacturer assigns the UID and the KU. The KU is decomposed into two parts, KU_1 and KU_2, such that $KU = KU_1$ XOR KU_2. The two parts are enciphered with the family key, KF, and are distributed to two different agencies. If law enforcement officials want to tap into a specific communication, they must get a court order and take it to both agencies. With the escrowed keys, they can reconstruct KU. Since KF is known, they can unlock the LEAF and the KS.

This section began hinting at a moral and ethical dilemma—that is, should the government have access to encrypted communications in order to effectively fight crime and terrorism or should citizens have a right to unrestricted use of powerful encryption? This is a tough problem. On the pro-Clipper-chip side, some argue that the police do not gain any new powers, since a warrant is still required. Hence, key escrow is a reasonable compromise between individual rights and the role of government to protect its citizens. On the other side, there is a great concern over the potential loss of privacy. Industry is concerned about the loss of access to strong cryptography. Restriction to Clipper technology could potentially weaken the ability to sell products in the international market place.

In the end, polls indicated that 80 percent of Americans opposed the Clipper chip. AT&T closed down its production line, and Congress failed to pass the most stringent of the proposed regulations. At present, the debate continues.

7.8   SUMMARY

Block ciphers are certainly more complicated than any of the classical ciphers we have seen so far. They are even more complicated than a contemporary version of a stream cipher. Not only are the ciphers themselves more complicated, but also the formal procedure for implementing a block cipher—the cipher mode—may also add complications. Bob and Alice were certainly impressed by the extent of bit manipulation involved in these ciphers. However, they needed to remember the lesson they learned from classical ciphers—complexity does not guarantee security. After all, they were impressed by many of the classical ciphers they chose to use only to have them all fall to the efforts of Eve. In this case, they made some poor choices in the name of simplicity, and Eve was able to exploit those choices and continue to read their messages. However, proper use of this class of ciphers could provide the level of security Bob and Alice had been looking for all along. The failures of Bob and Alice emphasize the necessity of not only selecting a powerful cipher, but also using it correctly.

Once again, Eve has learned the importance of known-plaintext–ciphertext attacks. Contemporary block ciphers are too strong to use brute-force attacks (if they are used correctly), and ciphertext-only attacks are no longer as feasible as they were against classical ciphers.

Overall, Bob, Alice, and Eve all learned that the strength of a cipher depends on a variety of factors, most of which are subjective. Among those factors are the following:

- The plaintext cannot be derived from the ciphertext without use of the key.
- There should be no plaintext attack that is better than a brute-force attack.
- Knowledge of the algorithm should not reduce the strength of the cipher.
- The algorithm should include substitutions and permutations under the control of both the input data and the key.
- Redundant bit groups in the plaintext should be totally obscured in the ciphertext.
- The length of the ciphertext should be the same as the length of the plaintext.
- Any possible key should produce a strong cipher.

Finally, both a new category and a new set of ciphers can be added to our overall cipher structure as shown in Figure 7.48.

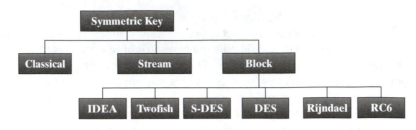

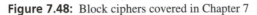

Figure 7.48: Block ciphers covered in Chapter 7

7.9   IMPORTANT TERMS

AES	Advanced encryption standard—after a long review and evaluation processes, Rijndael was selected
ASIC	Application specific integrated circuit
CBC	Cipher block chain—uses a block cipher much like an autokey cipher
CTR	Counter mode—uses a block cipher to generate a stream-cipher-like key
DES	Data encryption standard
Differential cryptanalysis	A chosen-plaintext attack on block ciphers
ECB	Electronic codebook—enciphers each block with the same key
FPGA	Field programmable gate array
ICM	Integer counter mode—uses a block cipher as a stream cipher
IV	Initial vector—used in some of the block-cipher modes to increase security
Linear cryptanalysis	A known-plaintext attack on block ciphers
Meet-in-the-middle attack	An attack on double-DES that encrypts in the forward direction and decrypts backward
OCB	Offset-codebook mode adds authentication to a basic block-cipher mode
OFM	Output-feedback mode uses a block cipher to generate the key for a stream cipher
Padding	Adding extra characters to the end of plaintext to match the final block size
Product ciphers	A cipher that uses more than one method, such as both substitution and permutation
Sbox	Substitution box used in block ciphers as a nonlinear transformation
TCP	Transmission control protocol

RESOURCES

In addition to the resources cited in the previous chapters, see also the following:
Advanced Encryption Standard Development http://csrc.nist.gov/encryption/aes/aes_home.htm

Biham, E. and A. Shamir, *Differential Cryptanalysis of the Data Encryption Standard* (Springer-Verlag, 1993).

Fergus, N. and Schneier, B. *Practical Cryptography* (Wiley Publishing, 2003)

The Block Cipher Lounge http://www.ii.uib.no/~larsr/bc.html

Verbauwhede, I., Schaumont, P. and Kuo, H. "Design and Performance Testing of a 2.29-GB/s Rijndael Processor," *IEEE JSOC*, vol. 38, March 2003.

PROBLEMS

1. What are the subkeys for a DES key of all 1's? all 0's? half and half?

2. S-DES has several weak keys. Find at least one (other than 0).

3. Break the following S-DES message:

   ```
   111000110011010111100000110001
   010010111000101010001111001011
   000011100000110100010010101011
   010001110110110010111011010001
   001010101101000100111100000001
   010000001000000010001010101110
   000011010001001010101110000000
   111110001111000010111001011110
   001011101101000100111100111000
   000011111001000000001010100110
   011111101011011001111
   ```

4. Bob and Alice tried double S-DES thinking that it would be twice as hard for Eve to break as single S-DES. Break their message:

   ```
   101001001000110110010011111101
   000000010110111110010001111
   100001011101000011010101001011
   010111000110100001010001111
   100011011011111011010000000011
   111110000101110100001000010111
   000101101100011010001011011011
   111000010001101101011100011011110
   11010000100100011111111010001
   1111001001110110101
   ```

5. Bob and Alice want to evaluate the S-DES cipher. They begin by determining the response of the cipher to a single bit change in the key. They found the average number of ciphertext bit differences generated by applying the following keys against each lowercase character: 28, 76, 84, 88, 92, 93, 94, and 124. That is, they ran a test in which the plaintext was the character "a" and tried each of the eight keys. Then they ran it again using "b" as the plaintext, and so on.

   (a) What did they find was the average bit change in the ciphertext?

   (b) Why did they select those eight keys?

   (c) What did they conclude about the performance of S-DES?

6. Bob and Alice decided to try a similar process to evaluate DES. First they wanted to test the strict key avalanche condition using the plaintext "This is a test" and tried the following keys: abcdefgh, qbcdefgh, and arcdefgh. What did they discover, and what did they conclude?

7. Finally, Bob and Alice tested the strict plaintext avalanche condition. They used the key "abcdefgh" and ran it on the following plaintext samples: "This", "Dhis", and "Txis". What did they discover, and what did they conclude?

8. Find the difference distribution table for DES Sbox 1.

9. Bob and Alice decided to test the randomness of the S-DES output. They entered the following plaintext:

   This is a test of s-des randomness. The ciphertext should appear to be a random set of binary bits if the cipher is to be trusted.

   They ran S-DES using the key "1011" and then applied the CAP tests to the ciphertext. What did they discover, and what did they conclude?

10. Bob and Alice repeated the randomness test on DES with the same plaintext. They used the key "retestit". What did they discover, and what did they conclude?

11. CAP allows you to implement S-DES in the output-feedback mode: in other words, as a keystream generator. Generate 1000 bits using the key "1103" and initial input "z". Run the randomness tests and report your conclusions.

12. Repeat Problem 11 using DES in the output-feedback mode (also available in CAP), using the DES key "abcdefgh" and initial data "abcdefgh".

13. Compare the impact of a single bit error in the ciphertext using ECB with that of using CBC.

14. For DES Sbox 2 with input 100100, determine the number of output bits that differ as each input bit changes—that is, how many of the output bits are different between 100100 and 000100 ...?

15. On a single graph, map the column number vs the Sbox value for each the four rows of Sbox 2. Comment on what you observe.

16. What is the first-stage output of AES if the input is "Alice just do it" using a first-stage key of 01 01 01 01 20 20 20 20 03 03 03 03 60 60 60 60?

17. Given an AES key of 30014fd1 69e31044 1782e4b1 23aa4018, what is the first-round key?

18. Break AES. Share the praise and acclaim with your instructor and the author.

Chapter 8

Public Key Ciphers

8.0   INTRODUCTION

One major problem with all the ciphers both classical and contemporary that have been covered so far involves the nature of key. They all have a single key that is used for both enciphering and deciphering. This may seem like a very useful and convenient feature, but the problem is that everyone who has legitimate access to the plaintext must have the key. Distribution of the key becomes a weak point in the cipher because all it takes is one careless user to expose the key and, in turn, all the ciphertext. This problem is addressed in a new form of cipher called a *public key algorithm*. First suggested by Diffie and Hellmann in 1976, these ciphers have two different keys: One is used for encryption and the other is used for decryption. The encryption key can be made public so anyone can use it. Only the decryption key is kept secret. These are also called *asymmetric key ciphers*.

Perhaps this problem can best be visualized by placing Bob in an imaginary world in which all the phones come in pairs with only a single button to maintain privacy. They don't have a standard number pad because each pair of phones connects only to each other. This means that, to talk to Alice, Bob must share a pair of phones with her. If Bob wants to talk to Paul, they have to share a different pair of phones. Eventually, poor Bob will be carrying around a ton of phones. (See Figure 8.1.) Of course, each connection is perfectly secure unless one of the phones is dropped or lost and is then found by Eve. This is exactly what could happen if Bob had to have a different complex key for every message he wanted to send. He would end up with an Alice key, a Paul key, and so on. Ultimately, he would either forget the key or write it down somewhere that Eve might be able to find it. Managing keys becomes a serious and difficult problem, much like having to carry dozens of phones.

Of course, Bob does not have to carry dozens of phones because in our world all he needs is one phone capable of dialing multiple numbers and a phone book that lists all the numbers he might need. Reality for Bob is pictured in Figure 8.2, in which he appears to be very relieved that he needs only a single phone. This is somewhat like the concept of a public key. Encryption keys are stored in a public area so anyone can look up a key when needed. This chapter explores the nature of this new class of ciphers and how they are commonly used.

Figure 8.1: Poor Bob

Figure 8.2: Relieved Bob

8.1   THE PUBLIC KEY PROCESS

Alice and Bob are looking into moving to a public key cipher precisely because of its multiple key structure. What they like about this new system is that they each will posses a secret key and a public key. Bob will give his public key to Alice and Alice will share hers with Bob. They could even publish them in a "phone book" of public keys. Eve can have both public keys and it will not compromise either Bob or Alice. The real advantage of a public key (PK) system is that once the public keys are shared, Alice can send a message to

Bob encrypting it with Bob's public key. Only Bob can decrypt the message because only Bob has the corresponding private key. This process is illustrated in Figure 8.3.

The requirements for a working PK system are as follows:

- It should be easy to generate both the public and the private key.
- It should be easy to encrypt and decrypt.
- It should be hard to find the private key from the public key.
- It should be hard to find the plaintext using the ciphertext and the public key.

The real contribution of the public key concept is that it reduces the number of keys that must be managed over a network of users. Using a symmetric cipher system such as AES, each pair of communication links requires a session key. For example, in a network of five users such as that shown in Figure 8.4, the symmetric cipher would require 10 secret keys overall and each user would have to remember (and keep secret) four keys. In the public key system, however, each user only has to remember their private key and can look up a public key when it is required. An added advantage for a public key system occurs when a new user joins the group. If a sixth user was added to the system shown in Figure 8.4, five new keys would be required (as shown in Figure 8.5). A public key system, on the other hand, would just require the addition of the public key of the new user to the listing of public keys. Another problem that the public key system solves is the establishment of keys. In the symmetric key system, each user has to agree on a common secret key value. If they are not careful, this could be a weak point in their overall cryptographic system. By contrast, in a public key system, each user sets up both their own private and public

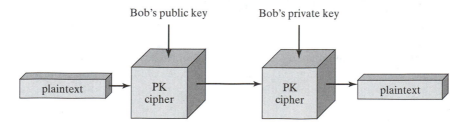

Figure 8.3: Public key process

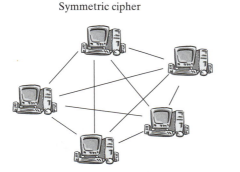

Figure 8.4: Key requirements

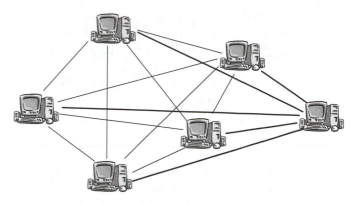

Figure 8.5: Adding a user

key—no communication between users is required. In addition, there are other uses of public key systems, including digital signatures, that will be covered in Chapter 9.

8.2   RSA

There are several methods and algorithms that implement the public key concept. Most are based on finding an intractable problem—that is, a problem which is difficult to solve. Problems such as factoring large numbers or finding the logarithm of a number have served as the basis for a public key cipher system. Always remember, however, that there is no proof that these problems are really intractable. They appear to be so only because years of experience with such problems have failed to produce a simple solution. Should such a solution be found, the cipher algorithms based on the solved problem will no longer be secure or useful.

One of the most common public key ciphers is called RSA (named after its inventors Rivest, Shamir, and Adleman). It is based on the concept of an exponentiation cipher that uses multiplication to generate the ciphertext. The process begins by translating the plaintext characters into numbers. This is done by converting their ASCII binary representation into the equivalent integer. The ciphertext is calculated by raising the plaintext integer to some power, e, and reducing the result, mod n:

$$C = P^e \bmod n.$$

The values e and n are the keys to the cipher. Of course, the process must be reversible if it is to be useful as a cipher. An exponentiation cipher is decoded using another key d such that

$$P = C^d \bmod n.$$

The value of d that works is found by solving

$$ed = 1 \bmod \varphi(n),$$

where $\varphi(n)$ is the Euler phi function. It is formally defined as the number of integers j such that j is less than or equal to n and $\mathrm{GCD}(j, n) = 1$. That is, the number of integers less than n that have no factors in common with n. If n is the product of two different primes p and q (that is, $n = pq$), then $\varphi(n) = (p - 1)(q - 1)$. A useful mathematical relationship involving $\varphi(n)$ is Euler's theorem, which states that if $\mathrm{GCD}(x, n) = 1$, then

$$x^{\varphi(n)} = 1 \bmod n.$$

As will be shown soon, this theorem is the basis for decipher method of RSA.

Rivest, Shamir, and Adleman took this basic idea and turned it into a formal public key cipher by defining a specific method to determine the values for e, n, and d. The value of n is determined by selecting two large prime numbers p and q such that $n = pq$. Since n is part of the public key, it is published. But both p and q must remain secret. Next, select another number, d, between $\min(p, q)$ and $(p - 1)(q - 1)$ that is relatively prime (it does not have any common factors) to $(p - 1)(q - 1)$. Calculate e so that it is the inverse of d when reduced mod $(p - 1)(q - 1)$—that is,

$$ed \bmod (p - 1)(q - 1) = 1.$$

Publish e as the other part of the public key, but keep d secret.

All this effort is just to determine both the public and private keys. The RSA encryption process now works just like an exponentiation cipher. The plaintext is divided into message blocks such that each block can be represented by a large number. The ciphertext block, c, is calculated from the message block m using

$$C = M^e \bmod n.$$

Since both e and n are public keys, anyone can create the ciphertext.

The RSA decryption process uses the private key d and calculates M by

$$M = C^d \bmod n.$$

This works because

$$C^d \bmod n = (M^e)^d \bmod n = M^{ed} \bmod n.$$

Since $ed = 1 \bmod \varphi(n)$, ed is 1 more than a multiple of $\varphi(n)$, so there must be an integer r such that

$$ed = 1 + r\varphi(n).$$

This means that

$$M^{ed} \bmod n = M^{1+r\varphi(n)} \bmod n = M^1 (M^{\varphi(n)})^r \bmod n = M(1)^r \bmod n.$$

Putting the pieces together yields

$$C^d \bmod n = M.$$

Since d is private, only the owner of d can decipher the ciphertext. The process is secure, because, to find d, p and q must be known. The only way to find those numbers is to factor n. If n is very large, factoring it is very difficult (as you will see later).

Bob and Alice want to try the RSA cipher, so they came up with a simple example to make sure they understood how it worked. Bob selected two small prime numbers, 11 and 23. The product of these two primes determines n:

$$n = 11 \times 23 = 253.$$

The private key d is selected so that it has no factors in common with $(p - 1)(q - 1)$ or, in this case, $10 \times 22 = 220$. There are many numbers that work, but Bob selects 19. The remaining part of the public key is e, which is determined by solving

$$19e \bmod 220 = 1.$$

The solution is $e = 139$. Bob only tells Alice the values of e and n: (139, 253). Alice decides to test the operation of this cipher by sending Bob the message "Hi". In ASCII, this message is given by the 16 bits 01001000 01011001. Translating these into two equivalent decimal numbers gives the message 72 105. Alice then uses Bob's public key to transform these two numbers:

$$72^{139} \bmod 253 = 2$$
$$105^{139} \bmod 253 = 101.$$

Bob receives the message (2, 101) and uses his private key to recover the original text:

$$2^{19} \bmod 253 = 72$$
$$101^{19} \bmod 253 = 105$$

Converting these two numbers into binary and translating the result from ASCII to characters gives Bob the actual message "Hi".

Bob and Alice discover that RSA works as advertised; however, they would never actually use such small numbers because Eve could easily discover the private key from the public key. For example, if Eve looked up Bob's public key (139, 253), she could try to factor 253 in order to discover p and q. The simplest method would be to divide 253 by every prime up to 16 (the smallest integer larger than the square root of 253). It would not take her long to discover that 11 divides 253 with a result of 23. Given this knowledge of p and q, she also knows that $(p-1)(q-1) = 220$. Now, since the value of e is known as well (139), all Eve has to do is solve the following equation to find d (the private key):

$$139d = 1 \bmod 220.$$

d is then easily exposed as 19. All this means is that if Bob and Alice are really going to use RSA, they must select two very large prime numbers so that n is nearly impossible to factor.

For example, Bob might select

$p = 3490529510847650949147849619903898133417764638493387843990820577$

$q = 32769132993266709549961988190834461413177642967992942539798288533$

so that n is quite large:

$n = 114381625757888867669235779976146612010218296721242362562561842935706935245733897830597123563958705058989075147599290026879543541.$

Actually, this is a poor choice for p and q, since this particular value of n was published by RSA Corporation as the RSA-129 challenge and it was successfully factored in 1994. In reality, Bob and Alice need to select primes with more than 100 digits if they want to be sure that Eve cannot discover their private key.

As a result, Bob and Alice face a host of problems before they can implement RSA: They need to be able to find large prime numbers; they need to be able to solve equations like $ed = 1 \bmod (p-1)(q-1)$ for these large numbers; and since handheld calculators and even standard computer programs cannot work with these large integers, they need some means to perform long integer arithmetic. In order to solve these problems, they need to explore some basic ideas in number theory like those presented in the next section of the book.

8.3   NUMBER THEORY—A VERY SHORT INTRODUCTION

The Phantom Tollbooth is the account of the travels of a young boy, Milo, through Dictionopolis and Digitopolis (two rather unusual cities). At one point in his adventure, Milo encounters a strange fellow called the Dodecahedron. During their conversation, Milo reveals that he found numbers to be rather unimportant:

> "NOT IMPORTANT!" roared the Dodecahedron, turning red with fury. "Could you have tea for two without the two or three blind mice without the three? Would there be four corners of the earth if there weren't a four? And how would you sail the seven seas without a seven? And did you know that narrow escapes come in all different widths?... Why, numbers are the most beautiful and valuable things in the world."

The Dodecahedron expresses an excitement about numbers that is shared by today's number theorists. Numbers come in all shapes and sizes: prime numbers, perfect numbers, amicable numbers, friendly numbers, lucky numbers, and powerful numbers. (These are all real categories.) The special properties of some numbers can be exploited to create powerful public key ciphers like RSA.

In order to tap into the real power of numbers, it is necessary to work with really large integers (100 digits or more). This requires special software and lucky for Bob and Alice, CAP has just what they need. Selecting the menu item Integer on the CAP main screen will open the Long Integer Routines window as shown in Figure 8.6. This package gives them a start, but to work with RSA they need to be able to calculate modular inverses and find large primes.

8.3.1 Modular Inverses

Setting up an RSA application requires selecting two large prime numbers (p and q) and a public key (e). The private key (d) is the modular inverse of the public key requiring a solution to the equation $ed = 1 \bmod (p - 1)(q - 1)$.

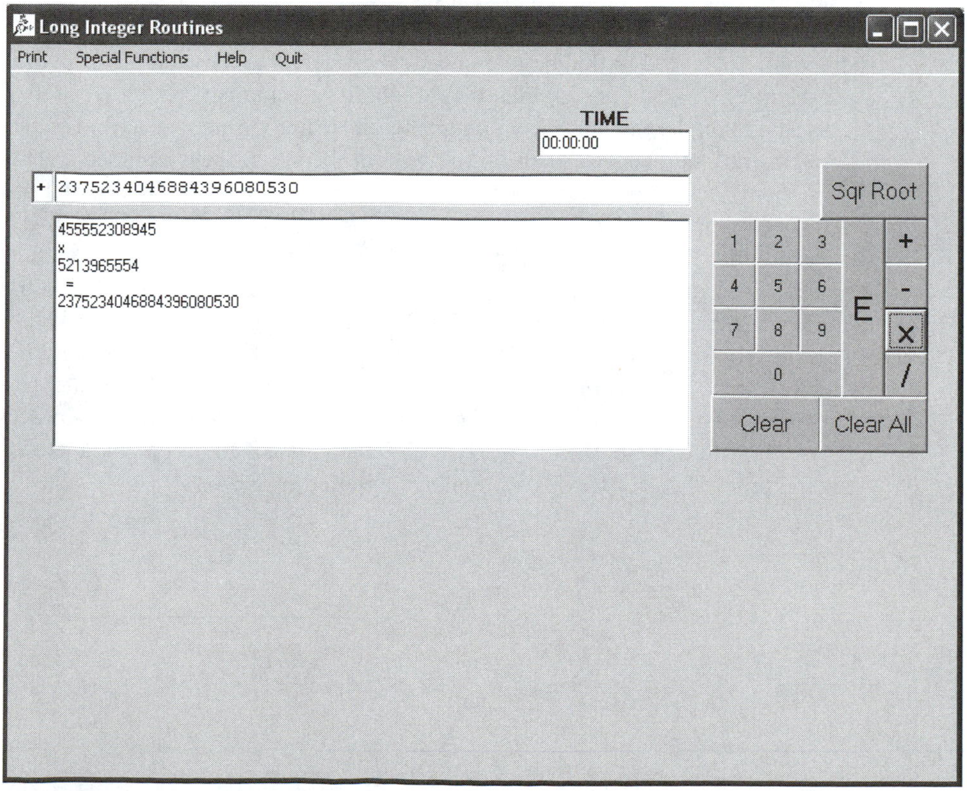

Figure 8.6: Long integer arithmetic using CAP

The solution is found by using a fundamental algorithm from number theory called *Euclid's algorithm*. Euclid's algorithm is used to find the greatest common divisor of two positive integers. The extended form of this algorithm will determine the modular inverse of a number. Given the problem $ed = 1 \bmod m$, the algorithm implements the following steps to find a value for d:

1. $(x_1, x_2, x_3) \leftarrow (1, 0, m)$ and $(y_1, y_2, y_3) \leftarrow (0, 1, e)$
2. If $y_3 = 0$, then stop there is no inverse; if $y_3 = 1$, then stop $d = y_2$ else continue
3. Let $Q = x_3$ div y_3 (integer division)
4. $(t_1, t_2, t_3) \leftarrow (x_1 - Qy_1, x_2 - Qy_2, x_3 - Qy_3)$
5. $(x_1, x_2, x_3) \leftarrow (y_1, y_2, y_3)$
6. $(y_1, y_2, y_3) \leftarrow (t_1, t_2, t_3)$
7. Go to Step 2

Figure 8.7 illustrates these steps to find the solution to $11d = 1 \bmod 51$.

While this algorithm is easy to implement by hand when the integers are small, it requires a computer for large integers. CAP provides the necessary tool in that case as shown in Figure 8.8.

8.3.2 Prime Numbers

The next problem Bob and Alice face is how can they find large prime numbers that may be used to create their public and private keys? It is easy to look up small prime numbers in a table and select two to use for an RSA key—but this is not acceptable from a security standpoint. They need to find large numbers and verify that they are prime in order to create a secure RSA key. For example, they might try the number 12553. (It's too small, but it's only an example.) Is it prime or composite (not prime)? One way to find out is to divide 12553 by every number less than its square root. If one of these numbers evenly divides 12553, then 12553 is not prime; otherwise, it must be prime. The square root of 12553 is 112.04, so this approach requires only 112 division operations (divide by 2, 3, 4, . . . , 113). It turns out that 12553 is indeed a prime number and it could be used to generate an RSA key. Since trail division worked so well on 12553, Bob and Alice decided to try a larger number—13,952,598,148,481. By hand, this would take a long time. However, CAP does have a trail division test available as one of the SpecialFunctions options on the Long Integer Routines window. Figure 8.9 shows the result of Bob and Alice's attempt to verify their suspected prime number. They didn't have the patience to wait for the process to finish, but who could blame them. Clearly trail division is not an acceptable method for verifying the prime status of the size of numbers required by RSA.

Q	X₁	X₂	X₃	Y₁	Y₂	Y₃
–	1	0	51	0	1	11
4	0	1	11	1	-4	7
1	1	-4	7	-1	5	4
1	-1	5	4	2	-9	3
1	2	-9	3	-3	14	1

Figure 8.7: Extended Euclid's algorithm

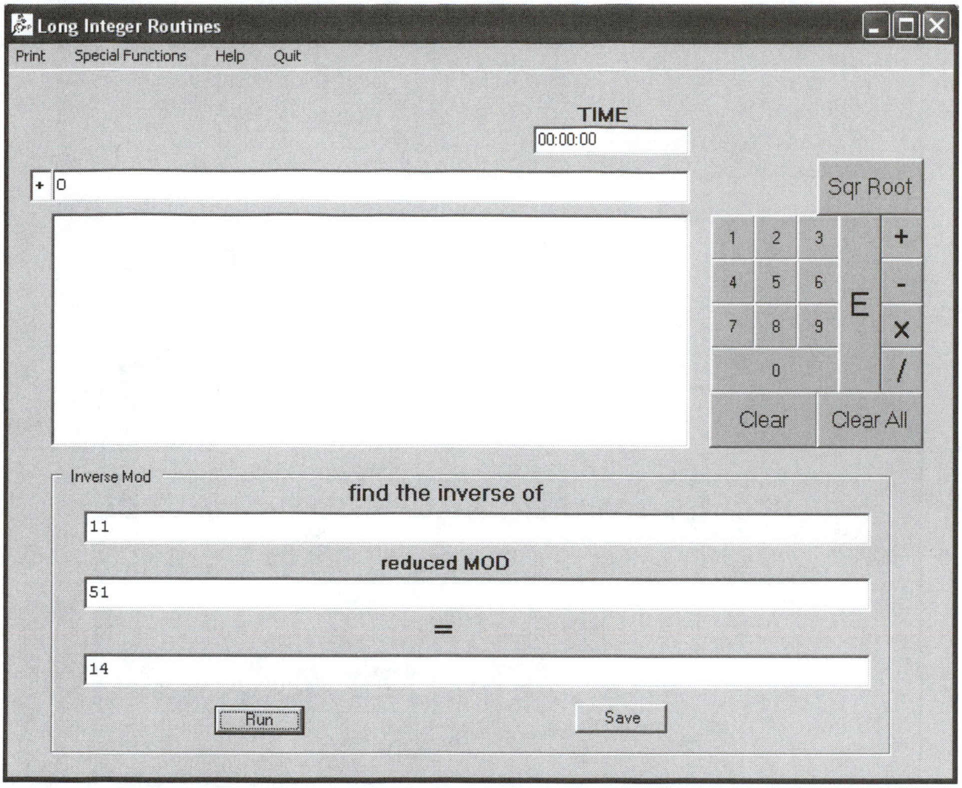

Figure 8.8: Using CAP to find a Modular Inverse

There is a trick that can slightly speed up trail division. Rather than divide by all the integers between two and the square root of the target, it is really only necessary to divide by all the primes in that range. Since all the primes may not be known, there is a simple formula that generates all the primes plus some composite numbers that would reduce the total number of trail divisions. The specification for this function is as follows:

- Divide by 2, 3, and 5
- Divide by $6k - 1$ and $6k + 1$ for all integers k

CAP provides this test as well and it does speed up the processes, but not by enough to make it feasible for the primes Bob and Alice require.

A faster, more efficient, prime number detector is required if Bob and Alice are ever going to use RSA. It turns out that a variety of prime number detectors exist that are based on an analysis of the properties of prime numbers. One method was developed by the 17th-century French mathematician Pierre Fermat. He noticed that, given two numbers, a base a and a prime p, where a is not divisible by p, it follows that $a^{p-1} = 1 \bmod p$. For example, select 6 as the base number and 7 as the prime number (6 is not divisible by 7). Then

$$6^6 = 46656 = 1 \ (\bmod \ 7).$$

This result is known as Fermat's Little Theorem. It suggests a method to verify the prime status of a number. If some number c is possibly a prime number, then select a base, say, 2,

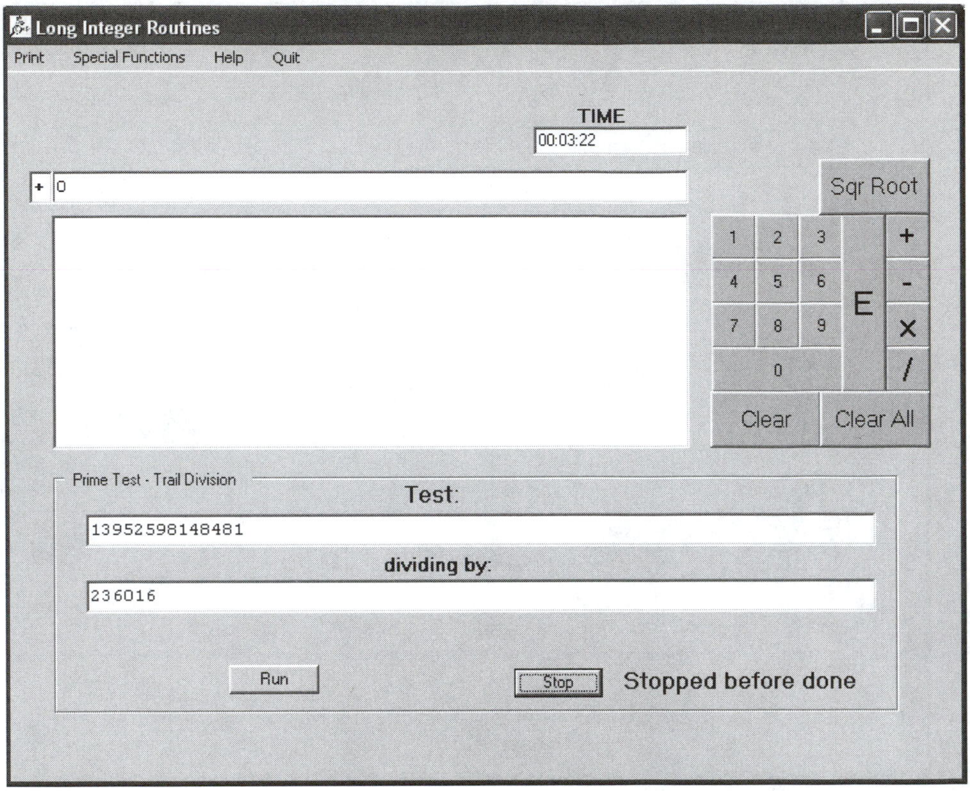

Figure 8.9: Trail division in CAP

and check to see whether $2^{c-1} = 1$ (mod c). Bob and Alice like this idea, so they try it on 341. Sure enough it turns out that $2^{340} = 1$ (mod 341). They decide that 341 is prime until another friend comes along and tells them to calculate 11×31. (It equals 341.) So 341 is not prime and this simple test failed on its first try. The problem is not with Fermat's theory; it is with the way it was used. It does not say that, if $a^{p-1} = 1$ (mod p), then p is prime. However, while it didn't work for 341, it does work for all primes. Composite numbers like 341 that appear on the basis of this test to be prime are called *pseudoprimes*. For example, 91 is a pseudoprime to base 3, since $3^{90} = 1$ (mod 91).

Perhaps the pseudoprimes could be avoided if the test were implemented twice using two different bases. That is, maybe a pseudoprime for base 2 will not be a pseudoprime for base 3. Since 341 is a base 2 pseudoprime, try base 3. In this case 3^{340} is not 1 (mod 341). It looks like a solution until 561 is tested. Since $561 = 3 \times 11 \times 17$, it is not prime, but it does pass Fermat's test for every base. It turns out that numbers which are pseudoprime for all bases are called *Carmichael numbers*, named after the American mathematician R. D. Carmichael who studied their properties in 1909. The bright spot is that Carmichael numbers are rare compared to prime numbers. There are only 2163 Carmichael numbers less than 25×10^9.

One approach to testing for primes would be to try Fermat's Little Theorem on a target number using several bases. If it passed all the base tests, then compare it to a table of Carmichael numbers. If it is not in the table, then it must be a prime number. This is one of the prime test routines provided in CAP. In Figure 8.10, it is used to verify that 41432541 is prime.

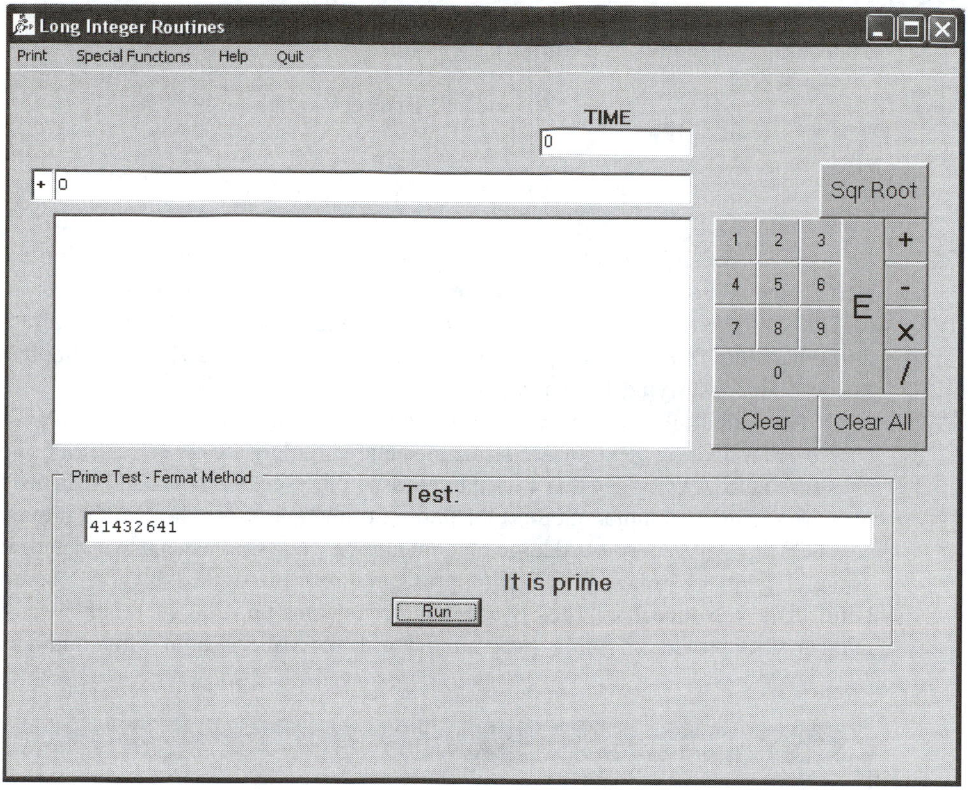

Figure 8.10: Fermat's method in CAP

The problem with this approach is that it is limited by the size of the Carmichael number file. A more general method is required if prime numbers of all sizes are to be quickly identified. Just such a method was discovered by Lehmann in 1982 and later, independently, by Peralta in 1985. This test is based on probabilities. That is, if some number, p, passes the tests the probability that p is not prime is very small. The approach used is to select 100 random numbers, a_i, in the range 1 to $p - 1$. Then p is probably composite if

1. $a_i^{(p-1)/2} = 1$ for all $i = 1$ to 100
2. or $a_i^{(p-1)/2} <> 1$ or -1 for all $i = 1$ to 100.

By contrast, p is probably prime if

$$a_i^{(p-1)/2} = 1 \text{ or } -1 \text{ for all } i = 1 \text{ to } 100 \text{ and it equals } -1 \text{ for some } i.$$

This works best if some of the smaller prime factors are first ruled out by division. CAP implements this approach as well.

The most widely used method is the Miller–Rabin test, another probabilistic primality test similar to the Lehmann test. It is based on the observation that, given an odd prime,

n, where $n - 1 = 2^s r$ (r is odd), and a random integer a such that $\text{GCD}(a, n) = 1$ (that is, a and n have no factors in common), then either

$$a^r = 1 \ (\text{mod } n)$$

or

$$a^{2^j r} = -1 \ (\text{mod } n)$$

for some j between 0 and $s - 1$. Hence, given a possible prime number n, find s and r; select a value a; and if the previous relations are true, then the probability that n is prime is 0.25. If both are false (the second for all j), then n is composite. If n passes all tests for m different values of a, then the probability that n is prime is $(0.25)^m$. CAP implements the Miller–Rabin test trying 100 values for a.

The real problem facing Bob and Alice is not so much one of testing individual numbers to determine whether they are prime; it is one of finding a large enough pair of primes to construct an RSA key. They don't want to guess numbers on their own and then test them. So they elect to use a common method for finding prime numbers. They find a program (CAP, anyone?) that will generate 100 large random numbers and stop when one is determined to be prime. Figure 8.11 shows a 15-digit prime number discovered by CAP based on the Lehmann test. Notice that it took over 6 minutes to come up with one relatively small prime number. CAP provides a similar program that uses the Miller–Rabin prime number test.

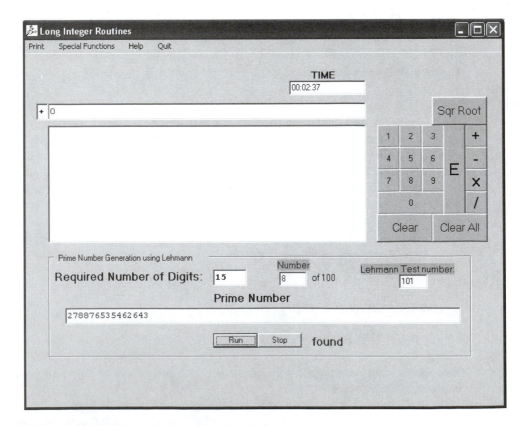

Figure 8.11: Finding a prime number using CAP

Not only do the primes selected for RSA need to be large enough to prevent a simple factor attack on n, the difference between them must be large as well. If p and q are close, then n can be factored using Fermat's algorithm (as will be seen in the next section). One suggested guideline is that the size of the smaller prime be 40 to 45 percent of the size of n. That is, if n is to have 100 digits, then p should have about 45 digits and q should have about 55 digits.

8.3.3   Fast Exponentiation

Besides finding large prime numbers and performing modular arithmetic, Bob and Alice face another problem using RSA—they have to raise large numbers to large powers. For example, how can they quickly and efficiently calculate

$$33890123410097^{23015} \bmod 131.$$

The straightforward approach would be to multiply 33890123410097 times itself 23015 times and then reduce the result mod 131. Keep in mind that requires 23000 multiplications by a 14-digit number. It is not doable by hand and is even slow (in computer time) on a computer. Lucky for Bob and Alice there are ways to speed up the process.

One simple way is to take the mod after each multiplication rather than waiting until the entire multiplication process is complete to reduce by the modulus. This is possible because it is true that

$$ab \bmod n = (a \bmod n)(b \bmod n) \bmod n.$$

This will reduce the size of the numbers at every step, but the number of multiplications required will still be the same.

It turns out that there is a way to reduce the number of multiplications using what is called *repeated squaring*. For example, 21^{16} would require 16 multiplications; however, since $16 = 2 \times 2 \times 2 \times 2$, the problem can be rewritten as

$$21^{16} = 21^{(2 \times 2 \times 2 \times 2)} = ((((21)^2)^2)^2)^2,$$

which reduces to only four multiplications. This will work for any exponent that is a power of two. But all is not lost; if an exponent is not a power of two, it can be broken down in a sum of powers of two. That is, if the exponent is 24, then $24 = 2^4 + 2^3$, so a problem like

$$21^{24} = 21^{(16+8)} = 21^{16}21^8 = ((((21)^2)^2)^2)^2 \times (((21)^2)^2)^2,$$

requires only eight multiplications rather than 24. To make it even easier, it is possible to reduce any number to a sum of powers of two by finding its binary representation (done at the beginning of Chapter 6). For example, the binary representation of 41 is 101001_2. In binary terms, 101001 is the same as decimal $2^5 + 2^3 + 2^0$, which is 41 (again). As a result,

$$21^{41} = 21^{32}21^821^1.$$

Using both repeating squares and reducing mod n after every multiplication will significantly reduce the workload required by a large multiplication problem. For example, $79^{51} \bmod 90$ would require 51 multiplications and the intermediate results would become quite large. However, fast exponentiation solves the problem as follows:

$$79^{51} \bmod 90 = 79^{32}79^{16}79^279^1 \bmod 90,$$

since $51 = 110011_2$. Expanding each exponent gives

$$79^{51} \bmod 90 = (((((79)^2)^2)^2)^2)^2 \times ((((79)^2)^2)^2)^2 \times 79^2 \times 79 \bmod 90,$$

which results in only 13 multiplications in place of a standard 51. This can be reduced even further by noting that finding 79^{32} requires finding 79^{16}. Completing the multiplications produces

$$79^2 \bmod 90 = 31$$
$$((79)^2)^2 \bmod 90 = (31)^2 \bmod 90 = 61$$
$$(((79)^2)^2)^2 \bmod 90 = (61)^2 \bmod 90 = 31$$
$$((((79)^2)^2)^2)^2 \bmod 90 = (31)^2 \bmod 90 = 61; \text{ this is } 79^{16} \bmod 90$$
$$(((((79)^2)^2)^2)^2)^2 \bmod 90 = (61)^2 \bmod 90 = 31; \text{ this is } 79^{32} \bmod 90$$

Now the problem is $31 \times 61 \times 31 \times 79 \bmod 90 = 19$.

8.4   RSA IN CAP

Using the prime number generator from CAP, Bob and Alice came up with their two prime numbers:

$$p = 232286714550223 \quad \text{and} \quad q = 816488284824217.$$

Using the long integer routines available in CAP, they constructed the other numbers required for RSA:

$$N = 189659381150564068093773150391$$

and

$$(p - 1)(q - 1) = 189659381150563019318773775952.$$

They select their value for d by finding a prime number larger than p to be sure that it is relatively prime to $(p - 1)(q - 1)$:

$$d = 1175885676400129.$$

Using the inverse mod feature of CAP, they find their secret key:

$$e = 53874618627671702415711710977.$$

After all that work, they are ready to use RSA. They begin by entering their plaintext and then selecting RSA from the CAP Cipher menu. As shown in Figure 8.12, Bob and Alice selected a block size of 32 bits and then entered their public key. Notice that it took almost

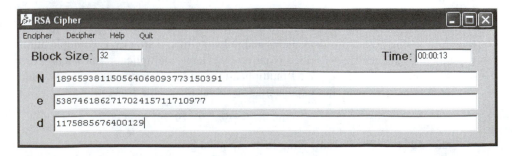

Figure 8.12: Example run of RSA

2 minutes to encipher a simple 70-character plaintext message. Performance is a serious issue with RSA, and it will be covered in more detail in the next section.

8.5   ANALYSIS OF RSA

In their first attempt to use RSA with a large (but not large enough) key, Bob and Alice encountered some difficulties. First, the key itself is large, impossible to remember, and difficult to enter without making a mistake. Second, the algorithm is slow—about 1000 times slower than DES. These problems only get worse when a realistic key is used. As a result, RSA is rarely used to encipher plaintext. Its major use is to provide a secure method for both key exchange and digital signatures. (See the next chapter for more details on these topics.)

Nevertheless, RSA remains an important cipher that has been put to use in the real world. Eve, suspecting that Bob and Alice have moved to RSA, launches a major effort to discover some weakness that she can exploit.

The first and most obvious attack on RSA is to factor the public key and discover the two primes p and q. The most straightforward method for factoring is trial division. Bob and Alice used trial division as a method to determine whether a number is prime. If it is not prime, then the process returns the factors.

Hoping that trial division will do the trick, Eve intercepts a message between Bob and Alice:

872113	423723	1722277	382609	1166418
489217	1346472	478777	1262541	2436322
2523374	2700185	1767245	1602334	1722277
2867006	1275413	1760613	2682469	755208

Eve looks up Bob and Alice's public key and finds the following listing:

$$N = 2949691 \quad e = 1801.$$

All she needed to do was to factor N into its two primes p and q. Using CAP it took less than a second to discover that one of the factors is 1031. Then, by division, the other factor was found to be 2861. Now all Eve had to do was follow the same steps Bob and Alice used to discover that the private key d is 201021. Using the private key, she reconstructed the following plaintext: "Alice I hope our key is large enough Bob". After Bob and Alice discovered that their correspondence was once again being read by Eve, they decided that they could no longer trust RSA with small keys. Even though it meant using large prime numbers, they had to make the change. When Eve checked their new public key, she found that it was now much larger:

$$N = 68969781959371 \quad e = 2623883$$

Running the fast version of trial division, Eve was able to find the prime factors of this new key (52013371 and 1326001), but it took almost 20 minutes. Realizing that Bob and Alice will eventually select a key large enough to make trial division unusable, Eve decided it was time to find an alternative method for factoring large numbers.

8.5.1   Large Integer Factoring

The search for more efficient methods of factoring large integers predates both computers and public key ciphers. Mathematicians have been exploring ways to factor for centuries.

One method was suggested in the 1600s by the French mathematician Pierre de Fermat. Given a number, N, Fermat's idea was to write it as the difference of two squares, namely,

$$N = x^2 - y^2 = (x - y)(x + y),$$

which immediately reveals two factors of N. The problem of factoring N becomes one of searching for the values of x and y. The algorithm works by guessing a value for x and calculating y using $y^2 = x^2 - N$. Since x must be larger than the square root of N, the first guess should be $x = \text{sqrt}(N) + 1$, which is used to find $z = x^2 - N$. If z is a perfect square, then the search is done; if not, then try the next value $x = \text{sqrt}(N) + 2$. Continue this process until either the factors are found or time runs out. CAP implements this routine—it can be found by clicking the Factor button under the Public Key segment of the Analysis menu. While it is much faster than trial division, it works best if the factors are similar in size. (Remember the guideline for selecting prime numbers at the end of Section 8.3?) In that case, they are close to the square root; hence, the length of the search is minimized. The sample CAP run shown in Figure 8.13 indicates that Fermat's method took almost 7 minutes to factor the number 6664407857. Running the same program on the number 268380942439 (two digits longer than the first sample run), CAP found the solution in only 2 seconds:

$$268380942439 = 511897 \times 524287.$$

Notice that these two prime factors are fairly close. In fact, the reason RSA suggests that the two primes p and q differ significantly is to avoid just such a factoring attack.

J.W. Pollard has developed several alternative factorization algorithms that do not require similar factors. One method, called the Pollard Rho factoring algorithm, is based on the search for two numbers that are equal when reduced mod a prime factor of n. It sounds stranger than it really is—in fact it is quite simple. Given n, the number we want to factor; p an unknown prime factor of n; and a sequence of numbers $x_0, x_1, \ldots x_m$ where

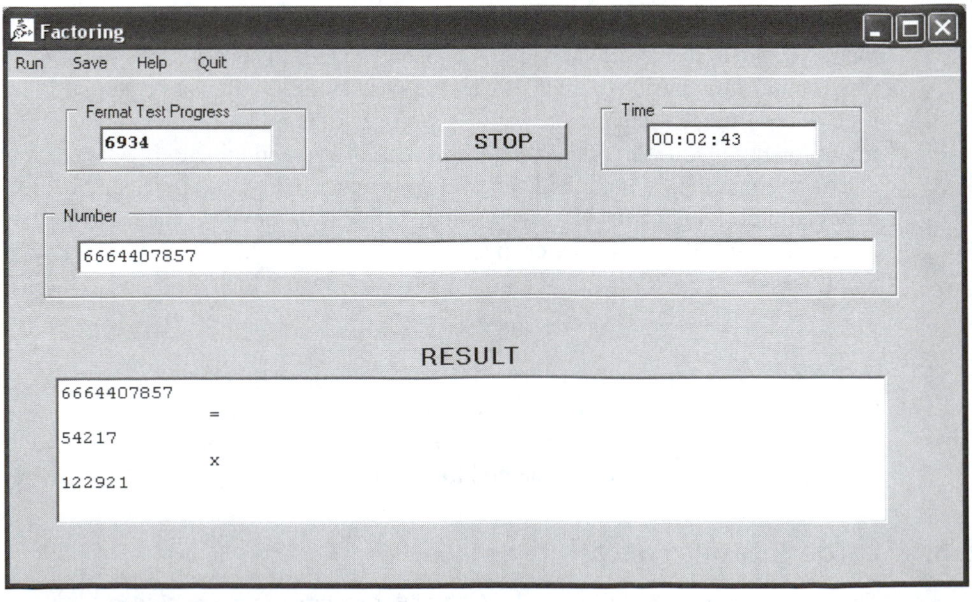

Figure 8.13: Factoring with Fermat's method in CAP

$x_{j+1} = f(x_j) \bmod n$, consider the sequence of numbers $z_k = x_k \pmod p$. Since the values in the z sequence are restricted to $0, 1, \ldots (p-1)$, they are likely to repeat sooner than the values in the x sequence, which range from 0 to $n-1$. When a repeat occurs in the z sequence ($z_i = z_j$ for some i and j), it means that $x_i = x_j \pmod p$. This in turn means that p divides $x_i - x_j$. It is already given that p divides n, so p must also divide the GCD($x_i - x_j, n$). If we are lucky, the GCD($x_i - x_j, n$) is not 1 or n; so it is a factor of n. This idea is implemented in the following algorithm:

Pollard Rho Factoring Algorithm

Input a composite integer n
Output a factor d of n
1. Set $a = 2$ and $b = 2$
2. For $i = 1, 2, \ldots$ do the following
    2(a) $a = a^2 + 1 \pmod n$, $b = b^2 + 1 \pmod n$, $b = b^2 + 1 \pmod n$
    2(b) $d = $ GCD($a - b, n$)
    2(c) if $1 < d < n$ then stop and return d
    2(d) if $d = n$ then stop, the algorithm has failed

This algorithm was used in 1980 to find the factorization of the eighth Fermat number:

$$2^{2^8} + 1 = 12389263615528987 \times p62,$$

where $p62$ is a 62-digit integer.

    CAP implements this algorithm—run the factor attack under the Public Key option, enter the number, and run Pollard Rho. As shown in Figure 8.14, Pollard Rho factored the number 6664407857 in only 2 seconds. (It took Fermat's algorithm almost 7 minutes.)

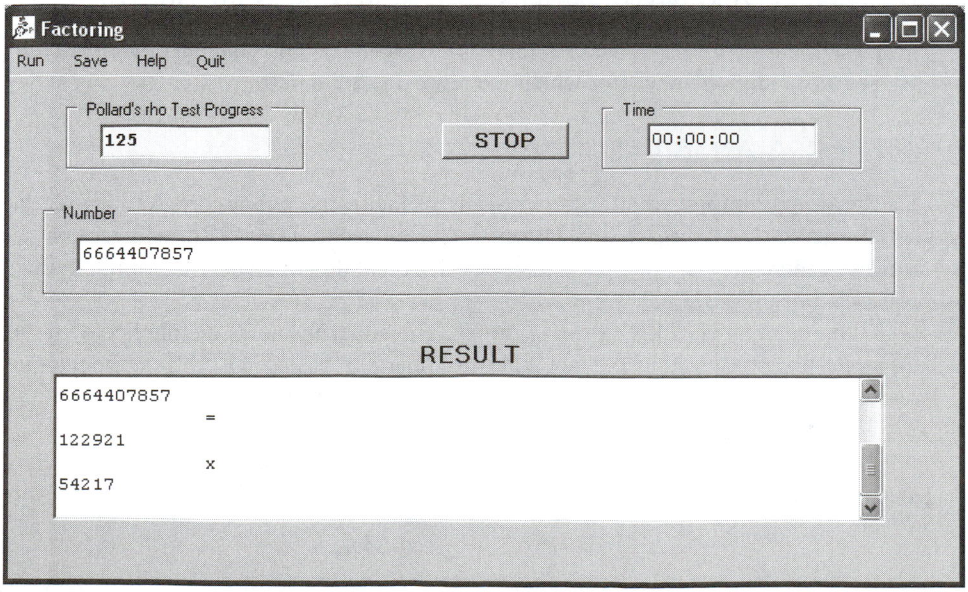

Figure 8.14: Example run of CAP's Pollard Rho routine

CAP implements two other common factoring algorithms (the reader is referred to texts on number theory for the details of their operation): Pollard's $p - 1$ and the continued fraction method. In addition to the four methods offered by CAP, some of the more powerful factoring algorithms in use today include the quadratic sieve and the number field sieve.

The history of RSA is one of constantly raising the bar on the required size of the prime generators because of the development of faster computers and new factoring algorithms. In a 1977 *Scientific American* column, Martin Gardner offered $100 to the first person that could factor RSA-129, the 129-digit number.

$$N = 11438162575788886766923577997614661201021829672124236256256184293570693524573389783059712356395870505898907514759929002687954354l.$$

In April 1994, Derek Atkins announced that

$$RSA\text{-}129 = 3490529510847650949147849619903834177646384933878439908205776 \times 3276913299326670954996198819083446141317764296799294253979828853.$$

This task was accomplished using the quadratic sieve algorithm running on volunteer machines that shared idle processing time across the Internet. There were about 1600 machines working for 8 months to complete the factorization.

RSA has offered cash rewards to the first person to factor one of a set of challenge numbers. In April 1996, RSA-130 was factored using the number field sieve. In August 1999, RSA-155 (512-bit) number was also factored using the number field sieve. That effort took 7 months and used the resources of 300 workstations and PCs plus a Cray supercomputer. As of February 2003, the smallest RSA challenge is the 174-digit number

18819881292060796383869723946165043980716356337941738270076335642298885971523466548531906060650474304531738801130339671619969232120573403187955065699622130516875930765025705905,

which will earn the first to factor it the sum of $10,000. The challenge numbers range as high as a 617-digit number (for which the reward is $200,000).

8.5.2 Other RSA Attacks

The most straightforward attack on RSA is to factor the public key. As long as the key length increases to surpass our current factoring technology, RSA will remain secure. However, there may be other ways to attack RSA that do not involve factoring. In fact, several have been discovered.

One method is called a *cycling attack*. The attacker knows the public key (e, n) and the ciphertext, c, as well as the fact that the ciphertext was produced from the plaintext by $c = m^e \bmod n$. It is also the case that there exists a number k such that

$$c^{e^k} = c \ (\bmod\ n),$$

which means that

$$c^{e^{(k-1)}} = m \ (\bmod\ n).$$

The attack requires calculating

$$c^e, c^{e^2}, c^{e^3}, \ldots,$$

all reduced mod n until the result is equal to c. Then the previous result is the plaintext. For a large n, this requires the same amount of effort as does factoring, so it is not considered to be a serious threat. That is, unless someone comes up with a way to find k, which does not require an exhaustive search.

RSA does not posses a quality called *semantic security*. This means that given a set of possible known messages, $m_0, m_1, \ldots, m_n$, and the ciphertext for one of them, c_i, it is possible to discover the value of i—that is, which of the n messages is encrypted into c_i. The process is easy—just encipher all n messages with the public key and compare the resulting ciphertext to c_i. Both the cycling attack and the lack of semantic security are not serious problems at this time. There are some other attacks that may be of more concern.

8.5.2.1 Side-Channel Attacks

Just like DES, RSA is subject to side-channel attacks. These are attacks that take advantage of information leakage, which might occur as the cipher is implemented. The oldest reported such attack took advantage of the sound of the Hagelin cipher machine. The Hagelin machine implemented a rotor cipher similar to the Engima. As the rotors moved, they produced a clicking sound. By monitoring the sound, it was possible to deduce the rotor settings.

A more contemporary side-channel attack, called *timing cryptanalysis*, was discovered by Paul Kocher in November 1995. Timing cryptanalysis requires that the attacker have the capability to measure the time it takes to encipher–decipher several messages. Given the timing results, the attacker uses the fact that if a bit in the secret exponent is 1, it takes longer to process the message than if the exponent bit is 0. By guessing each bit and comparing the time to complete the encryption–decryption using the guess to the statistical average time over several real messages, the attacker can discover the secret key.

There are several countermeasures that will hinder or invalidate a timing attack. One obvious method is to add random delays in the implementation of RSA. This will degrade performance, and since RSA is already quite slow, it may not be an acceptable solution. Another method is to use "blinding," which introduces two extra multiplications and hides the real timing. The blinding process applied to the decryption algorithm involves

1. selecting a random number r and
2. finding $m = r^{-1}(cr^e)^d \bmod n$ (instead of $m = c^d \bmod n$)

This process works because

$$m = r^{-1}(cr^e)^d \bmod n = (c^d \bmod n)(r^{-1})(r^{ed} \bmod n) = (cd \bmod n)(r^{-1}r^1 \bmod n)$$
$$= c^d \bmod n.$$

RSA Data Security (the company that held the patent on RSA) uses blinding in its implementation and finds that it adds about a 5 percent timing delay to the overall algorithm.

Another side-channel attack similar to the timing attack involves measuring the power draw as a device implements the RSA cipher. It seems that each operation consumes a different amount of power as indicated in Figure 8.15. By monitoring the power consumption over time, it is possible to determine each bit of the secret key, d, because if the bit is 1, there is an extra multiplication. An example of what a power analysis might produce is shown in Figure 8.16.

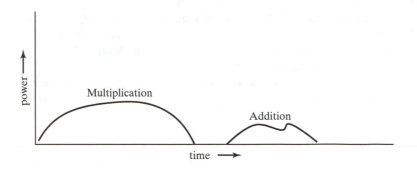

Figure 8.15: Possible power signatures of RSA operations

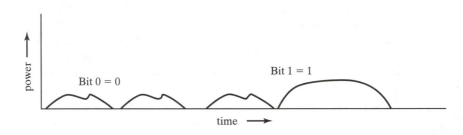

Figure 8.16: Discovering the bits of d

A possible countermeasure requires a careful analysis of the software instructions used to implement the cipher algorithm. Avoiding conditional branches will help—so will adding useless instructions.

8.5.2.2 Improper Use of RSA Attacks

There are also attacks that exploit the misuse of the RSA system, including a poor choice of the public or private key, or the broadcast of the same message with similar public keys.

If the private key, d, is too small, then it can be determined from knowledge of the public key (e, n). Since RSA is computationally intensive, there is some motivation to use small d's. A small d reduces the computation and hence the power consumption, making RSA more practical for low-power devices. The attack, originally suggested by M. Wiener and further developed by Boneh and Durfee, will discover d if $d < n^{0.295}$. As a result, if n is at the recommended level of at least 1024 bits, then d should be at least 300 bits long.

The partial-key-exposure attack is based on the choice of a small public key value, e. As with the choice of a small d, there is some motivation to select a small e. The smaller the value of e, the fewer multiplications are required to encipher, so the faster the encryption process is. The smallest possible e is 3, but for security reasons, e is often selected to be 65537. This value of e (rather than a large random e) can reduce the number of multiplications from 1000 to about 20. On the other hand, Boneh, Durfee, and Frankel have shown that, if n is k bits long and if the $(k/4)$ least significant bits of d are known, then all of d can found in time linear to $[e \log (e)]$. Hence, if e is small, then knowledge of a quarter of the bits of d will compromise the complete private key.

Another attack, called a *common modulus attack*, is also the result of a misuse of the RSA algorithm. Since finding large primes and hence a value for n that is secure can be time consuming, an organization might be tempted to generate a single value for n and then assign each user a different pair (d, e). The assumption is that Bob cannot read messages sent to Alice without Alice's private key. This is false, since Bob can factor n using knowledge of his public and private key. Once factored, Bob can find Alice's private key from knowledge of her public key.

This problem is even worse because an outside attacker (Eve) who does not have an assigned pair (d, e) like Bob can still break into an enciphered message. If Alice sends a message, M, to both Bob and Paul (remember, this is in an organization with a common modulus n for all their public keys), she will look up Bob's public key, $e1$, and Paul's public key, $e2$. Using these keys, Alice will create two different ciphertexts (one for Bob and one for Paul):

$$\text{for Bob—} C_b = M^{e1} \bmod n$$
$$\text{and for Paul—} C_p = M^{e2} \bmod n.$$

If Eve can get her hands on both ciphertexts and the two public keys have a GCD of 1 $[\text{GCD}(e1, e2) = 1]$, then all Eve has to do is find two numbers x and y such that

$$xe1 + ye2 = 1.$$

With x and y, Eve can recover the message M as follows:

$$C_b{}^x C_p{}^y = (M^{e1})^x (M^{e2})^y = M^{xe1+ye2} = M^1 = M.$$

As a result, never use the same modulus n with different exponents e.

8.6   ELGAMAL PUBLIC KEY SYSTEM

RSA depends on the difficulty of factoring large numbers for its security. There are other public key systems that depend on the difficulty of other kinds of operations for their security. Among these is the ElGamal cipher developed in 1985 by T. ElGamal. It relies on the difficulty of solving the discrete logarithm problem.

The discrete logarithm problem begins with a prime p and two integers a and b where $b = a^x \bmod p$ for some integer x. The problem is one of finding x—that is, of solving the equation $x = \log_a b$. If p is small, this problem can be solved by using an exhaustive search. For example, given $p = 17$, $a = 3$, and $b = 5$, find x such that $5 = 3^x \bmod 17$. Trying all possible values of x beginning with 1 until a match is found results in

X	1	2	3	4	5	
3^x	3	9	10	13	5	(MOD 17)

So $x = 5$. As long as p is small, this is an easy problem to solve by exhaustive search. When p is large, say a 100-digit prime, then this is as difficult to solve as the integer factorization problem.

Like RSA, the ElGamal system is a public key algorithm, so it has one set of key numbers that are published and another secret number that is used for deciphering. The keys are generated by selecting a large prime number p. It is recommended that $p - 1$ be divisible by another large prime. Compute a generator number g (more on this later) and select a random integer a less than $p - 1$. With these numbers, compute $b = g^a \pmod{p}$. The public key consists of the three numbers (p, g, b), and the secret key is the number a. To find a given the public key, an attacker must be able to solve the discrete logarithm problem.

If Bob wants to send a message to Alice, he begins by looking up her public key (p, g, b) and representing the message as an integer m in the range 0 to $p - 1$. He then selects a random key, k, that is less than $p - 1$. Using these numbers, Bob computes two numbers:

$$c_1 = g^k$$

and

$$c_2 = mb^k.$$

Bob then sends the ciphertext $c = (c_1, c_2)$ to Alice.

When Alice receives the ciphertext, she will recover the plaintext using her secret key, a, to compute

$$m = c_2 c_1^{-a} \bmod p.$$

This works because

$$c_2 c_1^{-a} = mb^k(g^k)^{-a} = m(g^a)^k(g^k)^{-a} = mg^{ak}g^{-ak} = m \pmod{p}.$$

For example, if Alice selected her initial prime number $p = 11$ (way too small for any realistic security), found the primitive element $g = 7$, and selected her random secret key $a = 2$, then she would compute her public key using $b = 7^2 \bmod 11 = 5$. She would then publish (p, g, b) as $(11,7,5)$, but would keep $a = 2$ secret. Now, if Bob wanted to send the letter "a" to Alice, he would first break it up into a set of numbers where each number is less than 11. Since the ASCII representation of "a" is 01100001, he might break it up into four messages (01 10 00 01) or in decimal (1, 2, 0, 1). Next, he would select a random number $k = 3$ and then compute and send the following to Alice:

m	c_1	c_2
1	$7^3 \bmod 11 = 2$	$1 \times 5^3 \bmod 11 = 4$
2	$7^3 \bmod 11 = 2$	$2 \times 5^3 \bmod 11 = 8$
0	$7^3 \bmod 11 = 2$	$0 \times 5^3 \bmod 11 = 0$
1	$7^3 \bmod 11 = 2$	$1 \times 5^3 \bmod 11 = 4$

The ciphertext is $[(2, 4)\ (2, 8)\ (2, 0),\ (2, 4)]$.

When Alice receives this message from Bob, she uses her secret key $a = 2$ as follows:

$(2, 4)\ m = 4(2)^{-2} = 4(4)^{-1} = 12 \bmod 11 = 1$ (4 and 3 are inverses mod 11)
$(2, 8)\ m = 8(2)^{-2} = 8(4)^{-1} = 24 \bmod 11 = 2$
$(2, 0)\ m = 0(2)^{-2} = 0(4)^{-1} = 0 \bmod 11 = 0$
$(2, 4)\ m = 1$

Alice reassembles the message into the letter "a".

It worked, but Bob made one fatal mistake. He used the same random value for k as he used for each m. In this case, if Eve could guess the first message number, then she could find b^k because $c_2 = m_1 b^k$. So $c_2/m_1 = b^k$. Using b^k, she can then find all the other message numbers. In the example, if Eve guessed that the first message number is 1, then she knows that $b^k = 4$. She uses this fact, the ciphertext for message 2–(2, 8), and the relationship $c_2/m = b^k$:

$$m_2 = 8\,(4) \bmod 11 = 2.$$

Hence, the rule is that every block must use a different random number k.

8.6.1 Generator Numbers

The only problem that Bob and Alice face in setting up the ElGamal system is finding a generator element that corresponds to their selected prime number. It turns out that it is not really necessary to use a generator, so any number would do. However, a poor selection would make the system easy to break.

Unfortunately, there is no known way to easily calculate a generator for a given prime number p unless the factorization of $(p - 1)$ is known. For the case in which it is known that the factors of $(p - 1)$ are $q_1, q_2, \ldots, q_r$, then a number g is a generator for p if, for all $i = 1$ to r,

$$g^{(p-1)/q_i} \bmod p \neq 1.$$

Of course, the problem with this method is that factoring a large number like $(p - 1)$ is difficult. Hence, the best way to find both a prime number p and its generator g is to first construct $(p - 1)$ with a known factorization.

One method to accomplish this involves the following steps:

1. Select a random number n which will determine the number of prime factors $(p - 1)$.
2. Select n random numbers $q_1, \ldots, q_n$. (Be sure to verify that they are prime.)
3. Select $n + 1$ random numbers $e_0, e_1, \ldots, e_n$ to serve as exponents.
4. Define the prime number, p, as

$$p = (2^{e_0} \times q_1{}^{e_1} \times q_2{}^{e_2} \times \cdots \times q_n{}^{e_n}) + 1.$$

5. Verify that p is prime.

If p is prime, then we have the factorization of $(p - 1)$, which can be used to find a generator number.

8.6.2 Using CAP to Implement ElGamal

CAP provides a version of ElGamal that includes a routine for selecting the keys. To access this routine, select ElGamal under the Cipher menu. Select Create under the Key menu item in the ElGamal window and the Create Key window will open. Begin the process of creating a set of numbers for your ElGamal key by entering the number and size of the prime factors of $(p - 1)$ and select Find p and q under the Create menu. CAP will find random primes of the specified size, random exponents for each prime, and multiply them to create $(p - 1)$. Next, it will use the Miller–Rabin test to determine whether p is prime. If so, it will use the factors of $(p - 1)$ to find a generator number, g. This entire process may take some time. Once it is done, enter a secret number and select Find b under the Create menu to complete the process. Be sure to save the key numbers using the Save option under the Create menu. An example run is shown in Figure 8.17. It took over 8 minutes to find the public keys:

$$p = 39823489096253$$
$$g = 874184$$
$$b = 10648334133598 \text{ (with secret key 14679)}$$

These key numbers are used by CAP in the ElGamal Cipher window to encipher–decipher messages in fixed blocks of size up to 32 bits. (The actual size depends on the size of p.) For example, using the three aforementioned public keys, CAP enciphered the message "This is a test of elgamal" into the following set of numbers:

```
4134442763715
18825904687947
27237957908646
19645981685387
16917762883314
3209378757176
25691232474630
1213006145262
7993144971816
3601640567706
2902376418316
17812051359532
2275290146625
38479927281019
```

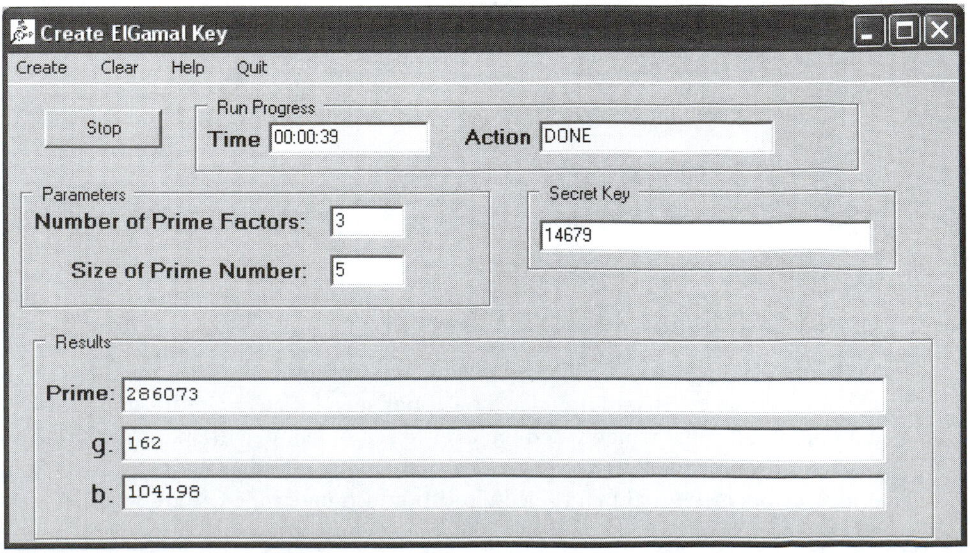

Figure 8.17: Creating an ElGamal key

8.6.3 Observations

The ElGamal cipher introduces some features that have not appeared in the other ciphers covered thus far. Most notable is the introduction of a random number in the creation of the ciphertext. This means that the same plaintext will result in different ciphertext, which is a real plus from a security standpoint. On the other hand, the ciphertext is twice as large as the plaintext, which increases the storage requirements and decreases the speed of data transmission.

8.7 KNAPSACK CIPHER

In 1976, Ralph Merkle and Martin Hellman were the first to suggest the possibility of a public key system. (It appears that the concept was known to British Intelligence in the early 1960s, but it remained classified until the 1990s.) They implemented a version of a public key system in 1978 based on the knapsack problem. The original knapsack cipher was cracked, so it is not used today (even though it was later revised to eliminate the problem). However, it is a interesting cipher to explore because of its adaptation of an NP-complete problem to cryptology.

The knapsack problem is easy to describe and visualize. Given a knapsack with a volume t and a set of items $1, \ldots, n$ with volumes $t_1, \ldots, t_n$, is there a subset of these items that completely fills the knapsack? For example, say the knapsack has a volume of 20 and there are 7 items with volumes 5, 3, 7, 1, 12, 15, and 19. Which items fit in the knapsack? In this case, there are several correct answers. Items 4 and 7 add up to a volume of 20, and so do items 1 and 6.

A more formal mathematical definition of the knapsack problem begins with a set of numbers $m_1, \ldots, m_n$, a target sum S, and asks to find the values of $b_1, \ldots, b_n$, where b_i can be 0 or 1 such that

$$S = b_1 m_1 + b_2 m_2 + \cdots + b_n m_n.$$

In terms of the knapsack problem, S is the total volume, and if $b_i = 1$, then the ith item is in the knapsack.

The Merkle–Hellman knapsack cipher encrypts a message as a knapsack problem. The knapsack is given as a list of numbers $m_1, \ldots, m_n$, the message block is a collection of n binary bits $b_1, \ldots, b_n$ and the ciphertext is the sum S previously given. For example, given the knapsack list (5, 14, 9, 23, 16, 7, 31, 27), the character "a" represented in ASCII as 0110 0001, the ciphertext is

$$S = (0 \times 5) + (1 \times 14) + (1 \times 9) + (0 \times 23) + (0 \times 16)$$
$$+ (0 \times 7) + (0 \times 31) + (1 \times 27) = 50.$$

Given just the ciphertext (in this case, 50), the plaintext can be recovered by solving the knapsack problem. In this case, that is not very difficult to do with an exhaustive search. Since the knapsack consists of only eight numbers, there are only $2^8 = 256$ possible combinations of 0's and 1's for the b's. But what if the knapsack contained 100 items? Then there would be 2^{100} possible combinations. Checking one million combinations a second, it would still take, on average, 5×10^{25} seconds to find the right one. That is equivalent to about 100 years.

The idea behind the knapsack cipher is to use the fact that it is hard to find the sum as a method to protect an encoding of information. Of course, a legitimate user must be able to decode the information within a normal lifetime, so there has to be a decoding algorithm that only the intended user could apply. Such a decoding algorithm is based on an easy knapsack problem. Easy knapsacks have a sequence of numbers that are superincreasing—that is, each number is greater than the sum of the previous numbers. Such a sequence is (3, 5, 9, 18, 38, 75, 155, 312). Notice that 9 is greater than 3 + 5, 18 is greater than 3 + 5 + 9, 38 is greater than 3 + 5 + 9 + 18, and so on. Now, to encode the character "R", use the 1's in the ASCII representation of "R" to select the numbers from the knapsack sequence to form a target sum. The ASCII representation of "R" is 01010010, so the target sum is 5 + 18 + 155 (using the example easy knapsack) or 178. For such a superincreasing knapsack, it is easy to recover the terms from the sequence that contributed to the sum, so it is easy to recover the character "R". In this case, 312 did not contribute to the target sum, since the target sum is less than 312. On the other hand, 155 had to contribute to the target sum, since the sum of all the elements of the knapsack sequence up to 155 is only 148, which is not enough. Knowing that 155 is part of the target sum of 178, it can be subtracted out, leaving 23. Now it is clear that neither 75 nor 38 contributed to the target sum because they are both larger than 23. So 18 must be part of the target sum. Subtracting 18 from 23 leaves 5, which must be the final term to contribute to the target sum of 178. So the transmitted character has the ASCII code 01010010 or "R".

The algorithm for solving a superincreasing knapsack (find the values of $b_1, \ldots, b_n$) with numbers $(m_1, \ldots, m_n)$ and a target sum of S is as follows:

for $i = n$ downto 1 do
    if $S >= m_i$ then
        $b_i = 1$ and $S = S - m_i$
    else
        $b_i = 0$

The superincreasing knapsack is easy to decode, which means that it does not protect the data. Anyone can recover the bit pattern from the target sum for a superincreasing knapsack if the elements of the superincreasing knapsack are known. Merkle and Hellman suggested that such a simple knapsack be converted into a trapdoor knapsack which is not superincreasing and so is difficult to break. Given a simple knapsack sequence $A' = (a_1', \ldots, a_n')$ the transformation to a trapdoor knapsack sequence, A, involves the following steps:

1. Select an integer $u > 2a_n'$.
2. Select another integer w such that $GCD(u, w) = 1$.
3. Find the inverse of $w \bmod u$.
4. Construct the trapdoor sequence $A = wA' \bmod u$.

For the previous example,

1. Select $u > 624$, say 672.
2. Select $w = 13$.
3. The inverse of $w \bmod u$ is 517 ($517 \times 13 = 1 \bmod 672$).
4. The trapdoor sequence is (39 65 117 234 494 303 671 24).

Using the trapdoor sequence, the character "R" becomes $65 + 234 + 671 = 970$. This cannot be easily decoded using the trapdoor knapsack sequence. However, if both the value of w^{-1} and of the original superincreasing sequence are known, it becomes easy to decode again. The target sum for the superincreasing sequence is found by calculating the product of the sum for the trapdoor sequence and w^{-1} then reducing it mod u—that is, $517 \times 970 \bmod 672 = 178$. Searching the superincreasing sequence for the terms that sum to 178 results in the recovery of the character "R". The secret key for this cipher consists of the underlying superincreasing sequence and the values u, w, and w^{-1}. The trapdoor sequence is published as a public key.

8.7.1 Breaking the Knapsack Cipher

Not only was the knapsack cipher the first to involve the use of a public key, it was also the first to be seriously compromised. Several different attacks on the original version of the knapsack cipher have prompted some revisions, but it has never been a popular system. In 1983, Shamir published his attack on the knapsack that did not require searching for a solution to the knapsack problem. Instead, he found a way to reconstruct the superincreasing knapsack. The lesson to be learned is that, even if a cipher is protected by some hard problem, it doesn't mean that there isn't a way to break the cipher without solving the hard problem.

One attack against a knapsack cipher that tries to directly solve the knapsack problem involves the use of a genetic algorithm (GA) to run a random search of possible solutions.

Genetic algorithms were developed by John Holland as a modification of what is called *evolutionary programming*. His idea was to construct a search algorithm modeled on the concepts of natural selection in the biological sciences. The result is a directed random search procedure. The process begins by constructing a random population of possible solutions. This population is used to create a new generation of possible solutions which is then used to create another generation of solutions, and so on. The best elements of the current generation are used to create the next generation. It is hoped that the new generation will contain "better" solutions than the previous generation. Remarkably, this turns out to be the case in many applications.

Three processes that have a parallel in human genetics are used to make the transition from one population generation to the next. They are selection, mating, and mutation. The basic GA cycle based on these three processes is shown in Figure 8.18.

A population consists of a set of binary strings. Each binary string represents one solution to the problem at hand and is called a *chromosome*. The first genetic algorithm step is to apply the selection process to this population. The selection process determines which strings in the current generation will be used to create the next generation. This is done by using a biased random selection methodology—that is, parents are randomly selected from the current population in such a way that the "best" strings in the population have the greatest chance of being selected.

The second step is the mating process. This determines the actual content of the binary strings in the next generation. The most common method used in GAs is called *crossover*. If the length of the parent strings is r, then a random number between 1 and $r - 1$ is selected, say, s. Crossover swaps bits s + 1 to s of the first parent with bits s + 1 to r of the second parent, thus creating two new children, as shown in Figure 8.19.

The final step is one of mutation. A fixed, small mutation probability is set at the start of the algorithm. Bits in all the new strings are then subject to change based on this mutation probability. Mutation is typically a very small probability event. If the mutation probability is 0.01, then each bit has 1 chance out of 100 of being complemented. These

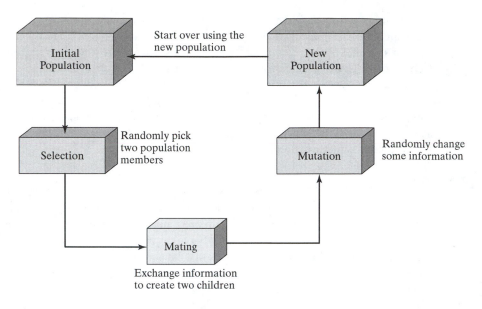

Figure 8.18: A genetic algorithm cycle

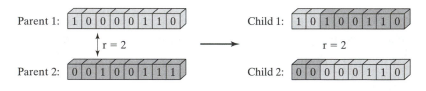

Figure 8.19: A crossover operation

three steps are repeated to create each new generation. It continues in this fashion until some stopping condition is reached (such as a maximum number of generations).

The representation structure for the knapsack problem is easy to generate because the problem naturally suggests the scheme. The binary bit pattern that represents the summation terms is perhaps the best structure. For example, given a knapsack with eight elements, (39 65 117 234 494 303 671 24), and a target sum of 970, a typical population element for the GA would be

1 0 1 0 1 0 1 0—add terms 1, 3, 5, and 7.

Once a representation scheme is selected for a genetic algorithm, it is also necessary to supply an evaluation function. This function is used to determine the "best" representations. For the knapsack cipher, the basic structure of the evaluation function is easy to determine. It should measure how close a given sum of terms is to the target sum for the knapsack. Within this general guideline there are a wide range of possible variations. An obvious fitness function for the knapsack problem would be a measure of the distance between the targeted sum and the sum of the terms in the current population element. In our little eight-element knapsack, the fitness of the population element (1010101) would be $|(39 + 117 + 494 + 671) - 970| = 351$.

The initial population for the GA is randomly generated and the fitness value of each population element is determined. Say a random population of six elements is generated and evaluated as shown in Figure 8.20. Given a population of chromosomes, each one with a fitness value, the algorithm progresses by randomly selecting two for mating. The selection is weighted in favor of chromosomes with a high fitness value. That is, chromosomes with a high fitness value have a greater chance of being selected to generate children for the next generation. For the example problem, the smaller the fitness value, the better is the element. In the initial random population, Elements 4 and 6 are the best, so they should have the best chance to serve as parents. Element 2 should have very little chance to pass its "genetic structure" on to the next generation.

Using a biased random selection method (biased so the best elements have the greatest chance of being selected), suppose that Elements 4 and 3 are chosen. Two children are created by throwing a random number between 1 and 7—say, 3—and swapping bits 4 to 8 between the two parents. The mutation process is applied to the parents, so that, say, bit 7 of the second child is randomly selected and complemented (1 goes to 0 in this case). The result of these two operations is shown in Figure 8.21. The average fitness of the two children is better than the average fitness of the parents even though neither child is as fit as the second parent. Over many generations, as the average fitness of each new population improves on the average fitness of the prior population, it is likely that a solution may be found.

8.7.2   The Knapsack Cipher in CAP

Much to the relief of Bob and Alice, CAP implements the knapsack cipher. Also, much to the delight of Eve, CAP provides a GA tool for breaking the cipher. Running the knapsack cipher in CAP follows the standard pattern for CAP ciphers—select Knapsack under the Cipher menu. The Knapsack window will open with slots for the elements of the key. CAP provides assistance in constructing a large knapsack—select Create under the Key option in the Knapsack window as shown in Figure 8.22.

An example of a CAP-generated knapsack cipher key created by Bob is shown in Figure 8.23. He wanted a knapsack with 50 elements, so he specified the first element (23).

	Population								Fitness
1	1	0	1	1	0	0	1	1	115
2	1	1	0	0	0	0	0	1	842
3	0	1	0	1	1	0	1	0	494
4	0	0	0	0	0	1	1	0	4
5	1	1	0	0	0	1	0	1	539
6	1	0	0	0	0	1	1	0	43

Figure 8.20: Sample population

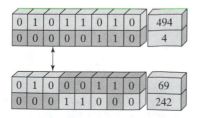

0	1	0	1	1	0	1	0	494
0	0	0	0	0	1	1	0	4

0	1	0	0	0	1	1	0	69
0	0	0	1	1	0	0	0	242

Figure 8.21: Crossover and mutation

Figure 8.22: Knapsack cipher in CAP

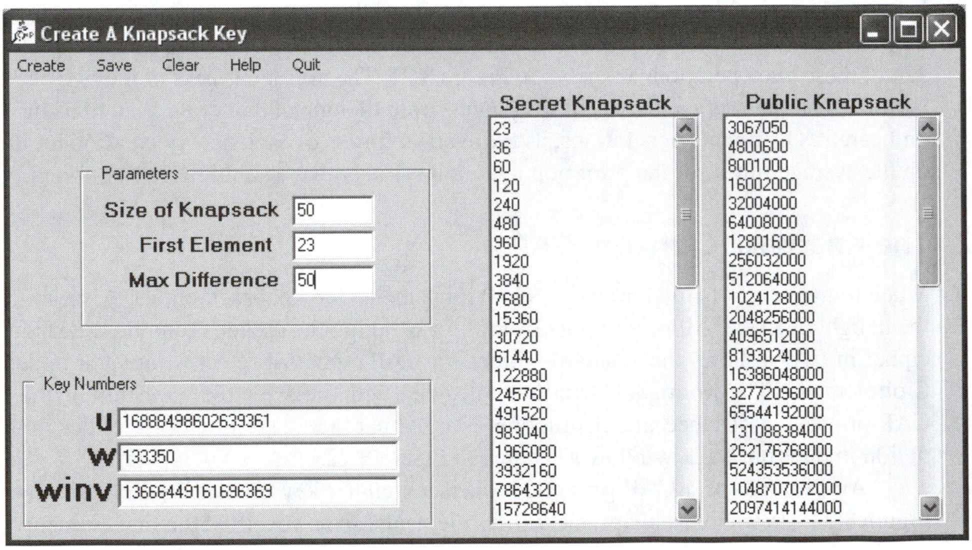

Figure 8.23: Knapsack key generated by CAP

To create a degree of randomness in the superincreasing knapsack, Bob entered 50 in the Max Difference field. Since the only requirement for a superincreasing knapsack is that each term is greater than the sum of the preceding terms, the Max Difference field is used to allow some variability in the difference between the minimum requirement for the size of a term and its actual size.

8.8   ELLIPTIC CURVE CIPHERS (ECC)

In 1985, both Koblitz and Miller independently suggested the use of elliptic curves in the development of a new type of public key cipher. An elliptic curve is a simple equation of the form

$$y^2 = x^3 + ax + b \pmod{p},$$

where p is a prime number or a power of two (it is sometimes called the order of the curve) and $4a^3 + 27b^2 <> 0$. The graph of a typical elliptic curve is shown in Figure 8.24. The

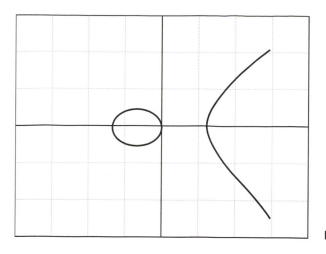

Figure 8.24: A typical elliptic curve

only points on the curve that are of interest are those with integer coordinates. The number of integer coordinates on the curve is finite and plays a role in evaluating the security of the cipher. In fact, the integer points can be combined in the form of an addition operation—one that is specifically defined for elliptic curves.

The addition operator on elliptic curves begins with two points, P and Q. The line through those points intercepts the curve at a third point, the sum of P and Q, and is defined as the reflection of their intercept point across the x-axis. It sounds more mysterious than it really is—a visual picture such as that in Figure 8.25 should help make the addition process much clearer.

For cryptographers, the real interest in elliptic curve addition is the process of adding a point to itself. That is, given a point P, find the point $P + P$, or $2P$. This is done by drawing a line tangent to P and reflecting the point at which it intercepts the curve as shown in Figure 8.26. P can be added to itself k times, resulting in a point $W = kP$. For example, Figure 8.27 shows the point $3P$.

A public key cipher must be based on a problem that is very difficult to solve. For the elliptic curve, that problem is as follows:

Given two points P and W, where W = kP, find the value of k.

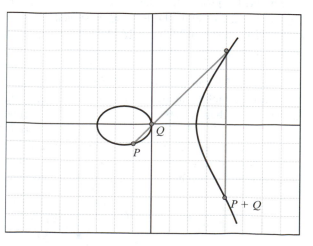

Figure 8.25: Addition on an elliptic curve

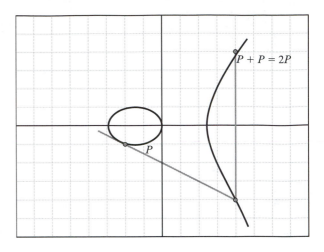

Figure 8.26: Adding P to itself on an elliptic curve

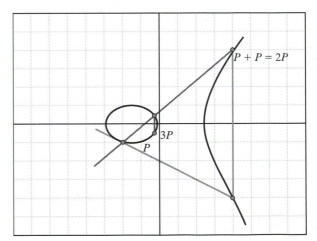

Figure 8.27: Finding the point $3P$ on an elliptic curve

This is called the elliptic curve discrete logarithm problem, ECDLP. (If this sounds like the ElGamal problem, you are right; they are related.) The ECDLP could be solved using an exhaustive search, starting with the condition shown in Figure 8.28: Add P to itself until the point Q is reached. However, for a large k, this is as difficult (or more difficult) than factoring k.

There are several ways in which the ECDLP can be imbedded into a cipher system. Bob and Alice decide to use one of the simplest implementations. Alice begins by selecting an elliptic curve and a point G on the curve. She then selects a secret number k that will be her private key. Her public key is G and P_A, where $P_A = kG$, which she gives to Bob. When Bob wants to send Alice a message, he converts the plaintext into a number m and finds a point on the curve P_m such that the difference of the x- and the y-coordinates equals m. He also selects a random number r. He then sends Alice the ciphertext, which consists of two points on the curve:

$$C = \{rG, P_m + rP_A\}.$$

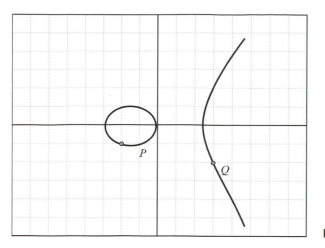

Figure 8.28: Q is what multiple of P?

Alice can easily decipher the ciphertext by multiplying the first point by her secret key and subtracting the result from the second point:

$$P_m + rP_A - k(rG) = P_m + r(kG) - k(rG) = P_m.$$

8.8.1 Observations

Although there are several algorithms that may be used to solve the ECDLP, the fastest is a version of the Pollard Rho method. However, for large key sizes, even the Pollard Rho method requires a large amount of computing time. In 2000, a 108-bit ECC key was broken using the parallel Pollard Rho method running on 9500 computers for 5 months, which is the equivalent of about 500 years of computing time on a single PC. A similar level of security for RSA would require a 600-bit key. Overall, it appears that ECC provides a higher level of security using smaller keys than does RSA.

A comparison between the bit size of keys for an equivalent level of security illustrates the advantage of ECC over RSA:

Security	RSA	ECC
Low	512	112
Medium	1024	161
High	3072	256
Very High	15360	512

Just like there are weak keys for DES, there are weak curves for ECC. For example, there is a class of supersingular curves that were shown by Menezes, Okamoto, and Vanstone in 1993 to be open to a subexponential time attack. This is called the *MOV attack* (after the authors of the paper). Hence, an acceptable curve must not be in the supersingular class, meaning that, to be used in an ECC, the curve must satisfy the following conditions:

1. If N is the number of integer coordinates, it must be divisible by some large prime r—that is $N = kr$.
2. If the curve has order p (using mod p operations), then r must not divide $p^i - 1$ for a small set of i (say i from 0 to 20).

Another set of weak ECC curves are called *anomalous curves*. These are curves for which the number of integer coordinates equals the order (using the values previously defined $N = p$). In fact, in 2000, to avoid weak curves, NIST recommended the following 10 general elliptic curves, 5 with a prime order and 5 with a binary order:

$$\text{Prime Order } p192 = 2192 - 264 - 1$$
$$p224 = 2224 - 296 + 1$$
$$p256 = 2256 - 2224 + 2191 + 296 - 1$$
$$p384 = 2384 - 2128 - 296 + 232 - 1$$
$$p521 = 2521 - 1$$

$$\text{Binary Order } p = 2163$$
$$p = 2233$$
$$p = 2283$$
$$p = 2409$$
$$p = 2571$$

8.9 PUBLIC KEY APPLICATIONS

Some of the most common applications of public key algorithms involve protecting the integrity of documents by providing the equivalent of a handwritten signature. As a result, a complete discussion of public key applications will have to wait until Chapter 9, in which the idea of a digital signature is introduced. However another common application of public key algorithms is their use to protect the integrity of symmetric block-cipher keys.

The problem with public key algorithms is that they are very slow compared to block ciphers. Hence, encrypting a large document with a public key system is sometimes just not efficient, especially when a symmetric block cipher can do it 10 to 100 times faster. On the other hand, the problem with a block cipher is that it is difficult to securely pass a key between two users. This is just not a problem with public key algorithms, since the enciphering key is always public. The solution to both problems is to use both algorithms—each in the most efficient manner. For example, if Bob wants to send Alice a large document as quickly as possible, he could encrypt it using AES and send it on to Alice. Of course, Alice needs the AES key that Bob used. If Bob just sends the key to Alice, he might as well not have encrypted the message in the first place—Eve will intercept both the key and the message. So Bob looks up Alice's public RSA key and uses it to encrypt his AES key. Alice uses her RSA private key to recover the actual AES key and then proceeds to decipher and read Bob's long document. Even though RSA is slow, it only has to encipher–decipher a relatively small AES key. Also, even though the AES key is difficult to remember, Bob can actually make one up for just this one message. He can then send it to Alice by using her public key, with a high degree of certainty that it will be secure. They win on both counts.

What should be noticed here is the issue of managing the keys between Bob and Alice. This is not the first time this issue has become important. It appears that key management is as important as the algorithm choice—and it is, as will be seen in the next chapter.

8.10 HISTORICAL DEVELOPMENTS IN PUBLIC KEY CIPHERS

It has generally been acknowledged that the concept of a public key system was first suggested by Merkel, Diffie, and Hellman in 1976 when they described the knapsack algorithm.

Two years later, Ronald Rivest, Adi Shamir, and Leonard Adelman published a paper on what came to be known as the RSA public key system. It wasn't until 1997 that the secret history of public key ciphers was finally revealed. Not to take anything away from the significant accomplishments of Merkel, Diffie, Hellman, Rivest, Shamir, and Adelman (after all, they independently discovered the fundamental concepts of PK ciphers), but it appears that James Ellis actually discovered the public key method in 1970 while working for the Communications–Electronics Security Group of the British Government Communications Headquarters (the successor to Bletchley Park). His work was not published until 1997 because it had been classified by the British government. In 1973, Clifford Cocks (also while working for the Communications–Electronics Security Group) published a classified paper describing the RSA cryptosystem.

This illustrates an ongoing problem in the field of cryptography. It seems that there are really two parallel efforts going on all the time. There is the classified work, which remains hidden, and there is the academic work, which is openly published.

8.11   SUMMARY

Bob, Alice, and Eve learned about a new class of ciphers, public key ciphers, that require two keys—one is public and the other is private. This is not the only unique feature of public key ciphers. Rather than relying on a complicated process of substitution and permutation for security, these ciphers rely on the difficulty of solving some mathematical problem.

All three also discovered the important role that mathematics plays in the development, analysis, and evaluation of this new class of ciphers. In particular, they gained a new appreciation for numbers and the science of number theory.

Specifically, Bob and Alice learned that for public key systems they need to generate complex keys in the form of very large numbers. This introduces a new set of problems: How do they manage these keys in a way that they can access them when they need them but Eve cannot? To solve this problem, they have to read the next chapter.

Eve learned that she not only requires patience to break this new class of ciphers, she needs to invest more time in the study of mathematics. Because the security of public key systems depends on the degree of difficulty associated with finding the solution to certain mathematical problems, Eve may be able compromise Bob and Alice's communications if she can find a clever way to take advantage of the increasing speed of computers in order to solve the targeted problem. Even if she doesn't succeed in a direct attack at the core of a public key algorithm, Eve also learned that there may be ways to compromise them by looking for information in a side channel.

Finally, another new category and a new set of ciphers can be added to our overall cipher structure as shown in Figure 8.29.

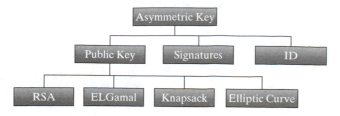

Figure 8.29: Classification of public key ciphers

8.12 IMPORTANT TERMS

ElGamal	A public key cipher whose security is based on the difficulty of solving the discrete logarithm problem
Elliptic Curve	An equation of the form $y^2 = x^3 + ax + b \pmod{p}$ in which addition of integer points on the curve may be used to create a cipher system
Euclid's algorithm	A method for finding the greatest common divisor of two numbers, the extended version will find modular inverses
Genetic algorithm	A random search algorithm based on the characteristics of natural selection in biology
Knapsack cipher	A cipher system based on the difficulty of solving the subset sum problem
Public key system	A cipher system with two keys—the public key is used to encipher plaintext, the secret key is used to decipher
RSA	A widely used public key system whose security is based on the difficulty of factoring large integers
Repeated squaring	A method used to reduce the number of multiplications required by RSA (and other algorithms that rely on multiplication)
Side-channel analysis	A method of breaking cipher by monitoring the characteristics of the cipher implementation such as power consumption or speed

RESOURCES

In addition to the resources sited in the previous chapters, check out the current RSA challenges at http://www.rsasecurity.com/rsalabs/challenges/factoring/numbers.html.

Boneh D., "Twenty Years of Attacks on the RSA Cryptosystem." *Notices of the American Mathematical Society*, 46(2):203–213 (1999).

Koblitz N., "Elliptic curve cryptosystems." *Mathematical Complication*, 48, pp. 203–209 (1987)

Miller V.S., "Use of elliptic curves in cryptography." Advances in Cryptology—Crypto '85, Lecture notes in Computer Science 218, Springer-Verlag (1986), pp. 417–426

PROBLEMS

1. Bob wants to use RSA with a block size of 10 to send the following message to Alice:

   Hi Alice it has been a while since I contacted you. I want you to know that everything is going fine and I will call you tomorrow. Bob

   Alice's public key is as follows: $n = 96498667$, $e = 94475891$. Create the ciphertext.

2. Given Alice's public key from Problem 1, find her private key and use it to decipher the ciphertext that Bob sent to her.

3. Which of the following numbers are prime (indicate the test you used for each one)?

   (a) 12253
   (b) 900213345
   (c) 17515889
   (d) 161270444129
   (e) 453851
   (f) 7670175557761

4. The following numbers are all prime:

   453851   1207039   32046463   398163641   1845277897   40847631499

   Graph the time it takes to verify that the foregoing numbers are prime against the number of digits. Use both trail division methods so there are two lines in the graph. What can you conclude about the two methods?

5. The following numbers are all prime:

   651247415327   8301310004401   18198400004401   449063710848593
   5264651305119901   68063301125552099   171382356359199751
   491377853869613295551   8560959889683060600941057

   Graph the time it takes to verify that the foregoing numbers are prime against the number of digits. Use the Fermat, Lehmann, and Miller methods so that there are three lines in the graph. What can you conclude about the three methods?

6. Eve intercepted a message from Alice to Bob enciphered using RSA with a block size of 16. She knows that Bob's public key is $n = 959455486236$ and $e = 27923157781$.

   The message is as follows:

   402570513855
   9110026864
   153439736421
   864921693668
   637925583027
   909658537600
   878879266527
   728359495475
   593068589632
   916200064152
   19746950663
   264468802305
   362546308473
   46544990900
   595811115816
   793018157000
   237037688464
   38552711197
   532693437264
   560347854564
   475636675945
   822754706889
   270893972249

   Find the plaintext.

7. Factor the following numbers (indicate the method used):

   (a) 15961
   (b) 76001
   (c) 175228969

    (d) 323235792283

    (e) 468603770014481

8. Factor each of the numbers that follow, and graph the time it takes to do so against the number of digits in the number. Use trial division (from the integer window of CAP) as long as it is feasible. Use the four methods available under the Factoring method (under Public Key Systems in the Analysis tools). You should have five curves on the graph. Comment on the results. Here are the numbers:

    (a) 503219

    (b) 1200559

    (c) 79811027

    (d) 545266873

    (e) 154306682903

    (f) 4775027828531

    (g) 526145434732711

    (h) 224192040175009871

9. Bob enciphered the following message and sent it to Alice using an ElGamal cipher and Alice's public key, which is $p = 11851409$, $g = 27046$, $b = 1848340$:

Alice, It took a while for me to generate my ElGamal key. Is that normal? Bob

Construct the ciphertext that Bob sent to Alice.

10. Graph the size of the primes vs the time it takes to find p and g for an ElGamal cipher in which the size of the primes ranges from 6 to 15 and the number of prime factors is 2. What do you conclude from the results?

11. Alice enciphered the following message and sent it to Bob using a 15-element knapsack:

Bob, these knapsacks are getting out of hand. What should we do? Alice

Bob's public key is

301
387
774
1548
3096
6192
12384
24768
49536
99072
50686
101372
55286
110572
73686

Construct the ciphertext that Alice sent to Bob.

12. How many multiplications will it take using fast exponentiation to find the value for $123^{79} \bmod 77$? How many multiplications does it save over doing it in a straightforward manner?

13. Discover a method to factor any size number in less than 10 seconds. Be sure to mention the names of your instructor and the author in your acceptance speech for the National Medal of Science.

Chapter 9

Key Management, Digital Signatures, Hash Functions, and Certificates

9.0   INTRODUCTION

When Alice and Bob began sending messages to each other, their only concern was that Eve not be able to read the contents. They tried several classical ciphers only to discover that Eve was able to break them. They moved on to more complicated contemporary ciphers and discovered that, if they were careful, they could prevent Eve from reading their messages. But a whole new set of problems began to emerge. One of the first was the problem of managing the large random keys required by the new ciphers. They had to use keys that were 56 to 256 bits long, and even if they worked with a Hex representation (blocks of four bits), the keys were long and nonsensical. (Try to remember 4ef0 124a 9732 cb44 5b01 6821 cc07 397f, which is a 128-bit key.) As a result, they were prone to write the key down and save it near their computer (under their keyboard for example—after all who would look there?). Clearly, managing the keys became a problem.

Even more sinister problems began to emerge. One day Bob received a message from Alice asking him to send her some important files. The message was enciphered using Bob's public key and told him that Alice had a new public key he should use to encipher the data he sent her. Bob used the new key, which was included in Alice's message, and sent the files. A week later, when he asked her about those files, Alice said she knew nothing about them. Worse yet, she said she had never changed her public key.

Later, Alice received an encrypted message from Bob authorizing the use of company funds to purchase a big-ticket item from a specific vendor. Alice, worried about what happened to Bob, called him to confirm that he had sent her a message. Of course, she did not want to discuss the contents of the message over the phone; otherwise, why would he have sent it in encrypted form? Bob confirmed that he did indeed send her a message, so Alice makes the purchase. The next day, Bob calls Alice to ask her why she purchased that large item when his message asked her to purchase a much less expensive version. Now it seems that Alice was the victim. From now on, neither Bob nor Alice trust the messages they receive from each other, even when they are enciphered using powerful algorithms. It appears that just encrypting files and messages is not enough—they need to restore a level of trust before any progress can be made.

They have discovered the hard way that even if Eve could not read their messages, it was possible for Eve to intercept a message and send on a modified version. How was Bob to be sure that Alice was the real author? Now, if Alice made some promises in her messages, could she repudiate them later—claiming that Eve made those commitments in her name? Suddenly cryptography became more than a means to hide information; it was important to use it to find ways to ensure the authenticity of messages and shared keys. It was time to go back to the books and explore a new application of cryptography.

Way back in Chapter 1, the main purpose of cryptography was to provide a layer of confidentiality to messages. This would ensure that only those authorized to see a message could actually read it. Now, a layer of integrity is also needed to ensure that, when deciphered, a message has not been modified or altered in any way. In addition, a layer of authenticity is also required to ensure that the author of a message is genuine. A message should be from the person who claims to have sent it, and the author should not be able at some later date to repudiate a message.

This chapter will show you how layers of integrity and authenticity can be added to a message as well as how keys can be efficiently and securely managed. It will directly address four kinds of attacks:

- Manipulation—the interception and modification of information
- Masquerade—pretending to be another user
- Replay—recording and replaying (at a later date) a communication
- Repudiation—the denial by a user of participation in part or all of a communication

9.1 KEY EXCHANGE

Remember the German's reason for setting a unique key for each Enigma transmission? They wanted to avoid using the same key again and again. It was a good strategy in theory; however, in practice it created a different weakness that the Allies were able to exploit. They had the right idea—don't overuse a key—but they adopted the wrong procedure for establishing a unique common key for each transmission. This remains a continuing problem in cryptography—how can a new key be securely shared with others?

For Bob and Alice, the first order of business was to come up with a way to manage the large keys they required in such a way that Eve could not interfere. While public keys could do this, the public key algorithms are slow. So Bob and Alice still wanted to use a faster block cipher that required a single key known only to them. Security also demanded that the key be changed on a regular basis. As a result, Bob and Alice need a secure method to generate a single key that only they could know without requiring them to meet in person.

It turns out that there are several key exchange algorithms available—most of which are based on a public key system. One of the first methods developed is called the Diffie–Hellman key exchange system. To set up the Diffie–Hellman (DH) protocol, Bob and Alice must first agree on two numbers: p, a large prime number, and g, a random number less than p. Both p and g are public, so Bob and Alice can select the numbers over an insecure channel. (They could send them to Eve, for that matter.) Alice selects a secret random number, a, and sends Bob the value $g^a \bmod p$. At the same time, Bob selects his own secret random number, b, and sends the value $g^b \bmod p$ to Alice. Alice uses her secret number and the value Bob sent her to calculate

$$(g^b \bmod p)^a \bmod p = k,$$

while Bob uses his secret number and the value Alice sent him to calculate

$$(g^a \bmod p)^b \bmod p = k.$$

They both end up with the same number, k, which becomes their common key.
  There are several observations that can be made about this process:

1. Neither Bob nor Alice has any idea what the final key will be.
2. Neither Bob nor Alice shares their secret number with each other.
3. Eve can have access to g, p, and the values $g^a \bmod p$ and $g^b \bmod p$ because the only way she can find k is to solve for both a and b, which is equivalent to the discrete logarithm problem.

  For example, if Alice and Bob agree on the values $p = 76825670157115949022871$ and $g = 129633$, then Alice selects her secret value 1567, Bob selects his secret value 3001, and they both calculate the number to send to each other. Alice determines that she must send 3748860625118221776574 to Bob, and Bob sends 34126923917580261813405 to Alice. The result is the following common key:

$$32347879715377627749156.$$

Now, this number that only Bob and Alice know can be used as a key for encrypting messages in a number of ways. For example, they could convert it to Hex and use the first eight Hex digits as a common DES key. Or they could use it to set up a stream cipher in which part of it represents the feedback loops and part the initial setting of the LFSR. The Hex representation of this key is as follows:

$$DB32A057D72A6FEB648.$$

If they are using DES, they might select the eight most significant digits as their key, in this case DB32A057.
  Bob and Alice quickly realize that these numbers are too large to work with by hand. Luckily they discover that CAP will do all the work for them, including translating the common key into Hex format as shown in Figure 9.1.
  The overall DH process is not tied to the use of exponentials. An elliptical curve cipher (ECC) version of the Diffie–Hellman scheme is also possible. In this case, Alice and Bob select a suitable curve, G, and base point, P. Each selects a secret random number. (Alice selects A and Bob selects B.) Alice sends Bob the value $P_A = AP$, and Bob sends Alice the value $P_B = BP$. They each used the value sent to them and their own secret key to compute the common ECC key: $K = ABP$.
  The Diffie–Hellman scheme is secure only if the public numbers are large. Even when large numbers are selected, the scheme is subject to a man-in-the-middle attack. The problem is that, since Alice and Bob are only communicating across an insecure channel, how do they know who is really on the other end? How does Alice know that Bob is the one that sent her the value $g^b \bmod p$? If Eve is able to intercept the messages between Bob and

Diffie-Hellman Key Exchange					_ □ ×

Run (Alice)   Run (Bob)   Convert Key   Help   Quit

Public Values

P 768256701571159490228871

g 1297633

Alice's Secret Value

X 1567

Bob's Secret Value

Y 3001

Alice's Shared Values

Send to Bob 748860625118221776574

Received from Bob 126923917580261813405

Bob's Shared Values

Send to Alice 126923917580261813405

Received from Alice 748860625118221776574

Alice's Key Value

KEY 323478797153776627749156

Bob's Key Value

KEY 323478797153776627749156

Figure 9.1: Example of Diffie–Hellman key calculation

Alice, she can set up two key exchanges—one with Alice and the other with Bob—in a way that both Alice and Bob think they have a joint key. This attack is illustrated in Figure 9.2.

An authenticated version of Diffie–Hellman is available to protect against a man-in-the-middle attack. It requires that both Bob and Alice have secret and public keys used to help set up the Diffie–Hellman procedure. As before, Bob and Alice openly agree on a prime p and a number g. Alice also has a large secret key, A, and a public key, g^A. Bob has a large secret key, B, and a public key, g^B. Both can use the other's public key and their

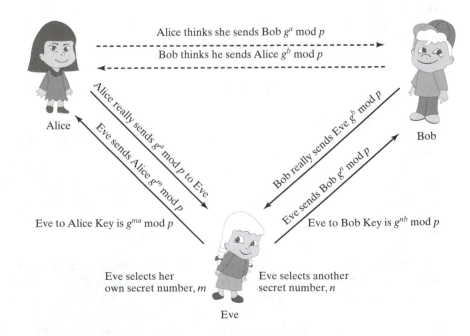

Alice thinks she sends Bob $g^a \bmod p$

Bob thinks he sends Alice $g^b \bmod p$

Alice really sends $g^a \bmod p$ to Eve

Eve sends Alice $g^m \bmod p$

Bob really sends Eve $g^b \bmod p$

Eve sends Bob $g^n \bmod p$

Alice

Bob

Eve to Alice Key is $g^{ma} \bmod p$

Eve to Bob Key is $g^{nb} \bmod p$

Eve selects her own secret number, m

Eve selects another secret number, n

Eve

Figure 9.2: Man-in-the-middle attack on Diffie–Hellman

own secret key to determine $K = g^{AB}$. Alice calculates $(g^B)^A$, while Bob calculates $(g^A)^B$. Since Eve does not know either A or B, she cannot determine K; so K serves as an authentication value. The DH procedure becomes

1. Alice selects a random number a.
2. She sends Bob g^{aK}.
3. Bob selects a random number b.
4. He sends Alice g^{bK}.
5. Bob computes the agreed-upon key as

$$K_{AB} = (g^{aK})^{K^{-1}_b} = g^{ab},$$

and Alice arrives at the same key value:

$$K_{AB} = (g^{bK})^{K^{-1}_a} = g^{ab}.$$

You have probably used the Diffie–Hellman procedure without be aware of it. It is one of the common options in the secure sockets layer (SSL) used to protect Web transactions. The task of the SSL is to set up an encrypted link between you and your selected website without requiring you to enter a cipher key. The result is that your computer and the Web server use Diffie–Hellman to establish a common key for the current Web session. Every time you access a secure website, a new key is automatically set up.

9.1.1 Internet Key Exchange Process

As noted in the previous section, the Diffie–Hellman procedure is used to set up a common key for a secure Internet connection. Back in Chapter 7 (Section 7.6.2, to be exact) the process of setting up a secure Internet link was discussed briefly. You were told to wait until Chapter 9 to see how the key was formed for the secure link. Well, your wait is over.

The formal process for such a connection in the IPSec protocol is called the Internet key exchange (IKE), and it is used to establish a security association (SA). For example, if Alice and Bob want a secure Internet connection, the IKE process would engage and exchange six messages between their machines. Note, Alice and Bob do not actually form or send these messages; they are part of the IKE automatic process. These six messages are shown in Figure 9.3. Alice's machine begins by sending an IKE SA proposal. This proposal lists the types of encryption algorithms that her machine is capable of implementing as

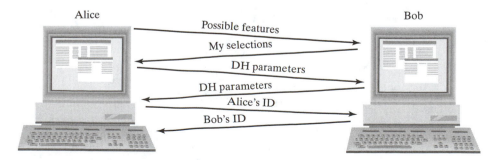

Figure 9.3: Internet key exchange process

well as other information that is vital to a secure link. Bob's machine responds by selecting the encryption algorithm and other features it can use from Alice's list. If there is a common set of methods between the two machines, then the protocol continues. The next two messages follow the Diffie–Hellman procedure. Alice's machine sends her part of the Diffie–Hellman secret plus a random value. Bob's machine responds with his part of the Diffie–Hellman secret and a random value. Now, both sides have a common secret key. Finally, Alice's machine sends its identity information and Bob's machine responds with its identity information.

9.1.2 Group Keys

Diffie–Hellman works fine for pairs of users, but there is a need for larger groups of users to securely establish a known key as well. Sometimes this situation arises when someone wants to broadcast a message to several different users. This is called a multicast, or one-to-many, communication link and will be covered in the next section. Other times, this situation arises when a group of users needs to carry on a secure discussion in a many-to-many communication link. In this case, every sender is also a receiver, and the process is called *peer-group communication*.

DH can be generalized to work in peer-group mode. For example, say Chris wants to join in with Bob and Alice. They need a common key, so they elect to use DH. All three agree on common values g and n. Alice begins by selecting a random number, a, and sends Bob the value g^a mod n. Bob selects his random number, b, and sends Chris the value g^b mod n to send to Alice. Finally, Chris selects a random number, c, and sends Alice the value g^c mod n. This completes the first step. Now Alice sends Bob the value g^{ac} mod n, Bob sends Chris the value g^{ab} mod n, and Chris sends Alice the value g^{bc} mod n. This completes the second step. For the third and final step, each one calculates the common key. Alice uses her random number and the final value Chris sent her to calculate $K = (g^{bc})^a = g^{abc}$ mod n. Bob uses his random number and the final value Alice sent him to calculate $K = (g^{ac})^b = g^{abc}$ mod n. Chris uses his random number and the final value Bob sent him to calculate $K = (g^{ab})^c = g^{abc}$ mod n. They all have the same key, but it is never transmitted directly, so it remains secure. Now they can establish a multicast or peer-group communication linkage. This process is illustrated in Figure 9.4.

While this offers Bob and Alice a straightforward generalization of the standard DH process, it does pose some problems. For example, if someone wants to join their group,

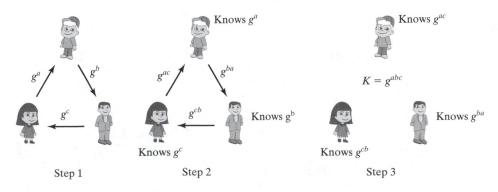

Figure 9.4: A group Diffie–Hellman process

they have to go through these steps again. Not only that, because there are four users involved, they have to go though four steps instead of three. If someone leaves the group, then the key assignment process must begin again as well. In short, this process does not offer the degree of flexibility required for large and variable-size groups.

Another, somewhat obvious, approach is to appoint a member of the group to be the group controller (GC). The GC shares a different key encryption key (KEK) with every member of the group. All the group members $(M_1, M_2, \ldots, M_n)$ share a single traffic encryption key (TEK), which is used to send encrypted, secure messages to each other. This model looks something like a star as shown in Figure 9.5.

When a new member joins the group, the GC sets up a KEK for her and determines a new TEK. The TEK is sent to each member, encrypted using the member's individual KEK. If a member leaves the group, the GC determines a new TEK and sends it to the remaining member's encrypted, of course, in each member's KEK. This method does not scale well. A group of size n requires n key encryption keys and one traffic encryption key, or $n + 1$ keys overall.

Overall, a good group key-management system should not only provide an efficient method to add or drop members, it should also provide four forms of security:

1. Group key security—it should not be possible for an outsider to discover the key.
2. Backward security—it should not be possible to determine previous group keys from knowledge of a subset of the current set of group keys.
3. Forward security—it should not be possible to determine any future keys from knowledge of a subset of the current set of group keys.
4. Key independence—it should not be possible to determine any group key from knowledge of a subset of the current set of group keys.

Kim, Perrig, and Tsudik presented a key-management scheme at a 2000 Association for Computing Machinery (ACM) conference that offered better scaling and a more formal procedure for joining and exiting a group. It is called a tree-based group Diffie–Hellman protocol (TGDH). The relationship between keys is represented in a key tree such as the one shown in Figure 9.6 for a nine-member group. Each key box in the figure contains two keys: a secret key, K_i, and public key (called a blinded key), BK_i. The root key, K_0, is the group key. Each member has access to all the blinded keys and to all the secret keys in the path from the root node down to the member. For the example, M_4 knows secret keys K_4, K_1, and K_0, as well as all the public keys.

To start the process of creating the keys, all members agree on public values for g and p as in the DH protocol. Then each member will select a secret random number. (Say, member M_i selects a_i.) If two members are children of the same key node in the

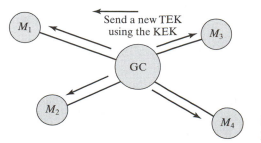

Figure 9.5: A star-shaped group key-management system

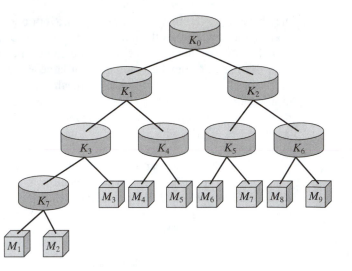

Figure 9.6: An example of a TGDH system

tree (as are M_1 and M_2), they will follow the standard DH protocol and create a shared secret key based on their individual random numbers. In the example (all values are reduced mod p),

M_1 sends M_2 the value g^{a1}

M_2 sends M_1 the value g^{a2}

Using these values, they calculate the secret key value

$$K_7 = g^{a_1 a_2}$$

and the public blinded key value

$$BK_7 = g^{K_7} = g^{g^{a_1 a_2}}.$$

The keys at each stage of the example are shown in Figure 9.7. The two children of each node establish the keys for the parent node using DH. For node K_3, the process looks like this:

M_3 sends k_3 the value g^{a1}

k_3 sends M_3 the value g^{k7}

The result is

$$K_3 = g^{a_3 K_7} \quad \text{and} \quad BK_3 = g^{K_3}.$$

Since every member knows all the secret keys in the path from their location up to the root node, every member knows the group key. They also have knowledge of intermediate keys, which could be used to form secure subgroups. For the example, M_1, M_2, and M_3 are the only members who know K_3, so they could use that key for secure communications among themselves.

If a member leaves the group, some of the keys have to be changed so old members cannot use knowledge of the prior keys to continue to eavesdrop on the group. In this case, a special member is appointed as the sponsor. The task of the sponsor is to broadcast the

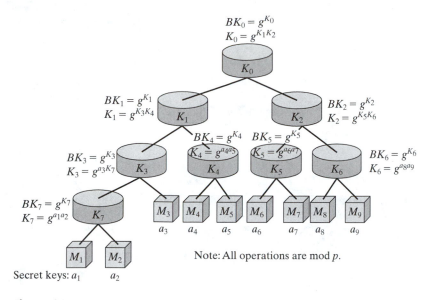

Figure 9.7: Keys in an example TGDH system

updated blinded keys so that the entire group can change their keys if necessary. For our example, M_7 leaves the group so M_6 becomes the sponsor. The two secret keys, K_0 and K_2, must be changed, since these are known to M_7. So M_6 will select a new random number, na_6, which will be used to update K_2. M_6 will broadcast the new BK_2 to every member so that M_8 and M_9 can update both K_0 and K_2 while the other members update just the group key K_0. The required changes are shown in Figure 9.8. Notice that only a few keys must be changed—this is really a very efficient method.

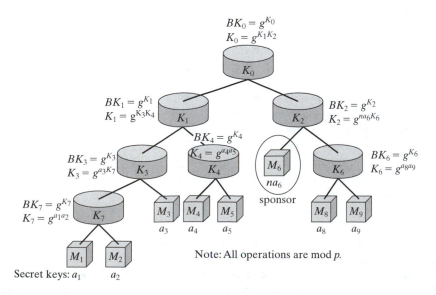

Figure 9.8: Rekeying when a member leaves

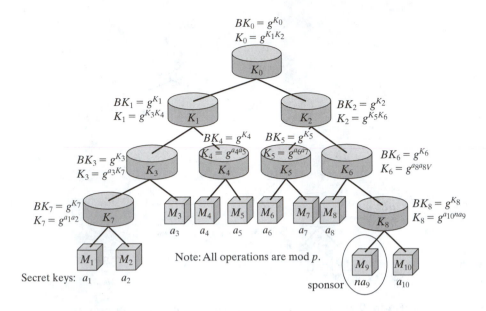

Figure 9.9: Rekeying when a member is added

Adding a new member to the group is also easy. As before, a sponsor is appointed who will update the blinded keys. For example, if M_{10} becomes a new member as shown in Figure 9.9, M_9 might be appointed the sponsor. In that case, M_9 would select a new random number, na_9, and use it to create K_8 and BK_8. This information is passed up the tree to create a new group key. Notice that, when M_{10} is added, he is not given any information that could reveal the prior keys. Every secret key in the path from M_{10} to the root is changed.

9.1.2 Broadcast Encryption

Up to this point, the assumption has been that multiple parties communicate with each other. They can share information back and forth in order to set up a key. But what happens when that is not the case? How can a key be established when one party can only transmit and another can only receive? This may seem like a unique and artificial condition, but it is actually quite common. Consider the operation of pay TV. Home viewers purchase a descrambling box and attach it to their TV. This box will accept an encrypted TV signal and decrypt it for viewing. How does the transmitting authority know which key to use to encipher the signal? How does the home box know the key for deciphering? The process of making this all work is called *broadcast encryption*.

The broadcast encryption problem is further complicated by the fact that it is usually only a subset of the users that are authorized to have access to a specific message. In the TV example, only a subset of the box owners may request a particular pay-per-view program, so only those owners should be able to decipher the TV signal. All other box owners should not be able to view the program for free. This is the case for those viewers who want to watch "The Sun Sets at Noon" as shown in Figure 9.10.

There are several methods of broadcast encryption that have been suggested and utilitized. One method would be to assign each TV box its own private key and then send out a customized signal encrypted with each private key to each box. With millions of home users, this would require that the same TV signal be encrypted and transmitted millions of times. There must be a better way.

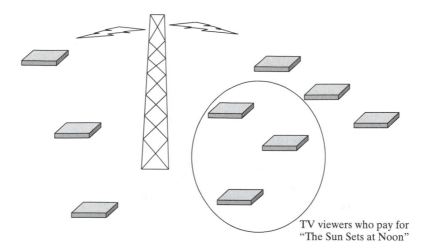

Figure 9.10: Broadcast subset

There is. An approach based on ideas similar to those found in the TGDH protocol covered in the last section has been developed. Given n devices, assume that each device has been assigned some secret information. (Device u is given I_u.) The devices are members of various subsets of n, $S_1, \ldots, S_m$. Each subset, S_j, has a long-lived key, L_j. Given a set of revoked devices R, the set of nonrevoked devices is $N \backslash R$, which consists of w disjoint subsets:

$$S_i, S_i, \ldots S_i \qquad \text{so} \quad N \backslash R = \cup S_i.$$

Each device in a given subset knows or can calculate the subset key L_i (for the ith subset). Every message is enciphered with a session key, K, by some algorithm F. The session key is encrypted for each subset using the subset key by some algorithm E. The message is then sent to all the devices in the form shown in Figure 9.11. The header identifies the subsets and provides an encrypted form of the session key, which can be decrypted by each subset. As a result, only those devices authorized to receive the message will have access to the session key.

The problem that must be solved before this method can work is how to assign keys so that subsets can be defined consisting of only the authorized devices. It turns out this can be done using a tree representation much like that of the TGDH protocol. This is called the *complete subtree method*. A full binary tree is constructed in which the leaf nodes represent the devices and the interior nodes hold a key value. An example of such a tree for eight devices is shown in Figure 9.12. Each device has its own key and knows all the keys in the path from the root to the device. For the example, Device 3 knows keys L_9, L_4, L_1, and L_0. Within this structure, it is easy to define a collection of subsets that includes only authorized devices. The process requires identifying the highest keys in the tree that are shared by authorized devices. For example, if a popular pay-per-view program like "Happiness Always Jumps the Tracks" is on, maybe users 1, 2, 3, 5, 6, 7, and 8 (all but 4) would be willing to pay the $50 fee to watch the movie. In this case, the authorized devices would be defined by three subgroups: $\{D_1, D_2\}$, $\{D_3\}$, and $\{D_5, D_6, D_7, D_8\}$. These three subsets are defined by the key set L_3, L_9, and L_2, as shown in Figure 9.13.

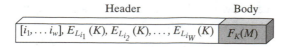

Figure 9.11: Encryption broadcast message form

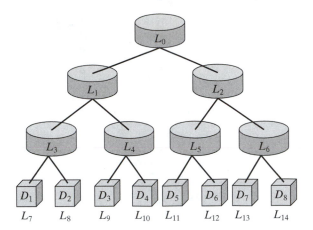

Figure 9.12: A full subtree for eight devices

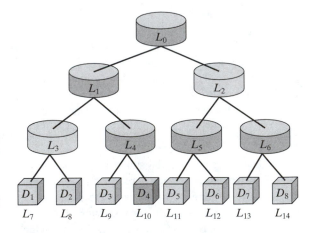

Figure 9.13: A large group of authorized devices

This turns out to be a very efficient method for broadcast encryption because, even if there are a large number of devices, each device only has to store a few keys. For example, if there are 16,384 devices, the tree has only 16 levels ($\log_2 n$, where n is the number of devices) so each device needs to store only 17 keys.

Before concluding this section on key management, it is important to note that very little has been said about the actual encryption algorithms. After eight chapters of material on how to encipher and decipher messages, it should be of some interest that the focus changes to handling and distributing keys. The lesson to learn here is that with contemporary ciphers, how you deal with keys is as important as which cipher you select.

9.2 AUTHENTICITY

During the Christmas holidays, E-mailboxes are filled with greetings just as regular mailboxes are filled with Christmas cards. The difference is that sometimes the greetings are more than what they seem. Bogus E-mail is sometimes sent telling the recipients to go to an innocent-sounding website like www.funholidaycards.com for a personal message from a friend. The site actually contains malicious code.

In 2002, instant message (IM) users were tricked into downloading malicious software by an E-mail warning them that their systems were infected. They were instructed to go to a certain website and download special software or they would be banned from the IM system. Of course, they really were not infected until they actually downloaded the bogus software.

Also in 2002, eBay customers received an E-mail asking them to update their financial information. They were directed to a website called www.ebayupdates.com. The website had the real eBay company logo and appeared legitimate. It was fake.

These three events may have nothing to do with encryption—after all nothing was enciphered. But they do have one thing in common: The E-mails were sent by imposters. Herein lies the problem with both digital documents and messages, even if they are enciphered. How do you know they are authentic? In fact, this was the same problem faced by those who plotted against Queen Elizabeth in 1587. Part of the evidence gathered against Mary Queen of Scots was the result of a fake message sent in her own code.

Bob and Alice face this problem when they send documents to each other. Using Diffie–Hellman or some variation of a key exchange protocol, Bob and Alice can be relatively sure that they share a secret key. So, the problem is no longer secrecy, it is authenticity. The issue of authenticity takes many forms. The simplest one is the concern over integrity—has the message been changed? It may even be the case that when Alice sends a message to Bob, she doesn't care if Eve can read it. She and Bob only want assurances that Eve has not changed the content of the message. In this case, they could add a message authentication code (MAC) to the end of the message. The value of a MAC depends on both the content of the message and a secret key.

For example, if Alice wants to send an authentic plaintext message to Bob, she might encipher it using the cipher block-chaining mode of DES. Since she is not concerned with secrecy, she doesn't send the ciphertext to Bob. Rather, she attaches the final block of ciphertext (her MAC) to the end of the plaintext message. When Bob receives the message, he runs it through DES and compares the final block to the MAC Alice sent. If the two match, then the message is assumed to be intact; otherwise, it is assumed that Eve changed it along the way. Since Eve does not know the DES key, she cannot create a valid MAC.

To achieve a level of authenticity and confidentiality, Alice could first encipher the plaintext with her private key and then encipher the result with Bob's public key. When Bob receives the message, he first deciphers it with his private key and then uses Alice's public key to recover the actual plaintext. Since only Alice knows her private key, the fact that the plaintext can be recovered using her public key is evidence that only Alice could have produced the message. Since only Bob knows his private key, only Bob can decipher the original ciphertext. This process is illustrated in Figure 9.14.

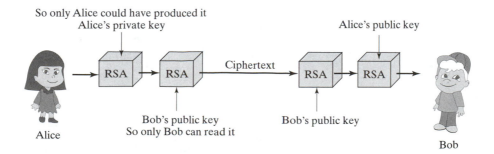

Figure 9.14: Using RSA for authenticity and confidentiality

A MAC will provide only a certain degree of authenticity, which means that a form of encryption must be added in order to gain a level of confidentiality. However, legal issues often demand more than just authenticity and confidentiality: Sometimes the messages sent between Alice and Bob must satisfy the same requirements as a formal signed document. This leads to the development of digital signatures.

9.3   DIGITAL SIGNATURES

The purpose of a digital signature is much like that of your own signature—it verifies the authenticity of a document or message in a legally acceptable fashion. In fact, both the U.S. Congress and the courts have granted digitally signed documents the same weight as paper documents that have a handwritten signature.

There are five qualities of paper documents that must be satisfied by an electronic document: unforgeability, authenticity, unreusability, unalterability, and unrepudiatability. *Unforgeability* is the proof that the signer and only the signer actually signed the document. *Authenticity* is the conviction of the recipient that the document came from the signer. *Unreusability* requires that the signature belong to only one document and not be applied to any other document. *Unalterability* requires that the document not be changed after it is signed. Finally, *unrepudiatability* ensures that the signer cannot later claim that he or she did not sign the document.

Using a public key protocol based on RSA (like the one suggested in the previous section) could satisfy all five requirements. However, the entire message must be enciphered by using RSA, which is slow. In addition, because of some of the possible attacks on RSA (such as the multiplicative attack, which will be covered later), enciphering a small segment is preferred. Hence, a digital signature is usually a small segment of ciphertext that depends on the entire plaintext. Given a message, m, the standard approach is to create a fixed-size message digest, $h(m)$, and then sign the digest, $S[h(m)]$. The signed message is sent as the pair $(m, S[h(m)])$. The message is verified by reversing the signature process to recover the value of $h(m)$ and applying h to the received message. If the two values are equal, then the message is authentic. This process is illustrated in Figure 9.15.

You might wonder why a hash value is signed and not just the entire message. In other words, why doesn't Alice just encipher the entire message with her private key? After all, when Bob deciphers it with Alice's public key, doesn't that prove that the message came from Alice? It turns out that it does not, because this type of "raw" RSA signature scheme is open to a multiplicative attack. It exploits the property that

$$(m_1 m_2)^d = m_1^d m_2^d \bmod n.$$

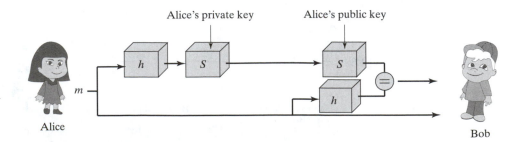

Figure 9.15: Using a digital signature

If Alice signed her message with her private key and sent it to Bob as $s = m^d \bmod n$, then Eve could forge her signature on any message. That is a powerful statement and a serious weakness. Say Eve wanted to forge Alice's signature on a message, f (for fake). She could succeed using the following steps:

1. Select an arbitrary message m_1 (a number in the range 1 to n) and compute a message $m_2 = f m_1^{-1} \bmod n$. This way $f = m_1 m_2$.
2. Trick Alice into signing m_1 and m_2 as s_1 and s_2.
3. Then the signature to f is $s = s_1 s_2 \bmod n$.

As a result, Alice must first hash her messages and sign the hash value.

Before examining hash functions in detail, it is worth noting that there is nothing about RSA that makes it the only candidate for digital signatures. Any public key algorithm could work in a similar manner. For example, an elliptic curve digital signature could be implemented in Figure 9.15 using the ECC public and private keys.

9.3.1   Hash Functions

The function h in the scheme shown in Figure 9.15 is called a *hash function*. A hash function converts any size of input into a fixed (smaller) size of output. There are six requirements for a hash function, h:

1. It should accept any length message as input.
2. It should produce a small fixed-size output ($\sim$100 bits).
3. It should be easy and fast to compute h for any input.
4. It should be a one-way function—hard or impossible to invert. That is, given $h(m)$, it should be very difficult to recover m.
5. It should be resistant to weak collisions. A collision occurs when two different inputs produce the same output.
6. It should be resistant to strong collisions—that is, it should be almost impossible to find two meaningful messages m_1 and m_2 such that $h(m_1) = h(m_2)$.

Hash functions are often used to protect password files. Your user password is hashed and only the hashed value is stored in the computer. This prevents someone from reading the file and learning your password. When you log on, the computer hashes the password you enter and compares the hash (not the actual password) to the stored hash value. If there is a match, then you are granted access.

For security purposes, there are three general properties which flow from requirements 5 and 6 from the previous list that a hash function should satisfy:

1. Preimage resistance—given $h(x)$, it is difficult to compute x.
2. Second preimage resistance—given x, it is difficult to find x' such that $h(x) = h(x')$.
3. Collision—it is difficult to find two messages x and x' such that $h(x) = h(x')$.

In 1979, Merkle proposed a general scheme for hash functions based on a data-compression function, f. The compression function accepts two inputs—a compression value (CV) of size n bits and a data value (M) of size b bits—and produces an n-bit output. What

Merkle suggested was that the data value consist of a message block and the process be iterated over all the blocks in a given message much like the system shown in Figure 9.16.

A simple hash function can be constructed using the XOR operation as follows: divide the message into fixed-size blocks, XOR the first element of each block to produce the first hash output, XOR the second element of each block to produce the second hash output, and so on. For example, with 8-bit blocks, the hash value for the message "Go now" (given in its ASCII code) is

G	0100 0111
o	0110 1111
n	0110 1110
o	0110 1111
w	0111 0111
	0101 1110 = 5E (hex).

Using only 8-bit blocks does not produce a collision-resistant hash value. In this case, both "bob" and "yes" have the same hash value (6F). However, larger block sizes may provide more resistance to a collision, so Bob and Alice decide to adopt this hash function. Bob sends a message to Alice acknowledging receipt of her secret key: "Alice, I just got your secret key." Lucky for them, they do not have to calculate the XORs for their messages, because CAP will do it for them. Bob selects the XOR Hash option under the Signatures menu, sets the hash size to 16 bits, records the hex hash value (021F as shown in Figure 9.17), and sends it along with the message to Alice. If Eve intercepted Bob's message and tried to substitute it

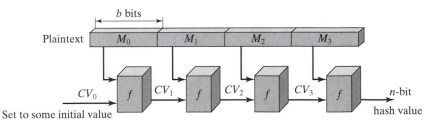

Figure 9.16: General iterative hash scheme

Figure 9.17: CAP implementation of a simple XOR Hash

with the message "Alice, I did not get your secret key", Alice would detect Eve's interference when she calculated the hash value for the bogus message (0D3E).

9.3.1.1   MD5

The simple XOR hash function does not provide enough security to serve as a digital signature. Several other more complicated functions have been suggested for this purpose. Among them is the algorithm MD5 (message digest 5) developed by Ron Rivest.

MD5 accepts a message of any length as input and produces a 128-bit message digest as output. Given a message of length L bits, there are three steps required to set up the algorithm. The first is to pad the message by adding extra bits onto the end of it. Padding is a common feature of most hash functions and done correctly it can add to the security of algorithm. For MD5, the message is padded so that its bit length equals 448 mod 512. (This is 64 bits less than an integer multiple of 512 bits.) Even if the original message is the desired length, padding is added. The padding consists of a single 1 bit followed by enough 0 bits to create the required length. For example, if a message consisted of 704 bits, 256 bits would be added on to the end (a 1 followed by 255 0's) to expand the message to 960 bits (960 mod 512 = 448).

Second, the original length of the message reduced mod 2^{64} is added to the end of the expanded message as a 64-bit number. In the example, the original size was 704 bits, which in binary is 1011000000. This is written as a 64-bit number (54 0's are appended to the beginning) and added to the end of the expanded message. The result is a message with 1024 bits.

Third, the initial input to MD5 is placed in four 32-bit registers A, B, C, and D, which will later hold the intermediate and final results of the hash function. The initial values (in hex) are as follows:

A = 67452301; B = EFCDAB89; C = 98BADCFE; D = 10325476.

Once these set-up steps are completed, MD5 will process each 512-bit block in four rounds. The four rounds are shown in Figure 9.18. Each round consists of 16 stages, each

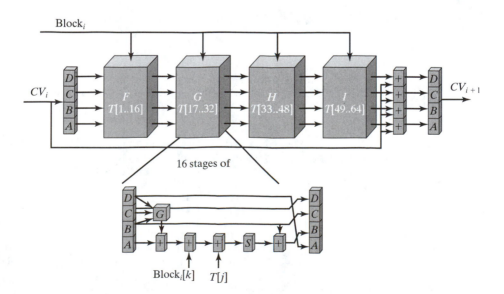

Figure 9.18: MD5 rounds and stages

of which implements a round-specific function (F, G, H, or I), a 32-bit addition to part of the message block, a 32-bit addition to a built-in value found in the array T, a shift operation, and a final addition and permutation operation. It really scrambles up the bits!

The round-specific functions accept three 32-bit words as input and produce a 32-bit output which is the result of a bitwise logical operation. The truth table shown in Figure 9.19 lists the output bits for each input bit combination. The 32-bit function output is added (mod 2^{32}) to the contents of the A register.

The 512-bit input block is divided into sixteen 32-bit words. Within each of the four rounds, each of the 16 words is used exactly once; however, the order of their use changes. For the first round (the one using function F), the 16 words of the input block are used in order—that is, $block_i(j)$ is added to register A, where j is the current stage. (j ranges from 1 to 16.) In the second round, $block_i(k)$ is added to register A, where $k = (1 + 5j)$ mod 16, in which j is the current stage. In the third round, $block_i(k)$ is added to register A, where $k = (5 + 3j)$ mod 16, in which j is the current stage. In the fourth round, $block_i(k)$ is added to register A, where $k = 7j$ mod 16, in which j is the current stage.

The new value in register A is then added (mod 2^{32}) to a constant element from the T array. The T values are derived from the sine function and are listed in Figure 9.20. The resulting value of A is then rotated to the left, and, like everything else in MD5, the rotation amount varies from round to round and stage to stage. The number of bits to rotate for each

b	c	d	F	G	H	I
0	0	0	0	0	0	1
0	0	1	1	0	1	0
0	1	0	0	1	1	0
0	1	1	1	0	0	1
1	0	0	0	0	1	1
1	0	1	0	1	0	1
1	1	0	1	1	0	0
1	1	1	1	1	1	0

Figure 9.19: MD5 round-specific functions

T[1] = D76AA478	T[17] = F61E2562	T[33] = FFFA3942	T[49] = F4292244
T[2] = E8C7B756	T[18] = C040B340	T[34] = 8771F681	T[50] = 432AFF97
T[3] = 242070DB	T[19] = 265E5A51	T[35] = 699D6122	T[51] = AB9423A7
T[4] = C1BDCEEE	T[20] = E9B6C7AA	T[36] = FDE5380C	T[52] = FC93A039
T[5] = F57C0FAF	T[21] = D62F105D	T[37] = A4BEEA44	T[53] = 655B59C3
T[6] = 4787C62A	T[22] = 02441453	T[38] = 4BDECFA9	T[54] = 8F0CCC92
T[7] = A8304613	T[23] = D8A1E681	T[39] = F6BB4B60	T[55] = FFEFF47D
T[8] = FD469501	T[24] = E7D3FBC8	T[40] = BEBFBC70	T[56] = 85845DD1
T[9] = 698098D8	T[25] = 21E1CDE6	T[41] = 289B7EC6	T[57] = 6FA87E4F
T[10] = 8B44F7AF	T[26] = C33707D6	T[42] = EAA127FA	T[58] = FE2CE6E0
T[11] = FFFF5BB1	T[27] = F4D50D87	T[43] = D4EF3085	T[59] = A3014314
T[12] = 895CD7BE	T[28] = 455A14ED	T[44] = 04881D05	T[60] = 4E0811A1
T[13] = 6B901122	T[29] = A9E3E905	T[45] = D9D4D039	T[61] = F7537E82
T[14] = FD987193	T[30] = FCEFA3F8	T[46] = E6DB99E5	T[62] = BD3AF235
T[15] = A679438E	T[31] = 676F02D9	T[47] = 1FA27CF8	T[63] = 2AD7D2BB
T[16] = 49B40821	T[32] = 8D2A4C8A	T[48] = C4AC5665	T[64] = EB86D391

Figure 9.20: MD5 constant values in the T array

Round	\multicolumn{16}{c}{Stage}

Round	1	2	3	4	5	6	7	8	9	10	11	12	13	14	15	16
1	7	12	17	22	7	12	17	22	7	12	17	22	7	12	17	22
2	5	9	14	20	5	9	14	20	5	9	14	20	5	9	14	20
3	4	8	16	23	4	8	16	23	4	8	16	23	4	8	16	23
4	6	10	15	21	6	10	15	21	6	10	15	21	6	10	15	21

Figure 9.21: Bit rotations in MD5

stage of each round are given in Figure 9.21. Finally, register B is added to register A and the registers are permutated.

After all four rounds, the original contents of $ABCD$ are added to the new contents of $ABCD$ to produce the output for the ith message block. This output serves as input to begin processing the $(i + 1)$th message block. The 128-bit content of $ABCD$ that remains after the final message block is processed form the hash value.

9.3.1.2 Secure Hash Algorithm (SHA)

Another hash algorithm was developed by NIST in 1993 called SHA. Two years later, it was revised into the form that is widely used today. The revised version is SHA-1, and it is the required hash algorithm for use in the digital signature standard.

It was modeled after MD4 a precursor to MD5, so it has a number of its features. It accepts an input message of any size and produces a 160-bit message digest. (MD5 only produces a 128-bit digest.) Like MD5, it works on blocks of 512 bits divided up into 32-bit words. It runs in four rounds with 20 steps per round.

The initial step requires that the message be padded so that its total length is a multiple of 512 bits using the same padding approach found in MD5. The initial input to SHA-1 is placed in five 32-bit registers A, B, C, D, and E, which will later hold the intermediate and final results of the hash function. The initial values (in hex) are as follows:

A = 67452301; B = EFCDAB89; C = 98BADCFE; D = 10325476; E = C3D2E1F0.

The message is divided up into blocks of 512 bits consisting of sixteen 32-bit words. The 16 words in the block are expanded into 80 words by a process of mixing and shifting defined by the following parameters:

> Initial Block— $M_0, M_1, \ldots, M_{15}$
> $W[0] = M_0, W[1] = M_1, \ldots, W[15] = M_{15}$
> $W[t] = W_{t-16} \text{ XOR } W_{t-14} \text{ XOR } W_{t-8} \text{ XOR } W_{t-3}$ for t from 15 to 80.

Rather than use 64 constants like MD5, only four constant values are added into the various stages. They are defined by the array K, where

$$K[t] = \text{5A827999 for } t \text{ from 0 to 19};$$
$$K[t] = \text{6ED9EBA1 for } t \text{ from 20 to 39};$$
$$K[t] = \text{8F1BBCDC for } t \text{ from 40 to 59; and}$$
$$K[t] = \text{CA62C1D6 for } t \text{ from 60 to 79}.$$

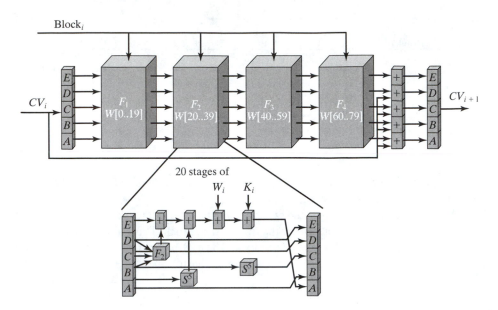

Figure 9.22: SHA rounds and stages

The block is processed in four rounds of 20 stages, each as shown in Figure 9.22. The two rotate operations indicated in the figure are defined as a rotate of 5 bits (S^5) and a rotate of 30 bits (S^{30}). Each round uses a different function given by the following table:

b	c	d	F_1	F_2	F_3	F_4
0	0	0	0	0	0	0
0	0	1	1	1	0	1
0	1	0	0	1	0	1
0	1	1	1	0	1	0
1	0	0	0	1	0	1
1	0	1	0	0	1	0
1	1	0	1	0	1	0
1	1	1	1	1	1	1

SHA-1 can be used to generate random numbers as well as to hash messages. Since random numbers play an important role in cryptography, it is worthwhile to consider how a hash algorithm can be used to construct them.

SHA-1 is modified slightly into a function $G(t, c)$. The first parameter, t, specifies the initial values of the five registers A to E. The second parameter, c, serves as the message to be hashed by SHA-1. The following algorithm will generate m random numbers based on a secret key, XKEY, and a set of optional seed values, XSEED_j ($j = 0$ to $m - 1$):

1. Select a secret key value, XKEY, the number of random numbers to generate, m, the maximum number of bits in each random number, b, and (if desired) a set of m seed values, XSEED_j, and a 160-bit random prime, q.

2. Initialize t to 67452301 EFCDAB89 98BADCFE 10324576 C3D2E1F0.

3. For $j = 0$ to $m - 1$, do

   (a) XVAL $= (\text{XKEY} + \text{XSEED}_j) \bmod 2^b$

   (b) $x_j = G(t, \text{XVAL}) \bmod q$

   (c) XKEY $= (1 + \text{XKEY} + x_j) \bmod 2^b$

The x_j's are the random numbers.

CAP implements this algorithm: Select SHA-1 Generator under the Random menu item to open the window shown in Figure 9.23. The random numbers could be used as is or CAP will convert them to a bit stream that could be used as part of a stream cipher.

While this text was being written, a new larger (and slower) version of SHA was released. SHA-2 is designed to work with the larger bit sizes that come with new algorithms like AES. SHA-2 is supplied in three versions known as SHA-256, SHA-384, and SHA-512. The names indicate the bit size. For example, SHA-256 works on eight 32-bit words as compared to the five 32-bit words of SHA-1 (which is only 160 bits). In SHA-384 and SHA-512, the word size is increased to 64-bits. Other differences include only one round, but more steps. For example, SHA-256 has only one round, which consists of 64 steps.

9.3.1.3 Comparison of MD5 and SHA-1

Since the message digest produced by SHA-1 is 32 bits longer than that produced by MD5, it is somewhat more secure against a brute-force attack. In general, it is believed that SHA-1 is resistant to cryptanalysis, while MD5 is possibly vulnerable. The hedges in the previous two sentences indicate that the security of these two algorithms is difficult to establish. However, since SHA-1 has more steps, it is slower than MD5.

9.3.1.4 Block-Cipher-Based Hash Functions

Both SHA-1 and MD5 were created from the ground up without using any encryption process. Given all that is known about the security and performance of contemporary block ciphers, the natural question to ask is: "Why not use a block cipher as the compression operation for a hash function?" For example, it would be very easy to implement the scheme shown in Figure 9.24 for a message consisting of n blocks using any of the block ciphers covered in Chapter 7. In this scheme, the IV is the initial value for the key, which is used to encipher the first message block. The resulting ciphertext is XORed with the message block and provides the key for use with the second message block. This process is continued with the final output providing the hash value. In fact, there are many ways in which a hash function could be

Figure 9.23: Using CAP to generate random numbers

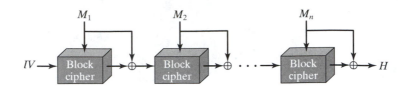

Figure 9.24: A block-cipher-based hash function

constructed using a block cipher. Several of these are illustrated in Figure 9.25. Actually in 1993, Preneel, Govaerts, and Vandewalle studied 64 such block-cipher-based hash functions and found that only 12 were secure. In 2002, Black, Rogaway, and Shrimpton revisited these 64 schemes and discovered that 20 actually were secure enough to be acceptable.

However, there are a variety of reasons why block-cipher-based hash functions are not used. One is that block ciphers like DES are only 64 bits wide, limiting the hash value to only 64 bits, which is generally too small for a secure hash value. In addition, the export of cipher algorithms is strictly controlled by the U.S. Government, which means that a hash function based on a block cipher would be subject to those same controls. Finally, the typical block cipher is too slow for efficient use as a hash function. In spite of these problems, there is some interest in using AES, since it has a larger block size and runs quite fast thereby overcoming some of the primary objections to block-cipher hashing.

9.3.1.5 Attacks on Hash Functions

Since a hash value is used to determine whether a message has been altered, the goal of an attack on a hash function is to produce an altered message with a hash value which matches that of the original message. For example, if Eve can find a pair of messages M_1 and M_2 such that $H(M_1) = H(M_2)$, and if Alice is willing to sign M_1, but not M_2 (even though Eve prefers M_2), then Eve has successfully attacked the hash function H. If Alice signed M_1 with her RSA private key and sent Eve the pair $(M_1, \text{Sign}\,[H(M_1)])$, Eve could claim in court that she received $(M_2, \text{Sign}\,[H(M_1)])$, since the hash of M_2 is the same as the hash of M_1.

The problem for Eve is how does she find two messages with the same hash value such that Alice would accept one and reject the other? She could begin by using a brute-force attack. That is, she could construct a set of acceptable messages $A_1, A_2, \ldots, A_s$ and a set of unacceptable messages $R_1, R_2, \ldots, R_s$. and then hash all the messages, looking for

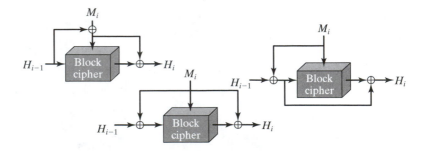

Figure 9.25: Other possible block-cipher-based hash functions

a pair with the same hash value. This may seem like an impossible task, but it turns out that Eve could succeed if the length of the hash value is small.

The feasibility of this type of brute-force attack is based on the solution to the birthday problem (sometimes called the birthday paradox because it is so unexpected). The birthday problem is formulated as follows:

In a room with N people, how large must N be so that the probability that two people celebrate their birthday on the same day and month is greater than 0.5?

Most people would assume that the answer to this question is a very large value when in fact it is quite small. The solution to this problem is usually presented as follows:

1. For the first person that enters the room, there are 365 distinct possible birthdays.
2. When a second person enters the room, there are 364 possible birthdays that do not match the first persons; so the probability of no match is 364/365.
3. When a third person enters the room, there are 363 possible birthdays that do not match either of the other two; so now the probability of no match is

$$\frac{(363)(364)}{(365)(365)}.$$

The probability of a match is

$$1 - \frac{(363)(364)}{(365)(365)}.$$

4. When N people are in the room, this generalizes to a probability of no match given by

$$\frac{(365 - N + 1) \cdots (362)(363)(364)}{(365)^{N-1}},$$

or a probability of a match of

$$1 - \frac{(365 - N + 1) \cdots (362)(363)(364)}{(365)^{N-1}}.$$

5. The value of N that makes the probability of a match greater than 0.5 is 23.

A good approximation to the solution to the birthday problem is $N = 1.17 * \text{sqrt}(n)$, where n is the number of possible outcomes (in this case, the number of possible birthdays or 365). The birthday problem can be restated in terms of an attack on a hash function as follows:

Given a hash function that produces a message digest of r bits, how many messages have to be examined so that the probability of two messages having the same hash value is greater than 0.5?

Since the message digest is r bits long, the total number of messages is 2^r. Hence the number of messages required is about $2^{r/2}$.

If Alice uses a hash function that produces a 16-bit hash value, all Eve needs to do is construct $2^8 = 256$ messages that are acceptable to Alice and another 256 messages that are not acceptable. There is a 50–50 chance that two of those messages produce the same hash value. This is done by generating similar messages that differ in eight words. For example, Eve might produce acceptable messages of the form

$$I \begin{Bmatrix} \text{promise} \\ \text{agree} \end{Bmatrix} \text{to} \begin{Bmatrix} \text{lend} \\ \text{loan} \end{Bmatrix} \begin{Bmatrix} 25 \\ \text{twenty-five} \end{Bmatrix} \text{dollars to my} \begin{Bmatrix} \text{good} \\ \text{best} \end{Bmatrix} \text{friend}$$

$$\text{Eve which she will} \begin{Bmatrix} \text{repay} \\ \text{return} \end{Bmatrix} \text{to me in} \begin{Bmatrix} 10 \\ \text{ten} \end{Bmatrix} \text{days or} \begin{Bmatrix} \text{less} \\ \text{sooner} \end{Bmatrix}$$

$$\begin{Bmatrix} \text{Yours,} \\ \text{Sincerely,} \end{Bmatrix} \text{Alice}$$

She might also produce unacceptable messages of the form

$$I \begin{Bmatrix} \text{promise} \\ \text{agree} \end{Bmatrix} \text{to} \begin{Bmatrix} \text{give} \\ \text{offer} \end{Bmatrix} \begin{Bmatrix} 25 \\ \text{twenty-five} \end{Bmatrix} \text{dollars to my} \begin{Bmatrix} \text{good} \\ \text{best} \end{Bmatrix} \text{friend}$$

$$\text{Eve as a} \begin{Bmatrix} \text{gift} \\ \text{present} \end{Bmatrix} \text{which she} \begin{Bmatrix} \text{should not} \\ \text{will not} \end{Bmatrix} \text{repay because I know she}$$

$$\text{needs this} \begin{Bmatrix} \text{help} \\ \text{aid} \end{Bmatrix} \begin{Bmatrix} \text{Yours,} \\ \text{Sincerely,} \end{Bmatrix} \text{Alice}$$

After hashing all 512 messages, Eve might discover that "I promise to lend 25 dollars to my best friend Eve which she will return to me in 10 days or less Yours, Alice" has the same hash value as "I agree to offer twenty-five dollars to my good friend Eve as a gift which she should not repay because I know she needs this aid Sincerely, Alice". If Alice signs the acceptable version, Eve can substitute the unacceptable version because it produces the correct hash value.

This all means that the size of the hash value has to be large enough so that Eve cannot feasibly check all the possible messages. MD5 has a hash size of 128 bits, so Eve would have to generate 2^{64} messages of each type. SHA-1 has a hash size of 160 bits, so Eve would have to generate 2^{80} messages. Neither is feasible.

9.3.1.6 Hash Functions in CAP

Bob and Alice decide to go with MD5 instead of the XOR hash, and it is very fortunate that they make the change because Eve is on the attack. One of the first messages Bob sends to Alice is "Alice, please meet with me next Tuesday in my office Bob". Bob sends the message in plaintext to Alice along with the MD5 hash value. Since CAP offers both MD5 and SHA-1, Bob is easily able to hash any plaintext message. Bob enters his message to Alice in the Plaintext box of CAP, selects MD5 under the Signatures menu item, and then selects Run in the MD5 window. (SHA-1 is implemented in CAP in the same manner.) The result is shown in Figure 9.26.

Bob signs this with his private RSA key set for 16 bits in CAP:

$$N = 259536431538907693211 \quad d = 48960441661.$$

Then he sends the plaintext message along with the following signed hash value:

"Alice, please meet with me next Tuesday in my office Bob".
135594961498378250638
560829401902021375805
126036030298687927000
146359889510644548489
243898624499816340 1
192894969220796395593
198148440850980822076
445471730783547319866
137644764749716115811
811780746351363731500
192894969220796395593
114438837427205627165
204086552991791154610
168969653468536651186
562901996368662771866
136285751850306590218

Eve intercepts the message before it gets to Alice. Since she does not like Alice, she decides to change the message so that Alice will miss the meeting. She sends the following message to Alice:

"Alice, please meet with me next *Wednesday* in my office Bob".
135594961498378250638
560829401902021375805
126036030298687927000
146359889510644548489
243898624499816340 1
192894969220796395593
198148440850980822076
445471730783547319866
137644764749716115811
811780746351363731500
192894969220796395593
114438837427205627165
204086552991791154610
168969653468536651186
562901996368662771866
136285751850306590218

```
┌─────────────────────────────────────────────────────────────────────┐
│ 🔲 MD5                                                    [_][□][✕]   │
├─────────────────────────────────────────────────────────────────────┤
│  Run    Save    Print    Compare    Help    Quit                     │
│                                                                       │
│                                                                       │
│       Hex Value:  ┌──────────────────────────────────────────────┐   │
│                   │ 44AB249A311961CAB959194A6A9252A4             │   │
│                   └──────────────────────────────────────────────┘   │
│  CompareValue:  ┌────────────────────────────────────────────────┐   │
│                 │                                                  │   │
│                 └────────────────────────────────────────────────┘   │
└─────────────────────────────────────────────────────────────────────┘
```

Figure 9.26: MD5 hash in CAP

Since Eve does not know Bob's private RSA key, she cannot change the signature. As a result her efforts to get Alice in trouble fail. When Alice receives the message, she runs it through MD5 to generate the message digest. Since she is compressing Eve's and not Bob's message, MD5 gives the value 452B456B494DACEDBCDCB4D87654529. Using Bob's public RSA key, she deciphers the signed message digest, which gives the value 44AB249A311961CAB959194A6A9252A4. She uses the comparison option available in CAP. Of course, the two values do not match, prompting Alice to contact Bob. Eventually, she received the correct meeting time.

9.3.2 Blind Signatures

Sometimes a document must be signed by a third party or witness in order to verify the identity of the author, but the contents of the document must remain private. In the world of ink signatures, this is often done by a notary public. This same process can also be implemented in the world of digital signatures.

For example, Alice wants to send a notarized message, m, to her bank, but she does not want anyone to see the contents of the message. She looks up the RSA public key of her local notary public—e and n. She selects a secret number b between 1 and n and converts her message into $m_s = (b^e m) \bmod n$. Alice takes m_s into the notary public along with proof of her identity. After verifying Alice's identity, the notary public uses her private key to sign $m_{sign} = (m_s)^d \bmod n$ and sends Alice on her way. Since the notary public has no knowledge of Alice's secret random number, b, he cannot recover the original message m. Neither does the bank know b, so Alice must remove all traces of b from m_{sign} before the message can be sent to the bank. She must do so without disturbing the notary public's signature. This is easily done because Alice not only knows b, but also knows $b^{-1} \bmod n$. The chain of events is almost like magic:

$$m_{sign} = (m_s)^d \bmod n = (b^e m)^d \bmod n = b^{ed} m^d \bmod n = b m^d \bmod n.$$

When Alice multiplies m_{sign} by b^{-1}, the result is a signed version of the message for the bank:

$$m_{bank} = b^{-1} m_{sign} = b^{-1} b m^d \bmod n = m^d.$$

Now the bank can verify the notary public's signature with the public key e and use n to recover the original message m.

CAP provides a tool for exploring the operation of blind signatures. For example, Bob wants to send the message "Alice, I am having this signed for verification Bob." He enters the message in the plaintext window and selects the Blind Signature option under the Signature menu. He looks up the public key of the trusted third party, enters it in the CAP form, enters a random number, selects Find Inverse under the Parameters menu, and finally selects Create under the Blind Message menu option. The result is shown in Figure 9.27. Of course, Bob would not have knowledge of the trusted third party's private key, even though it is entered in the CAP form. The Private Key option is there to allow CAP to perform all the roles in the blind signature process. Bob sends the blind message to the trusted third party and waits for the return of the signed version.

The trusted third party could use CAP as well. The blind message is entered into the form, and the Sign option under the Signed Message menu item is selected. The resulting signed message is sent back to Bob, who enters it into CAP and selects the Remove Blind option under the Signed Message menu item. Here is the message:

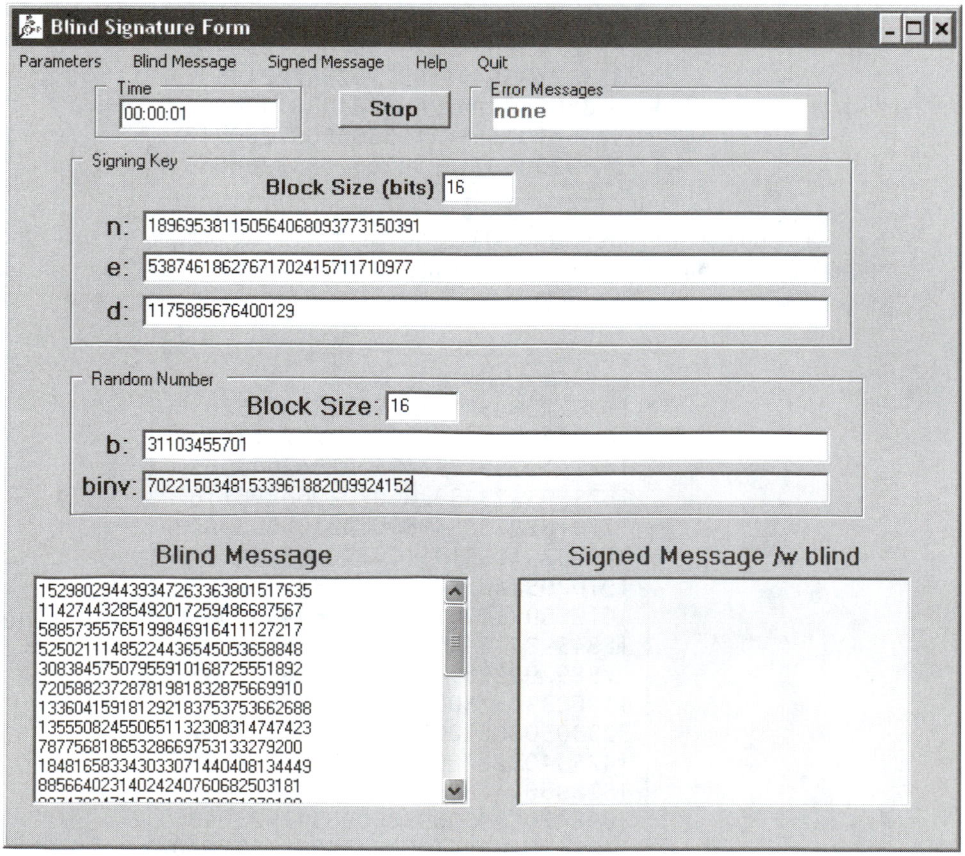

Figure 9.27: Blind signature form in CAP

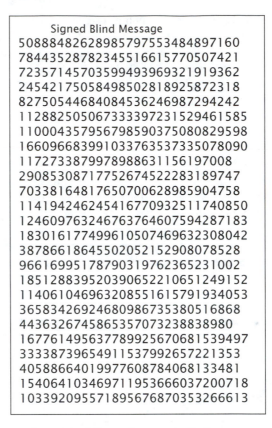

Signed Blind Message
50888482628985797553484897160
78443528782345516615770507421
72357145703599493969321919362
24542175058498502818925872318
82750544684084536246987294242
11288250506733339723152946I585
11000435795679859037508082959B
16609668399I033763537335078090
11727338799789886311561970OB
29085308717752674522283189747
70338164817650700628985904758
11419424624541677093251I740850
12460976324676376460759428718B3
18301617749961050746963230B042
3878661864550205215290807B528
96616995178790319762365231002
18512883952039065221065I249152
11406I046963208551615791934053
3658342692468098673538OSI6B68
44363267458653570723B838980
16776I49563778992567068I539497
33338739654911537992657221353
4058866401997760878406B133481
154064I0346971I95366603720071B
10339209557I89567687035326661B

The final message is sent to Alice, who can verify the message by using the trusted third party's public key to recover the plaintext. (Select Recover Plaintext under the Signed Message menu item.) The final message is as follows:

Final Signed Message
13232I5685218326593621099526S6
10694259445048893657797417432B
14274197091731495227842049665
1675593523339366070296889611I67
17701628738859800296390697997B
15908201083101106245193604201B
1910205845370015I886338407163
1618569711763410582644934B668
1884598428484528467762509B4366
2788929B2781410131684286399B
11960330518085629418097333625B
3233030800300702125363092769B
14253403287602086863957014299B
15289667478255845731340924437O
18984705295969300096347623O48
14281291658872604435885052769O
16216548031529487467909333643B
12449765676734525350863414512
15131722090396986416095289443B

```
46479872139487594967761149225
70237624261547572956815196007
81527750113764252079703308517
47920912866286144714326193307
39596335900630012149462505421
29788317029354015869982415072
```

9.3.3 Digital Signature Standard (DSS)

Just as there is a government-approved standard encryption algorithm (AES), there is a government-approved digital signature standard, called DSS. It was adopted in 1994 and remains under a cloud of suspicion because, unlike AES, the selection process was not public. However, DSS was the first digital signature system actually endorsed by any government, and it does offer an alternative to an RSA-type signature.

DSS is based on the El-Gamal public key system; however, it is strictly a signature algorithm and is not intended for encryption. As seen in Figure 9.28, it is also a complicated (but still fast) system that approaches the idea of a signature from a different perspective. For example, the final verification test is based on the value of r, which does not depend on the message. As a consequence, it is not obvious how the verification really works (but it does, as you will discover).

From Figure 9.28, it is clear that DSS uses a large set of parameters: p, q, g, k, x, and y. Some of these parameters are public, some private, but they all have certain required characteristics:

> p is a public 1024-bit prime number
> q is a public 160-bit prime factor of $p - 1$
> g is a public qth root of 1 mod p
> k is a private 160-bit random number
> x is a private 160-bit key
> y is a public 512-bit key, where $y = g^x \bmod p$

The four functions in DSS use these six parameters and the SHA-1 hash value of the message, h, to set up the overall verification process. The signature attached to the message consists of the values (r, s) determined by

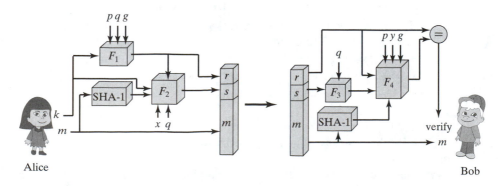

Figure 9.28: Operation of the digital signature standard

$$F_1 \; r = (g^k \bmod p) \bmod q$$
$$F_2 \; s = k^{-1}(h + xr) \bmod q.$$

The verification uses (r, s) as follows:

$$F_3 \; t = s^{-1} \bmod q$$
$$F_4 \; r' = (g^{ht} y^{rt} \bmod p) \bmod q,$$

where the message is verified if $r = r'$.

It almost seems like magic, but DSS works because of a straightforward mathematical derivation:

$$
\begin{aligned}
(g^{ht} y^{rt} \bmod p) \bmod q &= (g^{ht}(g^x)^{rt} \bmod p) \bmod q \quad \text{(substitute } y = g^x \bmod p) \\
&= (g^{(h+xr)t} \bmod p) \bmod q \quad \text{(combine exponents)} \\
&= (g^{kst} \bmod p) \bmod q \quad \text{(because } s = k^{-1}(h + xr) \bmod q) \\
&= (g^k \bmod p) \bmod q \quad \text{(because } t = s^{-1} \bmod q) \\
&= r.
\end{aligned}
$$

Like both MD5 and SHA-1, DSS presents some computational challenges. However, CAP provides an implementation of DSS—select Digital Signature Standard under the Signatures menu option. The window shown in Figure 9.29 will open. The menu list will lead you through the steps to create a signature. For example, to create the public key values p, q, and g, select the Create Global Keys option under the Keys menu. The DSS Key Generation window will open. Enter the required size for q in this window and step through the Create Keys options to arrive at a set of global keys such as those shown in Figure 9.30. With the global keys, a private key, and the hash of the message, the main DSS window will produce the two hash values (r, s). It also provides a test option to validate a message hash.

The original DSS approved in 1994 was amended in 2000, so there are now three officially approved digital signature methods: DSA, RSA, and ECDSA. The RSA digital signature method as expected uses RSA, but only on the hashed message. (Remember that a raw RSA signature is subject to a multiplicative attack.) In addition, the hashed message is padded to improve its security against known attacks on RSA. The formal procedure for an RSA signature of a message M with an RSA public key of (n, e) is as follows:

1. Compute the hash of M using SHA-1 $[h = \text{SHA}(M)]$.
2. Create a padded string $M = 6|PS|h|33CC$, where PS is the string of hex values "$BB \ldots BA$". The length of PS is selected so that the length of the entire padded string is the same as the number of bits in n.
3. Use the private key d to compute $s = M^d \bmod n$.
4. Send the original message M along with the signature s.

In this scheme, the last four padding hex values (33CC) identify the hash function as SHA-1. If a different hash function is used, a different four-hex-digit code number is added on to the end.

The elliptic curve digital signature algorithm, (ECDSA), which is now part of the DSS, involves a similar set of steps. It begins with ECC public and private keys. The

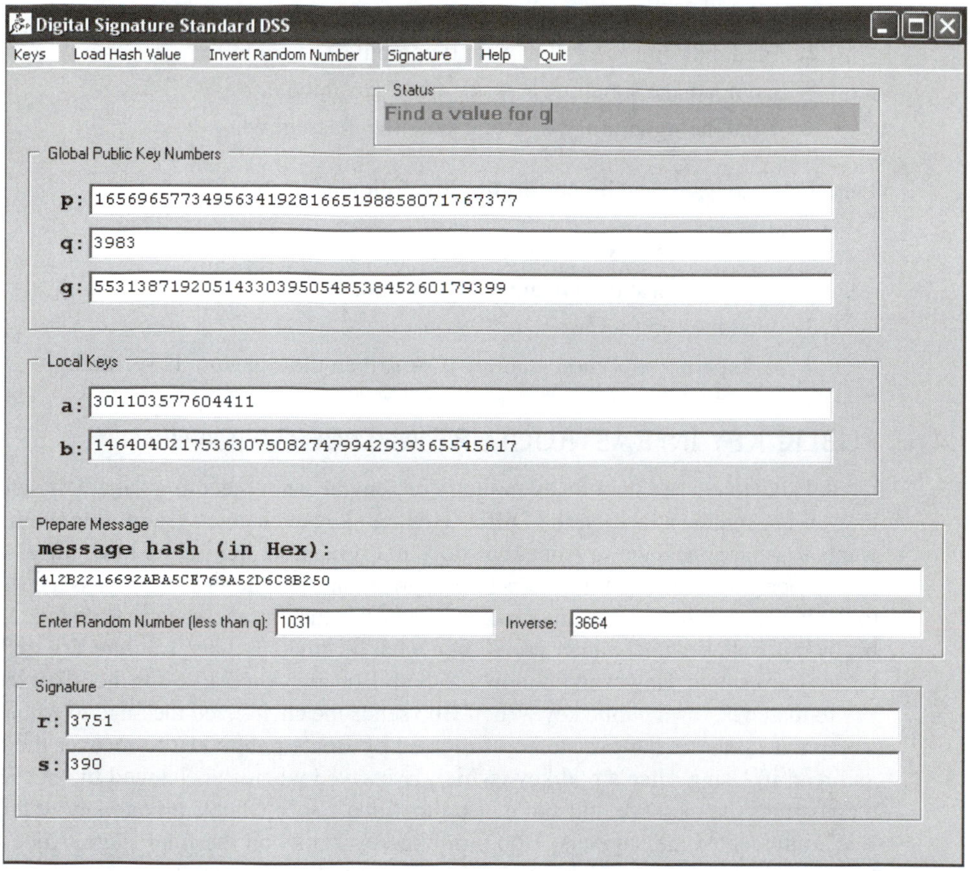

Figure 9.29: DSS in CAP

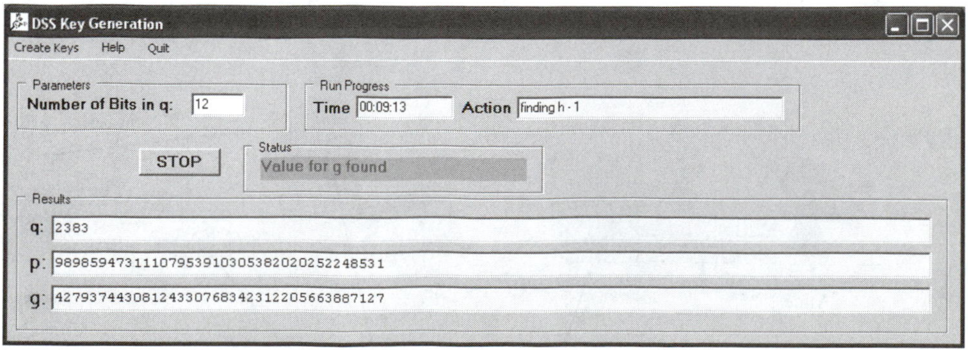

Figure 9.30: DSS Key Generation in CAP

known values are the order of the curve (n), the base point (P), the private key (d), the public key ($Q = dP$), and, of course, the message M. SHA-1 is used to create the hashed message [$h = \mathrm{SHA}(M)$]. The remaining steps for creating of the signature are as follows:

1. Select a random number k.
2. Find the point $kP = (x, y)$ and compute $r = x \bmod n$.
3. Compute the signature $s = k^{-1}(h + dr) \bmod n$.
4. Send the signature (r, s) along with the message M.

This signature is verified by performing the following steps:

1. Compute $w = s^{-1} \bmod n$.
2. Find $u_1 = hw \bmod n$ and $u_2 = rw \bmod n$.
3. Find the point $(x, y) = u_1 P + u_2 Q$.
4. Compute $v = x \bmod n$ and if $v = r$, then the signature is verified.

9.4   PUBLIC KEY INFRASTRUCTURE AND CERTIFICATES

Digital signatures and public key systems in general are subject to an attack much like the man-in-the-middle attack on the Diffie–Hellman key exchange system. For example, Bob wants to send a message to Alice, but does not remember her public key. Since Alice has posted her public key on the Internet so anyone can send her a secure message, Bob goes to the website with the key and copies it. To ensure that the message is unchanged, he uses his own private key to encipher it and then what he thinks is Alice's public key for the final layer of protection. However, unknown to both Bob and Alice, Eve has modified the posted key to match her own public key. When Bob sends the enciphered message to Alice, Eve intercepts it. She uses her private key followed by Bob's public key to recover the message and read it. Using Alice's real key (which Eve saved when she changed the posting), Eve reconstructs the message and sends it on to Alice. Since Alice's private key will decipher Eve's intercepted message and Bob's public key works on the final stage, Alice believes that the message is secure. This process is illustrated in Figure 9.31.

The problem that both Bob and Alice have is a matter of trust. They may trust each other, but how do they know that the person they are communicating with is really who

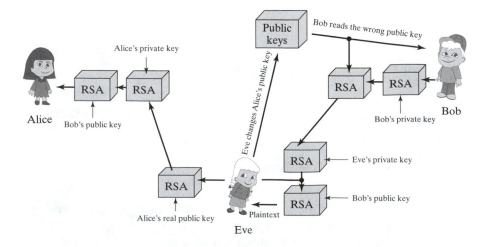

Figure 9.31: Attack on a digital signature protocol

they claim to be? How do Bob and Alice know that the public key they receive really belongs to the person to whom they are sending a message? If it is the case that Bob and Alice only communicate with each other, then they could use a key exchange procedure such as Diffie–Hellman. But the fact is that they are part of a larger community, and they want their public keys to be trusted and used within it. They need a mechanism to establish that trust.

The role of a public key infrastructure (PKI) is to establish a level of trust between users of a public key system. It does this by providing a secure method for publishing public keys. The two basic operations of a PKI are

certification (the process of binding a public key value to an owner); and

validation (the process of verifying that a certification is still valid).

A PKI consists of several parts: a certification authority (CA); a registration authority (RA); a repository; and an archive. The certification authority is a trusted third party that runs the PKI. The CA issues certificates, keeps track of old or invalid certificates, and maintains an archive of status information. The RA verifies the contents of a certificate for the CA. The repository is the database of certificates available to users.

9.4.1   Establishing a Certificate

Both Bob and Alice decided that they needed to have a certificate to maintain control over their public keys. Bob was the first to start the process. His efforts are shown in Figure 9.32. He selected a CA and sent in a request for a certificate. The CA responded with an application form. Bob filled out the form and, as instructed, generated a key pair using software

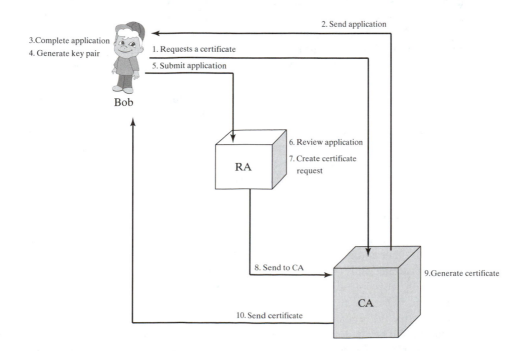

Figure 9.32: PKI operation

supplied by the CA as part of the application. The client software generated Bob's new keys, saved the private key on Bob's machine in a secure area, and created a password so that Bob could access the keys. Bob then signed and submitted the completed application, which included the new public key to the registration authority. The registration authority verified Bob's identity (more on this process later) and created a certificate request, which was sent to the CA. The process was completed when the CA generated the certificate, signed it with his private key, and sent it to Bob.

It is important to understand the details of this process because the usefulness of a certificate is based on the level of trust users have in the CA. For example, Bob and Alice must both trust the method by which the RA verifies their identity. Different RA's have different approaches. Some require the applicant to appear in person at a local office with proof of identity and his public key. Others may require the applicant to fax to them a copy of his driver's license and other identifying papers, along with his new public key. In this case, the RA will first send the applicant a request ID enciphered using the applicant's public key. The applicant must decipher and include the request ID along with the other documents.

9.4.2　Certificate Contents

Since there are several CA's, it is useful if they all produce similar certificates; otherwise, users could become confused while looking for the necessary information in a certificate. As a result, an international standard, X.509, has been established to specify the contents of a valid certificate.

The standard consists of 10 fields, some of which are optional. The first field is the certificate format version—currently there are three versions of X.509. (Version 3 is the latest.) This is followed by a certificate serial number, which is a unique number assigned by the CA to ensure that duplicate certificates are not issued. The next field is the signature algorithm field, which identifies both the hash method and the public key encryption algorithm used by the CA. The fourth field is the certificate issuer name. This is given by another international standard, X.500, and specifies the country code and the CA organization code. The fifth field is the validity period, which contains the date the certificate first became valid and the date it expires. The subject X.500 name is contained in the sixth field. The field of most interest to users is the seventh field, which contains the subject's public key and identifies the algorithm used by the subject. The next two fields are optional and consist of an issuer unique identifier followed by a subject unique identifier. These are used in the case of duplicate X.500 names for either party. The final field is the CA's signature. An example certificate is shown in Figure 9.33.

9.4.3　Using a Certificate

Once both Bob and Alice have received their certificates, they are ready to communicate with each other and the rest of the Internet world. A typical exchange between Alice and Bob is illustrated in Figure 9.34. Alice sends Bob a message signed with her private key. When Bob receives the message, he requests Alice's public key from the CA. The CA sends Alice's certificate to Bob signed by the CA's private key. Bob uses the CA's public key to verify the signature on the certificate. As a result, Bob is confident that he has Alice's public key and not the key of some third party (like Eve). Bob uses Alice's public key to open her signature and verify that the message was in fact sent by Alice and not tampered with during transmission.

Version	2
Serial Number	10035
Signature Algorithm	SH-1, RSA
Issuer DN	cu = US, o = VF
Validity Period	04/01/2003 08:00:00 04/01/2005 05:00:00
Subject DN	c = US, o = gov **cn** = John Smith
Subject Public Key	RSA, 5503 3997 . . .
Issuer UID	Usually omitted
Subject UID	Usually omitted
Signature	6A21 3E9F . . .

Figure 9.33: X.509 certificate format

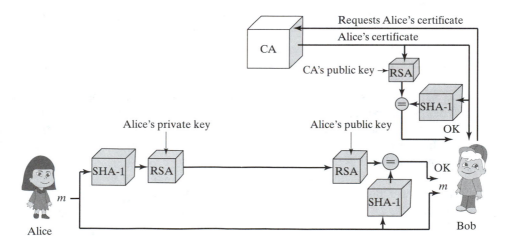

Figure 9.34: Using a digital certificate

Because Alice's public key correctly deciphers her signature and her signature matches the hash of the message he received, Bob trusts the content of the message. He trusts the source because the CA verified that the public key Bob used was indeed Alice's. It may seem like a complicated procedure just to communicate with each other. But in today's world, we need to be able to trust the information we receive, and sometimes that means things get a little more complicated.

9.4.4 Revocation of a Certificate

Sometimes a certificate must be withdrawn before its expiration date because of a suspected or detected compromise. Perhaps the owner of the certificate quit her job and is no longer associated with a specific company and her CA or an apparent misuse of the certificate was discovered. Anyone who might have accessed the certificate when it was valid needs to be aware of the revocation. There are several ways in which this can be done. Usually, the CA maintains a certificate revocation list (CRL) that contains a time-stamped list of all revoked certificates signed by the CA. The CRL may be updated hourly, daily, or weekly. It becomes the responsibility of the user of a certificate to periodically check this list.

9.5   APPLICATIONS

Several applications of contemporary ciphers were covered in earlier chapters, such as the use of RC4 in the wireless equivalent privacy (WEP) protocol, and the use of Diffie–Hellman in the IPSec protocol. Obviously, contemporary ciphers are more widely used than hinted at so far. Details of the use of these algorithms is perhaps best left to a text on network security; however, it is worthwhile to consider other applications, especially those that involve the full range of a cryptographic protocol.

9.5.1   Smart Cards

Almost everyone has (or has seen) a credit card. It is a wallet-sized plastic card with a name and number on one side and a magnetic strip on the other. In Europe, most magnetic strip cards have been replaced by smart cards; in the United States, the change over process is just beginning. As shown in Figure 9.35, a smart card has a small electronic device embedded in the plastic with six to eight contact pins. That device is actually a small computer with its own CPU and memory.

A typical smart card device has an 8-bit processor, serial input–output, a ROM to hold program data, a RAM to store computational data, and an operating system—all of this in an area less than 25 mm^2 in size. Some also have an FPGA-like device called an EEPROM that can store custom data–programs. The layout for a smart card microprocessor chip is shown in Figure 9.36.

Smart cards had their start in 1970 when they were first introduced in Japan. Today, more than a billion smart cards are manufactured worldwide every year, and their numbers are growing fast.

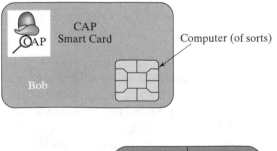

Figure 9.35: A typical smart card

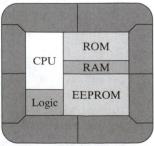

Figure 9.36: A typical smart card microprocessor chip

There are three basic types of smart cards. Contact cards such as the one shown in Figure 9.35 must be inserted into a card reader. Contactless cards are powered by radio frequency signal using inductive coils. These cards are read by passing them near a reading device (usually within two or three inches). The third type is a combi-card, which can be inserted into a reader or read by RF signals.

There are three primary functions of smart cards: (1) information storage and management; (2) identification of the cardholder; and (3) calculation (especially for encryption–decryption). These functions translate into a variety of applications such as storing money in the form of an E-wallet; storing passwords and cipher keys; or encrypting and decrypting data. They all have an obvious relationship to cryptography.

For example, a smart card may be used for network login. Instead of the more traditional approach of logging onto a network by entering your username and password, a smart card process could require you to first put your card into a card reader; then you may be confronted with a login window such as the one shown in Figure 9.37. The smart card stores a complex password in an encrypted format, but all the user has to remember is a simple PIN value. The end result is that, in order to gain access to a network, a user requires physical possession of the smart card and knowledge of the username and the PIN.

Smart cards can store more than just passwords. Given their processing capability, they can be used to sign documents such as E-mail. In fact, a smart card is an excellent device for securely storing the private key required for a digital signature. For example, Figure 9.38 illustrates the process of using a smart card to sign a document. The document is hashed, and the hash value is sent to the card reader. The smart card uses both the private key and the hash value to sign the document and sends the signature back to the system.

9.5.2   Secure Socket Layer

Back in Chapter 7 (Section 7.6, to be exact), the use of block ciphers in IPSec was discussed, but many of the details were left until later. Well, later has now arrived. IPSec is designed to work at the network layer providing a secure connection in which the network packet is encrypted using a block cipher. In this section, the details of a secure Web connection are covered through an examination of the secure socket layer or SSL. The task of SSL is to secure an application at the transport layer. (Refer to Section 7.6 for a review of

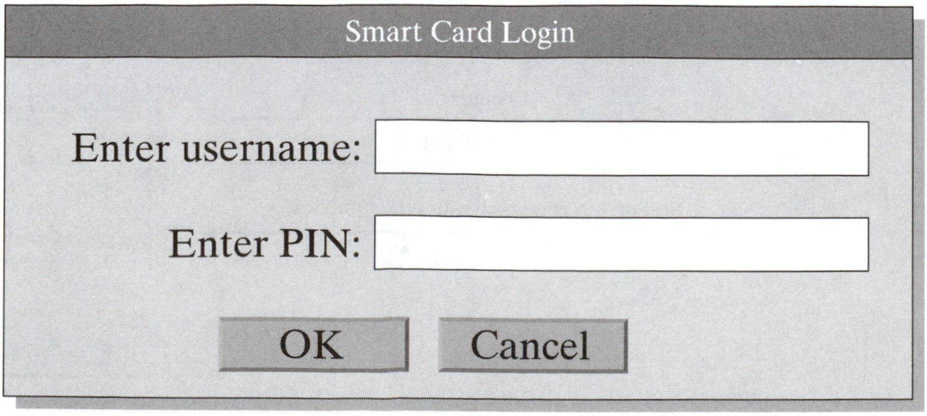

Figure 9.37: A possible smart card login window

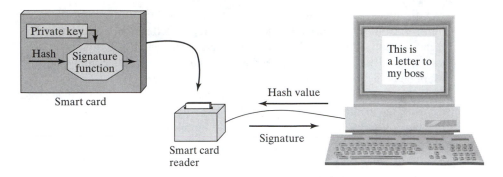

Figure 9.38: A smart-card-based digital signature

the layer architecture.) In fact, a slightly modified version of SSL is called TLS, or transport layer security.

SSL was originally developed by Netscape to provide authentication, integrity, and privacy to Web transactions. It accomplishes these by means of two protocols: the SSL record protocol and the SSL handshake protocol.

The SSL handshake protocol starts the process. It sets up a secure connection protected by a common set of algorithms and keys. Figure 9.39 shows how Bob might set up a SSL transaction with a website. It begins with Bob sending a "Client Hello" message to the Web server. This message contains information about the cipher suites (key exchange method, block cipher, MAC algorithm ...) that Bob can support. The server responds with a "Server Hello" message that selects a supported cipher suite for this session. If the server has a public certificate, it sends this to Bob along with its public key. Bob (or actually his browser) will verify the certificate and check to determine whether the CA's signature is valid. If everything checks out, Bob will generate a one-time, unique session key, encrypt it with the server's public key, and send it on. Now Bob is confident of two facts: (1) The identity of the server has been verified; and (2) both sides have a copy of a session key.

Actually, the SSL protocol is more flexible than the simple example of Bob logging on to a Web server. The "Client Hello" message offers one of several possible cipher suites. The encryption algorithms usually made available are DES, Triple-DES, RC2, RC4, and IDEA.

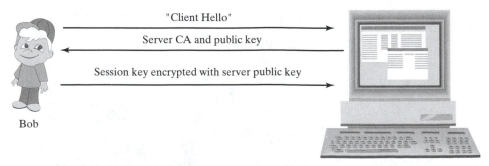

Figure 9.39: A simple SSL handshake

The way in which SSL responds to an algorithm choice raises an important issue that has been overlooked up to this point. That is the issue of the exporting encryption algorithms outside of the United States. It turns out that encryption algorithms are classified as munitions and hence are subject to strong export controls. If you ever wondered why some of the software you purchased came with a warning that it was intended for use only in the United States, now you know why. It appears that the material you have been reading about in this text is considered by the U.S. government to be equivalent to plans for building a nuclear weapon. Given the importance of information in our society, a good case can be made for that equivalency. This is just one more indicator of just how important it is to use what you have learned in a moral and ethical manner. From the standpoint of SSL, it means that it comes in two versions: a strong version that can be used in the United States and a weak version that can be exported overseas. Initially, the weak version was limited to 40-bit encryption, but that has now be extended to a 56-bit encryption. The strong version generally uses 128-bit encryption.

The "Client Hello" message also has the choice of offering RSA or DSA as the digital signature algorithm and MD5 or SHA as the hash function. There is more than one key exchange method available to SSL as well. Bob used RSA as the aforementioned key exchange method, but SSL is also capable of implementing several versions of Diffie–Hellman.

Once the handshake process is complete, data are transmitted between the user and the Web server using the specified keys and algorithms in the SSL record protocol. The record structure is shown in Figure 9.40. The data are fragmented into segments in which each segment is less than 16K bits. An optional compress operation is applied to each segment, and then the selected MAC format is calculated and attached to the fragmented packet. The selected encryption algorithm is applied, an SSL header is added, and finally the packet is sent on its way.

This process is reversed at the receiving end, where the application data are reconstructed. You should note that, while the process appears complicated, it just involves the application of the algorithms and protocols you have studied through this text.

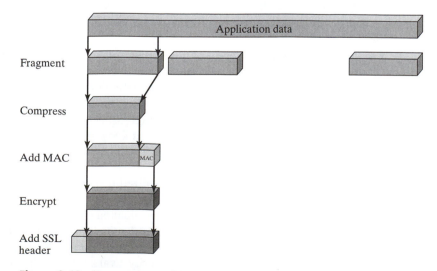

Figure 9.40: Constructing an SSL record

9.6   HISTORICAL PERSPECTIVE

There are two events relating to the implementation of cipher systems that are of both historical and practical interest. (Actually, there are more than two, but these two are very relevant to the material in this chapter.) The first is the story of the development of Pretty Good Privacy (PGP) and the other is the on-going development of the Common Criteria. Both illustrate the complicated and interconnected nature of cipher systems, political issues, key management, Internet security, and a host of other issues related to computer security and personal privacy.

PGP was developed by Philip Zimmermann in 1992 as a freeware e-mail encryption program. Philip Zimmermann was a computer security consultant and somewhat of a political activist. His overall goals for PGP were to use the best available cipher algorithms; integrate them into an easy-to-use application that would be independent of any operating systems; and make the entire system available at no cost to the end user. The original version of PGP used Zimmermann's own block encryption algorithm, Bass-O-Matic, but it quickly turned out to be too weak. So he replaced it with IDEA. His vision for PGP included more than just a block encryption algorithm. It now includes RSA for key encryption and SHA-1 for hash generation. (MD5 is also available.) They all work together and are available to a user through a simple command interface.

Philip Zimmermann's story is about more than just the creation of what is now a de facto standard for e-mail security. It is also a political story. It seems that when he created his first version of PGP, he ran into two problems: RSA was patented, and the U.S. government would not allow strong crypto to be exported. He chose to overlook both these issues and gave away his new program to friends. Since his friends were all within the United States, he did not run into direct conflict with U.S. laws, although the RSA Corporation was upset with his program. He eventually settled the issue with RSA, but the U.S. government was not pleased when PGP turned up on the Internet and hence was available outside the United States. Philip did not post it himself. It seems that one of his friends posted it to a Usenet discussion group. The result of that posting was that Philip Zimmermann became the target of a 28-month-long grand jury investigation. While the investigation was going on, Zimmermann became an Internet folk hero. The government finally dropped its investigation without comment in January 1996. The whole incident is just another example of the conflict between open cryptography and protection of intelligence-gathering processes.

On a lighter note, the other event of interest is the launching of the Common Criteria effort. It should be clear by now that there is more to cryptography and security in general than just selecting a powerful algorithm and finding a strong key. A complete cryptographic package may contain multiple algorithms, internal key-generation methods, and procedures for hashing and signing messages (much like PGP). The problem, as it always is in the field, is one of trust. How do you know that a security package is the right one for you? The answer to that question may be found in the results of the Common Criteria development effort.

In the early 1980s, the U.S. government realized that some standards needed to be developed and used to evaluate the quality of security products. One of the first such standards appeared in the Trusted Computer System Evaluation Criteria (TCSEC), which was called the "Orange Book." Later, a European standard—the Information Technology Security Evaluation Criteria (ITSEC)—was published with the same goal as the TCSEC. In 1993, the Common Criteria for Information Security Evaluation development effort was launched to create an international standard. The Common Criteria provide a basis for evaluating the security properties of more than just cryptographic systems—they encompass the whole range of information technology security products. Products are submitted by the manufacturer and are evaluated against the Common Criteria by an independent testing lab. The result of the evaluation is an evaluation technical report that, when certified, provides a level of assurance to users that the product does what it claims to do.

NIST also maintains evaluation criteria for cryptographic systems. The criteria are found in FIPS PUB 140-1 and FIPS PUB 140-2. The second is the most recent (in fact, NIST no longer validates products for FIPS 140-1). It is the most important for evaluating cryptographic products, and has much in common with the Common Criteria.

9.7   SUMMARY

Bob and Alice discovered that moving to more sophisticated and complicated ciphers meant that they had to manage large keys, which they could not memorize. As a result, while Eve might have a great deal of difficulty breaking their ciphers, she might find more success compromising their keys. So, they decided that they needed to come up with methods to share keys in a secure manner. One approach they discovered was to use a key exchange protocol such as the Diffie–Hellman to allow them to set up a common key over a communication link that might be tapped by Eve.

Another problem also arose—one of authentication. How could Bob be sure that a message from Alice was received unchanged or even was from Alice at all? To solve this problem, they found a number of ways to "sign" a document using hash functions and a public–private key system such that the signature could be verified later and the nature of the signature could also verify the stability of the message.

They still faced yet another problem. How could they be sure that any public key they looked up actually belonged to the people that claimed it was theirs? If they could be misled into using a fake key, they may compromise their messages. This led them to the use of a certificate authority who would verify the ownership of a given key.

Overall, all three (Bob, Alice, and Eve) learned that securing messages is more than an issue of encrypting plaintext. A truly secure system must include a mechanism for both managing keys and authenticating messages. A summary of the functions covered in this chapter is shown in Figure 9.41.

9.8   IMPORTANT TERMS

Birthday problem   Find the required number of people in a room that will
                                  give a 50–50 chance that two have the same birthday
Blind Signature   Signing a document without viewing its contents
Certification   The process of binding a public key value to an owner
DSS   the digital signature standard adopted in 1994

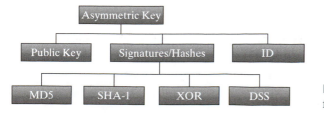

Figure 9.41: Typical signature–hash functions

MD5	A hashing algorithm developed by Ron Rivest
Padding	The process of adding extra bits to the end of a message before hashing
Public key infrastructure (PKI)	A reliable and secure system for establishing trust among the users of a public key system
SHA	The secure hash algorithm developed by NIST (updated to SHA-1 and now SHA-2)
SSL	Secure socket layer—used to provide application security on the Internet
Validation	The process of verifying that a certification is still valid

RESOURCES

Adams, C. and S. Lloyd, *Understanding PKI: Concepts, Standards, and Deployment Considerations*, 2d ed., (Addison-Wesley, 2003)

Smith, R., *Authentication* (Addison-Wesley, 2003)

Benantar, M., *Introduction to the Public Key Infrastructure for the Internet* (Prentice Hall, 2001)

Kim, Y., A. Perrig, G. Tsudik, *Simple and Fault-Tolerant Group Key Agreement Scheme*. In Proceedings of the Seventh ACM Conference on Computer and Communications Security, ACM CCS 2000 (ACM Press, November 2000)

Preneel, B., R. Govaerts, J. Vandewalle, "Hash functions based on block ciphers: A synthetic approach." In *Advances in Cryptology—CRYPTO '93*, Lecture notes in computer science (Springer-Verlag, 1994), pp. 368–378.

Besides some of the books already noted in previous chapters, a number of CA's provide information:

www.verisign.com

www.vasco.com

www.rsasecurity.com/products/keon/index.html

www.baltimore.com/servercert/webtrust.asp

www.cren.net/crenca/pkiresources/index.html

www.ncsa.uiuc.edu/UserInfo/Grid/Security/GetUserCert.html

www.entrust.com/corporate/index.htm

PROBLEMS

1. Describe how the public key authorization and confidentiality process introduced in Section 9.2 satisfies all five of the signature requirements listed in Section 9.3.

2. The simple 8-bit block XOR hash function used in Section 9.3.1 produced a collision on the words "bob" and "yes". Find two other words that also collide using this function.

3. Alice receives the following message from Bob:

   "Alice it's time for us to determine a new key, Bob".

   It came with the 16-bit XOR signature value of 6C2E. Is it a valid message?

4. Alice and Bob want to set up a new secret key using Diffie–Hellman. Their public key values are

   $$p = 26586842533836180377$$

   and

   $$g = 155801347.$$

Alice sends Bob the following value: 10029496837244214838.

Bob's secret number is 2667001284.

What does Bob send to Alice, and what is the secret key value?

5. Alice sent Bob the following message:

"Bob, let's meet at the usual place at noon tomorrow, Alice."

She used MD5 to hash the message and then enciphered the hash value using RSA with a 16-bit block size. Alice's RSA public key is as follows:

$$N = 18965938115056406809373150391$$

$$d = 1175885676400129.$$

Which of the following encrypted hash values represents the correct hash for the message, and where are the differences between the correct hash value and the incorrect hash value (i.e., how many characters and in which positions)?

(a) 47951043611207227029563446581
35288861891493485701518503049
54062023219871197095328143119
16978818009588536129702450088l
74251123619599524347993694299
36954262374929321715217941245
11449857985423730288736059989
13430732301535895640003706330
15538387441415917005048020880
16380990084490857536090312207
14496059682692065001869916532
9516360784477910751645627436
10391896936838748444791413970
76069742877585746560416877
15274949600990765506395807280
45748928547946983699201341618

(b) 47951043611207227029563446581
18416188265624588032188813765
90068264091116461532992522091
49869178049443931329254150168
74251123619599524347993694299
16303394419611060497597924532
81082243942335608898626549219
14034612409478606195792631614
65569882893207348447027812642
99525581119696307868751903848
74251123619599524347993694299
81082243942335608898626549219
10391896936838748444791413970
76069742877585746560416877
15274949600990765506395807280
45748928547946983699201341618

6. Bob wants to send an important message signed by a third party to Alice, but he does not want the third party to know the contents of the message. He hides the message by using the random number 100372401233791 and takes it to the Trusted Notary Public Service. Using a 16-bit RSA, the firm signs the message and returns it to Bob. The blind signed message is as follows:

758831624162631273354182016631663
459615541609941014497570342l
158728952869916178458012134745
118526025261370562318179750342
158728952869916178458012134745
182130930859830580308433590877
85592668333782584212284483527
162181093993910088901552861810
157303387376692959649495686256
120472171820911393013720567791
500916293463563371885464433383
179404390252689238651085585938
158728952869916178458012134745
165684201096296924481302834490
3300243716019418944529215980808
118526025261370562318179750342
158728952869916178458012134745
80157452348797548678511728170
459615541609941014497570342l
383997461634878144298079937990
180557696831286742925905739086
162724727974146105457778034593
100906556339429695230686193604
884393054869043024664110389940
164285278023193840937653051650
72106808602161891422961402423
945394377631775703385912767655

(a) What is the signed message that Bob sends to Alice?

(b) The public key for the Trusted Notary Public Service is

$$n = 18965938115056406809377315039l$$
$$e = 53874618627671702415711710977.$$

What is the actual message Bob sends to Alice?

7. Suggest a way in which the XOR hash could be used to generate random numbers.

8. Generate a set of five random numbers using the SHA-1 random-number generator. The secret key is 100003461.

(a) What are the five random numbers?

(b) Convert them to binary and run the random test set on the result. Is it truly random? Why or why not?

9. Bob sends this message to Alice: "Alice I agree to meet with you on Sunday at noon Yours, Bob". He signs it with an 8-bit XOR hash.

(a) What is the hash value?

(b) Eve intercepts the message and changes one important detail, yet her message has the same hash value. What message could Eve have sent to Bob?

10. It is possible to create a hash value using a classical cipher. For example, using a version of the Autokey cipher,

   (a) Select a keyword of length x.

   (b) Encipher the first x characters of the plaintext with a Vigenere cipher using a keyword.

   (c) Use the ciphertext characters as the keyword for the next block of x characters.

   (d) Repeat this process. (Add padding in the form of a string of y's to the end of the plaintext to ensure that the final block is of length x.)

   (e) The hash value is the ciphertext for the final block.

   Use this method with a keyword, and document how to find the hash for the following plaintext:

   "Alice, this is a test of a new hashing method. Bob"

   How does the hash value change if the plaintext is changed to the following?

   "Alice, this is the text of a new hashing method."

   Comment on this hash function.

11. Alice and Bob use the authenticated Diffie–Hellman method to set up a key in which $p = 3061$ and $g = 17$. Alice's secret number is 113 and Bob's is 211. Alice selects the random number 91. Bob selects the random number 11. What does Alice send to Bob? What does Bob send to Alice? What is their final key value?

12. Given the following group key structure with $p = 3061$ and $g = 13$, find both K and BK for each node:

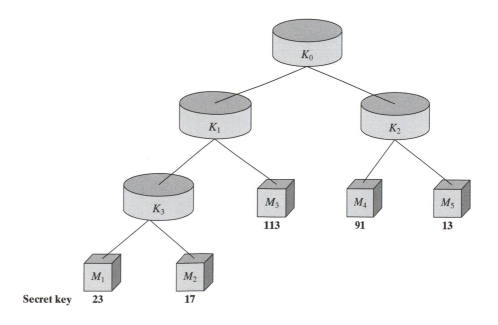

13. A new member wants to join the group formed in Problem 12. The result is the following structure:

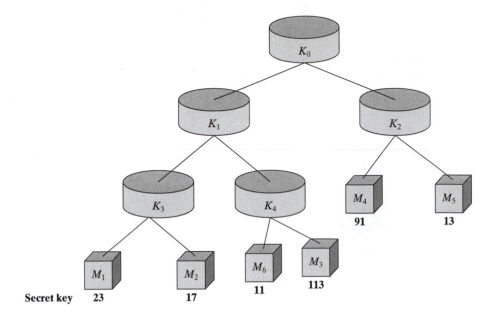

Secret key

Show the results of rekeying this system.

14. Develop a new Web security protocol and get it accepted worldwide. Name it after your instructor.

Part 3

The Future
of Cryptology

Part One examined the historical foundation of the science of cryptology. It revealed both the cleverness and the patience of the early leaders in the field. Part Two examined the current state of cryptology—one in which the computer is king, but both cleverness and patience remain vital qualities for developers.

With Part Three, we enter a strange new world—one in which common sense no longer applies. A world that appears to be more science fiction than fact. A world that will demand a new level of cleverness and patience to master. A world that turns cryptology upside down and rewrites the nature of codes, ciphers, and their analysis. It is the world of quantum physics.

Chapter 10

Quantum Cryptography

10.0   INTRODUCTION

Beginning with the use of simple substitution ciphers by Caesar and arriving at complicated substitution permutation networks that only a computer could love like AES, it would seem that the field of cryptography has come a long way. It may even seem like all that can be done in the future is more of the same. Nothing could be further from the truth. We are now on the verge of another revolution in cryptography (and computers in general) that will make the last 50 years look like a small improvement. It appears that computers are about to enter the strange world of quantum mechanics in which all our ideas about how the real world operates are turned upside down (and inside out). As they enter this new world, cryptography will also change in ways that we can only guess at now.

This is the world that Bob, Alice, and Eve are about to enter—so as Bette Davis once said, "Fasten your seat belts. We are in for a wild ride." (Congratulations to any movie buff who can e-mail me with the source of that quote.)

10.1   QUANTUM SYSTEMS—A BRIEF INTRODUCTION

Early in 1965, just after the initial technology for designing circuits on silicon was developed, Gordon Moore a cofounder of Intel, pronounced his famous "Moore's law," which now states that the number of transistors on a silicon die will double every 18 months. (His original prediction was that they would double every year.) It is anticipated that this process will continue into the next decade. However, Moore's law eventually will face a fundamental roadblock. As transistors become smaller and smaller, they consist of fewer and fewer atoms of silicon. Ultimately each device will contain (or operate on) just a few electrons. At this level, currents become erratic and the behavior of the device is no longer controllable. In addition, the insulators in the transistors stop insulating at a thickness of about 6 atoms. Moore's law applies to fiber-optic communication as well. Currently, about ten thousand photons are used to represent a single bit, but as communication becomes denser, fewer and fewer photons are necessary. Eventually, it will reduce to a single photon per bit, and our standard rules for evaluating bits will no longer apply. In order to continue making gains in computational power, a new approach to digital circuits must be developed. There are two methods currently being explored: the use of DNA and quantum computing. Of the two, quantum computing appears to have the most impact on cryptography.

10.1.1 Qubits

In the classical (nonquantum) world, voltages are used to represent binary bits. Transistors are used to logically manipulate the voltages and to implement Boolean functions. In the quantum world, a binary bit is represented by a qubit. A qubit is realized by any quantum system with two states. It could be an electron that has a spin-up and a spin-down state or a photon (a "particle" of light) that may be polarized in one direction or another. For example, an electron in the spin-up state could represent a binary 0, while an electron in the spin-down state could represent a binary 1 as shown in Figure 10.1. Qubit states are given by the notation $|0>$ and $|1>$, which are called kets. (The Dirac notation consists of quantum states defined by "bras" and "kets" in the form $<a|b>$.)

Just like the classical world, methods of measuring the value of a qubit and logically manipulating qubits are necessary if a quantum computer is to be constructed. Here is where the trouble begins—it turns out that, at the quantum level, measuring something changes it; in addition, bits can be manipulated in ways that violate common sense. In order to understand (if it is possible) these unusual properties of qubits, it is necessary to explore some the strange features of quantum physics.

10.1.2 The Weird World of Quantum Physics

Early in the 20th century, physicists began to explore the behavior of light, energy, and the particles that make up the atom in ways that had never been considered before. In the process, they opened up a Pandora's box of weird theories and unacceptable (at the time) predictions. All the rules changed—nothing behaved as it did in the larger world of baseballs and rocket ships. It began when the German physicist Max Planck discovered that energy came in fixed-size bundles that he called quanta. In 1905, Einstein predicted that light also came in fixed-size bundles. By the mid-1920s, everything we thought we knew about physics was changing. And it was only the beginning.

One of the most famous and still perplexing experiments that illustrated this strange new world was Young's two-slit experiment. The results of this experiment blurred the distinction between waves and particles. The experiment begins with a source of light traveling through a wall with two slits—the goal is to observe the light pattern on a second wall

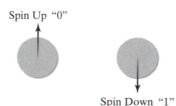

Spin Up "0"

Spin Down "1"   **Figure 10.1:** Electron spin qubits

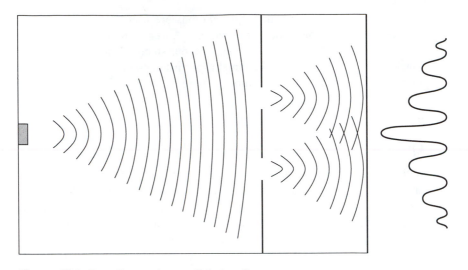

Figure 10.2: Two-slit experiment—light interference pattern

as shown in Figure 10.2. Since the wave can go through both slits, it will interfere with itself and produce a pattern of light and dark lines on the far wall.

This is not too surprising; after all, it is a wave that is passing through the slits. The real surprise occurred when the experiment was tried with electrons instead of light waves. When an electron is shot at the wall through two slits that are very close together, we would expect it to hit the far wall at one of two locations depending on which slit it passes through. That certainly makes sense; however, in the quantum world in which electrons exist, there seems to be no such thing as common sense. The results of the two-slit experiment using electrons are illustrated in Figure 10.3. It appears that the electrons are interfering with each other, but only one electron is fired at a time. So what really appears to be happening is that a single electron is interfering with itself, which means that the electron is going through both slits at the same time. It gets even more bizarre when we try to watch

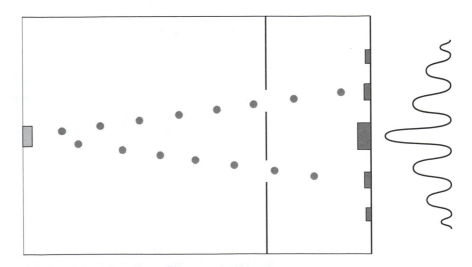

Figure 10.3: Two-slit experiment—electron interference pattern

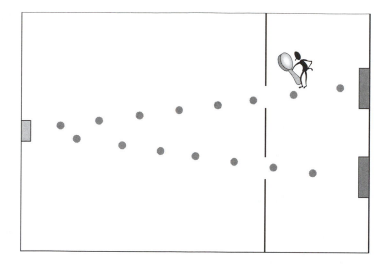

Figure 10.4: Two-slit experiment—watching the electrons

the electron as it goes through the two slits. If a sensor, such as that shown in Figure 10.4, is placed in the system, the interference pattern disappears and the electron travels through only one slit. It seems that when we watch it, it changes its behavior. The million dollar question is: "How does the electron know that someone is watching it before it goes through the slits so that it can change its behavior?"

The answer is that observing a quantum system affects the behavior of that system. The classical concept that we serve as outside observers, run experiments, and do not affect the outcome is not true at the quantum level. This may cause some concern for experimental physics, but as far as cryptology is concerned, it is the ultimate intrusion detection system (more on that later).

There are four additional bizarre features of quantum systems that are important to consider. The first is the principal of *superposition*, which states that if a quantum system can be measured to be in one of a number of states, then it can also exist in a blend of all its states simultaneously. This means that a qubit is fundamentally different from a binary bit. The binary bit is constrained to two values 0 or 1, while a qubit can be in state $|0>$, $|1>$, or some combination of these given by $a|0> + b|1>$. In other words, a qubit can be both "0" and "1" at the same time! This is the feature that makes quantum computers incredibly fast (more on that later as well).

The second bizarre feature of quantum systems is called *entanglement*. It seems that if two quantum particles interact, they can emerge from the interaction in some sort of "connected" state. If they are separated by any distance, they still have the capability to "communicate" with each other instantaneously. If one changes, the other will also change—allowing the transmission of information at speeds greater than the speed of light. The concept of entanglement serves as the basis for the study of quantum teleportation. (That is not a misprint.) Lest you think this is just theory—it has been experimentally verified. This means that two qubits can become entangled and (in a simplified view) be used to teleport binary information. We truly live in a surprising and strange world.

The third bizarre feature of quantum systems is called the *no-cloning theorem*, which states that it is impossible to create a perfect copy of an unknown quantum state. The fourth is the *uncertainty principle*, which states that it is not possible to know all the physical characteristics of a quantum system. The measurement of one characteristic will change another one.

10.2 QUANTUM FACTORING

The concept of quantum computing has been explored for quite some time, but before it could become a subject of serious study, someone had to come up with a practical application. In 1994, Peter Shor did just that while working at Bell Laboratories. He discovered a quantum algorithm that could factor large integers at high speed. It is called Shor's algorithm and it is based on a classical factoring method called *factoring via order finding*. Clearly, this algorithm could have a significant impact on cryptography. If a high-speed quantum-factoring system could be implemented, then ciphers such as RSA and elliptic curve will require even larger keys.

It turns out that the problem of factoring an integer N is equivalent to finding the period, r, of the sequence $x^0 \pmod{N}$, $x^1 \pmod{N}$, $x^2 \pmod{N}$, ..., where x is any integer coprime to N. (x and N have no common divisors other than 1.) The period, r, is the smallest integer such that $x^r = 1 \pmod{N}$ and it is called the order of x mod N. While r is not a factor of N, it is used to calculate the factors of N, which are given by $\mathrm{GCD}(x^{r/2} + 1, N)$ and $\mathrm{GCD}(x^{r/2} - 1, N)$. This is really just a mathematical modification of Fermat's factoring algorithm, which was covered back in Chapter 8.

For example, factoring 143 with $x = 23$ produces the following sequence:

$$1, 23, 100, 12, 133, 56, 1, 23, 100, 12, 133, 56, 1, \ldots.$$

The period of this sequence is 6, so the factors of 143 are given by

$$\mathrm{GCD}(23^3 + 1, 143)$$

and

$$\mathrm{GCD}(23^3 - 1, 143),$$

where $\mathrm{GCD}(12168, 143) = 13$ and $\mathrm{GCD}(12166, 143) = 11$.

CAP provides a feature that implements this algorithm. (Remember, it is not the quantum algorithm—it is the *basis for* the quantum algorithm.) Select the Integer option on CAP's main menu to open the Long Integer Routines window. Under Special Functions select Factoring - Shor's Algorithm. As shown in Figure 10.5, enter a value for N and either enter a value for x or allow CAP to select it. Click on Run to calculate the factors. (*Note*: The sequence is shown in the Results window.)

Peter Shor adapted this factoring algorithm to take advantage of two of the features of quantum computing: entanglement and superposition. The details of his algorithm involve mathematical issues that are beyond the scope of this book; however, the role of quantum systems in the algorithm can be explained in an accurate, yet somewhat simplified, method.

Given a number to factor, n, find an integer q that is a power of two and is between n^2 and $2n^2$. Select a random integer x that is coprime to n. These actions could be done on a classical computer. Now, create two quantum registers, A and B, such that A is large enough to store the integer $q - 1$ and B is large enough to store $n - 1$. As shown in Figure 10.6, set

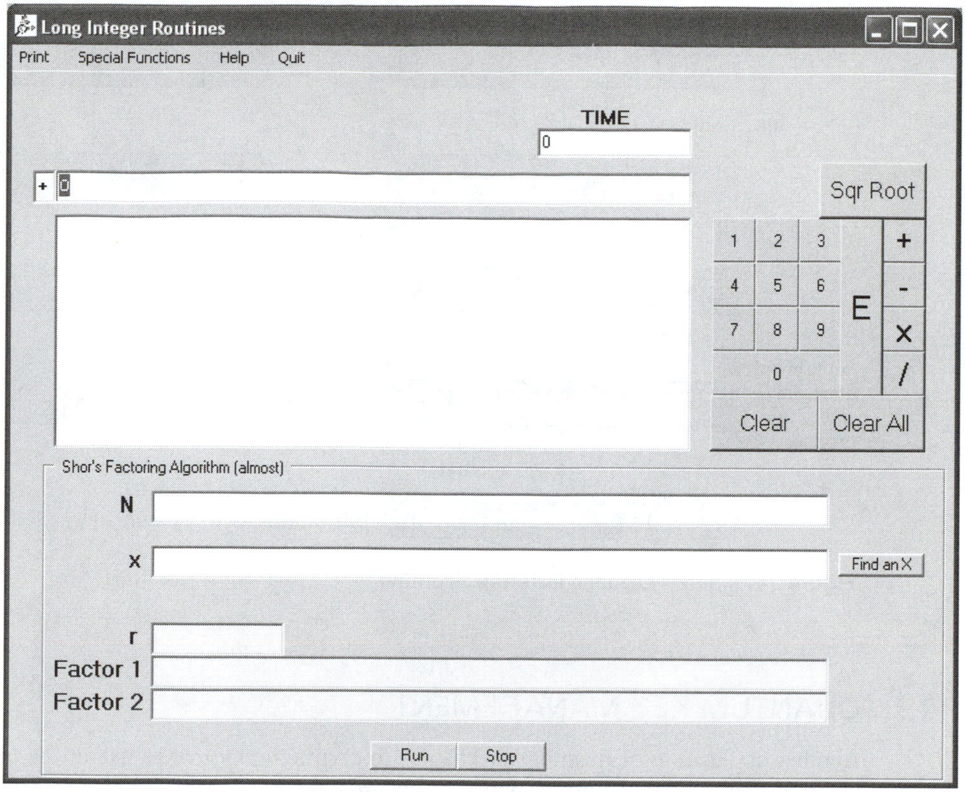

Figure 10.5: Running Shor's factoring algorithm in CAP

register A to some value y and register B to 0. Since A is a quantum register, until its contents are measured, the principle of superposition states that it contains all possible values for y. Apply the function x^y mod n to register A and store the result in register B. If you do not observe the result, B will also be in a superposition state and contain all possible function values (one for each possible value of y). The result is a massive parallel computation in a single step. In addition, the two registers are now entangled, so an observation on one will affect the values in the other.

Taking advantage of the entanglement of A and B, read register B. It will drop out of its superposition state and enter a state that represents a single value, say k. Since A is entangled with B, it contains a superposition of all the values of y such that x^y mod $n = k$. Performing a discrete Fourier transform on A (this is a way to analyze a function for periodic behavior) and reading A will cause it to fall into a state representing one of those values, say t. Now, t is an integer that is a multiple of q/r, where r is the period that we are looking for. Run this algorithm several times to gain several different values for t. A good guess for r can be found from the t values. Once r is known, it can be used to find the factors of n using the GCD calculation.

The whole process can be done in a few seconds, even for large N's. The result is a fast, efficient factoring algorithm that only awaits the construction of a practical quantum computer.

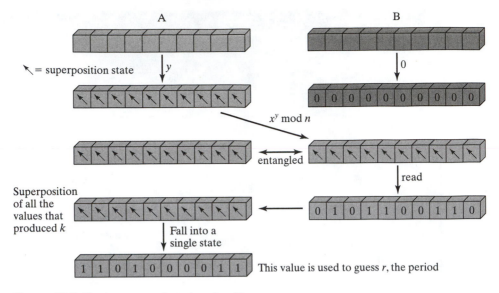

A B

$\nwarrow$ = superposition state $\quad\downarrow y$ $\quad\downarrow 0$

$x^y \bmod n$

entangled

$\longleftrightarrow$ read

Superposition of all the values that produced k

Fall into a single state

This value is used to guess r, the period

Figure 10.6: Shor's quantum factoring algorithm

10.3 QUANTUM KEY MANAGEMENT

Another application of quantum mechanics to cryptography makes use of the no-cloning theorem and the uncertainty principle to ensure the safe transmission of a secret key between two parties (say, Alice and Bob). The problem that Bob and Alice face is the same one covered in Chapter 9: How can they decide on a mutual secret key while remaining confident that Eve cannot discover or modify it? The solutions suggested in Chapter 9 involved the use of public key systems, digital signatures, certificates, or a key exchange algorithm such as the Diffie–Hellman procedure. Quantum systems offer another highly secure alternative.

The most common approach to quantum key management is called the BB84 protocol (named after Bennett and Brassard who published a paper on the procedure in 1984). The method uses photons (particles of light), so it is easily implemented along a fiber-optic link. It encodes the binary values 0 and 1 in the polarization (the direction of the electric field) of the photon. Photons can be polarized in the horizontal, vertical, or diagonal ($+45°$ and $-45°$) planes as shown in Figure 10.7.

Two filters can be constructed, one for horizontal and vertical polarized photons and another for diagonal polarized photons. If a photon passes through a filter that matches its polarization, it does not change. However, if it passes through a nonmatching filter, it randomly changes to one of the polarizations associated with the filter (as shown in Figure 10.8). The key point to remember is that the change is random.

Since the goal is for Alice and Bob to come to some agreement on a sequence of bits that will form their mutual key, they begin by deciding which polarization will be assigned

Figure 10.7: Polarized photons

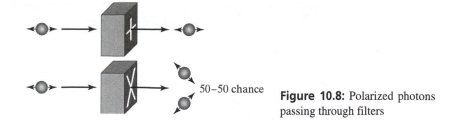

Figure 10.8: Polarized photons passing through filters

which bit value. For example, they may decide that a "0" is represented by both vertical and 45° polarized photons, so a "1" is represented by horizontal and −45° polarized photons.

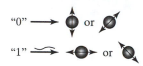

Now Alice selects a possible key bit and sends a photon with a randomly selected polarization to Bob. She notes the polarization. Bob receives the photon and randomly selects a polarized filter. He notes the filter type and the resulting bit value. (See Figure 10.9.) After Alice has sent all the photons, she contacts Bob over a nonsecure channel (perhaps the phone). Bob tells Alice the filter type he used for each bit and Alice tells him when his choice was correct. Those bits for which Bob selected the correct filter form the mutually agreed-on key.

For example, Alice generates 10 random bits: 1101000100 and 10 polarization patterns. As shown in Figure 10.10, she sends the first bit (a "1") using the −45° polarization and the second bit (also a "1") using the vertical polarization. At the receiving end, Bob selects the polarization filters in the order (x—angle, $+$ − horizontal, vertical): $+xx ++ xxx + x$ so he finds the bits 1001010101. When he calls Alice, they both discover that Bob made the correct choice on bits 3, 4, 5, 7, 8, and 9. Now they both know that the key is 010010.

10.3.1 Eavesdropping

If Eve is not trying to interfere with the process, then Alice and Bob have their secret key. What if Eve does listen in and, like Bob, randomly selects filters and generates bits? When she listens to the conversation between Alice and Bob, can she use that information to discover the key? The answer is no, and the reason can best be determined by assuming that Eve intercepts the photons shown in Figure 10.10, reads them as if she were Bob, and then sends her photons on to Bob. The overall result of this action is shown in Figure 10.11.

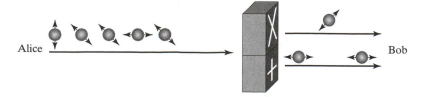

Figure 10.9: Alice and Bob deciding on a secret key

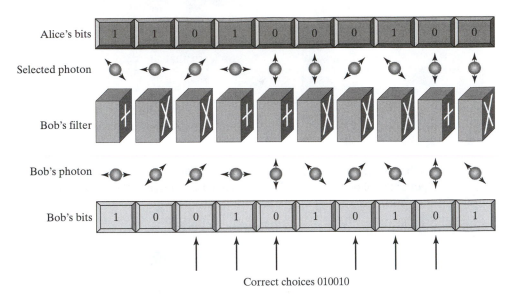

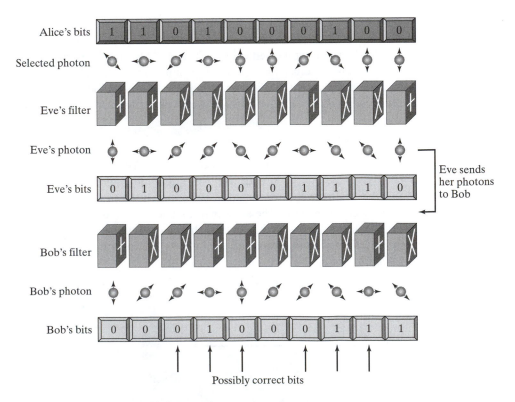

Figure 10.10: Deciding on the key bits

Figure 10.11: Effect of Eve's intervention

Of course, Eve does not know when her filter guess is correct and she can hardly call Alice to try to confirm her choices. She can, however, listen in on the conversation between Bob and Alice. In this example, she will learn that the correct filters are $x + x + +$ $+ xx + +$. Bob made the correct choices on bits 3, 4, 5, 7, 8, and 9. Eve knows that she made the correct choices on bits 2, 3, 8, and 10. Since Bob and Alice will only use bits that were correctly identified by Bob, Eve will only know two bits of the key (bits 3 and 8).

Not only will Eve not be able to determine the correct key, Bob and Alice will be able to detect her intervention in the process. Notice that in this example, Bob thinks the key bits are 010011 while Alice knows the key bits are 010010. The last bit is different even though Bob used the correct filter. The reason for the difference is that Eve used the wrong filter, so when Bob used the correct filter he had a 50–50 chance of either restoring the correct bit or creating the wrong bit. In this case, he created the wrong bit using the right filter. Bob and Alice can detect this change if Alice selects a small subset of the key and announces it to Bob. If bit 9 is part of that subset, then Bob tells Alice. Then they both know that someone must have intercepted the photons, so they cancel that key and try again. This process is called *key reconciliation*.

Just reading the bits of the small subset across a public channel could provide Eve with additional information, especially if the incorrect bits are not part of the subset. An alternative is for Bob and Alice to agree on small random subsets of the key bits and then compare only the parity of those subsets (i.e., count the number of 1's in the set—if it is an even number, then the parity of the set is even; otherwise, the parity is odd) . For example, if Bob and Alice have agreed on 20 bits for their secret key, but Eve has intercepted the exchange, there are undetected errors in Bob's key as shown in Figure 10.12. Because of Eve's work, Bob and Alice disagree on bits 2, 5, 8, 13, and 18. To expose any problems, Bob and Alice decide to run a series of parity checks. Over the public channel, they select bits 1, 3, 9, and 15 for the first test set. Without announcing the bits, they both return an odd

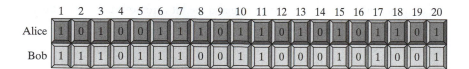

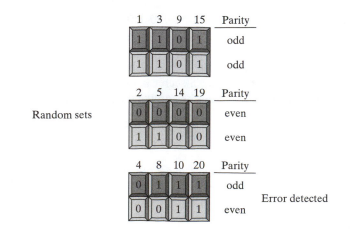

Figure 10.12: Key reconciliation using parity

parity, so everything looks okay so far. Their second test uses bits 2, 5, 14, and 19. This time they both agree on even parity even though Bob's bits are different from Alice's—they miss the actual error. However, on the third test they agree on bits 4, 8, 10, and 20. Now Alice finds an odd parity while Bob calculates an even parity. Eve's dirty work has been discovered and neither Bob nor Alice needed to expose any specific bit of the key.

Eve might try to get around this problem by copying Alice's photons, measuring one and sending the other one to Bob so he always receives the correct photon. What prevents Eve from doing this is the no-cloning property of quantum systems. Without complete knowledge of Alice's photons, Eve cannot copy them. To gain complete knowledge, Eve must measure them. Measuring them will change some of them, so she is back were she started and Alice and Bob can always detect an intervention.

10.3.2 Privacy Amplification

Privacy amplification was initially proposed by Bennett, Brassard, and Robert in a 1985 paper. It is a general process designed to allow people like Alice and Bob to derive a short secret key from a common bit string, which Eve also has some information about. This is certainly the case in the BB84 protocol.

After using the BB84 protocol, Alice and Bob discover that Eve has intercepted their photons and therefore has some partial information about the key bit string. They have the option of starting over and hoping that Eve gives up, or they can try to work around Eve's interference and still come up with a secure key.

They first need to detect and correct the errors introduced by Eve. This can be done by a modification of the parity-check process used to detect Eve's presence. Alice and Bob begin by dividing their key into blocks small enough that the probability of an error in a block is around 0.5. They then calculate and compare parities over the public channel. If the parities match, nothing is done. If they don't match, then the block is divided in half and the parity of each half is compared. The subblock with the error is again divided and the process continues until the error is discovered and the bit is removed. The bits are then randomized, the block size is increased, and the test is applied again. This is continued until at least 10 consecutive rounds produce no errors. A flowchart for this process is shown in Figure 10.13.

For example, if Alice and Bob produce the following binary patterns, there is a clear error in bit 11:

Alice 1 0 0 1 0 1 1 0 1 0 0 0 1 1 0 1 0 0 1 1
Bob 1 0 0 1 0 1 1 0 1 0 1 0 1 1 0 1 0 0 1 1.

Since Alice and Bob do not want to verify each bit over the public line (after all, that would defeat the purpose of constructing a secret key), they do not know that their two binary strings differ in bit 11. In this case, they divide the key into blocks of size 4:

Alice (1 0 0 1) (0 1 1 0) (1 0 0 0) (1 1 0 1) (0 0 1 1)
Bob (1 0 0 1) (0 1 1 0) (1 0 1 0) (1 1 0 1) (0 0 1 1).

They agree on even parity for blocks one and two, but Alice reports odd parity while Bob recorded even parity for block three. So they now know that there is an error in block three. They divide that block in half and report the parity of each subblock:

Alice (1 0) (0 0)
Bob (1 0) (1 0).

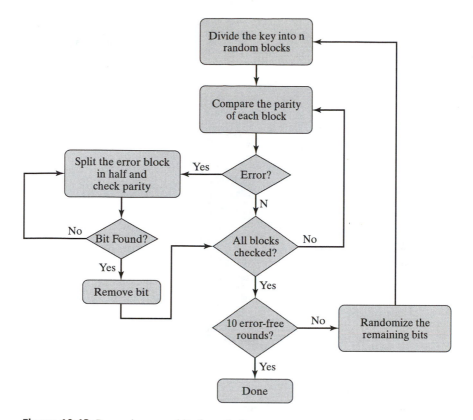

Figure 10.13: Removing error bits from the key

This time they agree on odd parity for subblock one, but disagree on the parity of subblock two.

By breaking subblock two into two blocks, they discover the error and Bob corrects it. They would now randomize the 20 bits and repeat this process until they had 10 error-free rounds.

Once Bob and Alice have a common bit string about which Eve might have partial information (say, Eve knows at most r bits of the n bit string), they need to construct a new key that minimizes Eve's information. This is the privacy amplification process, and one such method involves dividing the key into $n - r - t$ (t is an arbitrary parameter) different random subsets of length $s > r$. Bob and Alice will use the parity of each subset to create bits for a new key in which even parity is a 0 and odd parity is a 1. They do not report their parities—they don't have to, since both are using the same bit string to construct the parities.

For example, if Alice and Bob agree on the corrected bit string

$$1\ 0\ 0\ 1\ 0\ 1\ 1\ 0\ 1\ 0\ 0\ 0\ 1\ 1\ 0\ 1\ 0\ 0\ 1\ 1$$

and they suspect that Eve knows at most 3 bits, then by selecting $t = 5$, they construct 12 random subsets of the initial bit string each 4 bits long. Of course, they have to agree on which random bits go into each subset. Then they use the subsets parities to construct their final key—1001001110101—as shown in Figure 10.14. The final key is only 12 bits long; however, it is highly unlikely that Eve has any accurate information about the key bits.

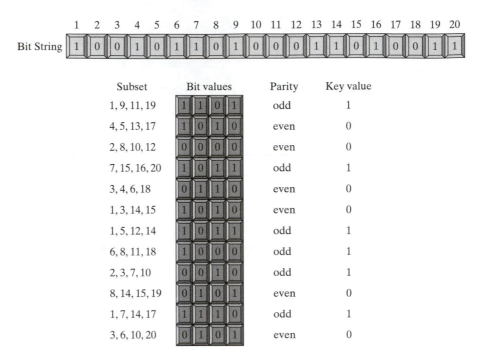

Figure 10.14: Constructing a key from parity information

10.3.3 Experimental Verification

Quantum key distribution (QKD) is not just a theoretical possibility—it has actually been implemented in the laboratory. Los Alamos National Laboratory demonstrated a QKD process across a 48-km optical fiber. At the University of Geneva, QKD experiments have been conducted over distances of about 70 km with bit rates of 100 Hz. These experiments and others indicate that QKD is a reality and it awaits further engineering design to make it practical.

10.4   SUMMARY

Cryptography has come a long way from the initial efforts to hide data by substituting one letter for another. Each stage in the development of cryptography has brought new challenges and required greater creativity and patience on the part of developers and users. The analysis of letter frequencies compromised most substitution ciphers, requiring the development of polyalphabetic and polygraphic systems. The discovery of patterns in ciphertext and the use of known words made even these ciphers insecure. The addition of transpositions and mixed transpositions–substitutions improved security once again, but the development of computer analysis weakened these systems as well. Today computers are used for both analysis and cipher implementation. Technology allows for the development of very complicated substitution–permutation patterns as well as ciphers based on difficult mathematical problems. The continued struggle between the search for new weaknesses and the development of more powerful ciphers continues. In the future, that struggle will enter a new realm—the strange world of quantum physics.

This is not the end of the story of cryptography; it is just the beginning. As long as we need to maintain privacy, as long as there are secrets, and as long as there is greed, we will need to hide information. In the ongoing battle between Alice, Bob, and Eve, there will always be another player behind the scenes—Paul (or Paula)—who will serve as the protector of data—the cryptographer. It is Paul's job to ensure that Alice and Bob have the most secure method available to protect their communications, which requires that Paul remain informed of all the efforts of Eve to break Alice and Bob's security. In some small way, perhaps, this book will inspire you to take over Paul's job. If so, I wish you good luck.

10.5   IMPORTANT TERMS

BB84	A quantum key distribution protocol developed by Bennett and Brassard in 1984
Entanglement	The ability of two qubits to share states over long distances
Key reconciliation	The process of comparing key bits to detect errors or interference by a third party
Qubit	The equivalent of a binary bit at the quantum level
Shor's algorithm	One of the first practical applications of quantum computing, a high-speed, large-integer-factoring algorithm
Superposition	The ability of a quantum system to be in all possible states at the same time

RESOURCES

There are a variety of good basic books on quantum computers that include useful information on quantum cryptology including the following:

Milburn, G. J., *Schrodinger's Machines* (W. H. Freeman & Company, 1997)

Brown, J., *Minds, Machines, and the Multiverse* (Simon & Schuster, 2000)

Siegfried, T., *The Bit and the Pendulum* (John Wiley & Sons, 2000)

Deutsch, D., *The Fabric of Reality* (Penguin Books, 1997)

PROBLEMS

1. Factor the numbers that follow using CAP's version of Shor's algorithm and graph the number of digits in the number against the time to factor. What do you conclude?

   (a) 481
   (b) 4169
   (c) 154811
   (d) 254497
   (e) 1096409
   (f) 16135487
   (g) 178443493

2. Given the following transmission, what would be the key that Alice and Bob finally agree on?

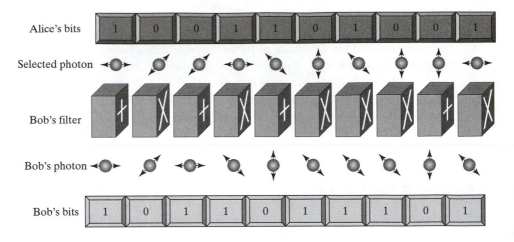

3. Bob and Alice agree on the following bits:

    Alice   1 0 0 1 0 0 0 1 1 1 0 1
    Bob   1 0 0 1 1 0 0 1 1 1 0 1

    There is an error (as you can see, but they cannot). Show the steps to locate and correct the error if they divide the key subsets of size 4.

4. Bob and Alice have corrected all errors and have agreed on the following binary string: 0 0 1 0 0 1 1 1 0 1 0 0 1 1 0 1. However, they know that Eve has some knowledge of this key (possibly 2 bits), so they select $t = 2$ and use 4-bit subsets constructed from the following bits selected at random:

    (1, 3, 10, 16) (2, 4, 11, 12) (3, 6, 8, 9) (5, 7, 14, 15) (4, 8, 13, 15) (5, 6, 7, 8)
    (2, 10, 13, 15) (1, 9, 11, 14) (6, 10, 12, 14) (4, 10, 11, 12) (5, 10, 14, 16) (3, 7, 9, 11)

    What is their final key?

Index

SINGLE PC LICENSE AGREEMENT AND LIMITED WARRANTY

READ THIS LICENSE CAREFULLY BEFORE INSTALLING THIS SOFTWARE. BY INSTALLING THIS SOFTWARE, YOU ARE AGREEING TO THE TERMS AND CONDITIONS OF THIS LICENSE. IF YOU DO NOT AGREE, DO NOT INSTALL THIS SOFTWARE. PROMPTLY RETURN THIS PACKAGE AND THE SOFTWARE AND ALL ACCOMPANYING ITEMS TO THE PLACE YOU OBTAINED THEM. *THESE TERMS APPLY TO ALL LICENSED SOFTWARE ON THE CD-ROM EXCEPT THAT THE TERMS FOR USE OF ANY SHAREWARE OR FREEWARE ON THE CD-ROM ARE AS SET FORTH IN THE ELECTRONIC LICENSE LOCATED ON THE CD-ROM:*

1. **GRANT OF LICENSE and OWNERSHIP:** The contents of this CD-ROM ("Software") are licensed, not sold, to you by Pearson Education, Inc. publishing as Pearson Prentice Hall ("We" or the "Company") and in consideration of your adoption of the accompanying Company textbooks and/or other materials, and your agreement to these terms. We reserve any rights not granted to you. You own only the disc(s) but we and/or our licensors own the Software itself. This license allows you to use and display your copy of the Software on a single computer (i.e., with a single CPU) at a single location for <u>academic</u> use only, so long as you comply with the terms of this Agreement. You may make one copy for back up, or transfer your copy to another CPU, provided that the Software is usable on only one computer.

2. **RESTRICTIONS:** You may <u>not</u> transfer or distribute the Software or documentation to anyone else. Except for backup, you may <u>not</u> copy the documentation or the Software. You may <u>not</u> network the Software or otherwise use it on more than one computer or computer terminal at the same time. You may <u>not</u> reverse engineer, disassemble, decompile, modify, adapt, translate, or create derivative works based on the Software or the Documentation. You may be held legally responsible for any copying or copyright infringement that is caused by your failure to abide by the terms of these restrictions.

3. **TERMINATION:** This license is effective until terminated. This license will terminate automatically without notice from the Company if you fail to comply with any provisions or limitations of this license. Upon termination, you shall destroy the Documentation and all copies of the Software. All provisions of this Agreement as to limitation and disclaimer of warranties, limitation of liability, remedies or damages, and our ownership rights shall survive termination.

4. **LIMITED WARRANTY AND DISCLAIMER OF WARRANTY:** Company warrants that for a period of 60 days from the date you purchase this SOFTWARE (or purchase or adopt the accompanying textbook), the Software, when properly installed and used in accordance with the Documentation, will operate in substantial conformity with the description of the Software set forth in the Documentation, and that for a period of 30 days the disc(s) on which the Software is delivered shall be free from defects in materials and workmanship under normal use. The Company does <u>not</u> warrant that the Software will meet your requirements or that the operation of the Software will be uninterrupted or error-free. Your only remedy and the Company's only obligation under these limited warranties is, at the Company's option, return of the disc for a refund of any amounts paid for it by you or replacement of the disc. THIS LIMITED WARRANTY IS THE ONLY WARRANTY PROVIDED BY THE COMPANY AND ITS LICENSORS, AND THE COMPANY AND ITS LICENSORS DISCLAIM ALL OTHER WARRANTIES, EXPRESS OR IMPLIED, INCLUDING WITHOUT LIMITATION, THE IMPLIED WARRANTIES OF MERCHANTABILITY AND FITNESS FOR A PARTICULAR PURPOSE. THE

COMPANY DOES NOT WARRANT, GUARANTEE OR MAKE ANY REPRESENTATION REGARDING THE ACCURACY, RELIABILITY, CURRENTNESS, USE, OR RESULTS OF USE, OF THE SOFTWARE.

5. **LIMITATION OF REMEDIES AND DAMAGES:** IN NO EVENT, SHALL THE COMPANY OR ITS EMPLOYEES, AGENTS, LICENSORS, OR CONTRACTORS BE LIABLE FOR ANY INCIDENTAL, INDIRECT, SPECIAL, OR CONSEQUENTIAL DAMAGES ARISING OUT OF OR IN CONNECTION WITH THIS LICENSE OR THE SOFTWARE, INCLUDING FOR LOSS OF USE, LOSS OF DATA, LOSS OF INCOME OR PROFIT, OR OTHER LOSSES, SUSTAINED AS A RESULT OF INJURY TO ANY PERSON, OR LOSS OF OR DAMAGE TO PROPERTY, OR CLAIMS OF THIRD PARTIES, EVEN IF THE COMPANY OR AN AUTHORIZED REPRESENTATIVE OF THE COMPANY HAS BEEN ADVISED OF THE POSSIBILITY OF SUCH DAMAGES. IN NO EVENT SHALL THE LIABILITY OF THE COMPANY FOR DAMAGES WITH RESPECT TO THE SOFTWARE EXCEED THE AMOUNTS ACTUALLY PAID BY YOU, IF ANY, FOR THE SOFTWARE OR THE ACCOMPANYING TEXTBOOK. BECAUSE SOME JURISDICTIONS DO NOT ALLOW THE LIMITATION OF LIABILITY IN CERTAIN CIRCUMSTANCES, THE ABOVE LIMITATIONS MAY NOT ALWAYS APPLY TO YOU.

6. **GENERAL:** THIS AGREEMENT SHALL BE CONSTRUED IN ACCORDANCE WITH THE LAWS OF THE UNITED STATES OF AMERICA AND THE STATE OF NEW YORK, APPLICABLE TO CONTRACTS MADE IN NEW YORK, AND SHALL BENEFIT THE COMPANY, ITS AFFILIATES AND ASSIGNEES. THIS AGREEMENT IS THE COMPLETE AND EXCLUSIVE STATEMENT OF THE AGREEMENT BETWEEN YOU AND THE COMPANY AND SUPERSEDES ALL PROPOSALS OR PRIOR AGREEMENTS, ORAL, OR WRITTEN, AND ANY OTHER COMMUNICATIONS BETWEEN YOU AND THE COMPANY OR ANY REPRESENTATIVE OF THE COMPANY RELATING TO THE SUBJECT MATTER OF THIS AGREEMENT. If you are a U.S. Government user, this Software is licensed with "restricted rights" as set forth in subparagraphs (a)-(d) of the Commercial Computer-Restricted Rights clause at FAR 52.227-19 or in subparagraphs (c)(1)(ii) of the Rights in Technical Data and Computer Software clause at DFARS 252.227-7013, and similar clauses, as applicable.

Should you have any questions concerning this agreement or if you wish to contact the Company for any reason, please contact in writing:

ESM Media Development
Higher Education Division
Pearson Education
One Lake Street
Upper Saddle River, NJ 07458